Social Problems and the

Social Problems and the City

NEW PERSPECTIVES

Edited by
David T. Herbert
and
David M. Smith

OXFORD UNIVERSITY PRESS

Oxford University Press, Walton Street, Oxford OX2 6DP

Oxford New York Toronto
Delhi Bombay Calcutta Madras Karachi
Petaling Jaya Singapore Hong Kong Tokyo
Nairobi Dar es Salaam Cape Town
Melbourne Auckland

and associated companies in
Berlin Ibadan

Oxford is a trade mark of Oxford University Press

Published in the United States
by Oxford University Press, New York

British Library Cataloguing in Publication Data
Social problems and the city: new
perspectives.
1. Great Britain. Urban regions. Social
problems. Geographical aspects
I. Herbert, David 1935 Dec. 24 – II. Smith,
David M. (David Marshall) 1936–
361.1'0941
ISBN 0–19–874145–6
0–19–874144–8 (pbk.)

Library of Congress Cataloging in Publication Data
Social problems and the city: new perspectives/edited by David T.
Herbert and David M. Smith. — 2nd ed.
Bibliography   Includes index.
1. Cities and towns—Great Britain.   2. Social problems—Case
studies.   3. Urban policy—Great Britain.   I. Herbert, David T.
II. Smith, David Marshall, 1936–
HT133.S65   1989   362'.042'0941 — dc10   88–38091
ISBN 0–19–874145–6
ISBN 0–19–874144–8 (pbk.)

Printed and bound in Great Britain by
Biddles Limited, Guildford and King's Lynn

PREFACE

It is now a decade since the first edition of this book was published, and it is timely both to take stock of the ongoing academic research into social problems and the city and to consider the current status of those problems. If the social problems of cities were matters of great concern at the end of the 1970s, they are certainly no less so at the end of the 1980s. During the last ten years British cities have experienced outbreaks of violence and riots of a scale and ferocity unparalleled during the present century. The 'new' symptoms of social malaise and disorder, such as hard and soft drug-taking, AIDS, and football violence, all tend to have strong links with cities and urban populations. As we approach the nineties commentators point more consistently and assertively towards the existence of disadvantaged groups within our cities. All of our major cities contain what may be regarded as 'problem areas' and 'problem groups' who carry in aggregate a disproportionate share of disadvantage and deprivation. The notion of targeting such areas and groups for special attention has gained greater credence during the 1980s. Alongside the growth in this awareness of disparities within cities has come a greater public perception of differences *among* cities. The image of a 'north–south' divide in Britain has become much sharper in recent years, providing a reminder of macro-regional differences in economic and (associated) social well-being. This kind of divide must not be overstated, for there are strong variations within any of these divisions, but the fact remains that 'problems' are more pervasive and affect greater proportions of urban populations in some parts of the country than in others.

A feature of the 1980s has been the growing belief that central government has not given high priority to the alleviation of social problems. This is clearly a matter of contention, and the government consistently points towards its spending record on the National Health Service and other welfare services as evidence of its firm intent. Overall the most consistent line in government argument has been that its task is to set the economy of the country on a firm footing, to control inflation and to stimulate economic growth; once these are in train the ability to provide better welfare services will have been earned and will follow. This type of thinking is reflected in some ways by academic studies which argue that if the economic problems of the inner city can be tackled, their amelioration can form a context for addressing the very evident social problems with which they are closely associated. During this period of economic priority, however, the social problems have grown and the welfare services have come under increasing stress. Crime continues its upward trend, waiting lists for hospital beds and housing grow longer, and social workers face overwhelming case-loads.

One school of thought would censure government for its failure to tackle the problems of the needy with more vigour, resources, and commitment. There is of course another view. That might recognize that the time had to come when the dependency of people on the state had to be lessened. The health-care problem, for example, might be seen as a 'bottomless pit' as long as the notion of 'free issue' or 'something for nothing' continues. At some time and in some form greater accountability must be brought into the welfare services, and there may be a need to reassess the extent to which government rather than other agencies and individuals accepts the responsibility for social problems and their amelioration. This debate is now in sharp focus. Whether it will prove conclusive and lead to any significant policy changes remains to be seen; considerable scepticism exists, fuelled by the observation that many of the social and structural problems in cities recur over time, and the state's response shows a similar level of repetition. What is clear is that both the social problems themselves and the attempts to manage them are currently in the full glare of public attention.

Whereas this book does follow its predecessor in attempting to convey something of geographical approaches to social problems and associated policies, it is less explicitly a work of geography, and geographers, than was the first edition. This in large part reflects the evolution of a geographical perspective which, although remaining true to its basic principles and methodologies, feels less obliged to follow traditional forms of analysis and presentation. The spatial concerns are here, as are the central interests in place and the urban environment, but these chapters cannot be accused of spatial chauvinism or any kind of obsession with spatial patterns and distributions for their own sake. A concern with broad and deep-rooted social processes and indeed with current 'policy climates' is typical of many chapters. From this understanding the distinctive flavour and perspective of social geography emerges, but the essential task is to understand the problem rather than to show its immediate association with geographical space.

Part of the consideration of social processes is prompted by the need to identify the preconditions of social problems, and on such a controversial issue it remains hard to find common ground in contemporary geography. There is nothing exceptional about geography in this respect: similar wide-ranging debates on the value of one approach as opposed to others can be found in almost all other disciplines. Philosophy

itself, towards which social scientists increasingly turn for epistemo-
logical guidance, thrives on a diversity of interpretations of the world.
This second edition continues to reveal a variety of individual perspectives. The '-isms' of the 1970s remain those of the 1980s, for the most
part, though perhaps better digested and held in clearer critical focus
than they were ten years ago. 'Mandarin dialect' doubtless persists, but
can be seen more readily for what it is.

This book draws on few of its original contributors. Apart from the
editors, there are but three survivors from the original list of fourteen,
and the editors themselves took a conscious decision not to feature as
individual chapter-writers. A purge of these proportions should not be
seen as any sign of dissatisfaction or lack of faith with our original
contributors, but rather as a determined attempt to give a new generation of researchers the opportunity to reflect on the social problems of the
city. There are now twenty-two contributors in addition to the editors;
this reflects the greater variety of topics which we now judge to be
relevant. There are issues such as drug abuse, alcoholism, and urban
disorder, which were not sufficiently in the forefront of geographical
research to include in 1979, but which clearly are so now. There has
been a ferment of research on themes of health care and the welfare
services which must be reflected in this collection. Issues concerning
gender in society have attracted much research work which must find
expression in any modern review of social problems.

The book that has emerged is not radically different in general structure from the original. Part I provides the background against which to
review more specific social problems. We now have more sharply focused
chapters on urban political processes and the social organization of cities.
Throughout this section, and elsewhere in the book, there is a consistent
weighing of problem against response, and to this extent social problems
and government policies become intertwined. Part II contains the bulk
of contributions which focus on specific issues. Our ordering of chapters
is not in any way critical, but it does seek a logical structuring and allows
some banding together of social problems which most closely touch upon
each other. Part III concentrates on policy issues in a more focused way
than the earlier individual chapters could achieve.

Finally, it must be stressed that this is in many ways a new book. It
reflects a new set of views by contributors who have made a significant
contribution to research in the 1980s. In that sense it does not *replace* the
1979 book, which remains a useful if time-specific collection of essays in
its own right. In another sense, however, we must see this text as a
successor volume which both takes forward an academic discipline's
perspective on the social problems of the city and presents a modern
update on the state of the art. The 'art' or 'science', however, can take

no great satisfaction from becoming more refined in its methods or more incisive in its understandings if the problems themselves, in and of cities, show no signs of diminishing.

D.T.H.
D.M.S.

March, 1988

CONTENTS

Contributors   xi

Introduction: Social Problems and the City   1
  David Herbert

PART I: BACKGROUND   15

1. Social and Economic Futures for the Large City   17
  Brian Robson

2. The Vulnerable, the Disadvantaged, and the Victimized:
Who They Are and Where They Live   32
  Paul L. Knox

3. Politics, Society, and Urban Problems: A Theoretical
Introduction   48
  Keith Hoggart

4. Urban Transformation: From Problems *in* to the
Problem *of* the City   60
  Roger Lee

PART II: SPECIFIC ISSUES   79

5. The Environmental Problems of Cities   81
  Ian Douglas

6. Resources and Finances for the City   100
  Robert J. Bennett

7. Health-Care Policy Issues   126
  John Mohan

8. Educational Change in the City   142
  Michael G. Bradford

9. The Housing Question   159
  Peter Kemp

10. Community Welfare Services in the Inner City   176
     Sarah Curtis

11. Social Problems of Elderly People in Cities   197
     Anthony M. Warnes

12. Women's Inequality in Urban Britain   213
     Jane Lewis and Sophie Bowlby

13. Urban Unemployment   232
     Ian R. Gordon

14. Economic Restructuring, the Urban Crisis and Britain's
     Black Population   247
     Vaughan Robinson

15. The Challenge of Urban Crime   271
     Susan J. Smith

16. Riots as a Social Problem in British Cities   289
     Michael Keith

17. Heroin Use in Its Social Context   307
     Geoffrey Pearson

18. Alcoholism and Alcohol Control Policy in the American
     City   323
     Christopher J. Smith

PART III: POLICY RESPONSE   343

19. Local Initiatives for Economic Regeneration   345
     Andrew P. Church and John M. Hall

20. Urban Policy? What Urban Policy? Urban Intervention
     in the 1980s   370
     John Eyles

Conclusion: From Social Problems and the City to the Social
Problem of Injustice   387
     David M. Smith

Index   397

CONTRIBUTORS

ROBERT J. BENNETT is Professor and Convener of the Department of Geography, London School of Economics. He was formerly a lecturer at the University of Cambridge and University College, London. His main research field is in intergovernmental finance, local government economics and public policy, and he has published books on *The Geography of Public Finance* (1980), *Central Grants to Local Government* (1982), *Intergovernment Finance in Austria* (1985), *Local Business Taxes in Britain and Germany* (1988).

SOPHIE BOWLBY is Lecturer in Geography at the University of Reading where she teaches social geography and the geography of retailing and marketing. She has been a member of the Institute of British Geographers Women and Geography Study Group since its inception and has been active in writing about and doing research on issues of feminist geography.

MICHAEL G. BRADFORD is Lecturer in Geography, University of Manchester. He graduated from St Catharine's College, Cambridge in 1967. His postgraduate research on urban consumer behaviour was carried out at the University of Wisconsin, Madison, and the University of Cambridge, where he obtained his doctorate in 1974. He has been at Manchester since 1971 where he has carried out research on education, housing and marketing. Two books, on the geography of education and human geography, are in press.

ANDREW P. CHURCH is Lecturer in Geography at Birkbeck College, University of London. Previously he was an Economic and Social Research Council 'CASS' postgraduate student at Queen Mary College, researching a Ph.D. thesis on the redevelopment of London Docklands. He is the author of several papers on inner urban regeneration.

SARAH CURTIS is Lecturer in the Department of Geography, and formerly Senior Research Fellow in Health and Health Care at Queen Mary College, University of London, conducting research into factors which affect the varying need for health and welfare service provision in different communities. Much of this work is funded by health authorities or the DHSS, with the emphasis on aspects of need relevant to resource allocation for health and social services. A text, *The Geography of Public Welfare Provision* was due for publication in 1989.

IAN DOUGLAS is Professor of Physical Geography at the University of Manchester. After graduating from Oxford, Ian Douglas specialized in humid tropical geomorphic processes during graduate work at the Australian National University. Observation of the geomorphic impact of people in Queensland's rainforests, followed by studies of fluvial erosion around Kuala Lumpur, led to a recognition of the environmental problems of cities. Subsequent work at Hull, New England and Manchester universities saw these ideas result in a book, *The Urban Environment*, and a series of papers on urban sedimentology. His research now relates to urban environmental problems in Manchester and Kuala Lumpur, involving a major rainforest geomorphology and hydrology programme in Sabah, Malaysia.

JOHN EYLES, formerly Reader in Geography at Queen Mary College, London, now teaches at McMaster University, Hamilton, Ontario. He has held visiting positions in Australia, Poland, New Zealand, and Israel. His research interests are in the fields of social geography and the geography of health care, in which his most recent book is *The Geography of the National Health: An Essay in Welfare Geography* (1987), as well as in theoretical and methodological issues of human geography, on which he has recently edited *Research in Human Geography* (1988).

IAN R. GORDON holds a Chair of Geography at the University of Reading and was formerly Reader in Regional Studies and Director of the Urban and Regional Studies Unit, the University of Kent at Canterbury. His recent research has focused largely on the functioning of urban and regional labour markets, including both fairly formal models of interaction and adjustment processes and work on appropriate policy responses to unemployment among disadvantaged groups. His chapter draws on work from two ESRC funded projects, on metropolitan labour market analysis and structural adaptation in two areas of London.

JOHN M. HALL is now Assistant Secretary (Policy) with the London Boroughs Association, but when writing for this volume was Lecturer in Geography and Director of the Centre for East London Studies at Queen Mary College (University of London), where his research interests included economic and social change, planning and management in the London region, especially policy impacts in East London and Docklands. He has been editor of *Area* (Institute of British Geographers) and of the *London Journal*, an interdisciplinary review of metropolitan society past and present. He is the author of *London: Metropolis and Region* and of *The Geography of Planning Decisions*.

DAVID HERBERT is Professor of Geography and Vice Principal at University College, Swansea. He has served on national committees for geography including the Social Science Research Council and the Institute of British Geographers: he is a member of the Sports Council for Wales and the Sports Council (Great Britain) Research Policy Group.

Current research interests cover social problems and the city and some aspects of leisure studies and recreational analyses. His books include *Urban Geography* and *The Geography of Urban Crime*. David Herbert has served as Visiting Professor in many North American and European universities and also at the University of Khartoum.

KEITH HOGGART is Lecturer in Geography at King's College, University of London. Educated at the universities of Salford, Toronto and London, Keith Hoggart has taught at King's College since 1978. He has also taught at the University of Maryland and Temple University, and has held a Commonwealth Scholarship to Canada and a Fulbright Scholarship to the United States. Editor, with Eleonore Kofman, of *Politics, Geography and Social Stratification* (1986) and author, with Henry Buller, of *Rural Development: A Geographical Perspective* (1987), his research interests are urban public finance and rural development.

MICHAEL KEITH is a Research Fellow in the Centre for Research in Ethnic Relations at the University of Warwick. He has published work on riots and uprisings in the 1980s and has completed a doctoral thesis on the events of 1981 in London. His current research involves a study of the relevance of 'Inner City' policy to issues of racism and racialization in British society.

PETER KEMP is Lecturer in Housing at the University of Salford. He was formerly a Research Fellow in the Centre for Housing Research at the University of Glasgow and, before that, a Researcher for SHAC (the London Housing Aid Centre). He has published articles on the housing market in the late Victorian city as well as on current housing policy issues, including co-operative housing, housing benefit, and the privately rented sector. He edited *The Private Provision of Rented Housing* (1988).

PAUL KNOX is Professor of Urban Affairs and Director of the Center for Urban and Regional Studies at Virginia Polytechnic Institute and State University. He has written several books, including *Urban Social Geography* (1987), and numerous papers on urban and regional development. In addition to his work on vulnerable and disadvantaged households in American cities, he is working on comparative approaches to postmodern urban change.

ROGER LEE is Senior Lecturer in Geography at Queen Mary College, London. As well as working on the historical geography of the welfare state, he is researching (with John Mohan) the uneven geography of public service provision in south-east England and problems of regional development and urban change in Western Europe. These interests and the social theory which helps in their understanding also inform his more widely based concern for economic geography.

JANE LEWIS is currently working as Labour Market Adviser in the Economic Development Division of the London Borough of Ealing. Before this, she worked as a lecturer in the Department of Geography at the University of Reading, teaching industrial and regional geography, and as a research officer for CES Ltd, having completed a Ph.D. in the Department of Geography at Queen Mary College, London, which examined the role of women's employment in post-war regional uneven development in Britain. She is a long-standing member of the Institute of British Geographers Women and Geography Study Group.

JOHN MOHAN is Lecturer in Geography at Queen Mary College, where he was formerly an ESRC Postdoctoral Research Fellow. He is currently working on spatial implications of restructuring in the health sector in England, following the regional and local impacts of changing government expenditure policies and changing patterns of employment along with private sector growth. He is joint author of *Commercial Medicine in London* (1985) and author of numerous articles on the geography of health care provision.

GEOFFREY PEARSON is Professor of Social Work at Middlesex Polytechnic in London. Educated at the universities of Cambridge and Sheffield and the London School of Economics, he then taught at University College, Cardiff, and at the University of Bradford where he was Reader in Applied Social Studies. His published work includes *The Deviant Imagination* (1975); *Working Class Youth Culture* (1976); *Hooligan: A History of Respectable Fears* (1983); *Young People and Heroin* (1986); and *The New Heroin Users* (1987).

VAUGHAN ROBINSON is Lecturer in Urban Social Geography at the Department of Geography, University College, Swansea. After graduating from St Catherine's College, Oxford, Vaughan Robinson undertook research at Nuffield College, Oxford, where he was subsequently elected to a Research Fellowship in Race Relations. Since taking up his current post he has written two books, *The Geography of Race in Post-war Britain* (1989) and *Transients, Settlers and Refugees: Asians in Britain* (1986). He has co-edited two books, including *Ethnic Segregation in Cities* (1981) and is the author of over thirty monographs and articles. His current research interests include the Vietnamese and Polish communities in Britain as well as changing patterns of urban and regional segregation.

BRIAN ROBSON is Professor of Geography at the University of Manchester and Chairman of its Centre for Urban Policy Studies. He was Chairman of the ESRC's Environment and Planning Committee, through which a major research programme evaluating inner-city policy was conducted. His most recent books are *Managing the City* (1987) and *Those Inner Cities* (1988).

CHRIS SMITH is at the Department of Geography and Planning, University of New York at Albany. A British graduate, he then attended the University of Michigan and has taught at the University of Oklahoma at Norman. His long-standing interest in social issues in cities has included mental illness and the effects of discharge of patients from institutions into the community, as well as alcohol-related topics. His research has always had strong policy dimensions and involved working closely with public agencies. Chris Smith has published extensively, including a monograph *Alcohol Abuse: Geographical Perspectives*, with Robert Hanham (1982).

DAVID M. SMITH is Professor of Geography and Director of the Health and Health Care Research Centre at Queen Mary College, London. His main research interests are in the geographical expression of social inequality, especially within cities, with particular reference to South Africa, the USA and the USSR. His books include *Human Geography: A Welfare Approach* (1977); *Where the Grass is Greener: Living in an Unequal World* (1979); *Apartheid in South Africa* (1987); and *Geography, Inequality and Society* (1988). He is co-editor of the *Dictionary of Human Geography* (1987) and *Qualitative Methods in Human Geography* (1988).

SUSAN J. SMITH is a member of the Department of Social and Economic Research and Research Fellow in the ESRC's Centre for Housing Research at the University of Glasgow. She began her post-doctoral career as a Junior Research Fellow at the University of Oxford (St Peter's College), and has held research and teaching posts at the University of California, Los Angeles, and at Brunel University. Her research interests and publications span the fields of victimization and the fear of crime, race and racism in Britain, and the methodology of the social sciences.

ANTHONY M. WARNES is Reader in the Department of Geography and Age Concern Institute of Gerontology, King's College, University of London. A human geographer with long-standing interests in social gerontology, his research has explored the geographical and applied policy dimensions of the mobility of elderly people, their housing circumstances and opportunities and the implications of rapid ageing in less developed countries. As Secretary of the British Society of Gerontology, and a leader in the new Age Concern Institute of Gerontology at King's College, he has been closely involved with the recent rapid development of social gerontology in Britain. His publications include *Geographical Perspectives on the Elderly* (1982) and *Human Ageing and Later Life* (1988).

Introduction: Social Problems and the City

David Herbert

Urbanization continues to be a pervasive force in virtually all parts of the world. Over the past decade its form has shown signs of change, though these may be differences in kind rather than of degree. Counter-urbanization, for example, has been closely studied as a 'new' phenomenon over the past decade, though whether it is significantly more than suburbanization and dispersal writ large is another matter. Recent demographic analyses of British cities suggest that during the 1980s there has been a significant slowing down in the outward movement of people from our metropolitan areas. New constraints upon such movement are emerging, which seem at present to be having some effect upon those who normally exercise the greatest amount of choice over where they should live and work. It is not yet clear whether these constraints will be short-lived, a temporary aberration of job and housing markets, or whether they signal some longer-term trend which will affect the shape and functional roles of our urban areas. Trends of this kind, however, whether real or apparent, seem to have a limited effect on the evident disparities which exist within societies and within our cities. Studies continue to show that some sections of society are significantly worse off than others; that the crude division between inner city and suburb still serves as a reminder of the gulf between the 'haves' and the 'have-nots'.

This term 'crude division', always appropriate in relation to the inner city/outer city dichotomy, has become more so in the 1980s. The inner city remains a problematic area, often coincident with areas of poverty with large numbers of deprived people and many indicators of social malaise. At the same time, however, it is increasingly necessary to remind ourselves of the problems of scale associated with area generalizations. The partial revitalization of inner-city areas throws this issue into a sharper focus. As capital investment returns in a selective way to those parts of the inner city which promise most in terms of profit and development, the infusion of new kinds of inner-city dwellers creates tensions in urban space, with close juxtapositions of very different urban environments and life-styles. Gentrification, a well-established phenomenon, has effected some of these contrasts, but more recent changes, such as the development of London's Docklands, have exaggerated their scale and content. The inner city can be seen as a mosaic, and as part of the urban area which contains a significant dynamic for change.

For many large cities, the real problem areas are as much on their peripheries as they are in the centre. We pay the price for bad planning, poor design, utilitarian principles, and under-resourced housing projects in some of the urban wastelands which peripheral estates have become. Many high-rise public-sector housing projects, located both in the inner city and in peripheries, have become more increasingly unattractive to residents and increasingly unacceptable as components of the urban fabric. In the British city at least, 'problem areas' exist throughout the whole urban area and cannot be easily generalized into spatial models of the kind which retain some validity in North American cities.

Although one can point to disadvantaged groups—and indeed to disadvantaged areas—within cities, it is still legitimate to ask the question 'Is there an *urban* problem?' Cities naturally contain the major concentrations of people in space but is the association of social problems with cities any more than the result of that concentration? Are the social problems finding clearest expression in cities simply because cities throw all kinds of human attributes into sharper focus? Herbert and Johnston (1976) clarified the point by making the distinction between problems *in* and problems *of* the city. They argued that problems *in* the city were in fact general problems affecting society as a whole: they appear to be urban simply because of their clustering in urban areas. Poverty, for example, is evident in many cities; we can often identify urban poverty areas, but it is by no means exclusively an urban problem. So, the argument goes, the concentration of poverty in cities simply reflects the concentration of population in cities rather than being created or exacerbated by urban places *per se*. The causes of poverty are therefore seen as lying in economic and socio-political structures rather than in spatial structures.

Herbert and Johnston regarded problems *of* the city as those brought about or exaggerated in some consistent way by the urban environments in which they occur. Louis Wirth (1938) argued that the size, density, and heterogeneity of urban settlements produced a particular set of life-style characteristics in cities; his thesis led to the long and inconclusive debate on an urban–rural dichotomy. That debate no longer has any great value, but the argument that cities have special features which contribute to the appearance of social problems persists. The internal spatial structures of cities are typified by forms of segregation, 'communities' within the city. There is evidence that locality or neighbourhood

effects emanate from these, adding to the accumulated negative exter-
nalities from which disadvantaged groups, segregated in the most
deleterious urban environments, suffer. Are there 'negative values'
associated with some residential areas which add to the problems of
growing up in the city (Herbert, 1976)? Are there built environments
which because of their effect on social, or anti-social, behaviour reduce
the quality of life for people who occupy them (Newman, 1972;
Coleman, 1985)? These questions are contentious and will remain so,
but it is clear that the urban condition, in its local manifestations, has
some effect on the extent to which social problems occur and the particular forms they take.

Geographical Perspectives

In the introduction to the first edition of this text the review of then
current geographical perspectives included a schema which sought to
encompass the variety of approaches to the study of urban problems.
Written at a time when the discipline was seeking to define its position
and to recognize a framework which held quite different approaches in
some kind of order, the schema did have some value for students. That
kind of detail is less needed now. It may be better simply to recognize the
fact that a diversity of approaches remains, and while there are some
excellent works which attempt to reconcile some or all of these (see, for
example, Harvey, 1985; Smith, 1986), the goal remains elusive. As
Harvey (1985, p. xvi) argues: 'The path between the historical and
geographical grounding of experience and the rigours of theory construction is hard to negotiate.' Susan Smith (1986, p. 195) moves
between the ecological and ethnographic traditions of the Chicago
School and the modern theories of structuration. In this she follows an
approach which: 'while focussing on the impact of crime, has been able
to follow the effects of structured inequality into the organization of daily
life in neighbourhood settings'.

It is this task of forming the link between structural theories and their
sources of explanation, on the one hand, and localities and their sources
of variation, on the other, which geographers are gradually coming to
terms with. A diversity of approaches, perspectives, value judgements,
and ideological stances still typify human geography and are reflected in
the chapters of this book. Rather than codify them into various boxes, it
is perhaps sufficient to recognize a number of broad divisions, each of
can be subjected to further, more detailed subdivisions. Jackson and
Smith (1984), for example, suggested a 'triad' of approaches—
positivism, structuralism, and humanism—which typified geographers.

This triad is as good as any in describing the current breadth and diversity of geographical research. Most, if not all, contributors to this text show some awareness of, and respect for, the context and comprehension which a structural perspective can offer; many use what are essentially positivistic methods and techniques in the empirical content of their studies. That humanism does not emerge in these essays in any significant way is in part a reflection of the state of that approach, which still has some way to go in moving from interesting semantics and case studies to more intellectually rigorous interpretations of the incidence of social problems in cities. Humanistic studies have yet to realize their full potential.

Organization of the Text

The book is organized to give first some general commentary on the state of our cities, to provide, second, a full set of close analyses of specific social problems and, finally, to give some attention to policy responses. As said in the preface, these are not hard and fast divisions in the text, as most contributors have necessarily referred to the policies, or lack of them, in their specific field of concern. Rather, related chapters are grouped together in a way which both presents a coherent whole and provides a work of reference for individual topics.

Brian Robson opens the book with a chapter on the 'Social and Economic Futures for the Large City'. His reflections are drawn from his close involvement with the inner-city studies funded by the Economic and Social Research Council, and his current interest in the 'management' of our larger cities. Robson's initial questions are whether the urban 'underclass' has a future at a time of widening economic and social disparities, and whether cities can survive as centres for tourism and entertainment in the absence of any growth in producer goods and services. This chapter is much concerned with the implications of policies which target inner-city areas for Urban Programme aid on the hand but reduce the rate support of these same areas on the other. There are conflicts to be resolved in our large cities—between central and local government and between economic and social goals. We need to develop policies in the absence of growth; waiting for growth to come may be a little like 'waiting for Godot'.

Paul Knox, in Chapter 2, poses some more traditional questions for a social geographer: who are the disadvantaged and where do they live? He reviews the roles of territorial social indicators, both objective and subjective, in locating and understanding social problems in cities. The critical distinction between 'people problems' and 'place problems' emerges in this chapter, and, implicitly, so does that between 'people policies' and 'place policies': these are not alternatives, but must always be seen as complementary approaches.

Keith Hoggart provides us with a more conceptual view of the theories of the state and the ways in which these must be understood as a precursor to any understanding of urban problems. These theories show that not only is the concept of 'urban' contentious, but so also is the notion of 'local'. Hoggart argues that we are some way from a convincing theory of political action. In practice, the perceived realignment of local–central relations may be little more than a change from an administrative political system to an ideological one.

Roger Lee sets the scene for a consideration of the problems in and of the city with three stories or vignettes. In Chapter 4 he illuminates the elusive link between theory construction and the realities of urban life. It was at the end of the nineteenth century that it became apparent that there was a problem of the city, and since that time the restructuring of the circuit of capital has had far-reaching implications for cities and the organization of urban space. A few cities have become nodal points in the global circulation of finance capital, while others show all the signs of abandonment by capital. Cities which become 'losers' are sometimes reconstituted in a new round of investment which identifies a different set of potentials. The imperatives of social reproduction enforce growth, stagnation, or decline unless the realization that society is made up of real people with real needs stimulates meaningful interventions and controls.

When urban geographers talk about environments in cities they almost inevitably talk in terms of the built environment, the social environment, or something which is the product of human rather than natural activities. It is proper, however, that we do recognize that cities 'rest' upon and within natural environments both affected by and in turn affecting them. At the beginning of Part II Ian Douglas provides us with a methodical review of the ways in which these interactive relationships between cities and their natural environments work. His focus is on environmental problems and the ways in which these arise. Such problems are associated with the sites of cities, with their surface areas, with urban form; they are exacerbated and sometimes initiated by resource uses, technological changes, planning policies, and the sheer impact of numbers of people. This chapter demonstrates the interdependence of conditions within the urban 'system' as a whole: we cannot ignore the natural environments in which social problems occur.

Urban finance has become one of the key points of debate between central and local government over the past decade. New York's fiscal crises of the later 1970s had reverberations in many other places, and the role of the US federal government was crucial. In Britain the financing of cities has moved through crises of similar kinds in the 1980s, as under different conditions of the central/local funding argument many large cities have come under extreme pressure. Bob Bennett reviews the financing of British cities, giving close attention to both the trends and their policy implications. He identifies at the heart of the crisis of urban funding not merely questions of the sufficiency of resources and of the nature of financial reform, but basic constitutional and political conflicts which call into question the relationship between central and local government. A new form of partnership is required, not only between central and local levels of the state but also between public-sector responsibilities and private-sector initiatives.

Issues of finance pervade the welfare services, but in none have the tensions become more acute in the 1980s than in the health-care services. John Mohan makes resource allocation procedures the central issue in his study of health-care services within British cities (Chapter 7). In part concerned with the quality and actualities of service in both the hospital and primary sectors, Mohan also raises a number of key questions. One of these concerns the impact of deprivation on both the demand and the supply of services—is deprivation a significant factor? Does a high level of use imply a high level of need? Again, how can one evaluate the infusion of private practice into health care? Does this lead to competition and a blurring of the boundary between private and public supply? The evidence points to the conclusion that resource allocation procedures need reform, but this and other changes must be so managed that they reduce rather than widen the present inequalities. Mohan calls for greater attention to public health issues, and his argument that 'environmental' improvements could well lead to improvements in health link with Douglas's portrayal of the hazards contained in urban environments.

Along with health care, education stands as an issue at the forefront of public concern. Funding is again an issue, and education forms such a major component of local authority budgets that it is almost inevitably a prime target for cuts. Michael Bradford shows that several of the key trends in education are tending to fuel the case for cost-cutting exercises and economies, and are at the same time leading to greater polarizations in the provision and quality of education and to sharper segregations among types of school. Bradford organizes his chapter around what he terms the 'six Cs'—contraction, cost-cutting, careerism, commodification, choice, and community control—which currently stand as issues in the education debate. As demographic changes and falling rolls raise the possibilities of school closures and amalgamations, the education budgets tend to shrink accordingly. Economic rather than welfare arguments are paramount, and school reorganization is dominated by financial arguments. Against this background some of the innovative reforms such as the national curriculum, greater vocational and technological training and community/parent control are being pressed forward. So far the potential of many of these is at least questionable, and the likelihood of greater rather than less social inequality in our cities as a result remains.

Housing is one of the oldest issues in welfare provision, and one in which the state has assumed a role for a long time. As Peter Kemp reminds us, the housing problem is never solved, it only changes. As with some of the other problems of the city, this one has a social construction— it is essentially a political, perhaps even an ideological, issue. Kemp reviews the progress of housing reform since the Victorian era and assesses the state of the housing problem now—what is the quality of our housing stock as the twentieth century draws to a close? Kemp's view is that housing may not be in crisis, but it is certainly not free of significant problems and is also undergoing some radical changes. There are run-down modern estates which now deserve as much attention as inner-city tenements; there is a thrust towards increased home ownership and the sale of council houses; and the move towards change in the rented sector may well give a different form to the housing question in the near future.

Community welfare services are designed to meet special needs. Many of us never need social work services, for example, and in that sense they are different from services providing for health, education and housing, which are universal needs. But it must be acknowledged that the lines of distinction are blurred: health is a factor in social needs, and those in poorest housing are often those who make demands upon social work services. Sarah Curtis focuses on some aspects of health and social services in inner London, showing that the issues which arise may usefully be seen as institutional problems, in the sense that they arise from the failure of 'agencies' to deliver services. Large parts of inner London remain typified by extensive disadvantages, and within its plural and multi-ethnic demographic composition there are groups specifically at risk. The problems grow as a return to the central city of young professionals reinforces the more articulate groups able to extract most from available urban services. Public services suffer from a lack of co-ordination; there are institutional feature which make it difficult for the system to work efficiently; and it is clear that to counter reducing resources, public health and welfare needs to be raised to a higher level of priority by decision-makers.

The term 'target groups' is one of convenience. It points to the existence of sections of society that may in some ways be especially vulnerable or have a past record of suffering a disproportionate share of disadvantage. Tony Warnes (Chapter 11) reminds us that old age is not in itself a social problem. It does however have a special link with social problems because increasing old age commonly leads to less mobility, more disability, and a more frequent need for medical and other social services. Further, two-thirds of Britain's elderly population are thought to live below or near·the margins of poverty. The populations of Western societies have aged significantly during the present century, and this has had a considerable impact on our cities. Most old people are urban dwellers, and although there is nothing like a 'geriatric ghetto' in cities, some patterns of concentration, especially in parts of the inner city, are evident. The housing market has responded with more sheltered homes and purpose-built accommodation, but the basic policy priority must remain that of providing an adequate retirement income. The shift from institutional care to a system of caring for the old in the community is proceeding in an *ad hoc* and inadequately planned way. Cities are not necessarily hostile environments for the elderly; they can and should contain the best range of caring services for a section of society which becomes increasingly dependent on the localities within which they live.

As women make up over half of the British population, they clearly can not be regarded as a minority group. Yet they qualify as a 'target group' by virtue of cultural norms and expectations, traditional roles, and the slowness of institutions to respond to the need to change; these all serve to place women at some disadvantage. Jane Lewis and Sophie Bowlby review the evolving theoretical positions on the place of women in society and identify the main areas of empirical evidence for inequality. There are issues of access, of roles within households and family structures, ability to compete for jobs and to achieve good conditions of work in the labour market, and to compete for services— especially housing. The time is ripe for action and new initiatives to remove the main sources of inequality.

Of the various indicators which are watched closely by the media as measures of the well-being of the nation, levels of unemployment have attained priority status; the unemployed deserve designation as a target group, and some cities undoubtedly contain large unemployed populations. Ian Gordan recognizes unemployment as a characteristically urban phenomenon which in the 1980s has come to typify cities affected by the decline of their heavy industries. In capitalist societies, labour power is regarded as a commodity and individuals compete for jobs in the labour market. The principal sources of explanation for urban unemployment are an aggregate gap between supply and demand, the attributes of individuals, and the structure of the labour market. From a case study of London, Gordon argues that local demand deficiency does not stand as a clear explanation and although racial factors are important the clearest reason for clusters of unemployment is the relatively weak competitive positions which inner-city populations occupy in the job market. Progress in alleviating the problem could follow from an improvement of these positions by adapting conventional labour market practices.

Few would deny that Britain's ethnic minorities constitute a target group, and Vaughan Robinson in Chapter 14 on the urban Black population clearly sees them in that light. Robinson relates the inflow of coloured immigrants and their subsequent assimilation into British society since the 1950s to broader processes of economic change and in particular to the economic restructuring process within Britain. He argues that Black labour was initially introduced to make up for the failure of the British economy to modernize and invest in more intensive production processes. As these processes have subsequently occurred, the urban Black population has emerged as the main loser. All Black populations suffer racial discrimination and social disadvantage and have not been allowed to compete on equal terms with the white population. Black populations still show a tendency to cluster in the inner areas of conurbations, but their 'geography' is becoming more complex, with, for example, up to 40 per cent of the main groups living outside large cities, and detailed segregations appearing within the overall immigrant group. Again, public policy is crucial and has so far followed the paths of controlling levels of in-migration and legislating against discrimination.

Crime is another up-front image of the urban condition, and Susan Smith begins Chapter 15 on urban crime with the unequivocal statement that the streets of British cities are getting meaner. In these new situations the traditional concerns of academic researchers become even more critical, it is more important than ever to question criminal statistics, to question the definition of criminality and to see crime as part of society. Too much research has focused on offenders as a 'breed apart', and the emphasis should shift elsewhere. The victims of crime are often those who suffer many forms of social deprivation. There is a need to link crime-prevention policies with the whole range of social policies, as they may well be concerned with the same set of problems. Aspects of life-style place some sections of the population at particular risk, and fear of crime needs to be managed in more positive and consistent ways. Fear relates above all to the marginality of people and their lack of power to control events around them. In all of this the role of the police is crucial, and the politics of policing and questions of accountability are key issues.

The urban riots of the early 1980s in several British cities have, perhaps more than any other factor, thrown the role of the police and their relationships with the Black population in particular into sharp perspective. Debates on the causes of the riots are intense and will continue to be so; official inquiries, such as that by Lord Scarman, throw light on the circumstances in which riots occur but cannot provide complete understanding. Michael Keith examines the evidence and assesses the debate on urban disorder. The range of causes is considerable, from individual incident to general social disadvantage, but somehow it has to be formed together into some general explanatory framework. The police find themselves at the 'coal-face'; their task is clearly to maintain law and order, but the manner in which they do this and the strategies they adopt are crucial.

Geoffrey Pearson tackles the difficult task of analysing the impact of drug abuse in our cities; again an issue which pre-occupies police and public alike. Pearson talks of a 'heroin epidemic' in Britain in the early 1980s, though stressing than it is not necessarily a national problem; it is localized in effect. Tracing the infiltration of heroin into British society and the range of policies aimed to curb its use and to penalize the providers, Pearson is dismissive of the idea that a drug-free society is at all attainable. Whereas control will continue to be the main explicit policy, drug abuse has to be seen in the context of the wider *mélange* of deprivation and social disadvantage from which it arises.

Alcohol abuse reaches out far more widely into society and has far more direct impact upon our urban populations than does drug abuse, yet it receives far less than its correct share of research attention. In Chapter 18 Chris Smith focuses on alcohol abuse and excessive drinking in American society, and reminds us that ten times as many people die from someone abusing alcohol than from the abuse of all the illegal drugs put together. In New York in 1983 there were over 12,000 alcohol-related accidents involving 876 fatalities and over 20,000 injuries; in addition to this awesome catalogue of death and injury, abuse of alcohol is linked with many other social problems. Attitudes towards alcohol abuse have changed over the past fifty years. Initially regarded as a crime, it has since been classed as a disease. Other 'models' used have included the social or integration models which support the idea of more responsible drinking, and the public health model based on the observation that the proportion of heavy or problem drinkers can be predicted from the overall level of alcohol consumption. The public policy aim must be one of social control, and various measures, such as taxing consumption, age-limits for drinkers, drink/driving legislation, and the control through licensing laws of the outlets, reflect this. Again the problem tends to emerge an an urban one, and it is acknowledged that the urban environment is optimal for drinkers, offering a wide variety of sources of supply. Chris Smith reminds us of the vested interests of the alcohol industry, the taxation revenue for the government and the resultant reluctance to press for radical change.

As already stated, a concern with policy is evident in most of the contributions to this book. The final two chapters, however, have the specific task of evaluating current policies that relate to the social problems of the city. The theme addressed by Andrew Church and John Hall, local economic initiatives, is a new focus which had little impact on British urban policy before the 1980s. Local initiatives can come from central or local government, from the public or private sectors, and often represent new forms of intervention designed to assist ailing urban economies. Church and Hall are concerned with the motives for such interventions, with the forms they take, and with their impact on cities. Academics have developed useful theories to explain local economic initiatives, but they are often most easily understood in pragmatic terms: agencies of various kinds have responded to the shock of urban riots, to the despair of high unemployment, and to the publicized plight of the inner city.

There are contrasts in the forms of intervention. 'New Left' local authorities may see the public sector as the vehicle for change, and this often contrasts sharply with a central government concerned to press for partnership involving strong private investment. Gains so far are limited if measured against the longer-term losses of cities, but the process may be moving into a new phase. The 'locality' issue is becoming important, and local leadership and drive, the ability to 'sell' your city, and becoming indicators of the different success rates among cities. As city leaders seek to attract capital and to change the image of their city with some new positive initiatives, a 'geography of enterprise' may well emerge.

The final chapter, by John Eyles, takes a broader view of urban policies, which includes an international perspective. His view is more pessimistic. Whereas the 1970s were typified by attempts by capitalist governments to engineer solutions to social problems, the dominant image of the 1980s is one of crisis, failure, and austerity. Certainly government has stopped pouring money into cities in the 1980s, certainly the focused social policies have slipped well down the list of priorities. In the 1980s the message is that economic well-being must be achieved before there is any amelioration of social problems. Fiscal austerity hits cities most dramatically, and welfare programmes in general are obvious targets for a policy which is guided by the principles of efficiency and effectiveness as measured by economic indicators. Urban Development Corporations have come to symbolize a new approach, in which free-ranging agencies dilute local control and define their own urban strategies. Economic regeneration and political ideologies have changed the nature and purposes of intervention, and the hallmark of the 1980s has been the dearth of urban policies which directly address the social dimension of urban problems.

In Conclusion

Any collection of essays must be characterized by some diversity of views, and this book is no exception. There are however, many strong and recurrent threads which run through the chapters, and show a high level of unanimity among academic researchers on social problems in the modern city. All our contributors, almost regardless of the theoretical positions which they wish to develop, are concerned to demonstrate the realities of urban problems, to show that they affect real people, many of whom suffer now from many forms of disadvantage. Geographers are not concerned to do no more than portray the extent of human misery, or to make the facts of spatial clusters and concentrations an end-product in themselves. The authors of this book are overwhelmingly concerned with processes, at a variety of scales, which contribute to the continuance of social problems. Some of these processes are inbuilt to the structures of our society: others emerge as the product of inept or misguided managerial decisions. Always it is those at the margins who suffer, those with least access to good jobs, to good schools, efficient hospitals, and other 'goods' of the urban system. Such people have least access to sources of power and control, and whatever the merits of current government policies or private intiatives, they must await their outcomes in the short term and rely upon normal democratic processes in the longer term.

　　Many of the contributors are critical of government policies. Particularly in the chapters on 'target groups' and specific social problems, the text becomes something of a litany. Every group is a priority, each social problem needs extra resources; one can find some sympathy for a government faced by a shopping list which never grows smaller and sometimes seems out of control. In Britain, central government has moved away from trying to tackle social problems head-on; the strategy is to increase the overall wealth of the nation, to 'get the economy right', before looking at what is affordable in terms of welfare services. Some of the major academic contributions to the policy debate in the 1980s have followed a similar line: 'A major aim has been to provide specific lessons for the improvement of the policies and practices of urban development which aim to strengthen urban economies and alleviate the economic distress caused by structural change while increasing employment and income opportunities for disadvantaged urban residents' (Hausner and Robson, 1985, p. 7). Minimal direct state concern with social problems has its precedents. In the United States, for example, the whole concept of welfare occupies a much lower scale of priority for both 'public' and 'government' alike. These precedents unfortunately do not always point to a better future. Despite economic regeneration, social problems often remain: American cities are models towards which few European societies would aspire.

This book recognizes deficiencies in attitudes and policies towards urban social problems. Its message is that although economic priorities are understandable, they do not obviate the need to address social issues directly in their own right. Government must retain its sense of responsibility and priority; the social problems of the city are real problems felt by real people.

References

Coleman, Alice (1985), *Utopia on Trial* (Hilary Shipman: London).

Harvey, D. (1985), *Consciousness and the Urban Experience* (Basil Blackwell: Oxford).

Hausner, V. A. and B. T. Robson (1985), *Changing Cities* (Economic and Social Research Council: London).

Herbert, D. T. (1976), 'The Study of delinquency areas: a social geographical perspective', *Transactions of the Institute of British Geographers*, 1(4): 272–92.

——and R. J. Johnston (1976), *Social Areas in Cities: Spatial Processes and Form* (John Wiley: London).

Jackson, P. and Susan J. Smith (1984), *Exploring Social Geography* (Allen and Unwin: London).

Newman, O. (1972), *Defensible Space: People and Design in the Violent City* (Architectural Press: London).

Smith, Susan J. (1986), *Crime, Space and Society* (Cambridge University Press: Cambridge).

Wirth, Louis (1938), 'Urbanism as a way of life', *American Journal of Sociology*, 44: 1–24.

PART I

Background

1

Social and Economic Futures for the Large City

Brian Robson

The future of large old cities in Britain still looks very bleak, even at the end of over a decade of inner-city policy. What shape will our cities be in by the end of the century? In the era of nineteenth-century industrialism, large cities could be seen unambiguously as places of production, offering benefits through the access which they provided to a large labour force and, through good inter-urban communications, to a large market. The promise, in the post-industrial age, was of the city as a centre of consumption, a view articulated by Castells (1977). The proponents of the post-industrial thesis (e.g. Bell, 1973) foresaw a future not only of increasing real income, leisure, and services, but also of decreasing inequality, through which ever-more people would enjoy the fruits of economic transformation. In practice, consumption has been privatized, has been disproportionately restricted to the affluent and, since the affluent are mobile and can consume in a variety of places other than the large city, the spatial and social divisions in society have increased so that there is now a large reserve army of the dispensable and unwanted found disproportionately in the large cities. So two questions arise: what is the future for the urban underclass, and can the city survive merely as a locus of tourism in the absence of growth in public goods and services?

Such questions involve both an urban and a regional dimension in the British case. Because of the peculiar geography associated with its industrial revolution, the growth of industry in Britain meant the growth of areas not previously in the heart of settlement, and hence the creation of the breed of industrial cities spatially eccentric to the older areas of investment in the south, south-west, and East Anglia. The concentration of large cities and the legacy of the older industrial heritage within the north and west has mean that, with industrial restructuring, the regional problem of 'north' versus 'south' has therefore compounded the problems of cities *per se*. We cannot consider the problems of cities in Britain without also discussing the problem of regional disparities (Champion and Green, 1988). In no other part of Europe is this consonance of urban and regional problems found to the same extent.

TABLE 1.1.	Indices of population and employment change in urban and
			rural areas, 1951–1981

	1951	1961	1971	1981
A. Changes in population of working age				
Inner cities	100	93	77	65
Outer cities	100	92	87	87
Free-standing cities	100	96	94	91
Towns and rural areas	100	106	114	117
B. Changes in employment				
Inner cities	100	89	71	55
Outer cities	100	97	97	93
Free-standing cities	100	93	91	85
Towns and rural areas	100	105	112	120
C. Unemployment rates				
Inner cities	133	136	144	151
Outer cities	81	82	88	101
Free-standing cities	95	107	112	115
Towns and rural areas	95	93	90	90

Note: All values are index values. For A and B the index of 100 is for the 1951 value of each type of settlement. For unemployment, the index of 100 is the value for Great Britain in each of the four years covered. Inner and outer city figures cover the 6 large cities (Greater London, West Midlands, Greater Manchester, Merseyside, Tyneside and Clydeside). 'Free-standing cities' are the next 17 largest cities.

Source: Begg *et al.*, 1986.

The decay of large cities and the disinvestment which they have faced in the post-war decades is suggested by the figures for employment and population in table 1.1. The loss in those three decades of over one-third of the population of the inner areas of the six large conurbations, and of almost one-half of their jobs, and the widening differentials in unemployment between inner areas and small towns and rural areas is dramatic. When the detailed figures from the 1984 Annual Census of Employment are eventually made public they will show the extent to which the economic disparities have continued to grow during the years of deep recession in the early 1980s. Such decay has prompted consider-able concern in central government, and a vast array of legislative instruments. While urban policy has been a faltering and uncertain element in government thinking, producing much rhetoric, there have been a number of excellent initiatives, some of which have achieved notable success in improving the physical infrastructure of cities. It is significant that many of the most successful schemes have capitalized on the potential of large cities as places of consumption, involving tourism or entertainment-based renewal or helping to introduce new private services; for example, the creation of the exhibition complex of G-Mex in Manchester, tourist attractions such as Wigan Pier, and housing schemes—often linked to waterfront developments as in the London and Liverpool Docklands—which have increased the social mix in a number of large cities, nowhere more so than in Glasgow.

Policy Approaches

Since the enhanced urban programme began in 1977–8, the sums of public money targeted to inner cities have grown impressively. From annual allocations of less than £40m, the Urban Programme has grown to annual sums of over £300m (table 1.2). To this have to be added other, often more considerable, resources which have disproportionately benefited cities. An example is provided by the job-creation schemes introduced through the Manpower Services Commission, much of whose budget, now exceeding £2.5b. has in practice been of especial benefit to inner-city residents. Indeed Kenneth Clarke, the government spokesman for the inner cities, claims that the total budget for urban expenditure as a whole, now exceeds £2b. The overall set of policy instruments within the urban programme is impressive if bewildering: Derelict Land Grants, Urban Development Grants, Urban Renewal Grants, Commercial and Industrial Improvement Areas, Enterprise Zones, Simplified Planning Zones, Urban Development Corporations, Partnership and Programme Authorities, Task Forces, City Action Teams.

TABLE 1.2.   Urban Programme expenditure in England, 1979/80 to 1986/7 (£ million)

	79/80	80/1	81/2	82/3	83/4	84/5	85/6	86/7
Partnership	110	116	118	143	133	131	125	127
Programme Areas	32	47	50	77	86	97	96	102
Other Designated	3	6	5	9	8	8	10	9
Traditional Urban Programme	30	33	42	47	53	47	44	37
Urban Development Grant	—	—	—	—	7	15	22	25
Other[a]	10	—	—	19	23	23	20	19
TOTAL	185	202	215	295	310	321	317	319

[a]includes Merseyside Task Force.

Source: DoE, 1987.

A frequent criticism of government policy has been that it lacks co-ordination, that the numerous ministries involved in aspects of urban policy have never aligned their respective approaches so as to develop a genuine *urban* policy. At national level there is undoubted force to this critique: the hoped-for 'bending' of mainstream expenditure to favour inner areas never really happened; central government departments have vied rather publicly for control of the overall programme; and, even though there is now a 'spokesman' from the Department of Trade and Industry and a cabinet committee chaired by the prime minister, it is clear that the two main departments involved have distinctive and not always complementary approaches. National policy will always be difficult to co-ordinate—even with the institution of City Action Teams, whose aim was precisely to help co-ordination—since the rather watertight nature of departments means that different fields of government activity develop hierarchies of priorities of their own. At local level, however, the lack of co-ordination can be seen as a positive benefit, since the welter of schemes has provided opportunities for the more alert authorities, individuals and agencies to stitch together some imaginative large schemes involving combinations of funding instruments such as Urban Programme resources and Enterprise Allowance Schemes. What would be helpful as a way of capitalizing on such initiative would be the wider publication of manuals of 'best practice' at local level.

The Limitations of Policy

Leaving aside the confusion that the 'alphabet soup' of initials of the numerous schemes can create, many of these central initiatives have achieved considerable impact within areas of some of the large cities, and to them have to be added the activities of local authorities in developing local economic development agencies. Nevertheless the overall impact has been less impressive than might have been anticipated. This may not be surprising, given the twin forces of industrial restructuring and the inheritance of old industrial structures with which policy has been faced. It could be argued that the resources devoted to urban renewal have not been commensurate with the need. It is, however, more to the point to argue that urban policy has suffered from a number of specific weaknesses of implementation and conceptualization that have blunted its impact.

First, and reflecting the lack of national co-ordination, much of the potential of the spatial targeting of resources has been simultaneously undermined by conflicts with other programmes. Local authorities in the large cities point to the withdrawal of rate support as a classic case of the other hand withdrawing what one hand has offered. For the period 1980/81 to 1982/3, for example, the Partnership Authorities (the seven English cities which were considered as having the most severe inner area problems and which consequently have been given the largest allocation of resources to spend through a partnership of central and local government) suffered a 25 per cent real reduction in rate support grant as against an average of only 13 per cent for all authorities (Buck, Gordon and Young, 1986, p. 115). In London, the designated inner area boroughs received some £300 million from the Urban Programme between 1979/80 and 1983/4, but 'lost' five times that amount through reduction in rate support grant over the same period (Lever and Moore, 1986. p. 145). Another example is the equally contrary impact of the investment of public resources in research and development and in public procurement by central government departments, where investment in the 'golden belt' of the Bristol–Cambridge axis has helped to channel economic growth into the M4 and M11 coridors of the southeast, and hence away from the older industrial urban areas (Boddy and Lovering, 1986).

Second, the conflicts between central and local government have diverted energy and resources away fròm tackling urban problems and into an unhelpful political flexing of muscles on both sides. That there are inefficient local authorities often motivated more by political ideology than by the best interests of their areas is indisputable. Some of the reports of the Audit Commission have demonstrated the considerable gap between best practice in 'good' authorities and the performance of the 'worst'. In London, for example, comparison of the eight boroughs of Brent, Camden, Hackney, Haringey, Islington, Lambeth, Lewisham, and Southwark with eight 'similarly deprived but better managed' London boroughs suggested that the first group spent £16.50 per house on refuse disposal as against £9.00 for the second group; that rent arrears were 20 per cent as against 7 per cent; that vehicle maintenance costs were over £1,000 per year as against under £700; and that the first group had negotiated deferred loan arrangements of some £550 million, a large part of which was to finance revenue expenditure (Audit Commission, 1987).

It has been in response to central government's increasing suspicion of the ability of some local authorities to manage economic development, and particularly to work with the private sector, that central government has developed agencies such as Urban Development Corporations to assume the traditional planning and management responsibilities of areas within those authorities. Nevertheless, the increasing and widespread hostility between central and local government has undoubtedly had a cost: that of diverting energy away from the co-ordinated implementation of renewal in many large cities. While the achievements of the Urban Development Corporations have been impressive—and nowhere more than in the London Docklands—to see such interventions as more than a short-term catalyst is to ignore the local democratic imperative which is rightly respected by local groups. It seems implausible that local authorities, in some form, will not play a central role as multi-purpose bodies in the delivery of services and the overall management of land in local areas. Indeed, some of the most innovative schemes of local economic development have been in their hands (Mawson and Miller, 1986), yet such local economic development has been undertaken in the absence of encouragement from the centre and in the guise of local enterprise agencies created through a variety of what amount almost to subterfuges by local authorities.

Third, and perhaps most damagingly, there has been a long-running dilemma in public policy between social and economic goals. At the start of the urban programmes, social aims—the building of community facilities, educational provision in the broadest sense, additional help with housing—played a substantial part in resource allocation, and this emphasis enabled the voluntary sector to play a significant and often innovative role in local areas. Since 1981, economic aims have consciously come to dominate expenditure. Resources have been channelled increasingly to the building of industrial premises, to the provision of basic infrastructure for business, to loans and grants for enterprise. The switch can clearly be seen, for example, in the Newcastle case, where 'social' expenditure comprised 59 per cent of the Urban Programme budget in 1979/80, but had fallen to 30 per cent by 1982/83 (Robinson *et al.*, 1987). Public policy has long—and damagingly—seen economic and social goals as alternatives, while publicly making the assumption that they are not incompatible. The practice of separation ignores at considerable peril the connections between the two. It seems inconceivable that economic growth can be sustained in the long term in the absence of social benefit being spread more widely among urban populations. The riots of 1981 and 1985 bear testimony to that, as indeed do the innumerable continuing sub-riots which occur with depressing frequency, or are only narrowly averted on innumerable occasions, in most of the big cities.

The Gloomy Scenario

The gloomy prospect that cities face is one of living with the ghetto, of the physical containment of the urban underclass, who might form 10 per cent of the national population but perhaps one-third of that of big cities. Unwanted, allowed to develop a subculture which sets them apart from mainstream society, such an underclass must form a recurring threat to the achievement of economic affluence for the majority. One increasingly plausible response may become that of containment, with a more rigid formal mechanism of policing and physical containment of such areas. And where better to contain than in the run-down housing estates on the fringe of large city centres, or in the girdle of deprived population lying outside the central city?

There is an assumption that if that scenario is to be avoided we need to encourage national economic growth. The options facing us can be seen (in figure 1.1) along two dimensions, one of economic growth and the other of policy. The conventional argument would have said that we must wait for economic growth before we can return to the 'normality' of the redistributive mechanisms represented by the policies of the 1960s. Current government belief in the efficacy of the market points in a similar direction, growth will trickle down and ultimately bring benefit to even the most deprived individuals and regions. Only with growth would we have the luxury of being able to pursue policies favourable to spatial equity. In other words, the track in figure 1 is from A to B to C. This I find unconvincing. What does national economic growth hold for the cities? We can formulate an answer by looking at the converse question. It is clear that the recent economic depression has, if anything, helped to *stem* the further loss of population from urban areas. Out-migration diminished. Champion's figures (in table 1.3) show that, compared with the decades 1971–81, the large cities in the following years of deep depression in 1981–5 lost *relatively* fewer people than did other areas. Rather than this being a sign of an upturn in the fortunes of cities, it can more realistically be interpreted as a consequence of the depression, during which, just as in the 1930s, people moved less or

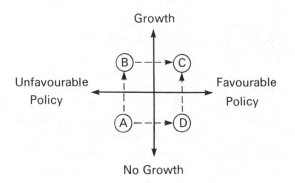

FIG. 1.1. *Alternative scenarios*

TABLE 1.3. Recent population change in large cities

City	Population change (% per year)		
	1971–81	1981–5	Shift
Greater London	−0.96	−0.14	+0.82
Birmingham	−0.68	−0.33	+0.35
Glasgow	−2.16	−1.30	+0.86
Leeds	−0.37	−0.25	+0.12
Sheffield	−0.51	−0.41	+0.10
Liverpool	−1.42	−1.22	+0.20
Newcastle	−0.89	−0.17	+0.72
Manchester	−1.37	−0.62	+0.75
Great Britain	+0.08	+0.11	+0.03

Source: Champion, 1987.

indeed migrated back to areas from which earlier they had come. Whereas in the decade 1971–81 overall household mobility showed annual levels of over 11 per cent, by the early 1980s the figure had dropped to below 10 per cent. This has been a result of people and of business no longer having the incentive to move elsewhere. The implication is that when renewed growth comes, the gates will be thrown open to a repetition of outward movement of investment, of people and of enterprise, and there are already many signs of this. One of the most striking is the flurry of proposals for out-of-town mega-shopping centres in most of the large conurbations. If approved, they would have the effect both of undermining the existing regional role of city-centre shops and of encouraging further investment—in housing, services and business—in suburban or out-of-town locations.

The indicators are that much of the proposed development of the foreseeable future similarly lies in schemes which will widen the regional and the urban/non-urban gulfs. Examples include: private new towns in the country such as Tillingham Hall or Foxley Wood; the already evident impact of the M25 around the London Green Belt; the effects of the Channel Tunnel; pressures for the further expansion of Stansted Airport; the increasing amounts paid in subsidizing public transport in London and in meeting the costs of London and south east weighting allowances, for which increasing numbers of businesses are paying sums of over £3,000; suggestions for introducing regionally differential rates of pay; the effects of the introduction of a poll tax whose domestic levels will work directly to the disadvantage of the poorer living in cities and whose non-domestic levels, while reducing the tax for large-city business, will reduce the local income generated for large cities since they will be redistributed on a per caput basis. All of these current and probable future developments suggest the possibility of yet further divisions in the formalization of a 'command centre' in the south and east and an area of low-wage routine production in the north and west, where the large cities are concentrated. This would entail the latter regions becoming more subject to the fluctuations of economic fortunes—a kind of on-shore Taiwan. The evidence that the wave of prosperity is now stretching further from London—has now reached the southern out-skirts of Birmingham—should be of little comfort to those in northern cities. It promises merely a repetition of the post-war experience of regional structural inequality—driven by the highly centralized nature of the economy.

If this is right, the track towards a more equitable future should certainly not be that of waiting for growth—not the progression from A to B to C in figure 1.1. Instead, even in the absence of growth, we need to develop policies which are beneficial to the distressed cities and regions in order that they can stand to benefit from the fruits of present or future economic growth. The track, in other words, should be from A to D to C.

What might this mean in policy terms? Three general elements may be emphasized. First is the need for us to be more alive to the spatially redistributive nature of many apparently neutral public spending decisions. Public spending—and the importance of public services for the job prospects of the less prosperous—plays a critical role both in directly creating jobs and in providing the infrastructure which can attract or repel private investment. As Short (1981) and Boddy (1987) have shown, much of the spending of central government departments has benefited those very areas which are already most prosperous. The development of regional audits is an essential first step in helping us to recognize the differential impact that such spending entails. Such audits might use-fully be accompanied by the legislative introduction of formal 'urban impact assessment' on the American model, although this must remain debatable, given the somewhat limited effectiveness of such legislation in America (Massey, 1980).

Second, and partly allied with this, is the need for political and administrative decentralization to reduce the damaging centripetal forces within the country. Such decentralization is important at both national and local levels. Nationally, so long as northern cities are seen as a mere adjunct to a south-east-dominated economy, the political clout of such areas is unlikely to increase. It is in this context that the argu-ments for the wider introduction of regional development agencies needs to be assessed. The much-vaunted successes of the Scottish Develop-ment Agency, for example, have been the product of its close association with the political power of the Scottish office. In England, regional offices of central departments such as Environment or Trade and Industry are clearly no substitute for genuine political devolution. Merely to establish development agencies in the English regions may help to create simpler 'one-stop shops' offering information and advice to potential investors, in place of the present confusion produced by the plethora of fragmented competing, multiple local agencies, but by themselves such regional agencies would not achieve the impact of the SDA unless there were also political decentralization or at least a regional presence in the Cabinet to add muscle to the case of northern authorities. That there is also a case for economic decentralization is most forcefully seen in the case of access to venture capital where, with the exception of such regional agencies as Investors in Industry, the concentration of venture capital banks is overwhelmingly in the south east. The effect has been that, especially when looking for smaller sums of capital, potential entrepreneurs outside the south east have found great difficulty in raising the necessary capital. The argument for *local* decentralization is equally compelling, as a response to the clear evidence of the alienation and dependency of so many residents of large cities. The accumulated experience of the Priority Estates Project and other local decentralization projects (DoE 1981; Hoggett and Hambleton, 1987) provides convincing evidence that the wider introduction of neighbourhood-based schemes focused on housing or a range of local social services would have inestimable benefits in giving local people greater control over their local environment.

The third point is the need for more effective *social* targeting of the benefits of growth. There is little evidence that present benefits trickle down to the poor or that spatial targeting (one of the main planks of inner-city policy) is synonymous with social targeting. Open labour markets and the operation of standard commercial criteria in job selection mean that few of the new jobs created through such valuable initiatives as Urban Development Grants are actually taken up by the long-term unemployed or the more deprived of the inner-city residents. Especially in *regions* of high unemployment, new jobs in inner areas merely suck in commuters from outside (Buck and Gordon, 1987). The evidence from Newcastle suggests that only 37 per cent of inner-area residents have benefited from inner-city jobs newly created by public spending under the urban and regional programmes (Robinson, Wren and Goddard, 1987). Similar figures have been shown for other large conurbations. This suggests the need for some form of specific social targeting. A variety of possibilities can be suggested: improved links between housing, transport, and job creation schemes; schemes which link training and job creation so as to enable inner-area residents to compete more effectively for new jobs; links with education as in the London Compact scheme whereby private-sector firms offer guaranteed job interviews to pupils from schools in East London in return for meeting agreed educational and training goals; or spatial ring-fencing of recruitment to develop forms of affirmative action to increase the proportion of local residents working in newly created employment (Robson, 1987*a*). Only with such a more *socially* conscious dimension will policy begin to address the need to connect the economic and social facets of the urban dilemma. Policy which is favourable to urban renaissance has to recognize that the residents of inner urban areas represent a potential strength if their energies can be engaged, or a potential threat if their interests are marginalized.

The Ebullient Scenario

The above presupposes that it is in our interests to attempt to 'save' our cities. As an unrepentent advocate of large cities (Robson, 1987*b*), it is unnecessary for me to spell out the arguments on both sides of that debate. What is needed, however, is to elaborate a justification of an economic future of large cities in a world in which heavy industry and a dependence on manufacturing is a thing of the past—or no longer a major feature of developed economies. The *consumption* rationale of large cities is certainly now well recognized. They can offer a concentration of entertainment, leisure-related opportunities, tourist attractions and high-class shopping facilities that has provided one of the obvious lynchpins of both local and central government renewal strategy. Albert Dock in Liverpool and St. Catherine's Dock in London are perhaps the two most dramatic instances of this. The combination of water frontage and architecturally interesting buildings has proved everywhere an irresistable spur to renewal. Even an inland site like the core of Greater Manchester has provided such opportunities (figure 1.2) with the redevelopment of Salford Docks (Law, 1987) and the start of redevelopment of the canal basin at the heart of Castlefield providing the centrepiece for an extensive series of renewal schemes, many of which aim at attracting new tourist traffic through the development of museums and of sites of architectural, archaeological, industrial, and literary or cultural interest. Such leisure-related activities clearly provide a spur for environmental renewal which can in turn attract a variety of private investment in housing and in offices, which both increase the social mix of inner-area residents and provide additional jobs, some of which are especially appropriate for the indigenous residents, many of whom lack formal skills. Allied with affirmative action to link local residents with new jobs, this must be part of the way to avoid the creation

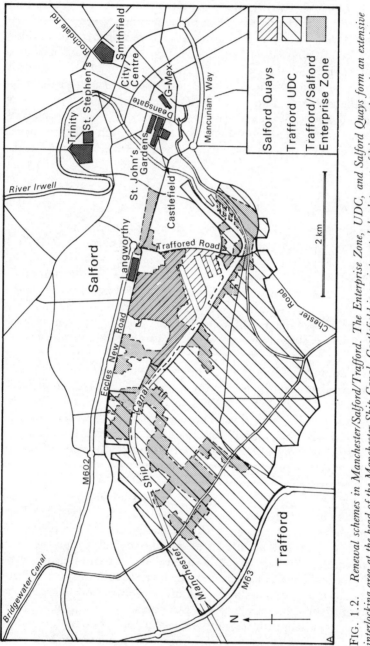

Fig. 1.2.   *Renewal schemes in Manchester/Salford/Trafford. The Enterprise Zone, UDC, and Salford Quays form an extensive interlocking area at the head of the Manchester Ship Canal. Castlefield is an integrated development of leisure and tourist attractions, incorporating industrial buildings, an archaeological site, and a major junction of canals. G-Mex is the conversion of the old Central Station into an exhibition hall. Smithfield is the conversion of old fish and vegetable markets into a mixed retail/industrial and housing complex. St Stephen's, Trinity, and Langworthy are ex-local authority housing estates which have been refurbished and privatized.*

of social and economic gulfs between the affluent and ghettoes of the unwanted.

However, there is a potentially wider reason for large cities than that of providing leisure and services. Their future *production*-related role can be seen in terms of their potential provision of an information-rich environment to which clusters of small and medium-sized firms can be attracted. Set against the long-standing trend of increasing gigantism in business, with the associated internationalization which has become one of the unchallenged 'facts' of economic development, a new phenomenon has become evident in the last decade: that of the fragmentation of corporate enterprise (Shutt and Whittington, 1987). Management buy-outs and the de-merger of businesses can be seen as a response to the increasing volatility of the business environment in which companies now operate: labour markets have become less controllable and, most importantly, markets have become more changeable and less easily manipulated by companies themselves. In the face of the risk associated with such uncertainty, corporate enterprise can be seen to have begun to externalize risk through a strategy of 'putting out' elements of production, and this has included the creation of smaller independent and quasi-independent firms as well as the creation of just-in-time systems and of flexible workforces. A key to the new flexible responses of businesses—to labour and to markets—is access to information; information about market trends, new technical developments, the implications and potential of new legislation. The model of Emilia Romagna, with its development of large numbers of small, linked firms, is increasingly being taken as one model of the future (Brusco, 1982). It is here that the potential importance of the new telecommunications technologies for the future economic renewal of large cities might lie. Current trends suggest that the investment patterns in advanced telecommunications are likely to lead to a further widening of the divisions between north and south and between urban and non-urban areas (Goddard and Gillespie, 1987). However, if concentrated investment of a broad-band fibre-optic network of advanced telecommunications were to be installed in one or more large cities, such areas could provide precisely the 'wired-up' information-rich environment that would offer an attractive context for new business investment by small firms. The implication is that policy should aim to select one or more large cities as the first fully 'wired-up' European urban locations, on the model of the Japanese development of Kawasaki (Batty, 1987).

Here is an alternative model for the big cities of the future, in which a combination of leisure and service provision on one hand and clusters of industrial villages on the other could capitalize on the potential benefits that dense urban settlement offers to a small crowded nation (TCPA,

1987; Breheny *et al.*, 1987). Such a strategy would also directly address the argument about the problems of centralization within the national economy, since such 'alternative magnets' would offer a more realistic, long-term way of eroding the overwheening dominance of London than would our present strategy of merely hoping that growth will spread from the south east and thereby reinforce the regional dominance that the area has long exerted.

Such a vision of what some of our large cities could become in the final decade of the century presupposes policy which is more coherent, more genuinely addressed to the *urban* dimension, and more alive to the need to blend the economic and social facets of the urban future. The alternative is clearly bleak for those who choose to live in or are trapped as residents of large cities. Yet it is in all our interests to recognize that stable solutions to the question of national economic growth and social well-being seem at best expensive and at worst implausible unless they take account of the needs of the less favoured in our society.

References

Audit Commission (1987), *The Management of London's Authorities: Preventing the Breakdown of Services*, Occasional Paper 2 (Audit Commission for Local Authorities in England and Wales, HMSO: London).

Batty, M. (1987), 'The intelligent plaza is only the beginning', *Guardian*, 17 Sept.

Begg, I., B. Moore and J. Rhodes (1986), 'Economic and social change in urban Britain and the inner cities', in V. A. Hausner (ed.), *Critical Issues in Urban Economic Development*, i (Clarendon Press: Oxford), 11–49.

Bell, D. (1973), *The Coming of Post-industrial Society: A Venture in Social Forecasting* (Basic Books: New York).

Boddy, M. (1987), 'High-technology industry, regional development and defence manufacturing: a case-study in the UK Sunbelt', in B. T. Robson (ed.), *Managing the City: The Aims and Impacts of Urban Policy* (Croom Helm: Beckenham), 60–83.

—— and J. Lovering (1986), 'High technology industry in the Bristol sub-region: the aerospace/defence nexus', *Regional Studies*, 20: 217–31.

Breheny, M., P. Hall, and D. Hart (1987), *Northern Lights: A Development Agenda for the North in the 1990s* (Derrick, Wade and Waters: London).

Brusco, S. (1982), 'The Emilian model: productive decentralisation and social integration', *Cambridge Journal of Economics*, 6: 167–84.

Buck, N., and I. Gordon (1987), 'The beneficiaries of employment growth, an analysis of the experience of disadvantaged groups in expanding labour markets', in V. Hausner (ed.), *Critical Issues in Urban Economic Development*, ii (Clarendon Press: Oxford), 77–115.

—— —— and K. Young (1986), *The London Employment Problem* (Clarendon Press: Oxford).

Castells, M. (1977), *The Urban Question* (Edward Arnold: London).

Champion, A. G. (1987), 'Momentous revival in London's population', *Town and Country Planning*, 56: 80–2.

—— and A. Green (1988), *Local Prosperity and the North–South Divide: A Report on Winners and Losers in 1980s Britain* (Institute for Employment Research, Warwick University: Warwick).

DoE (Department of the Environment) (1981), *The Priority Estate Project, 1981: Improving Problem Council Estates* (HMSO: London).

—— (1987), *The Urban Programme 1986/87: A Report on its Operations and Achievements in England* (DoE: London).

Goddard, J. B. and A. E. Gillespie (1987), 'Advanced telecommunications and regional economic development', in B. T. Robson (ed.), *Managing the City: The Aims and Impacts of Urban Policy* (Croom Helm: Beckenham), 84–109.

Hoggett, P., and R. Hambleton (eds.) (1987), *Decentralisation and Democracy: Localising Public Services*, Occasional Paper 28 (School for Advanced Urban Studies: Bristol).

Law, C. M. (1987), 'The redevelopment of Manchester Docks', paper given at the International Seminar on Waterfront Development and the Cityport Economy, Southampton, Nov.

Lever, W. F., and C. Moore (eds.) (1986), *The City in Transition: Policies and Agendas for the Economic Regeneration of Clydeside* (Clarendon Press: Oxford).

Massey, D. (1980), 'Urban impact analysis: the potential for its application in the UK, *Built Environment*, 6: 131–5.

Mawson, J., and D. Miller (1986), 'Interventionist approaches to local employment and economic development: the experience of Labour local authorities', in V. A. Hausner (ed.), *Critical Issues in Urban Economic Development*, i (Clarendon Press: Oxford), 145–99.

Robinson, R., C. Wren, and J. B. Goddard (1987), *Economic Development Policies: An Evaluative Study of the Newcastle Metropolitan Region* (Clarendon Press: Oxford).

Robson, B. T. (1987a), 'Local employment: a success story?', *Business in the Community*, 4 (Spring): 16–18.

—— (ed.) (1987b), *Managing the City: The Aims and Impacts of Urban Policy* (Croom Helm: Beckenham).

Short, J. (1981), 'Defence spending in the UK regions', *Regional Studies*, 15: 101–10.

Shutt, J., and R. Whittington (1987), 'Fragmentation strategies and the rise of small units: cases from the North West', *Regional Studies*, 21: 13–23.

TCPA (Town and Country Planning Association) (1987), *North–South divide: A New Deal for Britain's Regions* (TCPA: London).

2

The Vulnerable, the Disadvantaged, and the Victimized: Who They Are and Where They Live

Paul L. Knox

A fundamental part of the conventional wisdom about cities in Western societies is that they are necessary evils: places of employment and amenity that inevitably foster economic and social dislocation, materialistic and ego-centred values, and deviant behaviour. Popular literature, for example, tends to propagate the image of cities as arenas of conflict and desolation (Jaye and Watts, 1981; Lees, 1985); and evidence from attitudinal surveys suggests that most people in fact believe city environments to be unsatisfactory from almost every perspective—including income and employment criteria. In recent years this view has been reinforced by the experience of 'urban decline' associated with the economic transformation and spatial restructuring of the 'post-affluent' period (Gappert, 1987). Not only do cities have a disproportionate share of economic and social problems: they are also, most of them, increasing their share of society's disadvantaged, vulnerable, and victimized people.

Another part of the conventional wisdom about cities and their problems is that most of the disadvantaged, vulnerable, and victimized are highly concentrated in the slums, ghettos, and 'problem areas' that surround the central business districts of central cities. These neighbourhoods, it is asserted, are the ecological niche of an urban 'underclass'— a heterogeneous grouping of inner-city families and individuals who find themselves outside the mainstream of housing and job markets. Included in this subgroup are 'persons who lack training and skills and either experience long-term unemployment or have dropped out of the labour force altogether; who are long-term public assistance recipients; and who are engaged in street criminal activity and other forms of aberrant behavior' (Wilson, 1985, p. 133). Furthermore, the argument runs, the localization of the underclass in crowded, decaying, unhealthy, and under-serviced settings tends to compound and intensify economic, social, and behavioural problems. Substandard schools lead to a lack of occupational skills, which leads to low incomes; disorganized communities provide questionable role models; and so on.

This chapter examines the geography of social problems in detail, looking specifically at *who are* the disadvantaged, the vulnerable and the victimized in cities of different kinds and *where they live* within cities. The importance of these issues is twofold. In terms of theory and the search for an improved understanding of social problems, the geography of disadvantage, vulnerability, and victimization represents an important dimension of urbanization (Herbert, 1975): one that both reflects and conditions broader ecological and structural processes and outcomes. In this context, the validity of concepts of accelerating urban decline and of the ghettoization of an underclass is central to the debate over urban change, whether from ecological, neo-Weberian, or neo-Marxist perspectives. In practical terms, the geography of disadvantage, vulnerability and victimization is crucial to the tactics and strategies of a variety of public policies. The best examples are provided by policies of 'positive discrimination' in favour of deprived or disadvantaged cities or neighbourhoods. Among the implicit assumptions of such policies are: (*a*) that identifiable areas do in fact exist where a significantly high proportion of the population is disadvantaged (by whatever criteria); (*b*) that disadvantaged people and households are concentrated into such areas; and (*c*) that because of a neighbourhood or multiplier effect, the same resources can alleviate more problems when the target population is geographically concentrated than when it is scattered (MacLaran, 1981; Carley, 1981).

Territorial Social Indicators

It will already be clear that the description and analysis of the geography of social problems is surrounded by questions of definition and measurement. Social problems are both culturally and historically specific: 'Like the city itself, they reflect the prevailing values, ideology, and structure of the existing social formation' (Smith, 1979, p. 13). What constitutes disadvantage, vulnerability, and victimization is clearly relative, influenced by the level of economic and cultural development of the society concerned and, indeed, of the reference group of particular classes or individuals. Any attempt to describe or analyse the geography of social problems must inevitably confront these issues, while at the same time having to work within the limitations of the available data.

Until the early 1970s, the data collected on social problems, however defined, were rather patchy and often unreliable. Compared with economic accounting, the recording of social conditions was primitive. It was not until the events of the late 1960s—the rioting and disorder in American cities (associated with the blacks' struggle for civil rights), and the 'revolutionary' alliance between students and blue-collar workers in parts of Europe (associated with protest against the hegemony of 'Big Business' and 'Big Government')—that concern over social problems was translated into efforts to collect and monitor data on a greater number of social, behavioural, and environmental issues. As society in general became more sensitized to a wider range of social and environmental issues, geographers and other social scientists, in parallel with politicians and the media, began to examine these issues more closely. One major focus of interest was the distribution of 'bads' or 'ills' that were, apparently, the inevitable handmaidens of urbanization and economic growth. Concern for those places and social groups who found themselves the victims rather than the beneficiaries of economic change raised the question of how to identify the disadvantaged, the vulnerable, and the victimized. The collective response of academics, administrators, and policy-makers was manifested in the so-called 'social indicators movement', an unprecedented burst of investigation into the numerical measurement of social conditions (for a review of this literature, see Carley, 1981). David Smith did a great deal to demonstrate the value of *territorial* social indicators (Smith, 1973, 1975, 1977), and there is now a fair amount of evidence that derives from research at the inter- and intra-urban levels (Knox, 1987, pp. 139–49).

It must be acknowledged, however, that the use of territorial social indicators is subject to several important pitfalls (Knox, 1978; Visvalingham, 1983). Despite an increase in the availability of data relating to social problems, it is often difficult to find appropriate data at the required spatial scale. In particular, it is often difficult to assemble data that are unambiguously *normative*, in that they can be clearly categorized along a continuum from 'good' to 'bad', 'high' to 'low', etc., in relation to the concept being measured (Myers, 1987). This, in turn, is related to the difficulties of conceptualizing and operationalizing the issues at hand. What do we mean when we speak of 'deprivation', 'disadvantage', 'vulnerability', and so on? All too often, such terms are used without explanation, and the composite operational definitions that are presented seem to owe more to a combination of pragmatism and the values of the analyst than to theoretically grounded concepts or to the values and priorities of the people whose circumstances are at issue.

Problems such as these have stimulated interest in *subjective* social indicators: measures of people's priorities, attitudes, and satisfactions in relation to particular social concerns. Subjective social indicators seek to tap directly the problems experienced by people. Using subjective indicators means that the objective world is dealt with only indirectly, 'filtered through the individual's own perceptions and then weighed according to his expectations, experiences, attitudes and present circumstances' (Abrams, 1973, p. 35). From a phenomenological perspective, of course, the existence of variations in such feelings is by itself a sufficient justification for using subjective indicators; and indeed it is difficult to disagree— from any scientific perspective or political ideology—with the importance of people's reactions to their own lives. Most proponents of subjective social indicators, however, see them as complementary, rather than as alternatives, to objective indicators. The use of both, it is argued, affords a fuller and more sensitive portrayal of the issues. There are, neverthe-less, several practical problems that present significant difficulties in the use of subjective social indicators. In addition to the expense involved in conducting large-scale surveys with samples great enough to yield reliable estimates of variations between cities or neighborhoods, these include concerns over the reliability and comparability of data derived from psychosocial scales, and the interpretation of aggregated data from psychometric scales (Knox, 1979).

Inter-Urban Variations

It must be recognized at the outset that both the *nature* and the *intensity* of social problems vary a great deal between cities. A detailed survey of urban 'decline', 'distress', and 'disparity' in the United States, under-taken at the Brookings Institution, portrays a complex pattern (Bradbury *et al.*, 1982). Urban decline (measured by *changes* in unemployment rates, changes in real per capita income, changes in the incidence of violent crime, and changes in the public debt burden) and distress (meas-ured by *levels* of unemployment, violent crime, per capita income, older housing, and city/suburban tax disparity) were found to be wide-spread but at the same time were, apparently, mostly mutually rein-forcing, with some cities having a disproportionate share of economic and social problems. Boston and Cleveland, for example, fell in the most disadvantaged one-third of all cities on all nine components of the city distress and decline indexes: Dayton, Hartford, Newark, and Trenton scored eight out of nine; and Atlanta, Jersey City, Paterson, and Philadelphia recorded seven negative counts. Meanwhile, urban dis-parity (measured by central city/suburban differences in levels of unemployment, violent crime, per caput income, poverty, and old housing) was found to exhibit rather different patterns: some distressed and declining cities (Boston, Newark, and Trenton, for example) have a high degree of disparity; others (e.g. Jersey City, Knoxville) do not. Bradbury *et al.* conclude that, despite the overall prevalence of decline, distress, and disparity and a general tendency for them to 'bunch' together in certain cities, 'A tremendous diversity of urban conditions exists across the United States. Some cities fit none of the [overall] patterns—growing cities showing distress, troubled cities improving. Hence whatever processes generate "bunching" of conditions are neither inescapable nor universal' (1982, p. 64).

In the United Kingdom, inter-urban analyses of disadvantage and deprivation show a similar diversity accompanying the underlying 'bunching' of problems in the inner areas of the larger conurbations, particularly London and Clydeside (Holtermann, 1975; Bentham, 1985). Closer examination of these patterns suggests that much of this diversity may be associated with the existence of different *syndromes* of problems in different urban settings. Coulter's (1978) analysis of 1-km square census data for the seven largest British conurbations, for example, shows that the most common syndrome of problems involves overcrowding, low wages, unemployment, low levels of automobile ownership, and high levels of ill-health and is typically located centrally within the core of the conurbation. In addition, Leeds, Liverpool, Glasgow, and (to a lesser extent) Manchester all exhibit a further syndrome involving poor housing—mostly privately rented, furnished accommodation—associated with inner-city areas containing high proportions of one particular vulnerable group: New Commonwealth immigrants. Some conurbations also exhibit distinctive syndromes of problems which are associated with outer suburban areas. Some public housing estates in the outer zones of the Birmingham, Glasgow, and Manchester conurbations, for example, suffer particularly from a syndrome involving low educational achievement, low wages, and lack of cars. (See also Madge and Willmott (1981) for a comparison of the syndromes of deprivation in inner-urban neighbourhoods of Paris and London.)

As the existence of these syndromes suggests, analysing patterns of disadvantage more sensitively in terms of particular subgroups of the population can reveal further dimensions of variability. A good illustration is provided by the analysis by Donnison and Soto (1980) of the British urban system. They classified British cities into thirteen functional types: regional service centres, resorts, residential suburbs, new towns, London, Welsh mining towns, textile towns, heavy engineering/coal towns, central Scotland, inner conurbations, and two kinds of engineering town. At a more general level, they suggested, there is a twofold division between 'traditional Britain' and 'new Britain'. The significant feature about this division is that the communities of 'new Britain'—the new towns, residential suburbs, resorts, regional service centres and London—were generally more prosperous and equal: for any given occupational group, opportunity and affluence tends to be greater in the urban environments of 'new Britain' than in 'traditional Britain'. Perhaps the most interesting suggestion to emerge from the analysis, however, is that there exists a type of place—the 'Good City'— in which the most vulnerable members of society suffer disadvantages and victimization less than they do elsewhere, even though they represent a disproportionately large section of the total population.

Intra-Urban Patterns

At face value, the ecology of social problems is relatively straight-forward: the overwhelming impression conveyed by the available data tends to support the conventional wisdom of a marked concentration of social problems in older, inner-city neighbourhoods. The 'poverty areas' identified by the US Bureau of the Census provide good examples. These poverty areas were defined at the request of the Office of Economic Opportunity in order to provide information for the planning of anti-poverty programmes. They consist of census tracts with poverty levels of at least 20 per cent, using a definition of poverty that is related to a minimum food budget, adjusted for household size. In 1970, the poverty threshold for the average non-farm family of four was $3,742; in 1980 it was $7,412. As figure 2.1 shows, poverty areas are concentrated in inner-city neighbourhoods, although they tend to have spread outwards during the 1970s. These poverty areas also seem to be a locus of disadvantages of other kinds. Table 2.1 shows that the poverty-area populations of the hundred largest central cities in the United States in 1980 were characterized not only by much higher levels of poverty, near-poverty, and extreme poverty, but also by higher levels of unemployment and housing stress.

TABLE 2.1. Disadvantaged population in the hundred largest US central cities, 1980

	Inside poverty areas	Outside poverty areas
Extreme poverty ($<75\%$ of poverty level)	23.9	6.1
Poverty	33.5	9.2
Marginal poverty ($<150\%$ of poverty level)	49.1	17.1
Unemployment	12.3	7.4
Occupied units lacking plumbing	3.5	0.7
Occupied units overcrowded	11.2	6.0

Such statistics tend to reinforce the conventional wisdom. Likewise, John O'Loughlin's comparison of cities in Canada, the United States, and West Germany (1983) found a remarkable consistency in the degree of intra-urban inequality, in the spatial clustering of deprivation in inner-city neighbourhoods, and in the persistence, over time, of these disparities. There were, nevertheless, significant differences that seem to be the product of variations in urban historical development and in the nature of housing markets. In particular, deprivations were found to be less intense in the inner-city neighbourhoods of West German cities than in the North American cities in the study; partly, at least, because of housing shortages and controls on the use of suburban land for building—so that many inner-city neighbourhoods have been subject to infilling and rehabilitation by more affluent households. Where housing markets are even less perfect (in the neo-classical economic sense), patterns of deprivation depart still further from the conventional wisdom. In Glasgow, for example, where the public sector accomodates over 60 per cent of all households, pockets of deprivation are found *throughout* the city (Rae, 1983; Pacione, 1986, 1987; see also Sim, 1984).

Vulnerable populations

To the extent that urban, social, and economic change generates large numbers of people who are vulnerable to poverty and other forms of disadvantage—whether because of ethnicity, age, gender, household structure, educational experience, or immigrant status—we must recognize a problem of considerable proportions. In central Paris, for example, the population of just over two million includes large concentrations of immigrants (400,000), elderly persons (400,000), young singles (75,000), students from outside Paris (65,000), and several thousand physically or mentally handicapped people (Merlin, 1986). As with the already disadvantaged population, the spatial distribution of these marginal and vulnerable groups is largely a function of the structure and operation of housing markets, together with the organization of welfare delivery services (Jones, 1987; Wolch, 1980, 1981), so that the dominant patterns have been the familiar ones of localization in inner-city neighbourhoods, with some peripheral exclaves in cities where 'problem' households have been 'dumped' in peripheral housing projects. A recent comparative study of European cities found that vulnerable people seem to have become increasingly localized in inner-city neighbourhoods in some cities (e.g. London, Manchester, Rotterdam, Vienna) while in others (e.g. Göteborg, Köln, Paris, Strasbourg) new suburbanized patterns are emerging (Drewe, 1983; see also Winchester and White, 1988).

The victimized

Neighbourhoods where the victims of economic and social processes are concentrated are also the places where most of the victims of street crime and violence are to be found. A brief example will suffice here; patterns of crime are examined in detail in Chapter 15. In Chicago, more than half of the murders and shooting assaults in 1980 were concentrated in seven of the city's 24 police districts, areas with heavy concentrations of black or Latino residents. The most violent area of all is the overwhelmingly black Wentworth Avenue police district on the South Side. Within this four-square-mile area an average of 90 murders and 400 shooting assaults occur each year: one of every ten murders and shooting assaults in the whole of Chicago (Wilson, 1985, 1987). According to Wilson, many of the victims (and offenders) in the Wentworth district live in Robert Taylor Homes, the largest public housing project in the city, consisting of 28 16-storey buildings spread over 92 acres. The official population in 1980 was almost 20,000, but there were probably another 5,000 or more residents who were not registered with the housing authority. All of them were black and 72 per cent of the official population were minors. Median family income was less than $5,000; women headed 90 per cent of the families with children; 81 per cent of the households were receiving Aid to Families with Dependent Children; and unemployment was estimated to be nearly 50 per cent. Although only a little more than 0.5 per cent of Chicago's three million people live in Robert Taylor Homes, 11 per cent of the city's murders, 9 per cent of its rapes, and 10 per cent of its aggravated assaults were committed in the project.

Subjective responses

Although there is insufficient evidence from case studies to generalize about spatial patterns of people's feeling about their lives, it is clear that there is only weak correlation, overall, between such feelings and the intensity of local economic, social, and behavioural problems as measured by conventional, objective indicators (Allardt, 1981; Schneider, 1975). A detailed comparison of objective and subjective patterns of well-being in Dundee, Scotland, found that, despite broad correlations between objective and subjective measures of most aspects of personal well-being, residents of certain inner-city tenement districts appeared to be much more satisfied with living conditions, on average, than would have been anticipated from their objective circumstances; whereas the residents of newer owner-occupier neighbourhoods and some public housing projects were much less satisfied than would have been expected (Knox and MacLaran, 1978). Similar discrepancies were found in relation to other aspects of people's well-being, along with a marked tendency for higher (i.e. higher than 'expected') levels of satisfaction to be expressed in neighbourhoods dominated by ageing populations and lower levels in neighbourhoods populated by young families. The general lesson, it was concluded, is clear enough: 'some of the objective outputs of society (wages, consumer goods, health services, housing and so on) satisfy some groups of people whereas others do not, and there is no simple structure to these discrepancies' (Knox and MacLaran, 1978, p. 238). In many cases, however, it is possible to advance plausible explanations of the discrepancies between objective and subjective perspectives. The propensity of the elderly not to acknowledge problems and to remain relatively content in the face of hardship, for example can be attributed to a number of reasons: that today's elderly were socialized to be happy with their lot; that they compare themselves with other elderly people; that they are less ready to express 'failure' when questioned by strangers; that they remember the severe and almost universal hardships of the inter-war depression; that older people will have had more time to filter away from unsatisfactory physical and social environments; and that older people will have learned the emotional advantages of 'dissonance reduction'—liking what they have and not liking what they know they cannot get (Abrams, 1976; Campbell, Converse, and Rodgers, 1976).

People Problems versus Place Problems

Most of this, of course, supports the conventional wisdom of a ghettoized underclass: an image that has informed much of the discourse relating to urban problems. Yet this in some ways is a dangerous oversimplification, attributing more significance to spatial concentrations of the vulnerable, disadvantaged, and victimized than is warranted and inviting ecological fallacies (assumptions that individuals in a particular area share the overall attributes of the area as a whole). The truth is that, despite the marked spatial patterns described above, large numbers of disadvantaged, vulnerable, and victimized people do not live in distressed cities or problem neighbourhoods. Thus, for example, a study of deprivation at the enumeration district level in Britain found that the worst 15 per cent of the enumeration districts, ranked nationally on various criteria of deprivation, contained only 53 per cent of the households with no hot water supply, 64 per cent of those without a bath or shower, 36 per cent of the unemployed and 21 per cent of those with no car (Holtermann, 1975). In the United States, the poverty areas of the hundred largest central cities contained more than 60 per cent of the poor population in 1980, more than 70 per cent of the Hispanic poor, and more than 80 per cent of the black poor. There were, however, very great differences between cities, as table 2.2 shows. Such variability has prompted a debate on 'people poverty versus place poverty' (Edel, 1980; Hamnett, 1979; MacLaran, 1981). Concepts of 'poverty areas', 'problem neighbourhoods', and the like have been labelled as examples of 'spatial fetishism', while Agnew has pointed out that the distinction between people poverty and place poverty is itself ideologically biased 'against people in *social contexts* in favor of an atomized and reified view of people *in locations*' (1984, p. 43). Ottensman (1981), meanwhile, has drawn attention to the fact that there are substantial differences in terms of *what kinds* of poor persons and households live inside and outside the major concentrations of poverty. Table 2.3, drawing on the 'poverty area' data described earlier, shows this clearly.

TABLE 2.2.　The percentage of central city poor living in poverty areas in selected American cities, 1980

	Total	White	Black	Hispanic
Atlanta	82.7	46.7	89.2	73.8
Baltimore	79.5	53.0	88.2	81.9
Buffalo	68.1	47.7	87.1	87.6
Chicago	71.5	37.9	85.7	70.6
Houston	45.1	18.5	65.1	43.2
Kansas City	59.4	33.2	82.1	70.8
Los Angeles	60.8	42.4	81.3	70.1
Newark	88.9	70.9	94.2	88.4
Phoenix	40.6	25.0	76.9	69.0
St Paul	28.1	19.3	47.3	38.4
San Jose	22.2	17.6	19.9	31.8
Washington, DC	65.0	25.0	71.7	45.6
100 largest central cities	63.8	41.3	82.9	73.8

TABLE 2.3.　Population characteristics of the hundred largest US central cities, 1980

Percentages of	Inside poverty areas	Outside poverty areas
Black	52.5	13.2
Hispanic	20.3	8.7
Elderly	10.4	11.9
Aged less than 18	31.2	24.0
Persons in female-headed families	30.1	11.9

These issues can all be easily circumvented with research based on individual- or household-level data, though costs (for specially commissioned surveys) and confidentiality (in the case of census data) usually limit the practicability of such a straightforward approach. The one existing study of household-level census microdata to address the question of the localization of multiple disadvantage at the intra-urban scale deals with Scottish cities, where the scale of the public housing sector helps to ensure that multiply disadvantaged households are dispersed across entire urban areas, with some of the most striking concentrations of disadvantaged households being found in peripheral locations (Knox, 1986).

Changing Patterns

It is also important to recognize that some significant changes have been occurring the kinds of households that find themselves disadvantaged, vulnerable, or victimized in different urban settings. Several inter-dependent trends are relevant here, some of them mutually reinforcing while others are contradictory or compensatory. One fundamental process affecting the outcomes at issue in this chapter has been the economic shift within the world's core economies that has resulted in substantial changes in what is produced, how it is produced, and where it is produced. In particular, the decline of employment in manufacturing industries, together with corporate reorganization and redeployment, has resulted in pronounced regional and inter-urban shifts in prosperity and a selective decentralization of jobs and people at the metropolitan scale. Within cities, labour markets have become segmented and polarized, unemployment—particularly long-term unemployment and youth unemployment—has steadily increased, 'underground' economies have begun to flourish, and important changes have occurred in the welfare sector of the economy, with a general retrenchment being accompanied by changes in patterns of service delivery (de-institutionalization and privatization, for example) and by the emergence of a marked duality between welfare benefits that are conferred as a right and those that are discretionary and which, therefore, vary considerably from place to place (Pearce, 1983; Wolch and Gabriel, 1984).

Another fundamental process affecting patterns of disadvantage, vulnerability, and victimization is that of demographic change. William Wilson, for example, asserts that 'much of what has gone awry in the inner-city is due in part to the sheer increase in the number of young people, especially young minorities' (1985, p. 145). For some years now, the effects of the post-war 'baby boom' have been felt in labour, education, and housing markets; while increased longevity has resulted in large elderly and geriatric populations. Patterns of household and family formation have also changed. After the mid-1960s, improved methods of birth control contributed, among the majority white population at least, to delayed parenthood and, in turn, increased female participation in the labour market. A general increase in the rate of divorce has resulted in many more single-parent households; and changes in attitudes to marriage have resulted in a sharp increase in teen unwed motherhood (the incidence of teen pregnancies has remained fairly constant). Patterns of migration and immigration have also changed dramatically, with, for example, decreased flows of black migrants and increased flows of Asian and Hispanic immigrants to US central cities. Finally, urban land and housing markets have changed in ways that affect the geography of social problems. Gentrification, for example, has affected the ecology of inner-city neighbourhoods in some cities, while housing polices have tended to marginalize the increasing number of non-family households (Watson, 1986).

One of the most widely noted of these changes is the 'feminization of poverty' and the emergence of a 'new poor'. What has happened is that the composition of the poverty population has shifted, with a marked decline in the proportion of the poor who are rural, elderly and/or white, and a striking increase in the proportion of the poor population accounted for by blacks, by women and by children (Garfinkel and McLanahan, 1986; Hess, 1983; Hill, 1985; McDowell, 1983; Pearce, 1983; Rodgers, 1986).

What is less well documented is the spatial dimension of change. As we have seen (in figure 2.1), poverty remains very much an inner-city phenomenon, even though poverty areas tend to have spread outwards from their earlier cores. In most American cities, the poor were rather less concentrated in poverty areas in 1980 than they were in 1970 (table 2.4, column (*a*)), so that overall levels of spatial inequality have tended to decrease (O'Loughlin, 1983; Smith, 1985). Black experience has often been different, however. While black neighbourhoods in general have experienced greater relative improvements in socio-economic conditions than white neighbourhoods, inequality between black neighbourhoods has increased in many cities, a trend that is consistent, as Smith (1985) points out, with a selective process of upward and outward mobility on the part of *some* blacks that contrasts with the increasing localization of poor blacks—and female-headed households in particular—in the poverty areas of these cities (table 2.4, column (*b*)). If the notion of an increasingly ghettoized underclass is valid, then, it must be cast largely in terms of ethnicity and gender, and it must be carefully situated within geographical space. What is needed now are

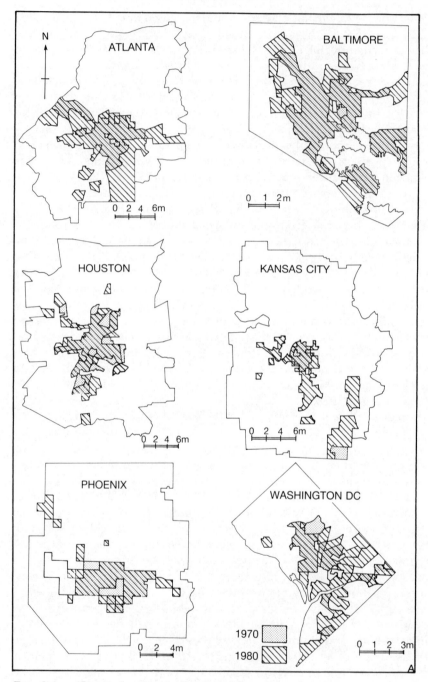

FIG. 2.1.   *'Poverty Areas' in six American cities*

TABLE 2.4. Percentage change in the localization of poverty in poverty areas of selected cities, 1970–1980

	Total population (a)	Black population (b)
Atlanta	−13.3	−15.0
Baltimore	−18.2	−11.0
Buffalo	−19.2	−1.0
Chicago	−18.8	−7.0
Houston	−11.4	23.0
Kansas City	−7.4	−2.0
Los Angeles	−17.6	−2.0
Newark	−11.8	−6.0
Phoenix	14.5	17.0
St Paul	21.2	24.0
San Jose	−16.4	24.0
Washington, DC	−7.1	−9.0

Note: Localization is based on a location quotient: % poverty in city's poverty areas/% poverty in city as a whole.

more detailed analyses of individual- or household-level data against which to develop a more detailed sense of just *who* is experiencing *what* problems in different urban settings and in different kinds of cities.

References

Abrams, M. (1973), 'Subjective social indicators', *Social Trends*, 4: 35–50.
—— (1976), *A Review of Subjective Social Indicators Research*, Occasional Paper 8 (SSRC Survey Unit: London).
Agnew, J. (1984), 'Devaluing place: "people prosperity versus place prosperity" and regional planning', *Environment and Planning D: Society and Space*, 2: 35–45.
Allardt, E. (1981), 'Experiences from the Comparative Scandinavian Welfare Study', *European Journal of Political Research*, 9: 101–11.
Bentham, C. G. (1985), 'Which areas have the worst urban problems?', *Urban Studies*, 22: 119–31.
Bradbury, K. L., A. Downs, and K. A. Small (1982), *Urban Decline and the Future of American Cities* (Brookings Institution: Washington DC).
Campbell, A., P. Converse, and W. L. Rodgers (1976), *The Quality of American Life: Perceptions, Evaluations and Satisfactions* (Russell Sage: New York).
Carley, M. (1981), *Social Measurement and Social Indicators* (Allen and Unwin: London).
Coulter, J. (1978), *Grid-square Census Data as a Source for the Study of Deprivation in British Conurbations*, Working Paper 13 (Census Research Unit: University of Durham).

Donnison, D., and P. Soto (1980), *The Good City* (Heinemann Educational: London).

Drewe, P. (1983), 'Structure and composition of the population of urban areas: 2. Northern and Central Europe', *Population Studies 7* (Council of Europe: Strasbourg).

Edel, M. (1980), ' "People" versus "places" in urban impact analysis', in N. J. Glickman (ed.), *The Urban Impacts of Federal Policies* (Johns Hopkins University Press: Baltimore), 75–91.

Gappert, G. (1987), 'The future of the metropolis and its urban design', in P. Knox (ed.), *The Design Professions and the Built Environment* (Croom Helm: Beckenham), 289–310.

Garfinkel, I., and S. S. McLanahan (1986), *Single Mothers and their Children* (Urban Institute Press: Washington DC).

Hamnett, C. (1979), 'Area-based explanations: a critical appraisal', in D. T. Herbert and D. M. Smith (eds.), *Social Problems and the City* (Oxford University Press: Oxford), 243–60.

Herbert, D. (1975), 'Urban Deprivation: definition, measurement and spatial qualities', *Geographical Journal*, 141: 362–72.

Hess, B. B. (1983), 'New faces of poverty', *American Demographics*, May, 26–31.

Hill, M. S. (1985), 'The changing nature of poverty', *Annals, American Academy of Political and Social Science*, 479: 31–47.

Holtermann, S. (1975), 'Areas of urban deprivation in Great Britain: an analysis of 1971 Census Data', *Social Trends*, 6: 33–47.

Jaye, M. C. and A. C. Watts (eds.) (1981), *Literature and the Urban Experience* (Rutgers University Press: New Brunswick, NJ).

Jones, J. P. III (1987), 'Work, welfare and poverty among black female-headed families', *Economic Geography*, 63: 20–34.

Knox, P. L. (1978), 'Territorial social indicators and area profiles', *Town Planning Review*, 49: 75–83.

—— (1979), 'Subjective social indicators and urban social policy', *Policy and Politics*, 7: 299–309.

—— (1986), 'Disadvantaged households and service provision in the inner city, in G. Heinritz and E. Lichtenberger (eds.), *The Take-off of Suburbia and the Decline of the Central City* (Steiner Verlag: Stuttgart), 253–65.

—— (1987), *Urban Social Geography* (2nd edn. Longman: London/Wiley: New York).

—— and A. C. MacLaran (1978), 'Values and perceptions in descriptive approaches to urban social geography', in D. T. Herbert and R. J. Johnston (eds.), *Geography and the Urban Environment*, i (Wiley: Chichester), 197–247.

Lees, A. (1985), *Cities Perceived: Urban Society in European and American Thought* (Manchester University Press: Manchester).

McDowell, L. (1983), 'Towards an understanding of the gender division of urban space', *Environment and Planning D: Society and Space*, 1 (1): 59–72.

MacLaran, A. C. (1981), 'Area-based positive discrimination and the distribution of well-being', *Transactions of the Institute of British Geographers*, 6: 53–67.

Madge, C., and P. Willmott (1981), *Inner City Paris and London* (Routledge and Kegan Paul: London).

Merlin, P. (1986), 'Housing politics in the old centre and the development of ghettos of marginal groups', in G. Heinritz and E. Lichtenberger (eds.), *The Take-off of Suburbia and the Decline of the Central City* (Steiner Verlag: Stuttgart), 228–34.

Myers, D. (1987), 'Community-relevant measurement of quality of life', *Urban Affairs Quarterly*, 23: 103–12.

O'Loughlin, J. (1983), 'Spatial inequality in Western cities: a comparison of North American and German urban areas', *Social Indicators Research*, 6: 185–212.

Ottensman, J. R. (1981), 'The spatial dimension in the planning of social services in large cities, *Journal of the American Planning Association*, April, 167–74.

Pacione, M. (1986), 'Quality of Life in Glasgow: an applied geographical analysis', *Environment and Planning A*, 18: 1499–520.

—— (1987), Multiple deprivation in Scottish cities: an overview', *Urban Geography*, 8: 550–76.

Pearce, D. M. (1983), 'The feminization of ghetto poverty', *Society*; 21: 71–4.

Rae, J. (1983), *Social Deprivation in Glasgow* (Glasgow District Council: Glasgow).

Rodgers, H. R. jr. (1986), *Poor Women, Poor Families* (Sharpe: New York).

Schneider, M. (1975), 'The quality of life in large American cities: objective and subjective social indicators', *Social Indicators Research*, 1: 495–509.

Sim, D. (1984), 'Urban deprivation: not just the inner city', *Area*, 16: 299–306.

Smith, D. M. (1973), *The Geography of Social Well-Being in the United States* (McGraw-Hill: New York).

—— (1975), 'Mapping human well-being', *International Social Science Journal*, 27: 364–71.

—— (1977), *Human Geography: A Welfare Approach* (Edward Arnold: London).

—— (1979), 'The identification of problems in cities: applications of social indicators', in D. T. Herbert and D. M. Smith (eds.), *Social Problems and the City* (Oxford University Press: Oxford), 13–31.

—— (1985), *Inequality in Atlanta, Georgia, 1960–1980*, Occasional Paper 25 (Department of Geography, Queen Mary College: London).

Visvalingham, M. (1983), 'Operation definition of area-based social indicators', *Environment and Planning A*, 15: 831–40.

Watson, S. (1986), 'Housing and the family: the marginalization of non-family households in Britain', *International Journal of Urban and Regional Research*, 10: 8–27.

Wilson, W. J. (1985), 'The urban underclass in advanced industrial society', in P. E. Peterson (ed.), *The New Urban Reality* (Brookings Institution: Washington, DC), 129–60.

—— (1987), *The Truly Disadvantaged* (University of Chicago Press: Chicago).

Winchester, H. P. M., and P. E. White (1988), 'The location of marginalized groups in the inner city', *Environment and Planning D: Society and Space*, 6: 37–54.

Wolch, J. (1980), 'The residential location of the service-dependent poor', *Annals, Association of American Geographer*, 70: 330–41.

—— (1981), 'The location of service-dependent households in urban areas', *Economic Geography*, 57: 52–67.

—— and S. A. Gabriel (1984), 'Development and decline of service-dependent population ghettos', *Urban Geography*, 5: 111–29.

3

Politics, Society, and Urban Problems:
A Theoretical Introduction

Keith Hoggart

Relations between societies, politics, and social problems are poorly served by theory. Undoubtedly, the links between superstructure (society), infrastructure (state institutions), and outcome (social problems) are complex, but no theoretical model convincingly integrates the three. To appreciate the underlying causes of this situation, it must be acknowledged that political scientists have shown scant regard for theories of the state. With some notable recent exceptions (e.g. Dunleavy and O'Leary, 1987), the theoretical perspectives of political science have been largely restricted to behaviour within governmental institutions, and have neglected associations with broader societal forces. Political scientists' interpretations of how society is organized all too frequently either are left as implicit assumptions or have been taken as equivalent to intra-institutional patterns (just because numerous groups compete for the control of an agency's decisions does not mean that this situation applies to society as a whole). Both these approaches are fundamentally flawed. As Cox *et al.* (1985) argued at length, theories which relate to all aspects of power in society (as those for the state or for political action intrinsically do) are inevitably contested and evaluative. By the very nature of power as a concept, it is not capable of formal or rational verification. This means that it is impossible to reach an all-inclusive (or generally accepted) analysis of power, and hence of the state.

Investigations which leave their assumptions about the state implicit too commonly shroud their analyses behind a cloak of 'objectivity'. This disguises underlying value dispositions that go a long way toward determining empirical conclusions. The same applies when researchers transpose observations from an institutional to a societal setting. Put simply, the same theoretical perspective is not necessarily appropriate for societal and institutional settings. Thus, while Marx saw the pre-eminent cause of state behaviour as (societal) class conflict, he also recognized that unless one class (or a smaller subclass) emerges as victorious, then the state is not an instrument of one social group. The state thereby has independence from class control. The end result for Marx was that state institutional power came to repose primarily in the bureaucracy (see Sen, 1982). Hence, while a class conflict perspective provided the dominant Marxian interpretation of state action, a comprehensive understanding of state behaviour require insights about the institutional behaviour of bureaucracies. (For a useful analysis of how societal conditions become integral to institutional behaviour see Batley, 1983.) This is not an endorsement for the merging of different theoretical models into a single 'super-theory'. A major weakness of theories of the state is that their incompatibility in underlying values (and assumptions) makes such a merger difficult, if not impossible. This can be illustrated by a consideration of the most widely accepted theories of the state.

Theories of the State

Marxist approaches

Probably Clark and Dear go too far when suggesting that: 'The only truly self-aware studies of the form of the capitalist State are to be found in the Marxist literature' (1981, p. 51). Yet the basic thrust of their assertion has much to commend it. A hallmark of the Marxist literature, which is largely absent in other research traditions, is a debate on the merits of theories of the state. Perhaps those who accept existing liberal-democratic ideals do not feel they need a theory of the state (Taylor, 1983), but if this is so they are abdicating their responsibility as researchers to improve our understanding of society. Furthermore, their research approach must be viewed as dishonest in so far as the supposed 'objectivity' of their investigations rests on an (unexamined) ideological viewpoint.

As the Marxist literature clearly shows, even within single research traditions major disagreements exist over the character and causal structures associated with the state. For Marxism, some reasons for these divisions are: (*a*) that Marx himself did not write an explicit theory of the state; (*b*) that discrepancies exist in Marx's earlier and later writings, and (*c*) that there have been significant changes in advanced capitalist societies since Marx wrote (Cox *et al.* 1985). Certainly, Marxists accept that in the long run state actions primarily benefit capital (the state's assumption of the role of enforcer of capitalist relations of property-ownership and market exchange is an obvious symbol of this, while its reliance for its income on the profits of capitalist enterprises acts as a powerful check on counter-tendencies; Offe and Ronge, 1982). Yet divisions exist between the 'capital logic' model (which conceptualizes the state as acting directly on behalf of capital) and the 'class theoretic' model (in which intra- and inter-class conflict induces state autonomy from capital). Although couched within a carefully argued case, the somewhat simplistic assumption of a direct correspondence between the interests of capitalists and state actions has raised severe doubts over the capital logic case (particularly because it implies that capitalists have a single 'interest' which the state serves). As for the class theoretic model, while it does not tie state actions directly to what is happening in the economy, it still assumes that the underlying logic of state actions is to defend capital and that individuals within the state have prior and superior knowledge about what the interests of capital are. This, plus its assumption about state autonomy, make the theory difficult to test empirically. Thus there has been little challenge to Saunders's assertion that class theoretic interpretations of the state are tautological (Saunders, 1982; Dearlove and Saunders, 1984).

A major problem arises with conceptualizing state autonomy from capital. Too readily in class theoretic analyses, if the state acts contrary to the 'interests' of capital, this is assumed to be because it has autonomy, yet if the state is seen to support capital, this is because it acts on behalf of capital. 'There is, one suspects, little that the state might do which could be used as a check on the validity of such a theory' (Saunders, 1982, p. 10). The force of this criticism is none the less weakened by its placing too great a reliance on Marxist theorizing, which focuses on the structure of society and not on immediate political events. Long-term benefits of state actions, and not the short-term outcomes of specific decisions, should thereby form the focus for an evaluation of Marxist theory. Indeed, as presently constituted, Marxist theorizing is poorly equipped to offer insights on short-term government policies.

Fundamentally, this is because structural conditions are not transposed directly into political outcomes. As Bornschier and Chase-Dunn explained: (1985, p. 15) 'Politics has a multiplicity of structural foundations. Together with the requirements of legitimacy which demand that the political system react to social problems, the multiplication of contradictory determinants implies a more or less independent action space for politics. Therefore, economic policy . . . can be regarded as a variable that cannot simply be reduced to structural features of the world economy'. A critical weakness in Marxist contributions to political analysis is that their advocates—like supporters of causes in most walks of life—tend to extend their argument beyond reasonable bounds. When producing empirical verification for their position, for example, 'Many writers of the Left endlessly rework discussions of the strategies of right-wing parties and leaders, especially in constructing hypothetical linkages between their actions and the "needs" of capital. In these accounts there is usually a very "loose fit" between the policies of parties or political leaders and capital "interests" ' (Dunleavy, 1986, p. 131).

In general, there is too great a tendency to adopt structuralist explanations of political action which effectively discount the causal effects of all factors save class structure and economic goals (an example is provided by Cockburn, 1977). This, however, is a problem of practice rather than theory. Investigations like that of Dickens *et al.* (1985), on housing in England and Sweden, show that a class theoretic framework can provide an effective interpretive device for explaining how nations produce dissimilar capital–labour compromises (and hence distinctive orientations in governmental policies). The key point here is that the class theoretic perspective pinpoints the emergence of dissimilar 'traditions' within state institutions (a very obvious difference in such traditions between Britain and the United States is the acceptance of a governmental-sponsored national health service in Britain, as opposed to the reliance on private sector hospitals and insurance schemes in the United States). At this level, Marxist interpretations have much to offer (as an example, capital–labour–state relationships in India do not comply with Marxist expectations unless the 'distorting' effects of pre-colonial social structures are acknowledged—see Sen, 1982). Structural impositions filter through to affect specific state actions, but they are only one of a number of influences. Social structures mould policy-making environments such that 'external' constraints become internal to organizations and administrative routines (Batley, 1983). At present, Marxist theory has developed few insights on this internalization process. Consequently, it is in a weak position when analyses focus on specific political actions.

Élitist and pluralist theories

Other major theories of the state, by contrast, focus directly on political behaviour. There are two major schools of such theories—the élitist and the pluralist. Stated at its simplest level, elitist theory holds that the state is controlled by a single social group, which bends state actions to its own advantage. Most commonly, the groups that are held to be such élites are capitalists and bureaucrats. So-called instrumental 'Marxist' ideas about how state actions coincide with the 'needs' of capital have close similarities with the capital logic school, but place more emphasis on the intervention of capitalists in the day-to-day running of state institutions. As with managerialist ideas about bureaucrats dominating governmental behaviour, as a general statement on political action the élitist expectation of universal control by one social group owes more to ideology than to reality. There is a tendency amongst those on the Left to see business-led conspiracies producing governmental policies which exacerbate social inequalities. In similar fashion, on the Right, preferences for lower taxes and less governmental controls often induce a neglect of demands for better public services from the general public (and capitalists) and produce exaggerated claims about the power of bureaucrats (especially over the growth of public expenditure; Larkey *et al.*, 1981).

These ideas are of course not without some empirical foundation: Thus, a variety of studies, most particularly in the United States, have shown that (non-elected) capitalists do exert controlling influence over the governments of some cities (see Friedland and Palmer, 1984). Similarly a variety of studies—perhaps most visibly demonstrated in land-use planning—report that bureaucrats control the agenda of public debate (partly through utilizing technical expertise to discount altern-ative solutions, partly through the controlled release of information), so their favoured solutions are adopted (see Page, 1985). However, the evidence is insufficient to support either élitist position. It only requires one point about each to illustrate this. The applicability of instrumental 'Marxist' ideas has declined as the scale of economic enterprises has increased. Although still lingering in some cities of the United States—aided by the regional character of many enterprises—there has been a withdrawal of business elites from local politics as the scope of their economic endeavours has shifted from city to national and international spheres. Single locations are now less important to large enterprises, so the advantages of close involvement in local politics have declined. This has led to a marked fall in direct business involvement in city govern-ment. As for bureaucratic control, it does not take much reflection to recognize that if public bureaucrats controlled governmental behaviour, they would not have permitted the cut-backs of the 1980s which have reduced the size and power of federal agencies in the USA and national and local departments in Britain.

This suggests that there are countervailing forces. The existence, indeed the glorification, of such forces underpins pluralist conceptions of the state. Why glorification? Largely because it is extremely difficult to disentangle normative beliefs about the desirability of such a society from evidence of its existence in the work of pluralist theorists. As Cox *et al.* (1985, p. 120) have pointed out, pluralist theorists have gone so far as to acknowledge that even if they found economic élites dominating the policy-making process (i.e. if there was support for instrumental 'Marxism'), this would not change their belief that pluralism was preval-ent. Furthermore, there are commonly huge (ideologically based) leaps of faith in pluralist writings. A classic example of this is found in R. A. Dahl's *Who Governs?* This study of New Haven was for a long time the (empirical) bible of pluralist advocates. Yet Dahl found that a few people dominated New Haven's policy-making procedures. A justification for calling this 'pluralism' was the belief (asserted rather than investigated) that these 'key' decision-makers made their decisions in the light of public preferences. This is because acceptance of this 'democratic creed' was the American way, and to 'reject the democratic creed is in effect to refuse to be an American' (Dahl, 1961, p. 317). Such idealized, ideologically inspired commentaries are a distinguishing feature of pluralist analyses. Frequently, advocates of this theory base their empirical work on detailed and impressive investigations of decision-making processes. As Dunleavy and O'Leary (1987, p. 70) rightly stated: 'pluralist research on state organizations and policy-making remains richer and demonstrates more of a concern for empirical accuracy than any other approach to the theory of the state.' However, whereas Marxist interpretations of the state suffer from their weak empirical investigations and an accompanying over-reliance on the importance of 'superstructure' in explaining behavioural events, pluralist advocates effectively ignore structural considerations (or, like Dahl, adopt convenient assumptions that discount their importance). Criticisms of key pluralist works have clearly shown that pluralist advocates are as 'guilty' as Marxists when it comes to over-interpreting results in order to justify their preconceptions. Even if pluralism can be said to exist within policy-making processes, the structural constraints of state policy-making can be such that a pluralist interpretation of the state is inappropriate. Generally, this is a feature of theorizing that pluralist advocates have chosen to ignore.

The Local State

Overall, investigations of the state stand on slim theoretical underpinnings. Yet, what applies to the state in general is even more strongly felt for urban studies. Not only is the concept 'urban', and particularly the idea of 'urban politics', somewhat contentious, but the very notion of a 'local' sphere for social action is open to differing interpretation (compare Savage *et al.*, 1987, with Urry, 1987). There is certainly little convincing theory on local government (let alone on the local state). What general models do exist offer little more than a description of existing local government structures. Of course, more than description *per se* is involved. Models like that of Tiebout (1956), for instance, over-emphasize the benefits to the public (or at least to sections of the public) and the democratic virtues of existing local government arrangements, whereas models like Saunders's (1981) dual state hypothesis point to the anti-democratic overtones of prevailing arrangements.

Neither of these two models, nor others on the local state, offer a convincing *explanation* for the structure or behaviour of local public institutions. This can be illustrated by reference to the dual state hypothesis. Although its relevance is largely restricted to Britain (just as the Tiebout model finds little utility outside the USA), this model was designed as a Weberian 'ideal type', so it is meant to provide a framework for analysing other nations. Saunders's interpretation of state organization is that (production-related) functions (which are critical to profitability) are kept in the hands of nationally elected or non-elected administrators, since this helps insulate them from public pressures and enhances the hand of capital. Meanwhile consumption-related functions, that do not directly enhance (and can be a restraint on) profitability, are kept at a local level, where citizen participation is greater. This is an appealing model, though it is somewhat superficial and does not to explain how structures emerged. Caveats can certainly be raised over Saunders's assertion that local government services are not significant for private sector profitability—local economic initiatives (Boddy, 1984) and public housing construction (Dunleavy, 1981) are two obvious exceptions. What is more, the 'needs' of capital are met by state institutions as much in enhancing production profitability as in 'placating' the general population. To undertake one without the other is a recipe for social unrest. Moreover, if 'consumption' functions are kept at a local level because public pressure helps maintain low taxes, why does central government reduce the effectiveness of this 'discipline' by awarding local authorities such large grants? (And as taxation levels directly affect profitability, consumption functions must be of concern to capitalists.) To explain the organization and operations of local public institutions, this model needs to account for dissimilar organizational principles in other nations. If local–central divisions within the state are promoted to strengthen the hand of capital, then why has this strategy not been adopted in other nations? In fact, one of the hallmarks of the United States (and some other nations) is the incidence of local pro-growth coalitions which owe their existence to municipal control over functions that directly enhance capitalist profitability (Kennedy, 1984). If a theoretical explanation for the local state is to be provided, it needs to draw out the reasons for differences in organization and practice.

To do this will require not *a* theory of the state, but theories of the state. As Duncan (1980, p. 25) correctly observed 'there is no theory of *the* state outside specific historical and spatial relations to social change. The state varies as this relation varies.' Put simply, conclusions reached about Britain cannot be assumed to be applicable to France. An illustration of this is seen in the relative impotence of British local government when conflicts arise with its national counterpart. Ashford made the point well when he suggested that 'What differentiates Britain from

France, which also has a unitary [governmental] system, is how easily national policy-makers can act without careful consultation with local government and how easily national objectives are imposed on this vast subnational structure' (1981, p. 68). Although roundly criticized when first made (largely for the simplicity of its structuralist framework), some commentators now see more justification in Cockburn's charge that: 'In spite of its multiplicity . . . the [British] state preserves a basic unity. All its parts work fundamentally as one' (1977, p. 47).

The policies of recent Conservative governments have done much to change analysts' minds. As Dearlove and Saunders expressed it:

The imminent demise of local government as a democratic and reasonably accountable system has been forecast many times before. Rate-capping makes such forecasts a reality, for it totally constrains a local council to follow the line being laid down at the centre by removing its one autonomous sphere of revenue. Effectively stripped of the power to raise taxes beyond a level determined by the centre, local authorities cease in any meaningful sense to function as systems of government and are reduced to the status of local outposts of the government in Westminster. (1984, p. 389)

Drawing on this statement, two points can be made about the unity of the state. First, the kind of property tax limitations that rate-capping has introduced in England are common in the United States (e.g. California's Proposition 13, Massachusetts's Proposition 2½, or New Jersey's 'Cap' Law), yet few hold that local government systems in the USA are marked by less autonomy than those in England. Second, the stronger involvement in local affairs of central government in Britain (most especially with regard to grants) actually handicaps its search for local compliance with its wishes. This is because national leaders carry a greater responsibility for local 'failures' (note, in particular, the way in which the Thatcher government became ineffectual when Liverpool City Council threatened to go bankrupt; largely because it could not extricate itself from being blamed for this council's plight—see Parkinson, 1985). As a consequence, despite the appearance of tighter central controls in Britain (most especially when compared with federal controls over municipal government in the US), the Reagan administration has been more successful in bringing about its targeted reductions in local expenditure than have recent British governments.

These points suggest that the unitary character of the British state has been somewhat exaggerated. Indeed, it is feasible to argue—though not as a complete picture—that the much-touted realignment in local-central relations since the first Thatcher government came to power (favouring increased centralization) is little more than a change from an administrative political system to an ideological one. Significantly, up to the mid-1970s, when academics were inclined to point to the vitality of local government autonomy in England, a key underpinning of the 'co-operative' atmosphere which pervaded local–central relations was the strength of 'policy communities' which forged alliances between local and central bureaucrats (and key politicians) over the promotion of specific services (like housing, highways or education; see Dunleavy, 1980). That academics were slow to recognize the importance of these policy communities meant that their significance began to be realized at the time when their role was being superseded by more overtly 'political' (or political party) criteria. This shift reached a new intensity with the election of the first Thatcher administration in 1979. Since then, long cherished ideas of professionalism and 'fair play' have come to be challenged as the government has sought a shift to the Right in the philosophy of public institutions. A key mechanism through which this has been achieved has been to ensure that vacant senior positions are filled by those who conform to the prime minister's ideological expectations. Hence, appointments to advisory committees have tended to go to Conservative party members (e.g. health members 'victims of Tory hit list', *Guardian*, 30 July 1984, p. 3) and the traditional lack of involvement by ministers in appointing top civil servants has been replaced by a more interventionist role (Ridley, 1983). The weakening of policy communities has been a direct consequence of this process. Since they had a tradition of promoting quantitative and qualitative service improvements, this brought them into conflict with the government's goal of reducing public expenditure. To pursue the government's broad objectives, the policy-making role of public sector professionals was reduced (the lowly position now afforded to professionals in education is seen by the imposition of a new core curriculum on schools and the removal of teachers' right to negotiate salaries and work conditions).

One consequence of the shift toward political party objectives has been a growing antagonism between local and national institutions of government. Yet, in a very visible way, the government's actions have not affected local authorities uniformly. Certainly, general reductions in local expenditure have been sought, as has a move to the Right in local policies (e.g. council-house sales). Effectively, however, 'restrictive' policies have been targeted largely at authorities controlled by the Labour party. Rate-capping, for instance, only affects a handful of councils a year,while the enforced sale of council homes was principally intended to change policies in Labour councils (note how largely right-wing councils in rural areas obtained exemption from sales because of their 'special needs'). Similarly, the abolition of the Greater London Council and the six metropolitan county councils was an important means of quietening some of the government's major critics.

These 'attacks' on left-wing councils have occurred because, at the same time as a more committed right-wing leadership controlled the national government, city governments were increasingly coming under the influence of a more committed Left. What is more, these councils actively challenged and embarrassed the government. This particularly applied to the government's belief that 'the market' would provide the answers to Britain's economic and social problems. As Dearlove and Saunders (1984, p. 391) noted: 'Every time a firm is saved by the intervention of a local council's enterprise board, or a group of workers is supported in setting up a producer co-operative, the potentiality of a socialised system of production is raised in people's minds while a doubt is sown regarding the inevitability of the market solution.' Being at the forefront of implementing creative accounting procedures, of promoting gay and women's rights and alternative employment strategies, and asserting that the maintenance of service standards is more important that tax cuts, left-wing councils challenged the government on a broad front. While it would be incorrect to hold that national policies have not placed general restrictions on the freedom of local councils (although the government has offered some compensatory new freedom, like removing loan sanctions in favour of a more flexible capital limits approach to infrastructural investment), it is New Left councils that have been most visibly affected, and researchers have tended to draw their conclusions on the general movement towards a unitary state from these. Most other authorities have been little affected by rate-capping, were selling council homes anyway, have not been abolished and did not levy supplementary rates. Critically, of course, it is in the New Left authorities that the densest concentrations of social problems are found.

The divisions that exist in local authority treatment by the central government are matched by divisions within the national government itself (and, more important in earlier decades, by dissimilarities in policy communities). Thus, there are frequent conflicts between national departments over local government policy. Disagreements between the Treasury and service departments over the funding of local projects provides a general example, with conflict between the DHSS and the Department of the Environment over who should supervise housing benefit payments providing a more specific example. There have also been substantial differences in the internal cohesion and political power of policy communities. For functions like highways, these communities have had a major role to play, whereas in housing, policy-making was fractured and open to more political party influence. The significance of these divisions lies in the fact that not only can the state not be considered as a unitary entity (in terms of organizational behaviour) across its local and national spheres, but that even within these spheres there are substantial differences in goals and power structures. This raises considerable problems for theory construction, which analysts have so far been slow to tackle (seemingly preferring to think more in terms of unitary blocks and uniformity of circumstance). Furthermore, in addition to considerations of structural restraints and organizational behaviour, as O'Leary (1987) has recently shown, significant political events are also conditioned by the personalities of powerful people. This adds a dimension to political understanding which has so far received scant attention. Altogether, analysts still have a long way to go before we have convincing theories of political action.

References

Ashford, D. E. (1981), *Policy and Politics in Britain: The Limits of Consensus* (Basil Blackwell: Oxford).

Batley, R. (1983), *Power Through Bureaucracy: Urban Political Analysis in Brazil* (Gower: Aldershot).

Boddy, M. (1984), 'Local economic and employment strategies', in M. Boddy and C. Fudge (eds.), *Local Socialism?* (Macmillan: London), 160–91.

Bornschier, V., and C. Chase-Dunn (1985), *Transnational Corporations and Underdevelopment* (Praeger: New York).

Clark, G., and M. Dear (1981), 'The state in capitalism and the capitalist state', in M. Dear and A. J. Scott (eds.), *Urbanization and Urban Planning in Capitalist Society* (Methuen: London), 45–61.

Cockburn, C. (1977), *The Local State* (Pluto: London).

Cox, A., P. Furlong, and E. Page (1985), *Power in Capitalist Societies* (Harvester: Brighton).

Dahl, R. A. (1961), *Who Governs? Democracy and Power in an American City* (Yale University Press: New Haven, Conn.).

Dearlove, J., and P. Saunders (1984), *Introduction to British Politics* (Polity Press: Cambridge).

Dickens, P., S. S. Duncan, M. Goodwin, and F. Gray (1985), *Housing, States and Localities* (Methuen: London).

Duncan, S. S. (1980), 'The methodology of levels and the urban question', Graduate School of Geography Discussion Paper 76 (London School of Economics: London).

Dunleavy, P. (1980), 'Social and political theory and the issues in central–local relations', in G. W. Jones (ed.), *New Approaches to the Study of Central–Local Government Relationships* (Gower: Farnborough), 116–36.

—— (1981), *The Politics of Mass Housing in Britain, 1945–1975* (Clarendon Press: Oxford).

—— (1986), 'The growth of sectoral cleavages and the stabilization of state expenditures', *Environment and Planning D: Society and Space*, 4: 129–44.

—— and B. O'Leary (1987), *Theories of the State* (Macmillan: Basingstoke).

Friedland, R., and D. Palmer (1984), 'Park Place and Main Street: business and the urban power structure', in R. H. Turner and J. F. Short (eds.), *Annual Review of Sociology 10* (Annual Reviews Inc.: Palo Alto, Calif.), 393–416.

Kennedy, M. D. (1984), 'The fiscal crisis of the city', in M. P. Smith (ed.) *Cities in Transformation*, Urban Affairs Annual Review 26 (Sage: Beverley Hills, Calif.) 91–110.

Larkey, R. D., C. Stolp and M. Winer (1981), 'Theorizing about the growth of government', *Journal of Public Policy*, 1: 157–220.

Offe, C., and V. Ronge (1982), 'Theses on the theory of the state', in A. Giddens and D. Held (eds.), *Classes, Power and Conflict* (Macmillan: Basingstoke), 249–56.

O'Leary, B. (1987), 'Why was the G.L.C abolished?', *International Journal of Urban and Regional Research*, 11: 193–217.

Page, E. (1985), *Political Authority and Bureaucratic Power* (Harvester: Brighton).

Parkinson, M. (1985), *Liverpool on the Brink: One City's Struggle Against Government Cuts* (Policy Journals: Hermitage, Berks.).

Ridley, F. F. (1983), 'Career service: a comparative perspective on civil service promotion', *Public Administration*, 62: 179–96.

Saunders, P. (1981), 'Community power, urban managerialism and the 'local state', in M. Harloe (ed.), *New Perspectives in Urban Change and Conflict* (Heinemann: London), 27–49.

—— (1982), 'The relevance of Weberian sociology for urban political analysis', in A. Kirby and S. Pinch (eds.), *Public Provision and Urban Politics* (Geographical Paper 80: Reading: University of Reading), 1–24.

Savage, M., J. Barlow, S. S. Duncan, and P. Saunders (1987), ' "Locality research": the Sussex programme on economic restructuring, social change and the locality', *Quarterly Journal of Social Affairs*, 3: 27–51.

Sen, A. (1982), *The State, Industrialization and Class Formations in India* (Routledge and Kegan Paul: London).

Taylor, P. J. (1983), 'The question of theory in political geography', in N. Kliot and S. Waterman (eds.), *Pluralism and Political Geography* (Croom Helm: London), 9–18.

Tiebout, C. M. (1956), 'A pure theory of local expenditures', *Journal of Political Economy*, 64: 416–24.

Urry, J. (1987), 'Society, space and locality', *Environment and Planning D: Society and Space*, 5: 435–44.

4

Urban Transformation: From Problems *in* to the Problem *of* the City

Roger Lee

. . . something fundamental happened.
(ILO, 1984, p. 36)

Three Short Stories

I

In January 1921 the City of Manchester was invaded. Some 320 burghers from the 76 municipalities of the economic region centred upon Manchester put their municipal transport systems to good use and converged upon the Town Hall of what was—once at least—the most revolutionary city. Their purpose was to 'prepare on broad outline a regional plan' (a contemporary novelty but hardly revolutionary) to provide for the 'progressive development of every part of this important region. . . . and to bring about the best possible conditions of life' (MDJTPAC, 1925, p. 9).

This remarkable objective could, it was argued, be achieved by 'proper and far-sighted planning . . . thereby [faithful echoes of the Manchester School] also obviating the expenditure of large sums of money' (MDJTPAC, 1925, p. 11). If the complacency of the participants in the Manchester meeting was staggering it is, perhaps, understandable. The contemporary power of local government was highly developed and still growing, and (or so it appeared to them) was underlain in greater Manchester by material supremity. They could see 'no comparable self-contained Region in which industry and commerce are so highly and completely developed' (MDJTPAC, 1925, p. 9).

The problem was that they were just a little out of time: revolutionary change had moved on. The Manchester meeting took place only months before the councillors of Poplar were about to invent Poplarism and seven years almost to the day after the new world of Fordism had been invented in Detroit. And greater Manchester itself was already past its best. In 1920, the year before the meeting, the membership of the Manchester Exchange had reached a precipitous peak: the export of cotton goods reached an all-time maximum value and was based on high technology production methods and organization; the extraction of surplus value—as measured by the payment of dividends—peaked in some 150 cotton spinning firms; and Manchester banks achieved their greatest turnover.

Contemplating their own proposals nearly seventy years later, the structure planners of Greater Manchester Council, the (now defunct) successors to the pioneering regional planners of greater Manchester, faced urban redundancy: 'the general picture is one of limited opportunities . . . for the plan to be realistic it must take account of constraints on resources over a period of at least 10 and up to 15 years ahead' (Greater Manchester Council, 1979, pp. 8, 6).

II

One of the most depressing journeys in Europe involves taking the tram from the heart of what must rank in the top three medieval cities in Europe to its post-war counterpoint to the east—which must count as one of the great follies of contemporary society.

The old city of Cracow was, despite its grotesque human tragedy, left physically more or less unscathed by the ravages of the Second World War. All the more then for the abrasive pollution of subsequent Polish development to devour. The tram provides a kind of urban journey in reverse as the blocks of flats in the unserviced suburbs of the new city of Nowa Huta press sullenly against the eastern boundary of Cracow. Here is a planned city of workers. The monumental southern entrance to Nowa Huta is defined in part by the sweep of tramlines from the city. They are intended to bring its residents to this central place where, in the Stalinesque Avenue of Roses, a statue of Lenin imposes its massive presence—a presence guarded from subversion by an ever-present and armed militia. Just around the corner a peasant woman crouches passively on the window-ledge of the largest store in town. She is selling four parsnips, three cabbages and a few bunches of late flowering daisies.

The eastern terminus of the Nowa Huta tram system is the city cemetery, an extensive, featureless and untended area looking across to what is, in the last instance, its major source of custom: the Lenin steelworks. There is not a church to be seen. The cemetery is filling with people who have lived and died here, and is visited by those that remain. Little groups of individuals gain access to the cemetery across the tramlines and a scrap of waste ground, past the wire fence and the unkempt and empty cemetery office. Meanwhile the tram loops back towards Lenin and the Avenue of Roses.

This place is less a city than a concentration of labour power, designed as a proletarian antidote to Cracovian cultural insistence and the nonconformity of the former capital of Poland. It was founded in 1949 on the economic base of a quite illogically located steelworks designed on good Fordist principles. Pollution from sulphur dioxide is about twenty times the national average, and its effects on mortality and illness entirely predictable: infant mortality is 40 per cent higher than the national average and occupational illness over 30 per cent higher. In the dozen or so years of the growth of an organized opposition in Poland, culminating in August 1980 with the establishment of Solidarnosc, Cracow/Nowa Huta remained in the forefront of the challenge to the state. A major centre of Solidarnosc during the fifteen months of its legal existence (Bivand, 1983), the voivodship incorporating Cracow/Nowa Huta succeeded in recording the lowest turnout in the highly symbolic elections to the Seym of October 1985.

III

Provided that a sense of inferiority can be resisted, one of the advantages of being a provincial rather than national or global city, of being the second city rather than the primate, is that local coalitions may always unite in the face of a common foe. Geopolitical self-consciousness is constantly asserted through the urban hierarchy. The danger, however, is provincialism and the adoption of local policies which isolate the locality from the wider context of which it is a part. For such reasons, no doubt, the counter-proposal of Birmingham City Council and the Birmingham Chamber of Commerce for a national exhibition centre to be located in the city was dismissed by the much more diffuse London lobby which assumed that such a facility must be located in the capital.

But the writing was clearly on the wall. A proposal to locate the exhibition centre at Crystal Palace had failed in 1962 for lack of local financial commitment, and in 1969 the selection of a site at Northolt in west London was overruled by the then President of the Board of Trade. He preferred the Birmingham proposal, which was not only locationally logical (the site is adjacent to an inter-city rail link, the M42 motorway and a regional airport subsequently reconstructed in the 1980s) but came with local money (Law, 1986).

There was rather more at stake here than mere inter-city rivalry. The city/regional interests focused on Birmingham are clearly intent on inserting a significant post-industrial flavour to a region archetypically linked with the new industries of the long boom and so suffering disproportionately during and after the crisis of the early 1980s. Even before the arrival of the National Exhibition Centre, the city corporation had in the 1960s helped both the BBC and independent TV companies to extend their studios in Birmingham beyond what was necessary for any mere regional commitment. In 1987, the city put in a bid to host the 1992 Olympic Games. The bid failed (on this occasion) partly, it was said by the protagonists, because the financial institutions of the City of London had been regionally chauvinist and had not offered sufficient financial backing for a project outside south-east England.

But the Labour-controlled city council did hold the first of what promises to be an annual Superprix on the streets of inner Birmingham in 1986. Hardly a mass spectator sport, motor racing relies on an extensive network of commercial relationships and attracts large numbers of spectators only at the big occasions like the British Grand Prix. The Birmingham meeting attracted 100,000 spectators. It was the centrepiece of a carnival which both involved the multi-cultural residents of the inner city whose streets and houses formed the theatre for the drama and controlled them, in a large-scale and highly organized event.

Most significant of all, perhaps, the coalition of local interests was mobilized once again in 1987 to extract extra financial subsidy from the Arts Council, in order to further the development of the City of Birmingham Symphony Orchestra under its artistic director, Simon Rattle, as the premier British orchestra, so taking advantage of the relative decline of the four London orchestras. Other moves are afoot to tempt financially restricted and locationally cramped parts of the London cultural scene to move base to the more expansive environment of Birmingham. Not the least of its attractions is the Convention Centre located at the centre of the city.

The city of production, with its long-standing local political consciousness, is being transformed into a city of communication and spectacle.

An Interpretation: The Centrality of Social Reproduction

It is not stretching credibility to breaking point to suggest that modernism (at least in its economic manifestations) was introduced to a startled world, then centred on Detroit, Michigan, when Henry Ford announced the $5-day on 5 January 1914. It is, perhaps, slightly more fanciful but not entirely beyond the bounds of reason and most certainly ironically symbolic of the new age to suggest that the progenitor of modernism was a little-known accountant by the name of Lee. John R. Lee was employed by the Ford Motor Company to resolve what was a serious social problem in the city of Detroit. This was not any old urban social problem but the central problem for capitalist society: the presence of restrictions upon the self-expansion of capital.[1] In the case of Ford, these restrictions on accumulation emanated jointly from the labour market and the size of the market for automobiles. Labour turnover was such that over 50,000 people had to be hired in any given year to maintain a labour force of 14,000 on the moving assembly line, while the price of automobiles was such that its market was restricted to the naturally limited number of the more wealthy.

It was Lee's ability that led him to propose a substantial and apparently paradoxical increase in wages and incentives to help resolve these problems. But it was Henry Ford's genius to realize that the problems of labour turnover and market size were two sides of the same coin, and that a doubling of wages, with the increase in demand that would follow, along with the imposition of an extensive system of social control of the productive and reproductive behaviour of the labour force, would solve both problems simultaneously. Fordism was born and a start made in providing the foundations of the long boom of the 1950s and 1960s.

Something fundamental had most definitely happened. And with it came the beginnings of a momentous urban transformation: social problems *in* the city—which themselves had provided the creatively destructive conditions in which urban government had been shaped in the nineteenth century—and the underlying threat of the urbanization of the proletariat, became elements of an even more all-embracing concern—the social problem *of* the city.

One immediate and constantly recurring implication of the solution adopted by Ford was the need—demonstrated already by his earlier innovations in production—to make space for his technology and method of production. His factories had, quite literally, to change shape (a new architecture had to be invented) and so had also to change location—from the inner, progressively, to the outer city. In Britain, the movement to Dagenham in 1929 of the Ford plant established in 1911 on the Trafford Park industrial estate south-west of Manchester (which, along with a preliminary flowering of a number of other representatives of the new industries of the inter-war period threatened briefly to sustain the city's industrial pre-eminence into the later twentieth century) served to emphasize not only the Fordist requirement for accessible green-field sites with (potential) access to socially controlled labour, but access to national and international markets and supplies. The disintegration of

---

[1] The grounding of social problems in production and reproduction rather than distribution is discussed by Lee (1979, ch.4). The reinterpretation of urban social problems presented in that essay has since been absorbed into the conventional wisdom: see, for example, Scott, 1986.

one old city and the disintegrated nature of the new urban fragment were accurate symbols of the fate of the products of the 'age of great cities', (Lawton, 1972). Detroit and Manchester were not alone: New York, Berlin, Paris, and London have all been subjected to the shock of the new urbanism (Ewers, *et al.*, 1986).

The point was, quite simply, that what was becoming an increasingly corporate circuit of capital was outgrowing the urban conditions of exist-ence which had been so vital during its competitive phase. The two-way formative relations between geography and capital accumulation had been expressed most emphatically in the urban system during the second half of the nineteenth century. 'Urban' populations in England and Wales already exceeded 'rural' by 1850, while in the United States the proportion of people living in cities grew from less than 11 per cent of the total population in 1840 to over 35 per cent in 1890 as, following the Euro-pean example, the number of cities of over 100,000 persons jumped from two to seventeen (Walker, 1978). At the same time, the map of world-standard big cities in Europe was transformed. The industrial cities of mass urbanization (Lee, 1979) threw off the shackles of their pre-industrial geographies and, in the symbiotic relationships between urban and industrial growth—often expressed under the rubric of external economies of scale—established the apparently overwhelming (but only temporary and only quantitative) pre-eminence of the north and the urban within the geography of European economic development (Lee, 1976).

Under these circumstances, it could hardly be said that the city was itself a social problem. However, the condition of the working class in cities, and the threat that the disorganized reproduction of labour posed to the reproduction of the circuit of capital as a whole in the absence of a coherent network of local government most certainly was (Fraser, 1979; Sutcliffe, 1982). Nevertheless, this problem generated a surprisingly slow (at least in the United Kingdom) process of reform in the emergence of the local state as a major force in regulating social reproduction and sustain-ing legitimation. The effects of the emergence of the 'free' market in hous-ing are, perhaps, the most dramatic example of what the 'freedom' of labour from the means of production means in practice. With housing no longer a responsibility of productive capital, labour was left to fend for itself in a generalized market for urban housing, so reducing direct costs to individual capitalists, but generalizing societal costs—not least those asso-ciated with the increasing separation of home and work—and opening up new areas for capital accumulation, class conflict, and state intervention in the provision of shelter (Vance, 1977, ch. 7).

The problem *of* the city began to emerge during the final decade of the last century—marked for some by the transition from the second to the third Kondratiev long wave (Gordon, 1986, ch. 1, Walker, 1978). Richard Walker, for example, suggests that 'the most significant reorientation of urban structure occurred as a result of the profound transformation to modern corporate capitalism around the turn of this century' (1978, p. 204). The trend towards capital concentration developed unevenly in time and space. Peter Dicken (1986, ch. 3) traces the origins of transnational productive investment back to the middle of the nineteenth century, but points out that the process of global investment really accelerated after the Second World War. By the late 1970s, the contribution of the largest hundred corporations to net manufacturing output varied between 30 and 40 per cent in the major industrial economies of the world (Armstrong *et al.*, 1984, pp. 216–18; Chapman and Walker, 1987). These trends imply a major quantitative and geographical restructuring of the circuit of capital. No longer tied to the external economies of scale provided by urban places, big capital is able to create many of its own material conditions of existence and to scour the world for productive sites, labour and resources. Productive decentralization has increased in scale from the predominantly urban to the global. Conversely, the co-ordination of global and international operations from the headquarters of these major firms requires highly centralized locations in capital and major world cities—so generating, as Stephen Hymer noted long ago (1972), a highly uneven process of urban development.

The restructuring of the circuit of capital has not only involved the increasing dominance of highly concentrated units of capital. Intertwined with the processes of restructuring based on the increasing concentration of capital is the sectoral and geographical reorganization associated with the development of new products and process technologies. One of the major sources of evidence to back the notion of long waves of economic growth is that it is possible to discern distinctive regimes of accumulation defined in part by their sectoral structure. The third Kondratiev wave, lasting from the late nineteenth century to the inter-war period, is dominated by the 'new' industries based on electricity, chemicals, and the motor vehicle, while the fourth—from which the contemporary world economy is struggling to escape—is based on electronics, petrochemicals, and synthetics.

Although it may be argued (e.g. by Massey, 1986) that, as a consequence of the growth of the new industries associated with the third Kondratiev wave, which favoured the south and east of Britain rather than the north and west, 'the geography of the country had to a large extent been reversed', the circuit of capital around the urban system remained dominated by finance capital—located predominantly in London. In fact, this domination had persisted throughout the nineteenth century and the industrial revolutions based upon steam and cotton, and railways and steel.[2] In Europe too, the industrially dominated urban system of the nineteenth century, although dramatic in its geography and qualitative impact, was remarkably short-lived; by the middle of the twentieth century it had returned to what some interpret as a medieval form of urban structure (Lee, 1976, 1979).

In some senses such geographical transformations have been even more marked in the USA. The Civil War appeared to resolve the competition between the established—and industrial—north-east and the resource-rich interior, and 'created a long period in American history of political-economic *domination* by the businesses and politicians of the Northeast'. This domination has, according to John Agnew (1987, p. 89), 'now come to an end. Since the 1940s but especially since the late 1960s, the western and southern regions have experienced much higher rates of growth and increased political influence relative to the Northeast.'

Perhaps the most dramatic symbol of such change was the fiscal crisis of New York City in the mid-1970s. But—and in line with the reproductive uses of crisis (Marcuse, 1981)—

a remarkable resurgence has reversed that perception. The city has regained or even enhanced its status as cultural leader and financial centre. Its renewed activity reveals itself through growth in population, investment, employment, and new construction. A magnet for global migration, it attracts multitudes of new immigrants who have invigorated many dying neighbourhoods; it heads the itinerary of millions of visitors, stimulating a hotel and restaurant boom. (Fainstein *et al.*, 1987)

And the reasons for this renaissance? They lie in the new geography of the circuit of capital: the globalization of finance capital (Thrift, 1986) and the emergence of three world financial centres—New York, Tokyo, and London—under a regime of liberalized and world-wide competitive relations in finance; the concentration of capital and the emergence of multinational and global capital with pronounced hierarchical and geographic divisions of corporate labour, in which the headquarters' functions tend to locate in major world cities (Dicken, 1986); and the new technology of service production—a response in part to the increased demand for and specialization of administration and producer services in a global economy of concentrated capital (Sassen-Koob, 1984). They lie too in the political mandate offered by economic decline for a public

[2] David Rubinstein (1981) traces the overwhelming dominance of London in terms of the holding of wealth and points out that, even at the height of industrialization in the nineteenth century, it was finance capital which appropriated most of the value being created through industrialization.

policy orientated towards the needs of capital and regressively opposed to labour. But they also lie in the new world of what some (e.g. Harvey, 1987) would call 'flexible accumulation'—the product of the fundamental events that transfixed the world economy in 1973–4 with the quadrupling of petroleum prices but which had, in reality, been undermining Henry Ford's version of capitalism for almost a decade.

Flexibility is a product of a number of interlocking forces: the possibilities (and, under the intensified competition of the end of the long boom and increased internationalization of the world economy, the necessity) of global choice; the decentralizing technologies of computer-based telecommunications with their associated adjustments to economies of scope (Scott, 1986) within firms and their potential for increased central control; the possibilities for fragmenting labour markets into cores and peripheries, so off-loading overheads on to the peripheral labour force; the increased social division of labour—most noticeable perhaps in the emergence of producer services as a distinctive and rapidly growing sector of advanced economies (Daniels, 1985; Gillespie and Green, 1987; Hall, 1987); and the reassessment of the efficiency of mass production (Piore and Sabel, 1984).

Associated with such changes is a marked increase in the velocity of circulation of capital, which brings its own competitive pressures and which facilitates rapid changes in urban fortunes; the resurgence of New York is a product of forces similar to those that have restructured what is, in many ways, its urban opposite—Los Angeles (Sassen-Koob, 1984; Soja 1987). Despite their archetypical contrasts in the 1970s, Houston was to follow Detroit into economic crisis in the 1980s (Hill and Feagin, 1987); decades of dereliction in the Docklands of London were transformed in the mid-1980s into a post-modern extravaganza of investment in producer services and the creation of high-status residential areas (Ambrose, 1986).

The progressive disengagement of capital from particular places (Lee, 1979) serves to increase the significance of differentiation for capital within what is a global urban system. Crucial features of this differentiation would include the capacity of cities to assume global control functions within the circuit of capital; the productivity, cost, and flexibility of their labour; the possibilities for private investment in the city to be subsidized by state intervention; and the attractiveness of the city as a centre of consumption and interaction—most especially of high-status housing, high-order retail goods and services and cultural artefacts and events—especially in urban spaces especially designed for the purpose (Knox, 1987). Paris provides an example of a city capable of differentiating itself in all four dimensions: a major capital city and an international if far from global centre of control; an unevenly productive urban region in which the planning authorities are attempting to reduce intra-regional inequalities by fostering employment and population growth in the less favoured east and investing heavily in high-speed mass transit facilities to ease the movement of labour into and across the city region; and a city both creating and re-creating a dramatic built environment for cultural and commercial consumption.

Such processes serve to distinguish cities in a high-speed and increasingly compressed world, where distance is less and less tyrannical and so provides less and less reason to prevent the geographical reorganization of the circuit of capital. The production of special urban built environments is one way in which ties to and the distinction of a particular place may help to slow down the process of change to a speed at which the locality is capable of managing it. And, in what is a competitive and therefore contradictory manner, localities may contribute to the management or postponement/displacement of the contradictions at the heart of the process of the accumulation of capital. But they must also pay for the privilege, the experience of differentiating cities in order to attract the circuit of capital is thereby also a process of regression in the distribution of income.

Furthermore, uneven urban development is not only increasingly compressed in time, it is also highly selective in space.[3] Within the United Kingdom, for example, Liverpool has simply been abandoned by the circuit of capital.[4] 'In the 1980s, the city is economically marooned: it is in the wrong place, based on the wrong kind of economic activity with an outdated infrastructure and an underqualified workforce. It is increasingly a branch plant economy which has become peripheral to the mainstream capitalist economy' (Parkinson, 1987). The residents of its hurriedly constructed and under-serviced outer estates (resonances of Nowa Huta here), like Kirkby, Speke, and Halewood, were decanted from the inner city as part of the Fordist processes of urban restructuring during the long boom. They now live lives in which many are deprived both of a livelihood in the capitalist economy and of support from a welfare economy devastated by the effects of the urban fiscal crisis. Likewise Middlesborough, a boom-town of the late 1960s and early 1970s—the product of large-scale Fordist industries like steel and chemicals—faced both a massive decline and

---

[3] And its uneven development is not merely a passive reflection of the assertions of the circuit of capital. The richness and significance of place in helping to shape the processes of social reproduction are revealed in the series of locality studies undertaken in the United Kingdom during the early 1980s (Cooke, 1988). The following paragraphs draw in part upon this work.

[4] For a discussion of urban redundancy, see Lee (1979). This notion of redundancy has since been taken up by, for example, Massey (1987).

internal restructuring of its labour market as global competition forced fundamental changes to the local circuit of capital in the town and its region. Job-cuts in the major industries were hardly compensated for by state-supported investment, regional development policy or, in the case of steel, nationalization. The growth of predominantly female service employment could come nowhere near to offsetting the decline of predominantly male manufacturing jobs (Beynon *et al.*, 1987).

These are stories of the abandonment and subsequent redundancy of urban places in contexts where the strength of external influences in the shape of the changing geographical trajectory of the circuit of capital could not be offset by internal pressure or even conformity with external demands. In other places the redirected circuit of capital may itself begin to reconstitute cities or at least provide the conditions in which reconstitution may be facilitated. The experience of Swindon in southern England moves from abandonment by a pre-Fordist industry focused upon railway engineering, through its replacement in the form of Fordist military–aeronautical engineering in a location strategically beyond the orbit of the London blitz and a British Motor Corporation (as the Rover Group then was) body pressings plant to post-Fordist developments. This process of restructuring has been fostered in part by a self-conscious local state, building on local defence connections and the rapidly diminishing distance between Swindon and London, to attract electronics and producer services as well as a Honda car-assembly plant. The introduction of this plant within the M4 corridor and close to the Rover Group's production complex at Oxford takes on added meaning in the context of productive co-operation between the British Rover Group and the Japanese Honda company. An automobile industry attempting to cope with global competition by adopting post-Fordist production techniques and labour relations and entering into transnational cost-sharing agreements poses a further threat to the industrial region centred on Birmingham and a challenge to the post-industrial transformation of that city.[5]

More generally, participation in the contemporary information-driven circuit of capital is highly selective (Hall, 1987). In the U K, Liverpool and London together hold the dubious distinction of being most sluggish in replacing manufacturing jobs lost with those related to the service—especially the producer services—economy. London, however, does at least start from a position of national dominance and world significance in such services, while Liverpool clearly does not. By contrast, provincial cities like Bristol, Cardiff, and most especially Edinburgh, have made much more rapid progress. Edinburgh is particularly interesting. Like

[5] With typical generosity, Phil Cooke drew my attention to this point.

Cardiff, it is a national capital but, unlike Cardiff, it is the capital of a nation with its own financial, legal, and educational system and so, as with capital cities elsewhere in Western Europe like Luxembourg and Brussels, continues to attract finance and control functions within the circuit of capital.

Furthermore, the poor employment performance of London and the other major conurbations is explicable in part by what may be interpreted as the geographical spread of the circuit of capital focused on them to encompass much of their surrounding regions. This process is especially marked in the case of London and the south-eastern region. Here, to the north, west and south-west of the metropolis, population and economic growth is particularly rapid in cities like Bournemouth/ Poole, Swindon, Milton Keynes, Peterborough/Huntingdon, and Ipswich, all cities which lie between about 100 and 160 kilometres from London. Thus it is hardly surprising to discover that the fastest-growing cities in terms of employment are in southern service, commercial, and manufacturing areas and in cities sufficiently close to London to be dominated by it. Nor is it surprising that producer services are growing most rapidly in southern towns and cities and in urban places outside but in touch with the major conurbations (Gillespie and Green 1987).

. . . and the Moral of the Stories?

One of the inescapable features of human life is its sociality.[6] As human beings we are incapable of existing outside or beyond society. Equally as human beings we are almost incapable of behaviour informed entirely by instinct. Thought, intention, plan, alternatives are features not merely of strategic junctures in our lives but of our everyday lives. So the societies that we live in are social products—we create and are created by them; and, in a process of perpetual motion, we continue to modify them both consciously and unconsciously. But we cannot escape their influence. A set of social relations provide the essential conditions of our existence.

At root, social relations provide a basis of communication and social interaction; they establish norms and define the boundaries of acceptable and even thinkable behaviour and social action.[7] But again we must insist that the establishment of a set of social relations is itself a social process governed by experience, thought, and the power of hegemony.

---

[6] A justification for this assertion is outlined in Lee (1989).

[7] A particularly clear example of the significance of what is almost a truism is provided by Milward and Saul's account of the social limits to agricultural improvement in pre-industrial Europe (1973, pp. 81–3).

Even in the highly integrated global economy of the contemporary world, there remain diverse forms of social relations, and their significance is demonstrated by the conflict between them. One of the most poignant contemporary examples is the struggle between aboriginal society and Western urban materialism in Australia, a continent which remains—and this adds to the poignancy—one of most empty land masses in the world. Both societies remain locked in what Robert Hughes (1987, ch. 3) calls the 'geographical unconscious'—a phrase he uses to describe the reactions of and to the first white settlers in Australia, but which is equally relevant today as mutual incomprehension continues to lead to social pathologies within both materialist and aboriginal Australia.

Unless social relations enable four fundamental processes to be fulfilled, social reproduction fails—and this is a failure often preceded by profound and violent social struggle. People must be able to engage in a productive relationship with nature to provide the material requirements of their lives. But to do so they must also be able to engage with each other in a sustainable manner. This sustenance may be provided by force (of ideology as well as of arms) but this is both wasteful of human, natural, and technical resources and difficult to sustain in a human society whose members are always capable of inventing and planning for alternatives. So two further conditions are necessary: space for individuality, and creativity. In one sense, these four conditions are mutually incompatible—a truism demonstrated by the course of human history—and yet, if social reproduction is to be sustained, they must be reconciled within particular forms of society. There are several ways of doing this—and, given the imaginative power of human thought, a persuasive ideology rather than physical violence remains the most compelling means of inducing such a reconciliation.

Capitalist society has proved to be particularly formative and dynamic. The historic significance of capitalism as a set of social relations has been captured most incisively by E. J. Hobsbawm (1962, p. 28). Assessing the emergence of industrial capitalism in Europe during the Industrial Revolution, Hobsbawm suggests with the greatest economy and precision that 'for the first time in human history, the shackles were taken off the productive power of human societies, which henceforth became capable of the constant, rapid and up to the present limitless multiplication of men, goods and services'. The shackles in question were the all-embracing social relations of feudal society, which had smothered thoughts of productive innovation. They came to be replaced, in a long-drawn-out and still not fully complete struggle, by the elegant simplicity of the mutual 'freedom' of labour and capital in capitalist society.

The material effectiveness of capitalism is as remarkable as it is uneven. Its dramatic potential was appreciated in the Manchester of the early 1920s even if the local implications of its geographical dynamic proved to be rather too dramatic for Mancunian comfort. The 'freedom' of capitalism compels competition (Brenner, 1977) and so necessitates accumulation for accumulation's sake, expansion for expansion's sake. It generates a powerfully restless geography—brilliantly described by David Harvey (1982, p. 373). It is a freedom which reduces human beings and the natural environment to commodities. Labour becomes labour power to be bought and sold in line with the requirements of capital; nature is transformed into a mere resource for, or potentially surmountable barrier to, productive activity. So, in appearing to provide a basis for social reproduction (and an apparently dramatically successful one at that), capitalism simultaneously undermines its own conditions of existence. It has, however, been limited in this process of destruction by its inability, finally, to control human beings (Urry, 1981). They continue to struggle to improve the conditions of their own existence and so humanize capital—at least in those parts of the world where labour has been able to offer resistance and organized opposition.

Nevertheless, even when the further penetration of human society is barred or severely limited, capitalism is able to feed off its own processes of uneven development. But at that point its dynamism is exposed as inhuman and senseless. It cannot resolve its crises but it can 'deconstruct' them and present a new interpretation to enable social acceptance. New urban forms may be created, for example, and may be endowed with great power in the ideological battle to sustain the hegemony of capitalist society through a process of reconstruction by labelling. The failed modern city aspires to post-modernism and so sets in motion—in Birmingham for example—a new round of competitive and uneven urban development. In succumbing to the requirements of social reproduction under capitalism, problems are redefined and may be relocated, but are rarely resolved, as resources must be reallocated for profitable use within the circuit of capital. Indeed, the very problems themselves may be used to support the need for the further allocation of resources to sustain or recreate a competitive position. Cuts in jobs, wages, and welfare may thereby come to be interpreted as natural and inevitable. And such an interpretation is easier to make when, as in Western Europe, the distribution of the costs of such policies are geographically separate from the benefits and so pose no real reproductive threat to the politics of capitalist restructuring.

If capitalist society succeeded in removing shackles, contemporary state socialist society replaced one system of exhaustive social control with another (Lee, 1989). This system now faces profound problems of reproduction as the undoubted economic achievements since 1917 (see, for example, Dicken, 1986, ch. 2) themselves create difficulties of economic co-ordination and control in what must become a more decentralized and innovative system of production. But the malaise appears to run more deeply. The contradictions of a production-orientated, centrally controlled and often grossly misplanned economic system— currently, 40 per cent of production from the socialized sector of the Polish economy is defective or shoddy (Simmons, 1988)—together with a profoundly insecure one-party political system, have served to repress individuality and creativity. The result is resentful and passive resistance among the population at large—especially in countries like Poland with a deep-seated cultural tradition and long history of external control— towards 'reforms' emanating from above and aimed, rhetorically at least, at decentralization and greater openness and freedom even within the daily business of making a living (Blazyea, 1987).

The intellectual and political challenge is—as ever—to refuse to be confused by labels and, more important, to present convincing alternatives rather than to accept or apologize for what we have now. But change has to be preceded by understanding. Essential to such an understanding is the recognition that social problems *in* cities cannot be resolved without a resolution of the social problem *of* the city. That in turn involves us in tracing the indirect and complex relations between dominant forms of social relations and the geography simultaneously made and used in what is, ultimately, the conduct of our daily lives.

But it also involves a recognition that the imperatives of social reproduction are imperative only if we accept them as such and forget that societies are made by people. Societies cannot be assumed away, but they can be changed. We have to start from the here and now rather than from some idealized alternative, and we must recognize the power and social distinction of the historical geography that has brought us to the here and now. The clock cannot be turned back: a return to an idealized past is neither possible nor desirable. The desire to return to the Victorian city, for example, is at best a grotesquely ill-informed anachronism. More realistically, it is another labelling exercise motivated by ideology. According to Margaret Thatcher (1987) the Victorian city was 'a complete, almost a city state, a complete ideal . . . They had this complete feeling that the city was the focus of their lives. . . . What I am trying to do is to rearrange things so that we kind of recapture that.' Engels would have difficulty recognizing in this account the cities that he studied first-hand and would abhor a return to those conditions.

So we must remember that the power which continues to drive our own geography is not an abstract force determining our actions, but a social energy 'embodied in real people and in a real context'. Edward

Thompson (1968, p. 9) goes on to say with incisive simplicity that social relations are not simply given: 'We cannot have love without lovers, nor deference without squires and labourers.' It follows that we cannot have urban problems ascribable to particular forms of social reproduction without a general acceptance of the social relations underpinning that process of social reproduction. And we cannot remove the cause of those social problems and build something better without the hard intellectual and social struggle to convince ourselves that there is—always—an alternative.

References

Agnew, J. (1987), *The United States in the World Economy: A Regional Geography* (Cambridge University Press: Cambridge).

Ambrose, P. (1986), *Whatever Happened to Planning?* (Methuen: London).

Armstrong, P., A. Glyn, and J. Harrison (1984), *Capitalism since World War II* (Fontana: London).

Beynon, H., R. Hudson, J. Lewis, D. Sadler, and A. Townsend (1989), 'Left to rot? Middlesborough in the 1980s', in P. Cooke (ed.), *Localities* (Hutchinson: London).

Bivand, R. (1983), 'Towards a geography of "Solidarnosc" ', *Environment and Planning D: Society and Space*, 1: 397–404.

Blazyea, G. (1987), 'The new round of economic reform in eastern Europe', *National Westminster Bank Quarterly Review*, Nov., 41–53.

Brenner, R. (1977), 'The origins of capitalist development: a critique of neo-Smithian Marxism', *New Left Review*, 104: 25–92.

Chapman, K., and D. Walker (1987), *Industrial Location* (Basil Blackwell: Oxford).

Cooke, P. (ed.) (1988) *Localities* (Hutchinson: London).

Daniels, P. W. (1985), *Service Industries: A Geographical Appraisal* (Methuen: London).

Dicken, P. (1986), *Global Shift* (Harper and Row: London)

Ewers, H. J., J. B. Goddard and H. Matzerath (eds.) (1986), *The Future of the Metropolis* (de Gruyter: Berlin and New York).

Fainstein, N., S. Fainstein and A. Schwartz (1987), 'How New York remained a global city 1940–1987', paper to the Sixth Urban Change and Conflict Conference, University of Kent, Canterbury, Sept.

Fraser, D. (1979), *Power and Authority in the Victorian City* (Basil Blackwell: Oxford).

Gillespie, A. E., and A. E. Green (1987), 'The changing geography of producer services employment in Britain', *Regional Studies*, 21(5): 397–412.

Gordon, G. (1986), *Regional Cities in the UK 1890–1980* (Harper and Row: London).

Greater Manchester Council (1979), *Greater Manchester County Structure Plan: Written Statement* (GMC: Manchester).

Hall, P. (1987), 'The anatomy of job creation: nations, regions and cities in the 1960s and 1970s', *Regional Studies*, 21(2): 95–106.

Harvey, D. (1982), *The Limits to Capital* (Basil Blackwell: Oxford).

—— (1987), 'Flexible accumulation through urbanization: reflections on "post-modernism" in the American city', paper to the Sixth Urban Change and Conflict Conference, University of Kent, Canterbury, Sept.

R. C. Hill, and J. R. Feagin (1987), 'Detroit and Houston: two cities in global perspective', in M. P. Smith and J. R. Feagin (eds.), *The Capitalist City: Global Restructuring and Community Politics* (Basil Blackwell: Oxford), 155–77.

Hobsbawm, E. J. (1962), *The Age of Revolution* (Weidenfeld and Nicolson: London).

Hughes, R. (1987), *The Fatal Shore* (Collins Harvill: London).

Hymer, S. (1972), 'The multinational corporation and the law of uneven development', in J. N. Bhagwati (ed.), *Economics and World Order from the 1970s to the 1990s* (Macmillan: Basingstoke), 113–40.

International Labour Organisation 1984 *World Labour Report 1. Employment, Incomes Social Protection, New Information Technology*, Geneva, International Labour Office, p. 36; quoted in Thrift, 1986.

Knox, P. (1987), 'The social production of the built environment: architects, architecture and the post-modern city', *Progress in Human Geography*, 11(3): 354–77.

Law, C. M. (1986), 'The geography of exhibition centres in Britain', *Geography*, 71: 359–62.

Lawton, R. (1972), 'An age of great cities', *Town Planning Review*, 43: 199–224.

Lee, R. (1976), 'Integration, spatial structure and the capitalist mode of production in the EEC', in R. Lee and P. E. Ogden (eds.), *Economy and Society in the EEC* (Saxon House: Farnborough), 11–37.

—— (1979), 'The economic basis of social problems in the city', in D. Herbert and D. M. Smith (eds.), *Social Problems and the City: Geographical Perspectives* (Oxford University Press: Oxford), 47–62.

—— (1989), 'Social relations and the geography of material life', in D. Gregory and R. Walford (eds.), *Horizons in Human Geography* (Macmillan: Basingstoke).

Marcuse, P. (1981), 'The targeted crisis: on the ideology of the urban fiscal crisis and its uses', *International Journal of Urban and Regional Research*, 5(3): 330–55.

Massey, D. (1986), 'The legacy lingers on: the impact of Britain's international role on its internal geography', in R. Martin and B. Rowthorn (eds.), *The Geography of Deindustrialisation* (Macmillan: Basingstoke), 31–52.

—— (1987), 'Thoughts from a train going north', *Area*, 19(3): 268–9.

MDJTPAC (Manchester and District Joint Town Planning Advisory Committee) (1925), *Report on the Regional Scheme* (MDJTPAC: Manchester).

Milward, A. S., and S. B. Saul (1973), *The Economic Development of Continental Europe 1780–1870* (Allen and Unwin: London).

Parkinson, M. (1987), 'Politics, money and economic decline: the Liverpool story', paper to the Sixth Urban Change and Conflict Conference, University of Kent, Canterbury, Sept.

Piore M. J. and Sabel C. F. 1984 *The second industrial divide: possibilities for prosperity* (New York, Basic Books).

Rubinstein, W. D., (1981), *Men of Property: The Very Wealthy in Britain since the Industrial Revolution* (Croom Helm: Beckenham).

Sassen-Koob, S. (1984), 'The new labour demand in global cities', in M. P. Smith (ed.), *Cities in Transformation: Class, Capital and the State*, Urban Affairs Annual Reviews xxvi (Sage: London), 139–71.

Scott, A. J. (1986), 'Industrialization and urbanization: a geographical agenda', *Annals of the Association of American Geographers*, 76(1): 25–37.

Simmons, M. (1988), 'Poles say Police Destroyed Party', *Guardian*, 16 Feb., p. 8.

Soja, E. (1987), 'Economic restructuring and the internationalization of the Los Angeles region', in M. P. Smith and J. R. Feagin (eds.), *The Capitalist City: Global Restructuring and Community Politics* (Basil Blackwell: Oxford), 178–98.

Sutcliffe, A. (1982), 'The growth of public intervention in the British urban environment during the nineteenth century: a structural approach', in J. H. Johnson and C. G. Pooley (eds.), *The Structure of Nineteenth Century Cities* (Croom Helm: Beckenham), 107–24.

Thatcher, M. (1987), quoted in 'The real state of the cities', *Guardian*, 25 Nov., p. 14.

Thompson, E. P. (1968), *The Making of the English Working Class* (Penguin: Harmondsworth).

Thrift, N. (1986), 'The geography of international economic disorder', in R. J. Johnston and P. J. Taylor (eds.), *A World in Crisis? Geographical Perspectives* (Basil Blackwell: Oxford), 12–67.

Urry, J. (1981), *The Anatomy of Capitalist Society* (Macmillan: London).

Vance, J. E. (1977), *This Scene of Man* (Harper and Row: New York).

Walker, R. A. (1978), 'The transformation of urban structure in the nineteenth century and the beginnings of suburbanization', in K. R. Cox (ed.), *Urbanization and Conflict in Market Societies* (Methuen: London), 165–211.

PART II

Specific Issues

5

The Environmental Problems of Cities

Ian Douglas

To ecologists and natural scientists, cities are the localities where people have most transformed nature, where a series of new habitats for all kinds of organisms have been created. To engineers and planners, cities may represent a culmination of human ingenuity in sustaining life in great concentration a long distance from the basic energy, water, food, and raw materials necessary to sustain it. This great dual transformation of nature involved in urbanization, the transformation of the site and of the natural flows of energy, water, food, and materials, inevitably brings with it many side-effects and unwanted problems whose resolution and reduction require technological and financial investment.

The environmental problems of cities relate to impacts of, and upon, climate, water, soil, biota, landforms, and human health. Many of them are interrelated, in that a site may have good attributes for a particular purpose, but technical change and urban expansion lead to those attributes becoming disadvantageous and then in turn to a set of environmental problems. In a simple way this may be illustrated by Sheffield, which grew up as an industrial centre from a series of industrial hamlets exploiting water power in the steep Pennine valleys descending to the River Don. This energy source was later replaced by coal and the focus of industry shifted down-valley to the Don River between Sheffield and Rotherham. Here the smoke from the great steelworks was trapped by the down-valley wind-flows and the frequent inversions in the lee of the Pennines, producing high levels of air pollution from suspended particulates and sulphur dioxide which severely affected the health and living conditions of local residents (Garnett, 1967). Subsequent changes in the economics and technology of steel manufacture and in fuel use for space heating, accompanied by clean air legislation, have led to much cleaner air in Sheffield since the 1950s. However, this interdependence of environmental problems with the site, technology, form, and economic life of the city is characteristic.

Such relationships between human and environmental factors, as they change through time, make the analysis of environmental problems difficult, as they are seldom simple, direct cause-and-effect issues. Resolution of one environmental problem may only produce another elsewhere, in the way that tall chimneys erected to disperse airborne pollutants to improve the air of cities from 1950 onwards may well have added to the long-distance dispersal of sulphur which aggravated the acid rain problems in Western Europe and north-eastern North America. Environmental improvement, by reducing effluents or requiring costly treatment of waste discharges, may impose extra costs on industry and commerce, forcing firms to reduce other costs, often by cutting jobs and saving on wage bills. Unfortunately, space does not permit a full analysis of all these ramifications of urban environmental issues in this chapter.

Knowledge of the type of environmental problem likely to arise from specific aspects of urban activity and morphology is useful to all aspects of urban studies. The great temptation for someone who is not an applied scientist is to think of the physical problems affecting the city as a constraint on development which can be overcome at the planning and construction stage, and the biological problems as easily controlled by pesticides and herbicides. Nature is far more cunning. The problems change as the city grows and its economic and social structure develop. Biological evolution does not stop at the Green Belt, but penetrates the food store, the house plants, the cellars, the attics, and the bodies of household pets and human beings. Removal of one pest may lead simply to its replacement by another. Although the city may be where people have most transformed nature, it is not a place where nature has been eliminated or even fully controlled.

To facilitate discussion, environmental problems will be considered here in terms of their relationships to: (*a*) the sites of cities; (*b*) the surface and extent of cities; (*c*) the three-dimensional form of cities; (*d*) resource use and the transformation of raw materials; (*e*) changes in technology, fuel use, materials, and chemicals; (*f*) planning policies; and (*g*) human health.

Environmental Problems Related to the Sites of Cities

'Know the ground your home stands on' ought to be common-sense advice to every house purchaser, but thoughts about the site are subdued by considerations of price, accessibility, rates, and school zoning when buying a home. Yet many examples exist of houses, offices, factories, and parts of cities which have severe foundation problems because of where they are built. The suitability of a site for construction will be determined by a variety of landform and soil characteristics. If the land is on a slope, the steepness and stability of the slope may be limiting factors. For example, around London slopes as gentle as 9° have failed because of the nature of London Clay. In areas such as Bristol, where resistant limestones overlie weaker rocks, removal or slumping of the underlying material may lead to cambering or valley-ward creep of the cap rock, with fissuring of the ground affecting structures above.

Particular problems arise in cities built on glacial deposits, as is the case of most British cities north of a line approximately from the Severn estuary to Harwich. Unconsolidated glacial materials make poor foundations generally, but often they are still relatively unstable, as the British landscape is still recovering from the last glaciation, its geomorphology not being at equilibrium with the present temperate climate. As the ice retreated from the lowlands of Britain, tundra conditions with massive frost action prevailed, most slopes becoming subject to solifluction, blockfield movement and landsliding. Many of the landslides that developed at that time can still be detected from air photos, but appear stable on the ground. However, when disturbed by construction work, these old landslides may move again, sometimes with severe effects.

North of Manchester, near Haslingden, construction began on a housing site at Ewood Bridge in 1973. Some sixty-six houses had been built, sold, or occupied, or were partially completed when movement of some floor slabs occurred and cracks appeared on some walls. Construction work stopped and the resale value of the houses fell dramatically. Local movement of the subsoil, possibly the reactivation of old landslips, had occurred. Eventually the local council decided that, while the existing structures could remain, the partially built houses should be demolished, and that the risk of further movement was too great to allow any further construction to proceed.

Dumping of waste on slopes of this type can produce even more disastrous consequences, the most tragic example of which was the Aberfan mud-slide and debris-flow in 1966. Glacial till (boulder clay), overlies strongly jointed sandstone, with beds of clay on the valley sides. The boulder clay does not allow much water to pass through, so that water in the sandstone emerging on the valley side above the clay beds normally runs beneath the boulder clay towards the valley floor. Dumping of mining waste on the valley depressed the boulder clay and kept the water in the sandstone under pressure. Following heavy rain, part of the coal tip slipped and water began to wash large amounts of material, including the boulder clay, down the valley side. Suddenly, the water under pressure in the sandstone was released, washing the slipped waste with it to form the debris-flow which engulfed part of Aberfan, especially the children in the school (Woodland, 1968). Waste tips and housing estates in such situations are still to be found in Wales and northern England and, given the stratigraphic situation, slipping could occur. Road construction across such unstable areas is particularly difficult, and electricity pylons resting on such slope deposits may have to be protected or jacked up at regular intervals.

The greater use of underground space in cities, for road and rail tunnels, car parks, and below ground level service areas and facilities, means that groundwater levels and surface materials have to be examined particularly carefully. The presence of old river channels with their coarse sandy deposits may still mean preferential lines of water movement. In one case, the siting of a major brick-lined sewer along a former stream channel at Farnworth near Manchester resulted, many decades later, in severe subsidence when the sewer lining gave way, and water rushed through the old stream deposits, carrying the overlying clay with it. The road above collapsed, creating a hole 40 m. long, 6 m. wide and 4 m. deep, with seventeen houses being damaged beyond repair (Douglas, 1985*a*).

Lest it be thought that ground problems are confined to central and northern Britain, it should be recalled that problems associated with the shrink-swell behaviour of clays, causing cracking and failure of building walls, foundations, and floor, are fairly common in southern Britain. Experiments at the Building Research Station at Watford showed vertical movement of up to 30 mm. in wet autumn conditions as montmorillonite clay mineral took up water and expanded. The exceptionally dry years of the 1975–6 British drought saw many cases of foundation movement resulting from clay shrinkage, and a tenfold increase in insurance claims for such damage (Douglas, 1985*b*). However, it is in the cities of the black soil plains of semi-arid regions that such problems are most severe, householders in Dallas, Texas, experiencing almost 8,500 foundation failures a year, 84 per cent of which are due to shrink-swell phenomena.

Karstic processes in calcareous rocks may pose severe environmental problems. In south-eastern England, collapses in the unconsolidated sediments overlying vertical pipes in the chalk occur periodically as a result of fluctuations in groundwater or changes in surface loading. Sometimes, material that has been used to fill an old chalk or limestone quarry has been levelled and reclaimed. Instances where the washing of such material into the karst fissures or cavern systems below occur from time to time, both over the chalk and the more massive limestone elsewhere in Britain. Sinkhole collapse is rare in the UK, but a serious problem in the eastern United States, parts of the Witwatersrand in South Africa and in east and south-east Asian limestone areas.

Environmental Problems Related to the Surface and Extent of Cities

Buildings and paved surfaces have albedos, or abilities to reflect incoming solar radiation, which differ from natural earth surface materials. The black, tarmacadam surface of a car park will absorb a large amount of heat and have a low albedo, but a light-coloured concrete pathway would store less heat. The overall impact of all these surface properties of a city, compared with the vegetated or water surfaces of the surrounding countryside, is to raise average temperatures in the city, especially at night. When added to the release from the conurbation of heat of fossil fuels, significant temperature differences occur, average maximum temperatures in London being 0.5 °C warmer than in the countryside, and minima almost 2 °C warmer (Chandler, 1965). This urban heat island effect is particularly noticeable in extreme conditions, especially during heatwaves. Heat causes great stress among people who are already ill or infirm, causing many to die before they would have done. Heatwaves are thus associated with excessive mortality. Using weekly mortality data, Macfarlane and Waller (1976) have shown that in 1975 in Greater London a temporary increase in mortality coincided with the heatwave of late July to mid-August, with a similar increase in late June and early July 1976, when temperatures reached 32 °C on 1 July.

Urban centres tend to become even warmer because of the heat generated by machinery. Attempts to cool buildings by air conditioning, and the use of reflective glass in modern buildings, tend to add to the external heat discomfort. In winter the warmth of the city influences the rate of snow melt and the incidence of frost.

The heat island also leads to a local wind circulation on days when there is no regional air movement. Surface winds tend to blow towards the city centre, then to rise over the city and descend outwards aloft towards ground level beyond the city. The rising air over the city carries particles with it which may act as condensation nuclei for water vapour, leading to cloud formation and possibly rain. Meteorologists argue about whether or not cities increase precipitation. Atkinson (1977) demonstrated that urban thunderstorms do occur in London, while Tabony (1980) claims that annual and seasonal rainfall trends in London do not display any features which can be attributed to urbanization.

Also associated with this urban air-circulation is the development of an 'urban dust dome' in which particulates are held in the air over the city, forming a haze. When the sun is strong, the effluents from motor vehicles are transformed into an orange-brownish-coloured photochemical smog, well known in cities in Mediterranean-type climates such as Los Angeles and Cairo, and in semi-arid zones such as Mexico

City and Tehran, but also present on occasional calm, warm summer days over British cities like London, Birmingham, and Manchester.

In addition to modifying the energy balance, the paved and roofed urban surface alters the water balance. As indicated above, rainfall, and certainly thunderstorm incidence, are likely to be increased. Rain falling on a paved surface tends to evaporate quickly. Initially much rain is held in shallow pools in a small depressions on the surface which then, as soon as the surface is warmed by the sun, evaporates. Large amounts of rain on paved surfaces run off directly to local drains and stormwater sewers, but this proportion may not be as high as might be expected, one London study noting that only 50 per cent of the rain on a 95 per cent paved area in London actually ran off, most of the balance returning to the atmosphere as water vapour (Oke, 1974).

With a paved, or partially paved, surface and artificial drainage, runoff patterns are altered and peak-flow characteristics changed (Leopold, 1968). Much depends on the proportion of paved area in a catchment. In areas with considerable amounts of garden and other green spaces, streams tend to show some increase in the rate at which runoff reaches the channel and an increase in the heights of peak flows from storms of moderate magnitude, but relatively small changes in the biggest stormwater discharges. For example, major floods, likely to occur only once in twenty years, on Canon's Brook in Harlow, Essex, are only minimally affected by urbanization (Hollis, 1974, 1975). In a rare, large flood event, the soil is so saturated that the whole catchment area is virtually impervious; there is no capacity for more water to enter the soil. In such circumstances, any extra water arriving at the ground surface must run off.

Some of this effect is apparent seasonally, high soil moisture levels in winter reducing infiltration capacities. Thus, from an analysis of fifteen years' records at Canon's Brook, Hollis (1977) found that urbanization had affected summer flows much more than winter flows. While there was little infiltration into wet clay soils in winter, in summer the dry soil allowed infiltration and so behaved very differently from the paved urban surface. Inevitably, the higher the proportion of a river basin that is paved, the more its runoff becomes quickly concentrated and the higher the peak flows. As the development of a city is a gradual process, over the decades more and more of a catchment becomes impermeable. Such a situation often means that bridges and culverts downstream in the older urban areas are no longer able to cope with increased peak flows. In Greater Manchester's southern suburbs, the Timperley Brook passes through a culvert under the Bridgewater Canal. When James Brindley built the canal in the eighteenth century, the surrounding area was all farmland. Now it is almost completely urbanized. Large thunderstorms over the catchment in the early 1980s produced such large volumes of peak flow that the culvert was unable to cope. Water backed up and nearby houses were flooded. The people near the canal were suffering from the urban development upstream; they were the victims of land-use changes several kilometres away. The culvert and adjacent stream channel had to be enlarged and local playing fields were adapted for use as temporary floodwater storage basins during runoff from the rare, extremely heavy rainstorms. This type of downstream, off-site impact of urban development often happens. Those who have to pay the costs are not those who benefit from the development.

The standard work on flood prediction in the United Kingdom recognizes that the only area where the percentage of urban area needs to be considered in forecasting peak discharges is the London area, the catchments of the rivers Thames and Lee. With so much modification of drainage in an area with a high proportion of calcareous rocks allowing much infiltration under natural conditions, urbanization has a much greater effect in this area than in the steeper catchments of wetter parts of the country.

Environment Problems Related to Urban Form

The architecture, built features and physical form of the city have a profound influence on its local environment. Structures interfere with air movements, altering local climates and creating microclimates, and affect living conditions for all organisms. An individual building will interfere with the wind pattern, one side perhaps being a windy side and another the protected side having only an occasional eddy swirling against it. when buildings are grouped together they complicate wind flows, with tall buildings lining streets creating 'urban canyons' which can be extremely windy if they are parallel to the dominant wind direction. Wind flows between buildings can create extreme gusts around corners and doorways. If multi-storey blocks form a virtual wall across the path of the prevailing wind, any gap between those buildings becomes a wind gap where velocities on windy days may be so high that it is difficult to walk into the wind. Not only is there human discomfort associated with urban winds, but also there are real economic costs associated with rates of cooling and heat loss from the walls of buildings exposed to strong winds. Individual homes or buildings with rapid air flow around them will lose heat more quickly than linked houses or clusters of buildings arranged so as to reduce wind speed and impede air flow. Clearly, urban design for winter warmth is not so effective for cooling on hot summer days, and different urban designs are needed to

TABLE 5.1. Types of urban land cover and biogeographic conditions

Nature of land cover	Type of location	Nature of biotic zone (after Dorney, 1979)	Type of urban eco-system (after Duvigneaud, 1974)	Trend over time
Paved, roofed, densely urban complexes devoid of open areas of vegetation and water bodies.	City central business districts. Large shopping centres and car parks. Some industrial zones.	Cliff/organic detritus	Anthropogenic	Birds and insects develop an increasing number of niches. Micro-organisms clonize.
Suburban mosaic of houses, roads, gardens, and mature trees.	Older, spacious inner suburbs.	Old urban savanna	Urbanophile	Already diverse and mature; future changes depend on management.
Corridor zones of wild plants.	Railway, canal, power line, and some arterial road reservations.	Grassland/weed complex.	Peripheral	Increasing biotic diversity unless interference occurs.
Landscaped parks and open spaces.	City parks, recreation grounds, golf courses.	Mowed grassland	Anthropogenic and modified natural.	Careful management keeps biotic diversity low.
Derelict land construction sites.	Abandoned industrial sites, old waste tips.	Abiotic/weed complex.	Urbanophile	Temporary opportunities for plant colonization removed when development is completed.

New suburbs, devoid of mature trees and high grassland: cultivated garden ratio.	Outer suburban areas, new housing estates, some modern industrial estates and office building complexes.	New urban savanna	Urbanophile	Biotic diversity increases as gardens become established. Rate of increase depends on occupants' attitudes.
Grassland on reclaimed soil with streets, car parks, and buildings but few or no mature trees.	Inner city redevelopment areas with large open spaces, modern flats or row houses, some new industrial estates.	New urban savanna/ mowed grassland.	Anthropogenic/ urbanophile.	Management tends to preserve low biotic diversity.
Small woodland and rural areas within the city.	Patches of woodland left as quasi-natural areas, urban commons or heaths.	Remnant ecosystem/ natural islands.	Relict	Old woodland diversity maintained if human interference is not increased.
Water bodies	Lakes, rivers and reservoirs.	Lake-stream/aquatic complexes.	Modified natural	Status dependent on management.
Wetlands and much-modified water bodies.	Marshes, sewage farms and gravel pits.	Derelict/weedy grassland and aquatic complex.	Urbanophile	If neglected, biotic diversity increases. Likely to be much disturbed.

Source: Douglas, 1983, p. 128.

ameliorate climatic conditions in areas of persistently hot climate.

Building layout and design also affects the biogeography of cities. Recent years have seen a growth in emphasis on the value of urban wildlife, especially the need to preserve tracts of wild land such as the Gunnersbury Triangle between suburban railway lines in London, or patches of wasteland along canals in Birmingham and Manchester. However, wildlife is not confined to patches of 'urban countryside', but exploits a whole range of habitat opportunities offered by buildings and other urban land uses. In any of the situations listed in table 5.1 wildlife can become a problem, but space permits but one illustration—the wildlife of the completely built-up urban areas.

Many ecologists have described the central business districts of cities as floristic deserts, unfavourable for plants, but supporting an insect, bird, mammal, and microbial life dependent on human activity. Yet even in the heart of the city there are plants in window-boxes, tubs, roof-top gardens, living rooms, offices and even bathrooms. Every plant is a potential host for insects and microbes. Older-style buildings often exhibit three sets of ecological conditions: the relatively high humidities of cellars; the warm, dry microclimate of living rooms; and the varying extremes of warmth and cold in attics (Duvigneaud, 1974). As building styles change, these habitat opportunities alter and the insect communities change, as Popham (1980) has demonstrated in Salford. The exterior changes in style also have an effect on wildlife. In the horse age, at the end of the nineteenth century, the house sparrow reached its peak population in British cities, grain from horse-feed providing abundant food. The widespread use of wood in building and the intricate architectural styles created abundant niches for nesting sites and roosting spaces. However, with the emergence of the motor car and smooth, modern building styles in the 1930s, the sparrow was forced to seek new food sources and nesting sites, and a noticeable decline in numbers occurred (Summers-Smith, 1963).

Habitat changes and social changes affect the relationships between people and wildlife in cities. The pigeon, long regarded as a favourable feature of Trafalgar Square and other open spaces in London, becomes a nuisance in excessive numbers and a real problem in areas such as major railway stations. When birds accumulate beneath roofs spanning rail tracks, sports arenas, or shopping centres, they are simply exploiting a habitat and food source opportunity, but they can be an annoying problem for facility managers. Other creatures can cause more serious problems. Rats constitute a serious public health hazard. Plague is spread from rats to people by the rat flea *Xenopsylla cheopis*, which is particularly serious in the black, ship, or roof rat (*Rattus rattus* L.). The common, brown, or Norway rat (*Rattus norveqicus Berkenhout*) is widespread, but in the United Kingdom in 1951 the ship rat was found in dock areas and in nearby buildings in Bristol and Avonmouth, Cardiff, Liverpool, Stretford (Trafford Park, Manchester), Barrow-in-Furness, Stornoway, Lerwick, Edinburgh, and perhaps Belfast (Bentley, 1959). In London it is concentrated in riverside and canalside areas. Central London provides conditions favourable for the ship rat not found elsewhere, with many multi-storey, centrally heated buildings, largely non-residential but interspersed with restaurants, canteens and other sources of food. As the ship rat is an indoor animal, it survives best where it can run from ship to vehicle to adjacent buildings or between buildings.

Changing technology and building styles are affecting the ship rat. With so much sea freight travelling in containers, fewer ship rats are reaching Britain. The replacement of the old dockland warehouses with new commercial and residential developments, as at Salford Quays, Manchester, or Canary Wharf, London, removes favourable habitats. The distribution of the ship rat has become more restricted, but it is likely to persist for a long time in dock areas of London, Bristol, Liverpool, and perhaps Edinburgh and Belfast, where the most favourable migration and habitat conditions are found. In other countries, especially in low latitudes, where sanitation and waste-handling facilities are less well developed, the ship rats, and associated plague-vector fleas, remain a major urban environmental problem.

More widespread, yet less dramatic, are the countless insects, fungi, moulds, mites, and bacteria that affect daily life in the urban environment. The dampness of poorly maintained inner-city properties brings about the growth of moulds that affect health and quality of life. Dust mites that thrive in even the most frequently vacuum-cleaned carpet aggravate allergies and may make some people extremely ill. Little attention is paid to how these organisms live and survive in cities, but without a biophysical analysis of their ecology, their role in social well-being will not be fully understood.

Environmental Problems Related to Resource Use

Two broad categories of resource use produce environmental problems in cities: the exploitation of water and mineral resources within the city, and the transformation of materials brought into the city. All cities require energy and water, many using fossil fuels and groundwater from beneath the city to sustain their growth. Groundwater is the major source of supply to many British cities, including London. Abstraction of groundwater usually leads to a lowering of the water table and the reduction of water held in voids between mineral particles. The weight of buildings above, increasing as the city grows and rebuilds, presses down on these now empty spaces, causing particles to become more closely compacted, leading to ground surface lowering or subsidence. Such subsidence is a major problem in cities such as Tokyo, Bangkok, and Mexico City, but is not without significance in British cities. Although land levels in London are affected by the geologic subsidence of south-east England and the southern North Sea, there is local subsidence owing to lowering of the artesian head (the level to which the water will rise under its own pressure if not confined by the overlying London Clay). Whereas the artesian head was up to 10 m above mean sea level in 1820, by 1936 it was 30 to 100 m below, greatest lowering being along an axis running south-westwards from central London towards Richmond (Poland and Davis, 1969). The gradual subsidence of the area beneath the city means that peak flows in the River Thames are now higher in relation to the city streets than they were a century ago, yet because of the draining and paving of the ground in the city, little of the peak flow infiltrates into the floodplain in the way it once did. As the Thames in London is tidal, a major flood can be produced when an exceptionally high tide caused by a storm surge in the North Sea meets a high flow from the land upstream. Tidal records show that high-water levels in London have risen relative to the land by about 0.85 m. per century, while at Southend the change is only 0.38 m. (Trafford, 1981). With a tidal height probability for a 1-in-200-year storm of 1.5 m. above the peak level in 1953, the flood risk to central London was so great that the tidal barrier was built across the Thames in Woolwich Reach at a cost of some £400m. (Horner, 1981), with an additional £270m. being spent on flood defences along the estuary downstream to prevent damage from the extra height of water held back by the barrier. In addition to providing defence against flooding, the barrier has the potential to provide benefits in terms of improved water quality, more water for industry, improved water transport facilities, amenities, and recreation opportunities. However, the cost reminds us of the expense of coping with environmental changes largely caused by urbanization.

London's threat from storm surge flooding is not unique; every town and city on an estuary around the North Sea faces a similar threat, tidal barriers having been built or planned at places like Hull and Great Yarmouth. However, these problems are small compared with those faced by cities likely to be affected by tsunamis, great tidal waves caused by submarine earthquakes or volcanic eruptions. A small ocean swell generated near a submarine event increases in height as it travels across the ocean at 700 km hr^{-1} to create waves of up to 15 m. in height such as that which destroyed much of Lisbon, killing 60,000 people in 1755 (Coates, 1985). Coastal cities like Tokyo, which have suffered subsidence, are particularly at risk from these hazards.

Groundwater abstraction also brings water quality problems. As water is drawn from the aquifer, flows may increase in velocity, transporting contaminants into the abstraction zone. On the slopes of the North Downs south of London, nitrate levels in soils increased during intensive agriculture. As London expanded and building activity spread up the slopes, soil disturbance during urban construction released nitrogen into groundwater. The nitrate subsequently moved slowly down the aquifer to abstraction wells, becoming a problem some fifty years after the disturbance (Young and Morgan-Jones, 1980). In other circumstances, nitrate contamination of groundwater is a major problem, with fertilizer use for agriculture, especially on the chalk outcrops of Humberside, as the major source.

Water is not the only liquid abstracted from underground. Abstraction of petroleum from beneath Wilmington and Long Beach in Los Angeles, California, caused subsidence of up to 1.5 m. by 1946 (Gilluly and Grant, 1949) but continued at up to 0.6 m. per year to reach almost 9 m. by 1970 (Coates, 1985). When the costs of subsidence damage had reached several million dollars, a programme of water injection to fill the voids was begun, reducing and arresting the fall of ground levels.

Mining is a major cause of subsidence, as anyone travelling on Britain's motorways through the Warrington, Cheshire, or Nottinghamshire-Derbyshire borders will recognize on seeing the deformation of the road pavement by settlement of old coal workings. The exploitation of the Roger Seam at Bradford Colliery just north-east of the centre of Manchester caused subsidence over 150 ha. in which a 283,000 m^3 gas holder became so tilted that only half its storage could be used, and the beds of the abandoned Rochdale Canal and River Medlock were so disrupted that there were fears of local flooding. When new housing estates were built in this area, Manchester City Council had to spend £3m. to avoid further subsidence damage. Similar problems are widespread in coalfield-based industrial cities.

Resource use in terms of manufacturing produces waste products and pollutants which are discharged to the air, the waters, and the ground. Air pollution is not only closely linked with the heat islands and wind circulations of cities, but also with the pattern and nature of emission sources. Once closely related to static point sources, it is now increasingly produced by motor vehicles. Most British cities have seen a dramatic decline in particulate and sulphur dioxide pollution, but an increase in oxides of nitrogen and lead.

Decreases in water pollution have been less dramatic, apart from the spectacular cleaning up of the River Thames. While factory effluents are more tightly controlled and inefficient small sewage treatment plants have been replaced by more efficient larger works, the growth of intensive livestock-raising units close to cities has produced high sewage loadings which still affect the quality of water in many rivers flowing through cities. Many coastal cities still suffer from a lack of sewage treatment and dependence on ocean outfalls which all too often result in sewage being washed back on to beaches. Several British coastal cities fail to reach EEC standards for the quality of bathing water. These pollution problems stem not so much from resource use, but from competition for the limited funds for capital expenditure on waterworks, on that part of the urban hydrologic system known as 'underground assets'.

Solid wastes are frequently dumped on land, into old quarries and gravel pits, or to fill low-lying areas such as old abandoned meanders in floodplains. Many authorities take large quantities of waste to landfill sites outside their area, the Greater Manchester Waste Disposal Authority taking 0.7 million tonnes of the 1.18 million tonnes of waste produced each year to disposal sites near Wigan and Chorley. Much of the remainder is dumped on the river Mersey floodplain, confining the area available to flood storage to the planned overflow basins such as Sale and Chorlton water parks, but having the net effect of accelerating river flow velocities and raising flood heights downstream.

While landfill can be beneficial, such as that used to expand Southampton Docks, or for constructing major airports, like La Guardia (New York), Changi (Singapore), and Kai Tak (Hong Kong), considerable problems of internal chemical changes, post-fill settlement and compaction and escape of leachates to underground waters exist. At a few tips, toxic chemicals are deposited and, although these are now usually tightly controlled, there are several examples, in Britain and other countries, of escapes of gas or noxious liquids from dumps that had been abandoned, sealed, turfed, and used for housing or other purposes years after tipping ceased. More widespread is the pollution of groundwater by leachates from dumps or from careless disposal of wastes. When sewage treatment was inadequate, this was a major problem in Britain: it still is in many large Third World cities.

Environment Problems Related to Technical Change

One of the most serious dangers of the static view of urban biophysical conditions espoused by some architects, planners, and social scientists is the failure to comprehend the way technological change affects the urban environment. In Britain, one of the most significant was the change from coal-burning for house heating and industrial energy to electricity, gas, or oil. Within twenty-five years, sulphur dioxide levels in the air over Manchester were reduced from 500 to 50 mg l^{-1}. However, at the same time taller power-station chimneys lifted sulphates aloft to be carried to the Lake District, southern Scotland, and further afield, where they fell as acid rain.

The hydrocarbons burnt in the burgeoning number of motor vehicles and stationary engines added new compounds to the air, making photo-chemical smog possible, given suitable weather conditions, in British cities. Lead, used as an 'anti-knock' device in petrol, became so significant a problem in the inner suburbs of cities, that a leading newspaper's property column on inner London reports lead levels as part of the local conditions. While urban air in Britain has generally become cleaner and less visibly polluted, the changing technology of chemical control of pests, use of aerosol sprays, and widespread use of trace elements such as lead, has produced an invisible pollution capable of altering the ecological balance of the varied urban habitats and provoking a number of hidden dangers.

The sophisticated chemicals that are part of our daily lives involve the carriage, in drums and tankers by road and rail, of large quantities of noxious substances. Many of these are carefully labelled and monitored under strict health and safety legislation, but there can be temporary parking of vehicles, overnight storage of drums, careless use in factories, and severe accidents in which containers burst. Storage problems for toxic chemicals gave rise to severe fires at Salford and at Stalybridge in Greater Manchester in the 1980s, but the dreadful gas clouds of Seveso in Italy and Bhopal in India should remind everyone of the care that must be taken with sophisticated modern chemical products.

The technical advances of the industrial revolution were highly successful in overcoming urban environmental problems, especially in providing safe drinking water and effective sewage disposal. However, many of these engineering works have had to take the strain of bigger cities and increased water use for over a hundred years. Now there are concerns about the safety of dams built in Victorian times, and the old sewers are beginning to collapse. In cities like Manchester, city centre streets are frequently closed to allow repair of sewer collapses and for renewal of the old brick-lined sewers which can no longer cope. In 1980 a sewer collapse in Richmond, Greater London, led to renovation and reconstruction of 550 m. of dual sewer (a 300 mm. foul sewage pipe and a 600 mm. storm-water drain) with a total cost in excess of £1m.–about £2m. per kilometre of sewer. The cost of replacing the entire British system would then have been over £30,000m. (Speed and Rouse, 1980). This need for renewal of the facilities maintaining environmental quality is only part of the total expenditure necessary for urban infrastructure replacement or repair. Victorian schools, hospitals, bridges and tunnels all need attention. The physical structures of the city cannot be taken for granted.

Environment Problems Relating to Planning Policies

Planning is one of the methods of alleviating urban environmental problems; indeed it may be argued that planning grew out of public health engineering as a direct response to nineteenth-century urban environmental problems (Douglas, 1983). However, planning decisions may in themselves introduce new environmental problems. In order to maximize the use of suitable residential land and to keep residential environments as quiet and traffic-free as possible, routeways for motorways and utilities such as electricity pylons tend to be confined to corridors, usually along less suitable urban land such as floodplains. Here there are problems relating to land use, stability of river channels, and retention of green space and urban countryside. The situation may be illustrated by the Mersey Valley, south of Manchester.

In the eighteenth century, before the Bridgewater Canal was built across the Mersey floodplain between Stretford and Sale, the river was highly active, frequently bursting its banks and flooding the turnpike road from Manchester to Chester. Floodwaters later threatened the new canal embankment, and eventually the channel upstream of the canal was embanked and an offtake weir constructed to allow floodwater to spill over into a new flood channel, taking the excess water under the canal and thereby reducing the risk of erosion. Later, the growing suburban municipal authorities dumped waste to form new embankments and raise the level of the floodplain. When new motorways round Manchester were needed in the mid-twentieth century, the only remaining open space was the Mersey floodplain. A great new embankment was built, not across, but along the floodplain. Floodways with offtake weirs and regulating outlets had to be built under the motorway to allow low-lying areas of the floodplain to continue to be used for flood storage. In addition, the large borrow pits from which material had been dug to build the motorway embankment were converted into permanent lakes, used for recreation, but with some capacity for flood storage. At the same time, overhead power lines were built along the valley, with pylons often sited close to the river. The main power and transformer stations are downstream of the controlled, channelized reach of the river affected by motorway developments.

In the downstream, unprotected reaches, bank erosion is severe, individual large floods eroding 2.5 m of bank in a single event. One electricity pylon was moved just before the ground beneath it was washed away, while another is being moved before it is undermined. The bank erosion is a direct consequence of upstream channelization to protect the urban area. All the rivers emerging from the western flank of the Pennines in the Manchester area have naturally unstable meandering channels. By controlling the tendency upstream, the available energy is expended at the first point downstream where erodible banks occur. Thus the policies of flood protection and utility corridors come into conflict with each other, while plans to use the land for recreation are undermined as the river erodes into playing fields.

Problems arising from the Impact of the Urban Environment on People

Contamination of air and water, crowding, and opportunities for disease carriers all make cities potentially unhealthy places unless public health installation and services are well maintained. Although most European, North American and Australian cities now have high quality public health facilities and good medical care, most of them contain pockets of poor conditions (owing to the physical state of housing, the contamination of the local environment, or to such factors in combination with housing policies and opportunities) where disease and ill health incidence is considerably above average. Increasingly it is recognized that the physical environment, including the state of housing, is seldom a cause of ill-health in itself but part of a complex of social, economic, and living condition factors which contribute to stress, maladjustment, and lack of well-being. People often have to live in unhealthy situations because they cannot afford to do otherwise. People who have difficulty in coping with life, through family breakdown, unemployment, misuse of drugs or alcohol end up in poor housing, where they become more disturbed and eventually mentally or physically ill. In assessing how the physical environment affects people we have to remember that the environment itself is altered by the people who live there.

One of the most difficult issues facing city managers, especially in Britain, is the degradation of the environment by people. Litter, graffiti, rubbish, vandalism, and wanton damage in many cities create the impression of a hostile (and therefore unsafe) environment. The psychology of this relationship probably finds its worst expression in the problem housing areas that most local authorities have—the places where they put the difficult families. Here sound physical structures, often recently renovated at considerable public expense, quickly become virtually uninhabitable as residents fail to care for the homes they rent and leave their surroundings in a mess. The boarded-up vacant premises of these problem estates indicate a major urban problem. In terms of environmental repair costs, they divert some of the resources needed to repair and replace the Victorian public health infrastructure. Yet this would seem to be a problem that a nation like Britain, if it paid a little less attention to increasing private wealth and a little more to eliminating public squalor, could solve.

The problems of urban living conditions are far more severe in cities like Calcutta, Dhaka, Karachi, Shanghai, and Sao Paulo. Here the majority live in areas lacking basic public health facilities. A major challenge of world development must be to improve conditions in these rapidly growing low-latitude cities. The risk of epidemics in these crowded urban areas is strong, and natural and people-made accidents, such as the earthquake and petroleum refinery fire in Mexico City in 1985, kill and injure far more people than are hurt in similar incidents in cities of Europe or the USA, Canada, and Australia.

Environmental problems of cities must be seen as interwoven with the economic and social life of cities. They are changing and evolving as the city itself changes. Many could be reduced if they were more carefully considered when planning and development control decisions are being made. However, elimination of a problem in one place may merely lead to the aggravation of a problem in another. Spatial and temporal analysis of environmental change is a proper part of the study of the great social phenomena called cities.

References

Atkinson, B. W. (1977), *Urban Effects on Precipitation: An investigation of London's Influence on the Severe Storm in August 1975*, Occasional Paper 8 (Department of Geography, Queen Mary College: London).

Bentley, W. E. (1959), 'The distribution and status of *Rattus rattus L.* in the United Kingdom in 1951 and 1956', *Journal of Animal Ecology*, 28: 299–308.

Chandler, T. J. (1965), *The Climate of London* (Hutchinson: London).

Coates, D. R. (1985), *Geology and Society* (Chapman and Hall: London).

Dorney, R. S. (1979), 'The ecology and management of disturbed urban land', *Landscape Architecture*, May: 268–72.

Douglas, I. (1983), *The Urban Environment* (Edward Arnold: London).

—— (1985a), 'Geomorphology and urban development in the Manchester area', in R. H. Johnson (ed.), *The Geomorphology of North-west England* (Manchester University Press: Manchester), 337–52.

—— (1985b), 'Cities and geomorphology', in A. F. Pitty (ed.), *Themes in Geomorphology* (Croom Helm: London), 226–44.

Duvigneaud, P. (1974), 'L'ecosystem "urbs"', *Mémoires de la société de botanique de Belgique*, 4: 5–35.

Garnett, A. (1967), 'Some climatological problems in urban geography with special reference to air pollution', *Transactions of the Institute of British Geographers*, 42: 21–43.

Gilluly, J., and U. S. Grant (1949), 'Subsidence in the Long Beach Harbour Area, California', *Bulletin, Geological Society of America*, 60: 461–530.

Hollis, G. E. (1974), 'Urbanization and floods', in K. J. Gregory and D. F. Walling (eds.), *Fluvial Processes in Instrumental Watersheds*, Institute of British Geographers Special Publication, 6: 123-39.

—— (1975), 'The effect of urbanization on floods of different recurrence water interval', *Water Resources Research*, 11: 431-5.

—— (1977), 'Water yield changes after the urbanization of Canon's Brook catchment, Harlow, England', *Hydrological Sciences Bulletin*, 22: 61-75.

Horner, R. W. (1981), 'The Thames barrier', *Journal of the Institution of Water Engineers and Scientists*, 35: 398-411.

Leopold, L. B. (1968), *Hydrology for Urban Land Planning: A Guidebook to the Effects of Urban Land Use*, US Geological Survey Circular 554.

Macfarlane, A., and J. Waller (1976), 'Short term increased mortality during heat waves, *Nature*, 264: 434-6.

Oke, T. R. (1974), 'Review of urban climatology 1968-1972', *World Meteorological Organization Technical Note*, 134.

Poland, J. F., and G. H. Davis (1969), 'Land Subsidence due to withdrawal of fluids, *Geological Society of America Reviews in Engineering Geology*, 2: 187-269.

Popham, E. J. (1980), 'The wild life of Salford', in H. P. White (ed.), *The Continuing Conurbation* (Gower: Farnborough), 184-90.

Speed, H. D. M., and M. J. Rouse (1980), 'Renovation of water mains and sewers', *Journal of the Institution of Water Engineers and Scientists*, 34: 401-24.

Summers-Smith, J. D. (1963), *The House Sparrow* (Collins: London)

Tabony, R. C. (1980), 'Urban effects on trends on annual and seasonal rainfall in the London area', *Meteorological Magazine*, 109: 189-202.

Trafford, B. D. (1981), 'The background to the flood defences of London and the Thames estuary', *Journal of the Institution of Water Engineers and Scientists*, 35: 383-97.

Woodland, A. W. (1968), 'Field geology and the civil engineer', *Proceedings, Yorkshire Geological Society*, 36: 531-78.

Young, C. P., and M. Morgan-Jones (1980), 'A hydrogeochemical survey of the chalk groundwater of the Banstead area, Surrey, with particular reference to nitrate', *Journal of the Institution of Water Engineers and Scientists*, 34: 213-36.

6

Resources and Finances for the City

Robert J. Bennett

Although cities contain some of the richest resources of an economy, often these resources cannot be fully mobilized in order to provide services or to overcome social problems. In stark contrast to their rich resources, cities often experience some of the severest problems of social deprivation, unemployment, crime, poor environment, homelessness, and low educational attainment. Because of this contrast some commentators have argued that what is required is massive redistribution between those with riches (higher income groups and economically expanding sectors) and those who are deprived. How could such a resource transfer be achieved? Even if it could be achieved, would its long-term outcomes be desirable, or are there more effective long-term reforms of resource allocation which are required to overcome the problems of the cities? In tackling these issues we are experiencing a new period of thinking about city problems in which questions concerning resources and their allocation are subject to radically new innovations and experiments.

The Mechanics of Resources

A city's resources, in the most general sense, are composed of the earnings of business as net worth, distributions to shareholders as dividends, and payment to economic factors (such as wages and rents). This total resource base makes up the gross product or economic base of a city, in the same way as gross national product (GNP) is defined for a country as a whole. Thus city resources depend ultimately on the level of local economic development which itself derives from its place in local, national, and international markets. Resource allocation within and between businesses, and between labour, owners of capital, and other economic factors is a question for market dynamics, relating supply and demand through price which reflects the relative scarcity of, or degree of control over, each economic factor which can be exerted. Resource questions in this sense are therefore ones of how markets operate, whether they are efficient, and the extent to which the outcomes are socially and economically desirable. This has not been the focus for most debates about resources in the city. But it should be the starting point, since, in Western economies, it is on the market allocation process that other resource issues depend.

The major policy question of a city's resources concerns how the base of market resources can be tapped for collective purposes, such as providing public services. Most analyses of resources in the city in this sense start from a pre-defined position of a specified tax or other financial source. This leads to analysis of how market resources (profits, distributions, wages, consumer sales, etc.) can be tapped to allow public services to be provided for purposes which the market will not directly cater for. Such are ones of market failure (situations in which exclusion from access to services or joint collective provision is required) which gives rise to the economic case for public goods and services; and where there is a major social need. These cases are often dealt with by public service provision, but there is a wide range of other means of providing for social goods and overcoming market failure. Alternatives to public service provision constitute a field of major innovation in OECD countries at present. Examples are regulation of private sector contractors (e.g. through 'contracting out' in refuse collection and transport, or control of standards in private education), co-operatives, associations and not-for-profit organizations (such as housing associations), voluntary services (as in old people's services), and mixed patterns of public–private partnerships (as in children's care and old people's care) (see e.g. OECD, 1987). Resources for these various forms of service provision are not defined solely as tax resources, but also as the ability to raise charges and voluntary contributions, the ability to regulate markets, and the potential mobilization of the manpower and management expertise.

For the purpose of funding public services, the resource base means the revenue base of central and local government. Here definitions are complex, since the revenue base depends on the precise revenue source discussed (e.g. an income tax will differ considerably from a property tax, and a tax differs greatly from a charge), the precise way in which the law defines that tax base (e.g. a property tax in Britain based on rental value is very different from property tax in the USA based on market values), and the structure of the market economy from which the revenues derive. I try to capture this relationship on the left-hand side of figure 6.1, which derives from the discussion by Smith (1977) and Bennett (1980). The economic base of a city provides a specified resource base only after a particular revenue source has been defined. The final level of available resources also depends on the ability of a city authority to vary its tax rate or revenue-take from the sources available to it.

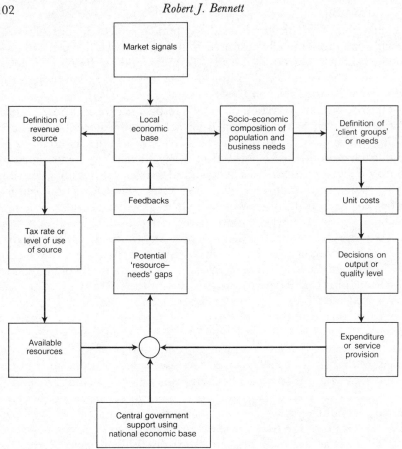

FIG. 6.1. *The local resource base of cities in relation to their economy, their revenues, and their socio-economic composition*

The revenue base also cannot be looked at independently of the 'need' for social or other spending. The definition of the concept of need is highly problematic, since there is no ready means of distinguishing needs from wants or desires (see Bennett, 1980, ch. 5). However, here the limited concept of 'need' related to a common service standard will be employed. In this sense, need is a measure of demand for resources. It derives from the socio-economic structure of the population of a locality, as well as the needs of businesses themselves (for infrastructure, utilities, security services, etc.). And socio-economic composition is largely an outcome of the structure of the labour market, which is in turn mainly derived from the economic base. Thus not only resources but also needs depend crucially on the market economy, the level of local economic development, and the place of the city in the national and international economic system. For a given local population a wide variety of 'client groups' exist which relate to the 'needs' for particular services. Some of these depend on demographic characteristics, e.g. old people's services, the educational needs of children, etc. Some services depend on socio-economic composition, e.g. income support; others depend on the environment, e.g. roads. The costs per unit of providing each service vary considerably between areas, mainly because of differences in the size and density of settlements, climatic effects on the costs of maintaining roads and buildings, and labour and resource costs. The interaction of unit costs with client 'needs' and with variations in local authority decisions on how they wish to provide a service (particularly local political priorities) leads to a final set of expenditure decisions, depicted on the right-hand side of figure 6.1.

A bringing together of local revenues and expenditures leads to the overall local authority budget. Any difference between revenues and expenditures is a potential resources–needs surplus or gap. In the long term there is a legal requirement for budgets to balance, so that resources–needs gaps usually result in needs unfulfilled because of insufficient financial resources. However, it is also possible for substantial deficits to be run, or for bankruptcies to occur, and this gives rise to the concept of 'fiscal crisis' which we confront in detail below.

Clearly the extent of such 'crises' or 'gaps' depends upon the extent to which central government becomes involved in supporting local resources, as shown in figure 6.1. If 'gaps' do exist, however, they are likely to lead to strong feedback effects on the economic base. Even if fiscal 'gaps' as such do not arise, any differences in public services in terms of their level, cost, or quality can be expected also to have feedback effects. An important form of such feedback is migration of population or businesses to other areas with higher quality services at the same tax cost, or to areas with the same quality of services at a lower tax cost, or to areas with a mixture of the two: so-called 'fiscal migration'. Migration is the most extreme response; more general feedbacks are the result of the effects on businesses or people that do not move. They will suffer unequal service levels, and/or unequal tax costs. For people the effect is public service 'welfare inequalities'. Although definitions here are difficult, the perceived form of inequalities will often reinforce, rather than diminish, existing social differences. For businesses, the effect is a variation in returns to different combinations of factor inputs, and changed profitability between localities from what would have occurred in a free market: so-called 'distortions'. Often also these effects are contrary to the directions of leverage on business profits or rates of return that would be desired on other policy grounds.

The Development of Resources

The actual pattern of city resources, possible feedbacks, and the extent of fiscal crises depends crucially on the structure of central and local government, the constitutional and legal framework, the political environment, and the vast array of administrative procedures that mediate the collection of revenues or provision of services. There will thus be considerable differences between one city and another, and particularly between cities in one country and another. Most discussions of these phenomena are dominated by the experience of the older industrial cities of the northern USA, particularly of New York City. This experience, however, is unlikely to have very direct relevance to the very different constitutional and political environments of Britain or Europe, or even to others parts of the USA. Let us first take the USA, however, as a paradigmatic case.

The development of the resources of US cities has been characterized by recurring financial crises in the older large metropolitan areas (see e.g. Sternlieb and Hughes, 1978; Clark and Ferguson, 1983). This has also attracted Marxian explanations (see e.g. O'Connor, 1973; Harvey, 1973; Hill, 1977). The organization of these older industrial cities of the USA is highly fragmented, uncoordinated, and strongly competitive between localities within the same labour market. Most local governments, whether city, county, township, or special purpose, have autonomous taxing powers, and make independent expenditure decisions. They may also use charges and fees. While almost all these governments use property taxes and fees, many use sales tax as well, and a small number, particularly large central cities, use income tax. In most states, local government has autonomy in definition (assessment) of the tax base. This is an important source of inequality and is a major contrast to most other countries, particularly Britain and Europe. As a result taxing systems differ greatly between cities and between states. In most states, the constitution is permissive of city financial decisions. Generally at least one half of local actions can be developed within a context of freedom to act. This is in marked contrast to Britain, where local authorities cannot act unless empowered to do so (the doctrine of *ultra vires*). The result is a system in which strong positive feedback can develop, which can lead to marked imbalances and continued divergence in fiscal burdens and benefits between areas. This is often particularly focused between central cities and suburbs, but there are also frequently marked imbalances between rich and poor suburbs as well as between metropolitan and rural areas.

The pattern of tax base and expenditure change in US cities and suburbs is shown in table 6.1. In the 1960s, and especially the early

TABLE 6.1. Per capita expenditure and revenue for the 37 largest SMSAs in the USA ($)

	Central cities				Outside central cities				Central city as % of outside			
	1957	1970	1977	1981	1957	1970	1977	1981	1957	1970	1977	1981
Population (000s)[a]	553	583	—	570	542	693	—	838	102	84	—	68
Per capita income	851	1351	—	6972	721	1636	—	7989	118	83	—	89
Total expenditure	196	524	1061	1453	154	385	761	1058	129	137	143	139
Non-educational expenditure	135	341	714	1023	74	174	388	586	202	207	201	184
Educational expenditure	61	183	346	420	80	211	372	471	80	86	93	91
Tax revenue	117	258	453	556	80	190	372	449	157	140	129	129
State and federal transfers	40	164	490	705	40	126	364	451	101	138	167	163
State aid[b]	—	123	297	441	—	122	306	372	—	107	127	126
Federal aid[b]	—	28	155	200	—	9	255	68	—	552	400	352

[a] 1960, 1970, 1980 in 85 largest SMSAs.
[b] 68 largest SMSAs.

Sources: ACIR, 1985; Bennett, 1987.

1970s, these imbalances in the US urban system were considerably reduced by numerous federal grant programmes. The most important were Revenue Sharing, Community Development Block Grant (CDBG), Countercyclical Revenue Sharing, Public Service Employment Program, and the Comprehensive Employment and Training Act (CETA). These had the dual effects of giving aid to fiscally stressed areas and creating leverage on the state government also to act. As shown in table 6.1, through the period from the Second World War until the middle 1970s, therefore, a steady increase in the level of state and federal resources progressively diminished the problems of fiscal stress and imbalance within the US urban system. Since about 1977, however, federal aid has been considerably reduced and the states have been relied upon to a greater extent to support intergovernmental programmes. Inequalities have, as a result, considerably increased.

In the case of Britain we are dealing with a simpler and more uniform system of urban government, in which grants have an even more dominant, and volatile, influence than in the USA. In Britain up to 1990 the aggregate tax base of local authorities is their rateable value, a tax on property. In the absence of revaluation, change in rateable values can be only modest, reflecting new or reassessed properties. Hence income can be increased at local level only by raising tax rates. After 1990 a new tax or 'community charge' (poll tax) is due to replace the rates. Using the property tax base it is possible to compare developments in the tax base, tax rates, and 'need' to spend using the estimates of budgetary change in the British urban system given by Bennett and Krebs (1988) and reported in table 6.2. The measure of need to spend reported here derives from Offord (1987), and is a standardized measure of need over time for seventy-six service subheadings (reported here only in aggregated form). The results are also reported for central cities and their functional city regions, equivalent to American SMSAs. In the table, changes in the main components of local authority budgets are translated to become changes in real rate poundages (local tax rates) over the period 1974 to 1985. A tax base increase represents an increase in available resources and hence results in a reduction in tax rates. Table 6.2 demonstrates that all areas experience tax base growth. Central cities have the lowest rates of increase, particularly in London and the large metropolitan areas, whereas the most rapid increases are in rural areas and city regions. For most cases this is mainly a result of growth of housing (domestic rateable values), but business tax base growth (non-domestic rateable values) is also significant. The whole pattern evidences the process of decentralization, or rural–urban shifts, which is common to the USA and many other Western countries. Over the same period total need to spend changes hardly at all, but major differences

TABLE 6.2.   Changes in tax rates resulting from different components of British local authority budgets, 1974–1985 (%)

	Tax base			Need	Change in RSG[a]	Change in expenditure	Total
	Domestic	Non-domestic	Total				
Highly urbanized areas							
Central cities	-2.7	-2.6	-5.3	-2.2	5.1	4.7	14.4
City regions	-5.1	-3.4	-8.5	1.1	8.1	3.9	7.2
Partly urbanized areas							
Central cities	-4.0	-4.9	-8.9	0.03	4.3	2.6	2.8
City regions	-6.5	-4.9	-11.4	4.4	7.0	0.5	4.6
London[b]							
Inner	-2.7	-2.4	-5.1	-10.1	-0.7	21.3	41.2
Outer	-2.3	-1.3	-3.6	-2.5	-4.6	10.6	10.1
London city region	-5.2	-3.4	-8.6	0.2	8.2	14.5	1.9
Rural areas	-5.6	-4.9	-10.5	3.9	8.8	-2.6	-0.02
TOTAL	-4.2	-3.7	-7.9	-0.06	5.3	8.5	8.5

[a] Rate Support Grant.
[b] The city of London and Westminster have been excluded.

Source: Simplified and recalculated from Bennett and Krebs, 1988, ch. 4.

are evident between areas. Large central cities, particularly inner London, experience declines in need to spend (giving tax rate reductions) of up to 10 per cent while outer metropolitan and rural areas experience 3–4 per cent growth in needs to promote services. Changes in central government Rate Support Grant (RSG) are an important element of instability in the overall pattern, and the table conceals the massive increases during 1974–9 which were superceded by cuts during 1979–85. An overall decline in RSG 1974–85 has been responsible for a tax rate increase of 5.3 per cent but accounts for 7–9 per cent increases in outer metropolitan and rural areas. In contrast inner and outer London, despite large cuts in RSG in recent years, have not lost the relative advantages they gained over the 1974–9 period, and hence still benefit in 1985 from a net reduction in tax rates, compared to 1974, as a result of changes in RSG. The most significant factor for many areas is the change in aggregate expenditure levels as a result of the exercise of local discretion to spend (this is the residual after all other factors have been removed). This accounts for an 8.5 per cent tax rate increase overall, but this reaches over 10 per cent for outer London and its region, and is over 21 per cent in inner London. In contrast, outer metropolitan and rural areas have slow expenditure expansion, and rural areas have actually cut expenditure by 2.6 per cent over the 1974–85 period.

The total pattern of change is dominated by the massive increase in tax rates of inner London, and to a lesser extent outer London and the larger central cities. Elsewhere aggregate financial changes in resources 1974–85 have been rather modest. The consequences of these tax rate developments have major impacts on people and businesses. The tax rate implications for householders can be judged from table 6.2: they indicate an emerging inequality between cities and other areas, with inner London residents particularly heavily burdened. For business activities Bennett (1986a) and Bennett and Krebs (1988) compare the effective tax rates, and rates of return, in different industrial sectors over time. They demonstrate that not only have effective tax rates on buildings except for shops increased substantially over time, but since an important 1974 change in the law with regard to the rating of plant and machinery, the tax rates on this component have also steadily grown. Industry faces a substantial tax on its wealth of 2–5 per cent; but most important, there is strong variation around this figure plus or *minus* 3 to 5 per cent between areas, depending on the industrial sector. Moreover, no more than 5–15 per cent of these differences can be shifted into prices (see Bennett and Fearnehough, 1987; Bennett and Krebs, 1988, ch. 6).

Public Resources and Social Dependency

The development of resources within US and British cities outlined above shows strong similarities, as well as important differences in detail, which derive from the different constitutional and administrative structures of city finances in the two countries. Of course public resource differences are only part of the wider question of total resource allocation between wages, capital, and other factors; and arguably public resource allocation can only have secondary effects on city welfare compared to the primary developments occurring in the market economy at national and international levels. But in so far as public resource allocation encourages greater welfare inequality, as well as possible positive feedbacks which stimulate rather than ameliorate social problems, there are serious grounds for policy concern; and here there are some close parallels between US and UK cities.

The most deprived areas of US cities represent a uniquely unattractive nexus of poor housing, education, and other public services, high relative local tax rates, high crime rates, racial tensions, and high unemployment. The unsurprising result is extensive migration of both people and businesses to suburbs, outer metropolitan areas, and indeed also regional shift away from decaying older industrial cities as a whole to newer locations in the south and west of the USA. Detailed analysis by Frey (1979, 1980) of the migration of people demonstrates that the *primary* explanation of these developments lies in the crime rate, deprivation, and environmental conditions of the inner cities. But important secondary factors are the higher city tax rates and quality of public services, particularly the quality of the school system. This migration is also strongly intercorrelated with racial factors, which have allowed the term 'white flight' to be used to characterize a large component of these moves. For businesses, again, we see a pattern in which primary causes of relocation are external to public resource allocation, but in which city 'fiscal climate', particularly relating to educational and other services valued highly by managerial decision-makers, is a significant secondary determinant of location. Recognition of the effect of fiscal factors represents a turnaround from the traditional wisdom of industrial studies in which local fiscal factors were found unimportant (see e.g. ACIR, 1967; Kierschnik, 1981; Harrison and Kanter, 1978; Bradbury *et al.*, 1981; Wasylenko, 1980, 1986). Similar factors affecting the migration of people and industry, particularly urban–rural shift (Keeble, 1980), are recognized in Britain, as evidenced in other chapters of this volume (see also Goddard and Champion, 1983; Champion *et al.*, 1987; Evans and Eversley, 1980; Young and Mason, 1983).

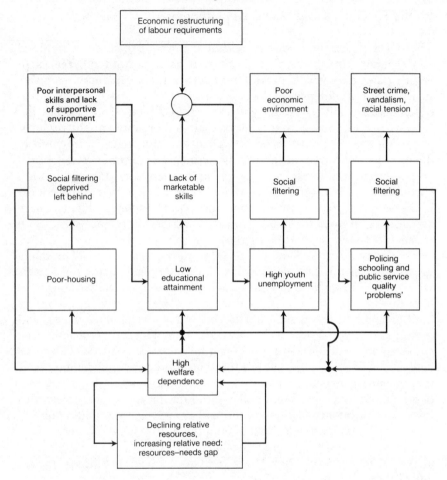

FIG. 6.2. *Economic restructuring, social filtering, public services, and the origin of welfare dependency*

This pattern of primary and secondary causes is being increasingly recognized as defining an emergent 'underclass': a vicious circle of positive feedback in which the social filtering of those able to migrate leaves behind an increasingly deprived population with progressively higher and higher dependence on public services and welfare support. The main components of this process are captured in figure 6.2. It is argued that poor housing, low educational attainment, high youth unemployment and public service problems (in policing, recruiting school teachers, quality of public transport, etc.) each contribute to further social filtering which generate further dependency, and so on in an immiserizing vicious circle until only an 'underclass' of the most deprived are left behind. The process takes place in the context of changes in the structure of the economy as a whole which makes the dependent groups less and less able to participate because of inappropriate training or labour skills. The public resource implications are an increasing needs–resources gap, since higher and higher burdens for public service support have to be borne on a diminishing resource base.

Although at its most extreme in the US, these problems can be readily seen in many British cities. For example, in large parts of inner London the demand for unskilled and semi-skilled jobs, which might have formerly employed some of these groups, has rapidly fallen: The number of jobs in construction alone fell by 126,000 in 1982–6. Unemployment is therefore high, particularly among young people: the inner London average in 1986 was 21 per cent, but it was 34 per cent for men aged 20–4, with highs of 46 per cent in Hackney and 44 per cent in Lambeth; and Afro-Caribbean unemployment at nearly twice this rate. Educational skills are low, and truancy is high (on average 35 per cent of fifteen-year olds on an average day). Despite much higher than average spending by the Inner London Education Authority, more than half of the new labour market entrants in Greater London have no 'O' level or equivalent CSE examination passes; this means that over 50,000 new potential employees per year in the metropolis have no recognized attainment skills. There are major problems of homelessness: over 5,000 families per night are accommodated in bed and breakfast accommodation in Greater London, and there is a council house waiting list of over 150,000 in inner London. There are major problems for the dependent and low paid in entering the private housing market because of rising costs; council house provision does not keep up with replacement of unfit dwellings, and the stock is deteriorating because of poor maintenance. In 1984 nearly half a million Greater London dwellings were unfit or in need of renovation, and the inner London average spending need was at least £4,000 per dwelling. The public resource implications of these problems in housing, general environment, and education are therefore huge. London presents an extreme problem because of its size: in 1981 it contained fifteen of the thirty most deprived local authority areas in England and Wales. The remainder were mainly central cities in Manchester, Liverpool, and Birmingham, but also included South Wales, Nottingham, Leicester and Slough (see Audit Commission, 1987).

The Policy Implications: I. Management

How can the required resources be marshalled to tackle the problems outlined above? Is it simply a question of pouring more public money into inner cities? It is at this point in the discussion that a sharp break has occurred in thinking. We tackle this issue here first as a management or administrative question, and then turn to its politics.

Increased resources alone do not tackle problems: to be effective they have to be appropriately applied. This is the management question. The Audit Commission (1986, 1987) has drawn attention to a major gap in the economy and effectiveness of public service provision between many central cities and other areas, but particularly between inner London and other relatively comparable areas. They concluded that there are major management deficiencies which contribute significantly to the vicious circle of dependency, outlined in figure 6.2, and which are contributing to an emerging needs–resources gap which may result in local authority bankruptcy. The cycle of management decline is depicted in figure 6.3. This is seen by the Audit Commission as primarily a problem resulting from attempts at 'management by elected council members', with a proliferation of committees and subcommittees which is expensive in officers' time, central overheads, and delays. It is difficult to recruit both officers and members, partly because of uncompetitive local government salaries for senior management offices, partly because

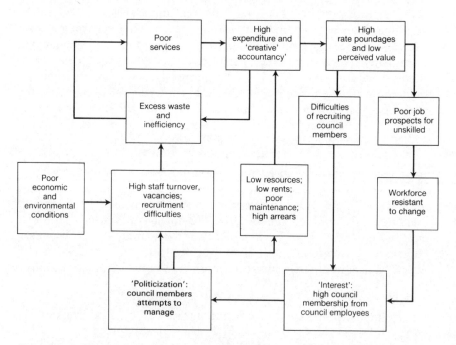

FIG. 6.3.   *The cycle of decline in management skills (modified from Audit Commission, 1987, p. 12)*

of continuous political interference by members in officers' decisions. Turnover of senior officers in London boroughs such as Camden, Hackney, Haringey, Islington, Lewisham, and Southwark was 40–69 per cent in the three years 1983–6, and less then 20 per cent of council members had more than four years' experience. These relationships are further compromised by labour relations problems in which employees are reluctant to adapt work practices. Elected members who are council employees or municipal trade unionists in inner London comprise between 33 and 50 per cent of the council, with 61 per cent in the former GLC (Walker, 1983a, 1983b). As a result they find it difficult to distinguish their roles as politicians, employees, and trade unionists. Hence many attempts to increase efficiency have resulted not in changes to work practices but in extra staff recruitment or salary regrading. The 'cycle of inefficiency' is therefore locked into a pattern in which higher expenditure becomes the inevitable solution to a problem. Given constraints deriving from central government as well as the size of the local tax base, this can often be accommodated only by debt finance. In effect the cycle of problems recognized in New York City's fiscal crisis and default in 1975 was being reproduced in 1983–7 in inner London and some other UK cities (see Morris, 1980; Brecher and Horton, 1985).

The Audit Commission (1987) evidenced these management deficiencies by comparing three groups of city local authorities. Group A included eight deprived London boroughs with suspect management records; Group B consisted of eight other London boroughs with similar problems of deprivation; and Group C included eight of the most deprived metropolitan districts outside London. Some of the comparisons are reported in table 6.3. This demonstrates the very high expenditures, levels of staffing and increases in staffing of Group A compared with either Groups B or C. These differences also apply to various detailed items of housing, social services, etc. Group A authorities are usually 50 to 100 per cent higher in costs or manpower than comparable authorities in London or elsewhere. The Commission concluded that 'large parts of London appear set on precisely a course which will lead to financial and management breakdown . . . [which] are *not* due solely to social and economic factors over which they have no control' (1987, p. 4). Although these aspects of the management problem are clearly rather special, they evidence a general pattern of economic and political pressures on city managers and councillors such that administration becomes one of the key aspects of city resource questions.

TABLE 6.3. Comparisons of management performance for eight inner London boroughs suspected of poor management (Group A), with eight other London boroughs (Group B), and eight metropolitan districts, all with comparable levels of deprivation

	Group A	Group B	Group C
Expenditure			
(£ per resident)[a]	336	226	152
Full-time employees			
(per 1000 population)	19	14	10
change in staff nos. 1980–6 (%)			
'white collar'	+ 19	+ 7	+ 9
'blue collar'	+ 4	– 16	– 14
central services	+ 18	– 14	+ 4
Housing management			
rent arrears (% of annual rent)	19.9	7.0	6.7
relet period (weeks)	20	13	9
management cost per dwelling (£)	201	206	101
Social Services			
cost per child in council care (£/week)	438	327	199
Refuse collection			
cost per premise (£)	16.5	9.0	11.2
Vehicle maintenance			
cost per vehicle (£/year)[b]	1123	830	700
Cash flow management			
income lost per £1000 demanded	86	81	69

[a]Excludes expenditure on police, fire, and education which are heavily statutarily constrained; corrected for staff cost differences.
[b]Uses data for inner London, outer London and metropolitan districts as a whole.

Source: Audit Commission, 1987, various tables.

The Policy Implications: II. Politics

The management problems briefly outlined above have not arisen by chance. Certainly there are difficulties in the comparison between local authorities produced by the Audit Commission and others; and certainly external socio-economic circumstances which affect the economic vitality of localities, local salary levels, and employment conditions also play important roles. Certainly also, central government's frequent changes to the structure of local authority finance in Britain have had a major disruptive influence on local authorities. But a major aspect of policy concern is that a significant part of the problem is self-inflicted as a result of the political stance taken by some local authorities. This is particularly characteristic of a group of local authorities often termed 'New Left' or 'Urban Left' (see e.g. Gyford, 1985; Boddy and Fudge, 1983). Finding a clear definition of 'New Left' presents many problems. There are certain clear members of this group at particular times: inner London through much of the 1980s, Walsall in the early 1980s, and Liverpool. These are in every sense 'self-defined' well publicized followers of a specific set of 'New Left' policies. However, even within this group there is enormous variety: the London Left being concerned primarily with equal opportunity issues (such as the rights of ethnic minority groups, women, homosexuals, lesbians), while Liverpool is Militant-Tendency inspired, with little concern for these minority issues, and Sheffield has developed a distinct character based upon municipal enterprise and local economic development initiatives. Any attempt to define 'New Left' areas will, therefore, embrace large internal variation. Thus Gyford (1985, p. 18) notes that local socialism is not a 'single coherent ideology', but a 'syndrome or set of associated characteristics'.

Nevertheless in the 1980–7 period there was an unquestionable core of about twenty local authorities which were in this category, and it included all eight London boroughs in the Audit Commission's Group A discussed earlier (namely Camden, Hackney, Islington, Lambeth, Lewisham, Southwark, Brent, and Haringey). All include the important characteristics of community action and 'community development; campaigns against spending cuts; . . . the radicalization of some of the local government professions; environmentalism, the women's movement', and in specific policies include 'a concern for . . . local economic planning, monitoring the police, women's rights, and racial equality; a disdain for many of the traditional ways of conducting local authority business; a view of local government as an arena both for combating the policies of a Conservative (central) government and for displaying the potential of a grass-roots socialism; and, perhaps most fundamentally, a commitment to notions of mass politics based on strategies of decentralization and/or political mobilization at local level' (Gyford, 1985, p. 18).

This interpretation of local socialism *requires* political intervention in management and entails resistance to efforts to encourage management effectiveness. For example Ken Livingstone, as chairman of the housing committee in Camden records that he 'reduced the number of meetings with the director of housing, and made contact with the third-tier officers, who took day-to-day management decisions. The more intelligent and active officers were keen to cooperate.' As leader of the GLC he 'wanted a new top administrative structure in which we could force early retirement on two-thirds of the chief officers, and chairs of committees would have a predominant role in administration of departments' (Livingstone, 1987).

The politicization of management, outlined in figure 6.3, has therefore been a desired objective of the local activists who sought to represent the local electorate's interests by resisting the Conservative central government's pressures. The 'New Left' response to resource pressure was not therefore a management one, but a political one. Until 1983 or 1984 this was primarily achieved by increasing local tax rates (rate poundages) in order to maintain or increase expenditure. Since 1984, with the implementation of central government's powers to rate-cap 'overspending' local authorities, the mechanism was increasingly one of 'creative accountancy'. All Group A local authorities in the earlier discussion were rate-capped in 1985/6. In order to evaluate the effect of these expenditure policies table 6.4 shows the development of local budgets from 1974 to 1985 in twenty-four authorities which had New Left councils in the 1980–5 period. The components of budget change are translated into percentage changes in rate poundages by the same method as that in table 6.2. The table demonstrates that in 1974 each area had comparable rate poundages, although inner London's was 20 per cent lower. By 1985 major changes had occurred: New Left inner London had tax rates 36 per cent higher than comparable areas, and other New Left councils had tax rates 13 per cent higher. These areas blame the central government manipulation of RSG. Certainly major reversals of RSG had occurred since 1979, but over the 1974–85 period changes in RSG are rather neutral. Moreover, New Left areas have benefited from a 5 per cent reduction of tax rates because of the increase in the tax base, and a 5.5 per cent (11.3 per cent in inner London) reduction in need to spend, owing to population decline. The main reason for tax rate change, therefore, lies not at the door of central government, but in the chosen policies of expenditure increase. New expenditures accounted for a 16.5 per cent increase in tax rates in New Left areas outside London, and a 26.4 per cent increase in inner London.

If expenditure increases drawn from the local rates kept New Left councils going until rate-capping in 1985, creative accountancy became the main mechanism thereafter, up to 1987. Table 6.5 gives the Audit Commission's (1987) assessment of the extent of 'creative accountancy' in the three groups of authorities discussed earlier. Creative accountancy involves three main mechanisms: use of balances accumulated from the past; borrowing to meet expenditures for maintenance that would normally be treated as revenue expenditures; and deferred purchase, where borrowing is used to fund expenditure with interest rolled up into a first payment two or three years later. The attraction of these methods

TABLE 6.4. Changes in tax rates (at 1985 prices) in New Left and other areas resulting from different components of local authority budgets, 1974–1985 (%)

	1974 rate poundage	1985 rate poundage	Tax base	Need	Change in RSG[a]	Change in expenditure	Total
All areas containing New Left							
New Left councils	181.4	226.2	−5.1	−5.5	0.2	16.5	24.7
other politics	180.5	200.9	−6.4	−2.2	3.1	6.6	11.3
Inner London							
New Left	155.3	237.0	−5.4	−11.3	−0.1	26.4	52.6

[a]Rate Support Grant

Source: recalculated from Bennett and Krebs, 1987, table 4.11, for 24 New Left councils.

Robert J. Bennett

TABLE 6.5. Estimates for three groups of local authorities of the extent of creative accounting and funding gaps, December 1986

	Group A	Group B	Group C
Creative accounting moves (£m.)			
Capitalization of maintenance 1984–7	180	55	195
Deferred purchase managements	550	175	180
TOTAL	730	230	375
Total per household (£)	1042	355	344
Estimated funding gap for 1987–8			
£m.	290	130	140
As % of annual revenue expenditure	30	21	10

Note: See table 6.3 for details of the groups.

is a deferral, through borrowing, of expenditures otherwise restricted by central government. It was hoped by these local authorities that the June 1987 General Election would yield a Labour government which would be prepared to use central largesse to bail them out. As can be seen from the table, for Group A authorities in particular (which are all inner London New Left) the use of these devices has led to a local debt burden two or three times as high as those of other areas. It amounts to a debt of over £1,000 per household for inner London, the repayments of which will absorb 30 per cent of the annual revenue expenditure for each year after 1987. Although major changes in New Left thinking and policy occurred after 1987, a large legacy of debt remains for the future. Anthony Crossland in 1976, on behalf of the then Labour government, warned councils that 'the party is over' and that they should hold back spending: in 1987 and 1988 the day of reckoning had arrived and major cuts in local spending were made in most New Left areas (for further details of this complex area see the discussion by Bennett *et al.* (1988).

Where Do We Go from Here?

The incapacity of British local government, at its extremes, to accept the need to balance the books is perhaps understandable. Green Paper, White Paper, or Committee of Inquiry into local government financial reform succeeded Green Paper in 1971, 1976, 1977, 1980, 1981, 1982, and 1986. Nothing seemed to change (for a review see Bennett, 1982). But suddenly in the mid-1980s, three sets of circumstances combined to rock the fabric of this formerly cosy area.

The first was the publication in January 1986, and subsequent implementation, of the government's Green Paper *Paying for local government*. This suggested three key changes to the present system: (*a*) that domestic rates on housing should be abolished as the main local authority independent tax resource, and replaced by a 'community charge' or poll tax levied on each adult; (*b*) that local authority power to levy an independent rate poundage on the non-domestic rates should be abolished and replaced by nationally uniform business rate poundages separately for the whole of England, Scotland, and Wales; (*c*) that the grant system should be greatly simplified to become distributed largely in terms of numbers of people, with an element remaining for special needs.

TABLE 6.6. The impact of the community charge compared to rate bills for different sizes of household and different rateable values of property in England (£)

	Poorest housing (RV < £75)	'Middle income' housing (RV £154–400)	'High income' housing (RV > £400)
Average rate bill 1986–87	114	449	1080
Average community charge 1986–7	205	205	205
Gain or loss by household size			
1 adult	– 91	244	875
2 adults	– 296	39	670
3 adults	– 501	– 166	465
4 adults	– 706	– 371	260

Note: RV: rateable value.

Source: Travers, 1988, p. 6.

These reforms were legislated for implementation in 1990 and will have a radical impact on the resource patterns of local authorities. Table 6.6 demonstrates the likely patterns of change. The poorest households will pay on average considerably more, whilst for middle and higher income groups the charge is largely neutral or gives very considerable benefit. This is the outcome of the explicit aim of increasing the number of local taxpayers: to raise the percentage of adults who pay tax under the rating system from 51 per cent (but less than 40 per cent taking account of social security and rate rebates) to 100 per cent under community charge. This, it is hoped, will greatly increase the accountability of local decision-makers to electors (taxpayers).

Thus the most radical element of the reforms is not the specifics but the objectives within which they are framed. These seek to create a different relationship between people, or families, and the state as a whole: a better *accountability*. The key sub-objectives are that city services should respond to real demand rather than to local bureaucratic agenda; that local government should be efficient and cost-effective rather than primarily seeking maintenance of municipal employment and work-practices; that a flexible approach to service provision and finance is possible, allowing full use of voluntary, not-for-profit or co-operative associations and private contractors rather than monolithic local government responses, particularly if driven by insensitive party political agenda. In short, the desire is for a better relation of decisions to individual demands and needs. All these desires are laudable, but it is highly uncertain that the poll tax will help to achieve them. Rather, it will, by placing the greatest burden on those least able to pay, tend to increase inequalities and encourage avoidance of payment by non-registration, thus undermining the accountability it seeks to improve.

Similar pressures for changes are occurring across most OECD countries (see OECD, 1987). In Britain the poll tax, reformed grants, uniform business rate, and the wider reforms of education, housing, and other city services are merely means of achieving a wider goal. These British reforms are, however, far more radical than those occurring elsewhere, and there is a real danger of 'throwing the baby out with the bathwater'. With respect to resources, for example, the more general change in other OECD countries is towards greater use of charges, while in Britain the poll tax will have on those who pay and induce affect and give incentives to groups by different from those who would be affected by a change.

The second change has been central government's political conception of how inner-city local authorities should respond to its perception of the needs of economic restructuring and stimulation of the market economy. As a result a wide policy package, across a range of ministeries, has sought to bring renewal of infrastructure and housing to inner cities, as well as attempting to overcome the barriers to economic development which the Conservative government has seen as underpinning the cycle of welfare dependency (the 'underclass') which is concentrated in the inner city. The major central government initiatives are Urban Programme Grants for capital projects (£297m. in 1986/7), within which Urban Development Grants can be used as 'seed money' to stimulate private enterprise (£25m. in 1986/7); Derelict Land Grants (£83m. in 1986/7); Enterprise Zones which give relief from local taxes and 100 per cent capital allowance against central corporation tax (worth approximately £70m. per year); Task Forces which, without separate financial resources, seek to stimulate private and public private development; Urban Development Corporations (£90m. in 1986/7) which seek to stimulate development and provide infrastructure and site clearance for business (the earliest (1981) are in London and Liverpool Docklands, with new UDCs created in 1987 in Tyneside, Teeside, the Black Country, and Trafford).

European Community Funds are also becoming an increasingly important source of funds for direct local government support, as well as offsetting a share of central government's Urban Programme expenditure. A wide range of other public/private initiative schemes such as that between the Department of Industry and Business in the Community also exist. In addition, reforms of education, vocational training, housing, policing, and other services are being implemented by central government and forced on often reluctant local authorities. The driving force of public policy in the city has now, therefore, become that of central government. This was begun in 1980/1 and has markedly accelerated since 1987. The consequence has been a domination by the concern to create the right conditions for economic growth and change, and to focus this adjustment on the economic development, or redevelopment, of the city. Within this process the local authority administrators, politicians, and managers of cities are having to respond to the pressures to adopt a new relationship with central government: more of agency than local political autonomy; and concerned primarily with the economic base and its efficient development rather than with social policy. This represents a major change in goals, with inevitable tensions, but it does redirect attention to the ultimate determinant of a city's resources: its net worth and returns to economic factors in conditions of international economic change.

These changes in goals represent a sea-change in resourcing the city in Britain which are also occurring in other countries. They are a response to a third circumstance: a shift in the dominant political or *policy culture* that mediates between political leaders, interest groups, administrative and municipal employees, on the one hand, and individuals and families on the other hand. This change in the policy culture of city finance has been reviewed by Bennett (1986*b*). In the USA, for example, Clark and Ferguson (1983) argue that the 'New Deal Democrats' that instituted the War on Poverty programmes in the mid-1960s have been replaced by what they term 'New Fiscal Populists'. In the earlier period the politicians depended heavily on organized groups of unions and civil rights and ethnic organizations, but overlooked the 'silent majority' of individual citizens, particularly the middle class. As a consequence 'New Fiscal Populists' have been able to draw on the interests of individuals as taxpayers and consumers which have emphasized market forces as instruments of policy, rather than organized groups; and they have argued that services can be maintained only by shifting the burden of support from taxes to charges and quasi-fee systems of public finance, improving efficiency of delivery, contracting out service provision, and replacing public by private services. The result has been pressure to diminish tax burdens on people and businesses, reduce the level of intergovernmental support borne on federal and state tax bases, and seek to maintain public services by market-like forces.

In Britain this has been represented by the emergence of a 'fiscal conservatism' in central–local relations (see e.g. Dunleavy, 1984). Bureaucracies are increasingly seen as budget-maximizers which have crippled market power. The need then is to induce 'market discipline' into government: at central and local level. Within this view local government can offer market opportunities by encouraging migration to better mixes of taxes and/or services in accord with preferences. In the more extreme forms of 'new right' philosophy (e.g. Scruton, 1980), the emergence of greater fiscal imbalances is seen as inevitable, and even desirable.

This is not the place to argue the case for or against fiscal conservatism. Here there is only space to note that the political adjustments will be difficult. Inner cities in Britain have become 'political ghettos' where it is not easy for voters, let alone municipal employees, councillors, and managers, to accept that work practices and social structures no longer fit into the dominant economic climate, particularly if the main proponent of change is a Conservative central government with which there is fundamental ideological disagreement. In these circumstances it is difficult to see how, within the existing institutional arrangements for financing local government, the fiscal problems of inner cities can be overcome by local action and the improvements necessary in city resource bases and quality of services can take place. It is clear that many New Left local authorities have been willing, in 1987 and 1988, to enact severe cuts in budgets. However, changes in management and work practices have been met by stiff resistance. The emerging local 'fiscal crisis' and 'service crisis' is not, therefore, primarily one of resources, nor will it be solved primarily be financial reforms (although such reforms are very necessary). Rather the crisis is a political and constitutional one, requiring a new partnership of local and central government and of public and private initiatives. The adjustments this requires of local government depend in Britain upon a political adjustment which must be radical and will be painful. The final outcome will depend on the extent to which, on the one hand, fiscal changes can successfully stimulate better management practices, improved efficiency of service delivery or substitution by non-state market goods, and on the other hand, urban regeneration policies can successfully stimulate sufficient growth in robust economic activity in disadvantaged regions and inner cities, to change the incentives to local political and economic trends.

References

ACIR (1967), *State-level Taxation and Industrial Location* (US Advisory Commission on Intergovernmental Relations: Washington, DC).

—— (1985) *Significant Features of Fiscal Federalism*, 1984 edition (US Advisory Commission on Intergovernmental Relations: Washington, DC).

Audit Commission (1986), *Report and Accounts, Year ended 31 March 1986* (HMSO: London).

—— (1987), *The Management of London's Authorities: Preventing the Breakdown of Services* (HMSO: London).

Bennett, R. J. (1980), *The Geography of Public Finance: Welfare Under Fiscal Federalism and Local Government Finance* (Methuen: London).

—— (1982), *Central Grants to Local Government: The Political and Economic Impact of the Rate Support Grant in England and Wales* (Cambridge University Press: Cambridge).

—— (1986a), 'The impact of non-domestic rates on profitability and investment', *Fiscal Studies*, 7: 34–50.

—— (1986b), 'The effect of urban administrative structures on fiscal development of cities and city region in the USA, Britain and Germany', *Political Geography Quarterly*, 5: Supplement, S119–34.

—— (1987), 'Recent development in fiscal structures of cities and city regions', in *DISP Nr. 88 Dokumente und Informationen zur schweizerischen Orts-, Regional- und Landesplanung*, ETH Zurich, NR 88, 10–19.

—— (1988), Policy Review Section, 'Local government finance: the inevitable day of reckoning', *Regional Studies*, 22 (3): 1–3.

—— and Fearnehough, M. (1987), 'The burden of the non-domestic rates on business', *Local Government Studies*, 13 (6): 23–36.

—— and Krebs, G. (1988), *Local Business Taxes in Britain and Germany* (Nomos: Baden-Baden).

Boddy, M., and C. Fudge (eds.) (1984), *Local Socialism? Labour Councils and New Left Alternatives* (Macmillan: Basingstoke).

Bradbury, K., A. Downs, and K. A. Small (1981), *Future for a Declining City: Simulations of the Cleveland Area* (Academic Press: New York).

Brecker, C., and R. D. Horton (eds.) (1985), *Setting Municipal Priorities 1986* (New York University Press: New York).

Champion, A. G., A. E. Green, D. W. Owen, D. J. Ellin, and M. G. Coombs (1987), *Changing Places: Britain's Demographic, Economic and Social Complexion* (Edward Arnold: London).

Clark, T. N., and L. C. Ferguson (1983), *City Money: Political Processes, Fiscal Strain and Retrenchment* (Columbia University Press: New York).

Derrick, P. (1988), Policy Review Section, 'Local fiscal crisis: diagnosis and remedies', *Regional Studies*, 22(3): 6–9.

Dunleavy, P. (1984), 'Analysing British politics', in H. Drucker, P. Dunleavy, A. Gamble, and G. Peele (eds.), *Developments in British Politics* (Macmillan: London).

Evans, A., and D. Eversley (1980), *The Inner City: Employment and Industry* (Heinemann: London).

Foster, C. D. (1988), Policy Review Section, 'Accountability in the development of policy for local taxation of people and business', *Regional Studies*, 22(3): 13–18.

Frey, W. H. (1979), 'White flight and central-city loss: application of an analytical migration framework', *Environment and Planning A*, 11: 129–47.

—— (1980), 'Status selective white flight and central city population change: a comparative analysis', *Journal of Regional Science*, 20: 71–89.

Goddard, J. B., and A. G. Champion, (1983), *The Urban and Regional Transformation of Britain* (Methuen: London).

Gyford, J. (1985), *The Politics of Local Socialism* (Allen and Unwin: London).

Harrison, B. and Kanter, S. (1978), 'The political economy of state job creation incentives', *Journal of the American Institute of Planners*, 44: 424–35.

Harvey, D. (1973), *Social Justice and the City* (Edward Arnold: London).

Hill, R. C. (1977), 'State capitalism and the urban fiscal crisis in the United States', *International Journal of Urban and Regional Research*, 1: 76–100.

Keeble, D. E. (1980), 'Industrial decline, regional policy and the urban–rural manufacturing shift in the UK', *Environment and Planning A*, 12: 945–62.

Kierschnik, M. (1981), *Taxes and Growth: Business Incentives and Economic Development* (Council for State Planning Agencies: Washington DC).

Livingstone, Ken (1987), *If Voting Changed Anything they'd Abolish it* (Collins: London).

Morris, C. (1980), *The Cost of Good Intentions: New York City and the Liberal Experiment 1960–75* (Morton: New York).

Nicholson, C. (1988), Policy Review Section, 'Local budgetary development, relative efficiency and local fiscal crisis', *Regional Studies*, 22(3): 9–13.

O'Connor, J. (1973), *The Fiscal Crisis of the State* (St. Martins Press: New York).

OECD (1987), *Managing and Financing Urban Services* (Organization for Economic Co-operation and Development: Paris).

Offord, J. (1987), 'The fiscal implications of differential population change for local authorities in England and Wales', University of Cambridge, Ph.D thesis.

Regional Studies (1988), Policy Review Section, 'Local Fiscal Crisis: the policy imperatives', *Regional Studies* 22(3).

Scruton, R. (1980), *The Meaning of Conservatism* (Macmillan: London).

Smith, D. M. (1977), *Human Geography: A Welfare Approach* (Edward Arnold: London).

Sternlieb, G., and J. W. Hughes (eds.) (1978), *Revitalizing the Northwest: Prelude to an Agenda* (Rutgers University Center for Urban Policy Research: New Brunswick, NJ).

Travers, T. (1988), Policy Review Section, 'Local taxation and services: present and future', *Regional Studies*, 22(3): 3–6.

United Kingdom (1986), *Paying for Local Government*, Cmnd. 9714 (HMSO: London).

Walker, D. (1983*a*), *Municipal Empire: The Townhalls and their Beneficiaries* (Maurice Temple Smith: Hounslow).

—— (1983*b*), 'Local interest and representation: the case of "class" interest among Labour representatives in Inner London', *Government and Policy: Environment and Planning C*, 1: 342–6.

Wasylenko, M. J. (1980), 'Evidence of fiscal differentials and intrametropolitan firm relocation', *Land Economics*, 56: 339–49.

—— (1986), *Local Tax Policy and Industrial Location: A Review of the Evidence* National Tax Association Tax Institute of America, Proceedings of 68th Conference (NTA: Columbus, Ohio).

Young, K. and C. Mason (eds) (1983), *Urban Economic Development* (Macmillan: London).

7

Health-Care Policy Issues

John Mohan

This chapter considers inequalities in the distribution of health care in urban areas, and policy responses. Three key issues are discussed: acute hospital services; primary care; and the possibility of greater private provision of services.

One problem common to all health-care systems is that there is no agreement about what constitutes 'need' for health care. While the additional demands placed upon health-care systems by some groups (for instance the elderly) are not disputed, there is disagreement about the relative needs of different communities. A controversial topic at present is whether social deprivation, typically concentrated in urban areas, generates additional need for health care. Furthermore, the social and cultural characteristics of individuals living in urban areas—notably members of immigrant groups—may prevent them from making use of the available resources (Donovan, 1986).

Because determining need for care is difficult, allocating health-care resources within urban areas is a complex task. Furthermore, providers are heavily constrained by the historical legacy of services, which may be judged both inappropriate and overprovided relative to contemporary requirements. The management of change is consequently difficult, and it is complicated by the division of responsibility for health-care provision between different statutory authorities and by the understandable attachment of urban communities to 'their' health services, so that change may be fiercely resisted. Because of this division of responsibility, and also because much ill-health is capable of being prevented, there have recently been moves towards a broader conception of strategies for health in urban areas, which have echoes of the nineteenth-century public health movement.

Urban Hospital Services

The pattern of hospital services inherited by the NHS was a very uneven one: inequalities existed both between and within regions (Nuffield Provincial Hospitals Trust, 1946); hospital services were concentrated in major urban centres but there were also intra-urban variations in provision (Abel-Smith, 1964; Pickstone, 1985). The 1962 Hospital Plan proposed to equalize access to health care via a programme of new capital investment, the aim being to develop a system of district general hospitals (DGHs) serving populations of 100–150,000 throughout England and Wales (Allen, 1979; Fox, 1986). Concentration was deemed essential in the interests of medical education and the efficient use of scarce medical staff. This plan therefore reproduced the dominant view of Western scientific medicine, and debates about hospital policy strongly reflected medical influences, often being concerned with the arrangement of facilities that would best suit the requirements of medical practitioners. In particular, there was fierce resistance to the idea of dispersing medical schools from London (Rivett, 1986). The implicit assumption was that the type of health care being provided was unproblematic; the only problem was its distribution.

Despite the laudable aims of the plan, its full implementation was thwarted by public expenditure restraint, disagreement about the optimum size of hospitals, and a reluctance on the part of governments to close peripheral hospitals, so that, by the early 1970s, substantial inequalities in hospital provision remained (Buxton and Klein, 1978). Furthermore, population change, especially inner-city decline, had left behind substantial concentrations of hospital capacity relative to the falling populations of such areas. The 1974–9 Labour government was elected on a manifesto which, by comparison with earlier programmes, was radical and included at least some commitment to policies designed to reduce inequality. The Labour government therefore set up the Resource Allocation Working Party (RAWP) to investigate methods of allocating health service resources in a manner responsive equitably and efficiently to social need. The RAWP report (DHSS, 1976) advocated a population-based formula, modified to take account of age and sex composition and also of standardized mortality ratios (SMRs) as a proxy for morbidity. After evaluating the position of the fourteen regional health authorities (RHAs) in England relative to their 'target' levels of revenue, RAWP proposed a transfer of resources in net terms away from London and towards the north and west of England.

There have been extensive debates on RAWP. In particular it has been attacked on a number of technical grounds, and these are relevant because of what they reveal about the problems of allocating health service resources in urban areas. The key issues here are the impact of social factors on need for and utilization of services; the effect of supply on utilization of services; and the costs of providing medical care in urban areas (for more detailed discussions see Buxton and Klein, 1978; RSHG, 1977; Smith, 1981; and Mays and Bevan, 1987).

The original RAWP formula made no allowance for social factors. Several commentators have argued that greater weight should be given to social conditions in allocating health-care resources (see Mays, 1986, 1987; Mays and Bevan, 1987; Woods, 1982). There are two principal positions in this debate. The first argues that need for health care is simply a function of morbidity and that it can therefore be estimated by the level of morbidity in an area or by proxy measures such as the SMR used in the original RAWP formula. On this view, social factors do influence morbidity, but their effect is taken into account by the use of SMRs. The second view is that social factors produce higher levels of morbidity and that social deprivation generates additional costs because, for example, people's home circumstances make it impossible to discharge them from hospital quickly, or because social deprivation results in a lower threshold for hospital admission. The latter means that a person may be admitted to hospital earlier than someone living in a more favourable environment—for example, in better quality housing. The view taken by RAWP was that the influence of social factors was reflected in SMRs and that there was a high degree of correlation between SMRs and social factors anyway, which supported this idea.

The case for including a deprivation factor has commanded a wide range of support. The vociferous medical lobby from the areas deemed to be 'overfunded' were most prominent, arguing the case for a deprivation weighting in the columns of *The Times* (Woods, 1982). They were joined by local authorities who were convinced that additional funds were required to meet the needs of inner London (GLC, 1985). Implicitly the argument was that the nature and extent of urban deprivation imposed demands on the NHS that went unrecognized in the RAWP formula. Nevertheless, according to Mays (1987), the suspicion remained that the deprivation arguments concealed a defence of the status quo by those with a direct interest in its maintenance, especially in view of the lack of hard evidence about exactly how social deprivation was translated into need for health care. At the time of writing, the debate rumbles on in the context of a review of RAWP (NHS Management Board, 1986); it seems likely that some allowance for social factors will be introduced, partly because of the financial pressure on many inner-city district health authorities (DHAs).

The analysis of need for health care is further complicated by the effects of supply on utilization of health services. Urban areas traditionally exhibit high levels of hospital utilization, but they also have high levels of provision of hospital services (Abel-Smith, 1964; Pickstone, 1985; Rivett, 1986). In what sense, if any, do high utilization rates indicate high need for health care? There are at least three opinions.

Firstly, high utilization rates are said to reflect the effect of social factors on morbidity, which leads residents to place greater demands on hospital services. This is essentially the argument that social factors should be recognized in resource allocation (see Jarman, 1983). Secondly, utilization rates are said to be high because, in the absence of good-quality primary care, people make use of hospitals as an alternative, a pattern of health service use which may be inappropriate and expensive. This was the position taken by the Jarman and Acheson reports on inner-city primary care (DHSS, 1981; Jarman, 1981). Thirdly, utilization rates are said to be high because supply creates its own demand and so, irrespective of the quality of primary care services, residents will use hospital services.

The problem is disentangling the complex interrelationships between these issues. One issue concerns the relationship between primary and secondary care. It seems entirely plausible that, if local primary care is poor, individuals will use hospitals as a source of primary care. The policy prescription which flows from this is that improving primary care will relieve pressure on urban hospitals. However, in opposition, improving urban primary care might actually generate still more pressure on hospital services, by unlocking 'need' that is presently unmet or suppressed by the existing supply of services.

A related difficulty is determining what effect supply has on utilization. If interaction between objects is proportional to the size of those objects and inversely proportional to the distance between them, one would expect areas with high levels of supply of services to exhibit high utilization rates. Actually demonstrating this is difficult, because we cannot allocate supply of health services to small areas. But at a national level this is simple enough, and, at the level of regional or district health authorities, one might argue that, subject to cross-boundary flows, there is a supply of beds that is available to the resident population. For smaller areas, such as electoral wards, this does not apply; we cannot say how much supply is available to each area. We might observe a high level of hospital utilization from a particular electoral ward in a locality near a number of hospitals, but we could not unambiguously attribute this to supply factors, since supply of services is not partitioned geographically: each small area competes with others for the available supply. Nor do utilization data help very much anyway, because by definition they refer to successful bids for the available supply; they give no guide to potential utilization, i.e. that which did not compete successfully for the available supply. In the absence of any direct measure of need for services, the only way to account for the influence of supply factors seems to be to introduce them to explain variations in utilization that are not statistically explained by social factors and/or SMRs. This, at least, was the thinking behind the recent research underpinning the review of the RAWP formula.

A further problem with the RAWP formula is the way it accounts for cross-boundary flows of patients. Under the NHS, patients can be treated at any hospital, and clinicians may refer patients to any hospital. This generates flows of patients across the boundaries of health authorities. Such flows may be substantial: half the DHAs in the Thames RHAs, covering south-east England, have cross-boundary flows exceeding 30 per cent of their caseload, though net inflows are much smaller.

The method by which DHAs are compensated for such flows is, in essence, quite simple. They receive funding which reflects their resident population plus adjustments for net inflows/outflows, costed at national speciality rates. The problem is that urban DHAs—such as those in inner London—exhibit high hospitalization rates, which may be due to a combination of supply and social factors (see above). Target levels of spending therefore underestimate the cost of treating the population of such areas, because the allowance for the resident population assumes utilization at national average rates. There is no point in DHAs treating inflows of patients cheaply, since they receive compensation for inflows, so they must either treat their resident population cheaply (e.g. as day cases), or else reduce the hospitalization rate of their residents (Bevan and Brazier, 1985). Arguably their best bet would be to treat only residents from other districts, but this is nonsensical. What they should *not* do is to restrict treatment to their *own* residents: this may ease short-term financial problems but it will worsen their financial position in the long-term, because reduced net inflows will eventually be reflected in reductions in revenue allocations. The system of incentives to DHAs with high cross-boundary flows is therefore perverse (Brazier, 1987). On the assumption that the simplest alternative—to eliminate cross-boundary flows altogether—is undesirable on the grounds of freedom of choice, alternatives need to be explored; these usually involve some form of market-based incentives to DHAs (see below).

There are grounds, then, for the refinement of the RAWP formula and for the introduction of new forms of accounting for cross-boundary flows of patients. Some refinements may be overdue, for the application of RAWP is currently posing severe problems for district health authorities. These are deemed to be overfunded: several DHAs in inner London, where large concentrations of acute hospital services remain in areas whose populations have fallen, are currently receiving levels of revenue at least 10 per cent above their theoretical targets. In the name of equity, these DHAs are to be brought to target levels of revenue within ten years; they face budget reductions in real terms of 1–2 per cent per annum. In common with all DHAs in England, they are at the same time being asked to develop priority services, for instance for drug misusers (see Ch. 17) as well as to transfer resources to community-based services (see Ch. 10). Urban DHAs, especially those in inner London, are also having to cope with the high costs of treating AIDS patients. The net effect is to increase the pressure on these authorities to rationalize services. While various measures are being taken to contain costs, the principal effect has been a rapid concentration of acute hospital services on the main hospital sites; many small, single-speciality units have been closed (ALA, 1986; London Health Emergency, 1987). Yet the savings that this process should have yielded have not, in fact, materialized (King's Fund Centre, 1987), and further stringent cost-cutting measures seem likely. These problems are not confined to inner London (see Davidson, 1987), and sub-regional resource allocation formulae are having a similar impact in other regions, for example in Newcastle (Newcastle Health Concern, 1986).

Finally, these arguments pose several questions about the nature of health-care policies. One implication of the debate about the influence of supply on utilization of services is that, as far as possible, access to services should be equal throughout the country. Even if one accepts the premise that equality *per se* is desirable, and by implication rules out alternative goals for national health-care systems, this leaves one with difficult policy choices. Should all areas be levelled up, involving massive public expenditure; or should everywhere be levelled down, imposing large-scale reductions in services and also in employment in urban areas? It is also questionable whether fine-tuning the formulae used for resource allocation is in fact a useful exercise. Minor amendments to the RAWP formula may ease the pace of change in some health districts, but some commentators feel that this will make little difference unless DHAs are given genuine incentives to plan services rationally rather than make *ad hoc* cuts in their budgets for local acute services (Bevan and Brazier 1987).

More generally, these debates might lead one to raise questions about alternative forms of health-care policies. For example, if social deprivation genuinely influences health status and service use, this could perhaps more appropriately be dealt with via community-based services. Arguably, health-care policy should be much broader in its remit than the provision of public health services, and the problems of some urban areas have led to calls for a 'public health movement', which are discussed in the concluding section.

Primary Health Care

Good quality primary health care is the cornerstone of the World Health Organization's (WHO) policy on health services. However, there is considerable variability in the provision of health care, and policies to rectify imbalances have met with variable success.

The problems of urban primary care came to national attention when the Royal Commission on the NHS (Merrison, 1979) noted that in inner city areas the NHS 'was failing dismally to provide adequate primary care'. Two important research projects on primary care in London were subsequently conducted: one focused on identifying the problems that existed (Jarman, 1981) while the other was broader in scope and made detailed recommendations on how to improve inner city primary care (DHSS, 1981).

Jarman's (1981) survey of the GP service revealed high proportions of single-handed GPs and of elderly GPs; few GPs were practising through group practices or from health centres; and NHS list sizes were low. The latter point does not necessarily imply good access to GP services. GPs may limit the size of their NHS workload at their discretion; statistics on list sizes say nothing about surgery opening hours, which may be inflexible and/or inconvenient; and low list sizes also mean that, under the present methods used to control the distribution of GPs, no new GPs may be allowed to practice in an area.

The Acheson report (DHSS, 1981) reached similar conclusions about the distribution of GP services, but also identified the institutional and organizational problems associated with inner-city primary care. The points it highlighted were: the high degree of population mobility, so that *non-registration* was a problem; the high proportion of *elderly GPs* and the practice of *twenty-four hour retirement*, under which GPs can notionally retire for twenty-four hours, then resume work having qualified for their pension and with remuneration for their NHS work; the inability of the designated areas policy (Butler *et al.*, 1973) to achieve a redistribution of GPs in London, since this policy implicitly assumes that GPs with small lists are open to new patients and that the whole population is registered; and the use of deputizing services.

The response to the problems of inner-city general practice has, however, been limited and partial (Rhodes *et al.*, 1986). The improvement of inner-city primary care has considerable resource implications in terms of compensation payments to GPs for early retirement, capital investment in premises, and incentives to practise in such areas. This, plus the government's anti-public expenditure policies and their unwillingness (before the 1987 General Election) to tackle the problems of inner-city decline (except by means of private sector-led development—see Ch. 19) meant that large-scale expenditure was a remote possibility. Furthermore, if, as was initially suspected, the problems were confined to London, incentives which were available only in London would be opposed by the medical profession. On the other hand, subsequent evidence from Manchester suggested that the problems were not unique to the capital (Wood, 1983*a*,*b*), and so any commitment to *inner-city* primary care would have resource implications stretching far beyond London. There are also important problems of providing good quality primary care in 'outer city' areas (CES, 1984), and the picture presented by the Jarman and Acheson reports of a poor GP service in inner-city areas may be oversimplified (Powell, 1986). The government's response to the Acheson and Jarman reports—an allocation, in 1983, of £9 million—thus represented a 'piecemeal, uncoordinated approach which was short term and temporary' (Rhodes *et al.*,1986, p. 61).

What alternative policies might be pursued for inner-city primary care? On the basis of a national survey of the social factors thought by GPs to influence their workload, Jarman (1983, 1984) argued that areas with high levels of social deprivation imposed considerable additional demands on GPs and the NHS generally. Jarman developed the 'underprivileged area' (UPA) score, a composite indicator based on census data which indicates relative levels of social deprivation. It has been criticized for its apparently arbitrary selection of variables and for compositing variables in an additive manner for no obvious reason (Thunhurst, 1985), but by being based on survey data, it has at least some purchase on the reality of GPs' workload. Using some variant of this criterion, perhaps linked to data on GP workload, could represent an advance on the designated area policy, which has arguably outlived its usefulness; under this policy the sole criterion is the average list size of GPs in an area, and the policy has no powers of positive direction.

There have also been proposals to reorganize primary care services on a 'patch' or 'locality' basis (Cumberlege, 1986; DHSS, 1986). The idea is to identify and respond to local needs in a more flexible way, reflecting a growing awareness of local inequalities in health status (see, among many studies, Thunhurst, 1985; Townsend *et al.*, 1988). By co-ordinating the efforts of health and local government agencies in providing services, problems arising from lack of co-ordination will be avoided. It is ironic that this is happening at a time when resources are limited, because constraints on NHS and local government budgets will mean that little cash is available to fund such developments. As yet, however, it is too early to evaluate locality initiatives.

The problems may not be solved by more refined spatial resource allocation methods alone. A crucial issue in the distribution of GPs is the autonomy afforded to them by their contract with the NHS. In particular the incentives to take on additional NHS patients are weak, and it has been argued that the GP's receipts from capitation fees should form a much larger proportion of his or her income. Furthermore, only recently have steps been taken to compel GPs to retire at seventy. Perhaps the greatest single problem in attracting GPs to inner-city areas is the lack of suitable practice premises. The supply may be limited in inner-city areas; property may be unaffordable or unsuitable, and there is a risk of financial loss in investing in such property. The shortage of suitable accommodation and the difficult working conditions make recruitment difficult. Recent proposals for future primary care service may have little impact. There has been talk of additional financial incentives for inner-city practice, but these proposals contained no hint of additional public expenditure on capital investment in inner-city primary care, merely hinting that some money would be made available to individual GPs to assist in acquiring premises (DHSS, 1986). Nor was there any suggestion that GP contracts would be substantially altered—for example, by introducing stronger powers of direction of GP personnel.

Private Funding and Provision of Health Services

Several states have responded to the problems of funding a comprehensive welfare state by opening up more space for the private provision of health services (Le Grand and Robinson, 1984; Klein and O'Higgins, 1985). This has been because of different combinations of demographic change, economic problems (balance-of-payments difficulties, unemployment, and inflation), and political changes at the level of central government. In Britain, the Conservative government has encouraged the growth of private health care, without yet going as far as some advocates of privatization have wanted. This section concentrates on the likely impact of private provision of acute hospital services and on the effect of measures designed to promote competition within the NHS.

Growth in private acute hospital care has been rapid; there are now 10,000 acute hospital beds in the private sector in Britain. The beneficiaries of private health care—those with private medical insurance—are concentrated in south-east England, especially in the commuter zones around London (OPCS, 1986). Private hospital developers have concentrated on major urban centres, with locations near NHS general hospitals being particularly prized (Mohan, 1985). The private sector workload consists largely of cold acute elective surgery performed mainly on middle-class patients (Williams *et al.*, 1984*a,b*; 1985). Even though there is now a substantial private sector presence in most major British cities, its contribution to local health problems is limited. There have also been criticisms that the private sector deprives the NHS of scarce, trained staff such as senior nurses (see Griffith, Rayner and Mohan, 1985, pp. 153-5).

The real significance of private health care may lie less in its scope than in its wider ideological and social effects. Government encouragement of the private sector may herald the introduction of a greater element of competition into the British health-care scene. Talk of a 'dual' (Klein and Day, 1985) or 'two-tier' (Hunter, 1983) health-care system is justified because of the substantial private sector presence in some localities. Collaboration between the public and private sectors is increasing (Mohan, 1986; Mohan, forthcoming; Rayner, 1986), and utterances by the Secretary of State for Social Services, John Moore, indicate that such schemes will be encouraged in future. We can therefore anticipate a steady blurring of the boundaries between public and private health care.

In particular, there has been much discussion of the possible introduction of market-based schemes for resource allocation in the NHS, to give service providers incentives to keep costs as low as possible. The most likely options are a system of 'internal markets' in the NHS, and the US-inspired Health Maintenance Organization (HMO).

Under the internal market mechanism (Enthoven, 1982), health authorities would have the choice of whether to provide all services themselves or to buy them from other DHAs or the private sector. The idea is that competition would keep costs down because, as providers, DHAs would have to offer services at competitive prices, while as customers they would attempt to seek good quality, cost-effective suppliers for their populations. The argument for this rests on the evidence of substantial variations in the costs of NHS treatment in different part of the country. This is not an open market solution, because: emergency and urgent cases would be excluded; clinicians would be unwilling to ask sick or elderly patients to travel long distances; the number of specialized services would be limited since there are usually only a few centres (e.g. for cardiothoracic surgery) in each RHA; and, politically, DHAs would be reluctant to make redundancies to take advantage of cheap suppliers elsewhere (Brazier, 1987). Hence competition would be limited. Ethical problems would also arise. At present decisions on whether or not to treat patients are made by clinicians alone, but the extensive use of contractual arrangements under cross-charging would mean that access to treatment would depend on explicit rationing decisions by the DHA. In spatial terms, some DHAs would be unable to compete as well as others because of high levels of morbidity and dependency among their patients, or because of the age and condition of their capital plant, and this would certainly work against inner city areas.

The HMO concept involves annual per capita payments for each patient covered by the HMO; the HMO is then responsible for purchasing a package of care for each of its patients. The HMO would purchase health care from hospitals—either public or private. The bigger the gap between the payment for each patient and the cost of treating that patient, the more profit the HMO would make; while, for hospitals, the incentive would be that costs would need to be kept as low as possible to attract custom. The experience of HMOs in the USA suggests that they work well in prosperous middle-class suburbs, where large profits can be made because the population—well-off middle-class young families—make minimal demands on the HMO. However, patients who are expensive to treat in a given year may be refused by the HMO in the following year. HMOs would seem likely to exacerbate spatial inequalities in the distribution of services, since they depend on market segmentation and exclusion in order to make profits (Petchey, 1987).

More generally, it is debatable whether the lessons from America are really applicable to the British NHS. The much-vaunted virtues of the American health market-place—choice and speed of treatment—result at least in part from the enormous funds spent on health care (some 10 per cent of a massive GNP). Furthermore, even spending on this scale fails to provide adequate health services for some 30 million citizens, a substantial proportion of whom are low-income urban blacks or hispanics. If the solution to the NHS's problems is really to be greater competition in order to give health authorities real incentives to reduce costs, a logical starting-point might be to inquire whether present cost variations genuinely reflect inefficiency—rather than, for example, spatial variations in personnel costs, or in the cost of running hospitals, many of which were built in the nineteenth century. Propositions that the NHS is inherently inefficient have yet to be proven convincingly.

Conclusions

The conclusions from this brief review relate to the problems of an area-based approach to resource allocation in the NHS, the difficulties of managing change in the public services, the weaknesses of possible alternative institutional structures for delivering health services, and the need for a broader-based approach to issues of urban health and health care.

It is almost a truism of urban policy debate that spatial resource alloca-tion procedures rarely reach all those people whose problems they claim to address, and so improved health will not necessarily follow from alloc-ating more resources to 'needy' areas. The interest in better targeting of resources has ironically come at a time when money is scarce, so targeting is deemed essential to maximize results. Implemented on their own, better spatial resource allocation policies within the NHS will achieve little without more serious challenges to institutional arrangements—for example, greater control of clinical budgets within DHAs. Having said that, a useful research priority would be the extension of community health surveys on a national sample basis, since this would provide much better indicators of morbidity and therefore of need than are available at present.

Secondly, it is now clear that allocating resources in a manner responsive to need is posing severe difficulties in the context of a health service budget that is at best static. The crucial shift in the implementation of RAWP—from differential growth to differential reduction—is forcing health authorities into extremely difficult financial circumstances and compelling them to take decisions which are certain to affect services (NAHA, 1987). Furthermore, savings are not materializing from economy measures on the scale required by current resource allocation policies (King's Fund Centre, 1987). This is forcing health authorities, especially in London, into a vicious circle: resources cannot be released fast enough for the development of suitable community services; this means that patients have to be kept in hospital longer, thus representing an inefficient use of resources; this in turn is costly and exacerbates the authorities' financial position and lengthens waiting lists. The key lesson from this is that if redistribution is to be pursued and if, at the same time, health authorities are expected to promote better community and primary care services, they cannot be expected to achieve these tasks while simultaneously reducing their budgets by up to 20 per cent over a ten-year period. Funds must be sufficient to allow this transition to take place in a smooth, planned manner. This is not only a matter of calling for more resources. If the 'cinderella' services are to be improved, part of the money will have to come from acute sector budgets. This will demand critical cost–benefit evaluation of different types of medical and surgical procedure, perhaps by the Quality-Adjusted Life Year (QALY) system, under which decisions on priorities are made according to the relative costs of producing life years per patient. Such methods are in their early stages as yet, but they hold out some promise of deciding questions of priority. The problem is likely to lie in introducing such methods and gaining the agreement of the medical profession. The need to challenge medical autonomy and make clinicians accountable for their own budgets is agreed upon by politicians of both Left and Right, but the problem remains—how to do it.

One further implication of the arguments summarized in this chapter is that health problems in urban areas can only be tackled by far-reaching changes in health service organization. For example, one way to improve inner-city primary care would be via a much more *dirigiste* policy with regard to GP personnel. Such a policy would, however, require a major reduction in the autonomy of general practitioners. Likewise, making clinicians accountable for their own budgets would not only throw much more responsibility upon them, it would be perceived as a threat to clinical freedom. A move towards market-based incentives, along the lines of the USA's health-care system, would most likely exacerbate, rather than ameliorate, problems of spatial inequality. The extensive media coverage of the 'crisis' in the NHS in January 1988 seems to have prompted, on the government's part, not so much a realization of the need for additional expenditure as a sense that radical policy options, such as market-based incentives, can once again be placed on the health policy agenda. In this sense, the government may be prepared to make a fundamental break with the consensus on which the NHS was founded.

There are good reasons to suppose that simply to implement internal reforms of the NHS would, however, be inadequate. The achievement of documents such as the Black Report (Townsend and Davidson, 1982) was to demonstrate that, despite thirty years of the welfare state, class inequalities in health status were undiminished. Such debate goes on (e.g. Carr-Hill, 1987; Le Grand, 1982; Townsend, 1987; Townsend *et al.*, 1988; Whitehead, 1987), and has confirmed that social and environmental causes lie at the root of urban health problems. To solve such problems requires much more than administrative reform of the NHS, and so there has been an attempt to argue for a revived 'public health movement' along the lines of that of the nineteenth century (see Draper and Scott-Samuel, 1986). This would recognize the responsibility of a plethora of agencies for health and would institute positive policies for prevention and for environmental improvement. Several local government agencies have set up programmes on these lines, and the WHO's 'Healthy Cities' project is very much in this spirit. Such programmes would, of course, require substantial public investment. There has been some government recognition of public health issues recently, but the report of a committee set up to examine them merely recommended that each DHA employ a public health specialist whose principal duty would be to monitor local trends in health status. More wide-ranging proposals —for example for public expenditure on environmental improvements —were notable by their absence (*Committee of Inquiry*, 1988). Yet proposals for action on public health can draw on the historical legacy of the Victorian era (see Kearns, 1988), a legacy which suggests that the broader challenge of public health represents a real alternative to present policies, and thus merits serious examination.

References

Abel-Smith, B. (1964), *The Hospitals 1800-1948* (Heinemann: London).

ALA (Association of London Authorities) (1986), *London's Health Service in Crisis* (ALA: London).

Allen, D. (1979), *Hospital Planning: The 1962 Hospital Plan for England and Wales. A Case Study in Decision-Making* (Pitman Medical: London).

Bevan, G., and J. Brazier (1985), 'Subregional RAWP—Hobson's Choice?' *Health and Social Services Journal*, 95 (4963): 1064-5.

—— —— (1987), 'Financial incentives of sub-regional RAWP', *British Medical Journal*, 295: 836-8.

Brazier, J. (1987), 'Accounting for cross-boundary flows', *British Medical Journal*, 295: 898-900.

Butler, J., J. M. Bevan, and R. Taylor (1973), *Family Doctors and Public Policy* (Routledge and Kegan Paul: London).

Buxton, M. J., and R. Klein (1978), *Allocating Health Resources: A Commentary on the Report of the Resource Allocation Working Party*, Research Paper 3, Royal Commission on the National Health Service (HMSO: London).

Carr-Hill, R. (1987), 'The inequalities in health debate: a critical review of the issues', *Journal of Social Policy*, 16: 509-42.

CES (Centre for Environmental Studies) (1984), *Outer Estates in Britain*, Occasional Paper 23 (CES: London).

Committee of Inquiry into the Future Development of the Public Health Function (1988), Cd. 289 (HMSO: London).

Cumberlege, J. (1986), *Neighbourhood Nursing: A Focus for Care* (HMSO: London).

Davidson, N. (1987), *A Question of Care: The Changing Face of the National Health Service* (Michael Joseph: London).

DHSS (Department of Health and Social Security) (1976), *Sharing Resources for Health in England* (DHSS: London).

—— (1981), *Primary Care in Inner London* (the 'Acheson' report) (DHSS: London).

—— (1986), *Primary Health Care: An Agenda for Discussion*, Cmnd. 9771 (HMSO: London).

—— (1987), *Promoting Better Health* (HMSO: London).

Donovan, J. (1986), *You Can't Buy Sickness, It Just Comes* (Gower: Farnborough).

Draper, P., and A. Scott-Samuel (1986), 'Whatever happened to public health?', *Health and Social Services Journal*, March, 322-3.

Enthoven, A. (1982), *Reflections on the Management of the NHS* (Nuffield Provincial Hospitals Trust: London).

Fox, D. M. (1986), *Health Policies, Health Politics: The British and American Experience 1911-65* (Princeton University Press: Princeton, NJ).

GLC (Greater London Council) (1985), *A Critical Guide to NHS Resource Allocation in London* (GLC: London).

Griffith, B., G. Rayner and J. Mohan (1985), *Commercial Medicine in London* (GLC: London).

Hunter, D. (1983), 'The privatisation of public provision', *Lancet*, 1: 1264-8.

Jarman, B. (1981), *A Survey of Primary Care in London*, Occasional Paper 16 (Royal College of General Practitioners: London).

—— (1983), 'Identification of underprivileged areas', *British Medical Journal*, 286: 1705–9.

—— (1984), 'Underprivileged areas: validation and distribution of scores', *British Medical Journal*, 289: 1587–92.

Kearns, G. (1988), 'Private property and public health reform in England, 1830–1870', *Social Science and Medicine*, 26(1): 187–99.

King's Fund Centre (1987), *Planned Health Services for Inner London: Back-to-Back Planning* (King Edward's Hospital Fund: London).

Klein, R., and Day, P. (1985), 'Towards a new health care system', *British Medical Journal*, 291: 1291–3.

—— and M. O'Higgins (eds.) (1985), *The Future of Welfare* (Basil Blackwell: Oxford).

Le Grand, J. (1982), *The Strategy of Equality: Redistribution and the Social Services* (Allen and Unwin: London).

—— and R. Robinson (eds.) (1984), *Privatisation and the Welfare State* (Allen and Unwin: London).

London Health Emergency (1987), *Hitting the Skids: A Catalogue of Health Service Cuts in London* (London Health Emergency: London).

Mays, N. (1986), 'Standardised mortality ratios, social deprivation or what? Accounting for morbidity in RAWP', in N. Mays, J. Brazier, and G. Bevan, *Reviewing RAWP* (Social Medicine and Health Services Research Unit, St. Thomas's Hospital: London).

—— (1987), 'Measuring morbidity for resource allocation', *British Medical Journal*, 295: 703–6.

—— and G. Bevan (1987), *Resource Allocation in the Health Service: A Review of the Methods of the Resource Allocation Working Party*, Occasional Papers in Social Administration 81 (Bedford Square Press: London).

Merrison, Sir A. (chair) (1979), *Report of the Royal Commission on the NHS* (HMSO: London).

Mohan, J. (1985), 'Independent acute medical care in Britain: its organisation, location and prospects', *International Journal of Urban and Regional Research* 9(4): 467–84.

—— (1986), 'Commercial medicine and the NHS in south-east England: the shape of things to come?' in J. Eyles (ed.), *Health Care and the City*, Occasional Paper 28 (Department of Geography, Queen Mary College: London).

—— (forthcoming), 'Rolling back the state? Privatization of health services under the Thatcher governments', in J. Scarpaci (ed.), *Privatization of Health Services: An International Survey* (Rutgers University Press: Rutgers, NJ).

NAHA (National Association of Health Authorities) (1987), *The Financial Position of District Health Authorities: Autumn Survey 1987* (NAHA: Birmingham).

Newcastle Health Concern (1986), *Cause for Concern: The State of Newcastle's NHS* (North East Trade Union Studies Information Unit: Newcastle).

NHS Management Board (1986), *Review of the Resource Allocation Working Party Formula* (DHSS: London).

Nuffield Provincial Hospitals Trust (1946), *The Hospital Surveys: The Domesday Book of the Hospital Service* (NPHT: London).

OPCS (Office of Population Censuses and Surveys) (1986), *General Household Survey 1984* (HMSO: London).

Petchey, R. (1987), 'Health maintenance organisations: just what the doctor ordered?', *Journal of Social Policy*, 16: 489–507.

Pickstone J. (1985), *Medicine and Industrial Society: The Hospital Services of the Manchester Region* (Manchester University Press: Manchester).

Powell, M. (1987), 'Territorial justice and primary health care: an example from London', *Social Science and Medicine*, 24: 1093–103.

Rayner, G. (1986), 'Health care as a business: the emergence of a commercial hospital sector in Britain', *Policy and Politics*, 14: 439–59.

Rhodes, G., U. Prashar and K. Young (1986), *After Acheson* (Policy Studies Institute: London).

Rivett, G. (1986), *The Development of the London Hospital System, 1823–1982* (King Edward's Hospital Fund: London).

RSHG (Radical Statistics Health Group) (1977), *RAW(P) Deals: A Critique of the Resource Allocation Working Party* (RSHG: London).

Smith J. (1981), 'Conflict without change: the case of London's health services', *Political Quarterly*, 52: 426–40.

Thunhurst, C. (1985), 'The analysis of small area statistics and planning for health', *Statistician*, 34: 93–106.

Townsend, P., and Davidson, N. (1982), *Inequalities in Health: The Black Report* (Penguin: Harmondsworth).

—— (1987), 'The geography of poverty and ill-health', in A. Williams (ed.), *Health and Economics* (Macmillan: Basingstoke).

——, P. Phillimore, and A. Beattie (1988), *Health and Deprivation: Inequality and the North* (Croom Helm: Beckenham).

Whitehead, M. (1987), *The Health Divide: Inequalities in Health in the 1980s* (Health Education Council: London).

Williams, B. T., J. P. Nicholl, K. J. Thomas, and J. Knowelden (1984*a*), 'Contribution of the private sector to elective surgery in England', *Lancet*, 14 July, 88–92.

—— —— —— —— (1984*b*), 'Analysis of the work of independent acute hospitals in England and Wales, 1981', *British Medical Journal*, 289: 446–8.

—— —— —— —— (1985), 'Differences in duration of stay for surgery in the NHS and private sector in England and Wales', *British Medical Journal*, 290: 978–80.

Wood, J. (1983*a*), 'Are the problems of primary care in inner cities fact or fiction?', *British Medical Journal*, 286: 1109–12.

—— (1983*b*), 'Are general practitioners in inner Manchester worse off than those in adjacent areas?', *British Medical Journal*, 286: 1249–52.

Woods, K. J. (1982), 'Social deprivation and resource allocation in the Thames regional health authorities', in D. M. Smith *et al.*, *Contemporary Perspectives on Health and Health Care*, Occasional Paper 20 (Department of Geography, Queen Mary College: London).

8

Educational Change in the City

Michael G. Bradford

From the mid-1970s onwards, both in Britain and the USA, public discussion of education has been preoccupied with contraction, cost-cutting, careerism, commodification, choice, and community control—'the six C's'. This has been in stark contrast to the previous two decades, when the debate concerned equality of opportunity and equality of outcome (Williamson and Byrne, 1979). The debate has then predominantly turned from social issues to economic ones. Where social and economic processes are both involved and often intertwined, the issues have been interpreted in economic terms, and economic rather than social criteria have dominated decisions, as they have in other areas of policy during the period. The more the issues are interpreted as economic rather than social, then the greater is the call for the private rather than the public sector to tackle them. This chapter traces the move from social to economic, and indeed from educational to political, and observes the social inputs to and consequences of these mainly economic issues. In reviewing the above six Cs, it argues for greater social and even economic awareness when tackling them, and for an agenda which is dominated by educational and social rather than economic and narrowly political influences.

During both periods the educational debate has been at its most intense within cities. In the sixties the spatial, social and economic residential segregation of most cities, in both countries, highlighted the problems of equality of opportunity for children from different socio-economic and racial backgrounds. In the 1970s the dramatic demographic decline of large and medium-sized cities, especially their inner areas, accentuated the problems of contraction. In Britain in many cities, especially again their inner areas, political differences between local and central government on public expenditure have produced great tension between providing the locally desired educational service and reducing overall expenditure as required by central government.

In both countries the economic recession of the late 1970s and early 1980s, with its associated high youth unemployment rates, has been felt most in large cities, especially in northern Britain and the 'rust-belt' of the USA. This economic malaise has further highlighted their poor economic performance over a longer period, relative to competitors such as Japan and West Germany. Poor economic performance has been attributed to educational weaknesses by numerous reports in the USA from national commissions, business groups, political groups, educational and citizen organizations (Carnoy and Levin, 1985), and by various groups and successive governments in Britain, especially since the Callaghan speech at Oxford in 1976, when the Labour Prime Minister took the schools to task for being so unrelated to wealth-creating processes. It is not surprising, therefore, that the call in both nations to raise educational standards and to shift the emphasis in education to producing a workforce that could respond to the needs of employers and the economy was particularly concentrated, not necessarily in, but on to, those cities.

The perceived need for education to be more career- and vocationally oriented and to provide both work and social skills for the economy has been paralleled by demands, especially but not exclusively from the New Right, to allow market forces to operate in the education system. Education becomes more like a commodity than a public service. Under market forces, consumer sovereignty would operate through parental choice of schools, not just between state and private institutions, but within the state sector. The degree of choice is potentially greater and therefore more of an issue in cities because of the density of school population and the greater number of schools. In Britain the greatest growth and levels of private education are in Greater London (Bradford and Burdett, forthcoming). Choice, both within and between sectors, and the operation of market forces, are therefore much more possible in the largest cities. Given their continued spatial segregation, it is also here that choice, and community control are most likely to be associated with selection and segregation between schools on ethnic and class grounds.

In discussing the educational issues of contraction, cost-cutting, careerism, commodification, choice and community control in Britain, this chapter demonstrates how educational problems are exacerbated in an urban domain. It also shows how those issues interact with social, economic, and political processes which operate within cities and at the national scale, both influencing and being influenced by urban experience.

Contraction

Demand for education is more directly dependent than most services on demographic change. The almost continual decline in the birth-rate in

Britain from 1965 to the early 1980s began to affect primary schools in the early 1970s and secondary schools in the late 1970s. Until that decade, the post-war and 1960s' baby booms had led to a national context in which there was a continuing expectation of an expanding education system, with growing numbers of pupils and teachers, and increasing resources for curricula development. This context in part accounts for the slow response of local authorities to declining secondary school rolls, even though they had the primary sector acting as an early warning system. Local authorities, however, have not been the only organizations to respond slowly to an environment of contraction, closure, and rationalization after being used to one of expansion, new facilities and development: many large companies have been equally slow.

The rolls of schools in large and medium-sized cities, particularly in their inner areas, decreased even more markedly than those in other areas because of net outmigration, especially of women of child-bearing age. In Manchester, for example, the population declined by 18 per cent between 1971 and 1981, while its primary school population fell by 33 per cent. The eleven-year-old intake to maintained secondary schools for metropolitan local education authorities (LEAs) as a whole peaked in 1976, and declined by just under 30 per cent to 1986; while for non-metropolitan counties it peaked a year later and fell by only 20 per cent. The decline has been most marked in the eighties, with a 24 per cent drop from 1981 to 1986 for the metropolitan LEAs and a 17 per cent fall for non-metropolitan ones. Generally, then, the problem has occurred slightly earlier and been more pronounced in large urban areas.

The extent of demographic decline also varies considerably between metropolitan areas, with Merseyside suffering the greatest loss (37 per cent from 1976) and West Yorkshire the least (23 per cent). The greatest variation, both in timing and extent, has been within the old metropolitan counties, with Merseyside again being prominent: Knowsley has lost 53 per cent of its intake since 1976, while St Helens continued to gain pupils until 1983, since which time it has seen a 20 per cent loss. A similar picture of dramatic, if not quite so extreme, change is found in Greater London, with well over 40 per cent losses from 1976 in Haringey, Brent, and the Inner London Education Authority (ILEA), in contrast to declines from later peaks in 1978 and 1979 of over 25 per cent for Bexley, Bromley, Enfield, Havering, and Waltham Forest, and less than 20 per cent for Sutton. The wealthier outer metropolitan boroughs therefore had some time in which to learn from the inner areas' experience, and even then faced less severe problems.

These figures for LEAs obviously conceal even more dramatic losses in pupil numbers within LEAs. Clearly this is particularly the case for primary schools with their smaller catchment areas, which are more readily identifiable with neighbourhoods. The rapidity of neighbourhood change through redevelopment and out-migration has contributed to anomalies. As Brown and Ferguson (1982, p. 179) note, 'Liverpool was not the only authority to have built a new school to find the catchment area depopulated as a result of planning and housing decisions inspired by national and local changes in political direction and policy.' The lack of foresight of some LEAs in responding to birth-rate changes was compounded by the lack of co-ordination between departments within the local authorities. The same blinkered view, not though simply within the LEAs, has characterized possible responses to these changes in demand.

The reduction in intake in both primary and secondary schools was initially seen as a means of reducing overcrowding, which in some areas had long been a problem. For primary schools, in particular, it is possible to appreciate the delayed response of many authorities. In the outer suburbs of Greater Manchester, for example, the local concern of the mid-1970s was the restriction on access to some primary schools because of overcrowding. Entry was delayed and redirected. Within two years that problem had ceased, while within five more years, the local political issue revolved around the amalgamation of schools. Change was rapid and in a new direction.

Cost-Cutting

The responses to the demographic decline became inextricably entwined with the reduction of local authority expenditure. The expected educational demand for much lower pupil/teacher ratios, which the falling intakes allowed, was not loudly heard. This might have occurred if the fall had been smaller and more gradual. As it was, the demographic decline straddled the 1976 downturn in public expenditure that followed the International Monetary Fund (IMF) loan. Responses to demographic change became part of the cost-cutting exercise that most local governments were forced to undertake from then onwards, as their Rate Support Grants were reduced. Perhaps not coincidentally, 1976 was the year in which James Callaghan chose to launch the 'Great Debate' in a speech at Ruskin College, Oxford, in October when, among other things, he questioned whether the education service was giving 'value for money', a criterion that was to become even more popular after 1979. Since the much publicized Black Papers (Cox and Dyson, 1969a, 1969b, 1971; Cox and Boyson, 1975) had earlier cast doubt, with very little evidence, on many of the teaching methods that necessitated and/or benefited from smaller classes, there was insufficient overall political will to use the demographic opportunity to restructure education *within* existing schools. The prevailing wisdom of the sixties that an increasing per caput investment in education was an indispensible condition for the achievement of greater equality of opportunity and national economic prosperity (Brown and Ferguson, 1982) had been overturned, at least at the national level.

At the local level many people in an education service which in numerous areas had only recently committed itself to comprehensive schools, felt that further upheaval in the school system was undesirable, as was any reduction in the opportunities for children from poorer backgrounds. Economic arguments, however, dominated the decisions. Central government (DES, 1977, 1978, 1979) and some educational research (Briault and Smith, 1980) continued to focus on falling school rolls and to encourage school closure and amalgamation at both primary and secondary levels. Some of the criteria applied to the reorganization of education for sixteen- to nineteen-year-olds in the late seventies and early eighties, namely the availability of a variety of subjects and a combinations of subjects, were also applied to younger age groups, and used as reasons for closing small schools which could not provide such a variety (Briault and Smith, 1980). This educational argument sits uneasily beside the supposedly 'better' private sector, with its numerous small schools, and indeed with the condemnation by some critics of comprehensives, which is often based on the problems of some *large* inner London schools. Given these external pressures, and faced with politically sensitive domestic rate rises because of high inflation and reductions in the Rate Support Grant, it is not surprising that many local authorities, in seeking areas in which they could reduce expenditure, turned to education. Education counts for by far the highest proportion of local government expenditure, and falling rolls presented an obvious opportunity for rationalization and restructuring between schools.

It should be clear from what was said above that some authorities were hit by the problem earlier and to a greater extent than others. They were also differentially affected by reductions in central government Rate Support Grant. In many cases the greatest enrolment decline occurred in areas of greatest grant loss, partly due to the grant's link to population and partly to the reformulation of the grant in 1982 so that it acted to encourage reduced spending. Inner-city authorities with their numerous social problems were particularly high spenders, especially on education. Penalties for overspending and rate capping restricted even more the local authorities' room for manoeuvre. While many were slow to respond to the falling rolls, some were reluctant to respond by closure because of the social impact. Nearly all have eventually done so. Most authorities proceeded on an *ad hoc* basis, closing a school here and amalgamating others there. Factors determining selection were as likely to be political, a weak or retiring head for example, as educational. Some drew up a plan for the whole authority and presented it to the public for their response. Bondi's analysis of Manchester's primary level plan and consultation exercise in 1982 (Bondi, 1986) warrants detailed examination because it presents strong evidence for the dominance of economic rather than educational or social criteria in the rationalization of schools. It also illuminates how urban politics operates.

The spatial distribution of proposed closures and amalgamations withdrew places in proportion to the expected decline in local demand to the end of the 1980s. Superficially this seems fair, but enrolments had fallen most in the most disadvantaged areas of Manchester, and had been most buoyant in the better-off ones, with consequently differential potential impact on different social groups. The narrow aim of reducing provision according to demographic decline overrode other possible objectives such as improving community facilities in poorer areas or removing the worst school accommodation. It also failed to consider the alternative policy of changing future demand through housing policy.

In selecting particular schools for closure or amalgamation the plan failed to apply objective criteria. Analysis of the proposals reveals that the major factors affecting closure were high vacancy rates, origins in the nineteenth century, and to a lesser extent high unit premises costs, which all appear in the criteria stated by the LEA. A major unstated factor, as important as any other, is school size. An educational argument for a maximum class size of thirty was transformed into an economic one of a minimum school size of 180 (six forms of thirty). Economic rather than educational and social factors dominated the overall distribution of proposals and the selection of particular schools.

The public consultation was largely a legitimation exercise (Bondi, forthcoming). The criteria used to produce the plan were not on the agenda, and the public were only asked to respond on the proposals affecting their school. The local communities were almost constrained into a pluralistic position, where defence of their school meant attacking others. Despite this, many groups markedly restrained from such competition, but only one small group tried to respond to the plan city-wide and to assess the criteria used. The plan had already been agreed and developed in consultation with church bodies and teacher unions, so this consensus, reached through corporate means, only allowed a limited area for pluralistic politics to act and almost ensured fragmented opposition. The idea of a dual state, with pluralism dominating local consumption issues while corporatism operates at the national level on mainly production issues (Saunders, 1981), is not borne out for this issue. Corporatism and managerialism set the limited agenda for pluralism.

The success of responses to the plan reflected biased pluralism, with, not surprisingly, middle-income groups and/or professionally led groups being most successful. Although in this case it is difficult to disentangle whether it was the professional occupation or gender of the leaders that was significant, it is worth mentioning that, for an issue dominated by female involvement, male-led groups were most success-ful, at least partly reflecting the dominance of male professional officers with whom they were dealing. Professional male leadership in lower-income areas produced successful campaigns, and this was largely owing to the tactics that they were able to employ. The most successful tactics for all groups were what Bondi (1988) has termed the 'factual' and 'political' approaches as against the unsuccessful 'public opinion formation' approach. The first uses the formal channel of consultation, presenting researched and reasoned reports as well as letters of protest. The political approach applies to those who successfully involved the active support of their local councillors, while the third encourages the public to oppose the plans through media-catching tactics, such as demonstrations and public rallies. Part of the bias in the pluralism was then associated with tactics employed, which were in themselves influenced by available resources.

This case-study shows how a plan of contraction based on economic principles led to differential social effects, and how the political responses to it were limited by the incorporation of potentially powerful opposition and the channelling of the community voice. It also demon-strates the bias in political influence of certain social groups and leaders.

The closure and amalgamation of schools and the reorganization of sixteen-to-nineteen-year-old education has been dominated by financial arguments, which central government has continually pressed and made necessary by their reduced grants. Yet the delay in the secretary of state's decisions on local proposals has hindered financial efficiency and prolonged uncertainty. The lack of consistency in the decisions has also made local management more difficult. Increased central control in response to what is, with very little evidence, popularly perceived as local inefficiency, has not been marked by central efficiency or consistency.

Careerism

At the same time as economic and political change has reduced the amount of finance going to education, it has stimulated demands for greater economic relevance in the curriculum and for greater links between schools and industry. Careerism or vocational education has been seen to have three purposes: making pupils able to get jobs, making them better performers in jobs, and making them more aware of the world of work (Dale, 1986). The renewed move towards careerism in Britain and the USA is partly a response to their economic decline in the late seventies and early eighties, and partly a reaction to the perceived or publicized 'failure' of schools to bring about the social changes and educational advances that were the objectives of the 1960s. Even though there is evidence of some success in improving attainment across the board, and making progress towards the aims of the 1960s, some teachers have welcomed the vocational initiatives and change of emphasis. Such initiatives have provided resources during a period of scarcity and career opportunities in a contracting profession. They have also given much-needed improved status, as they are fashionable objectives, replacing to some extent the unfashionable ones associated with social justice. Contraction and cost-cutting have then provided a context in which careerism has been more easily introduced.

Links between schools and industry have proceeded in Britain at different times and in different ways via such programmes as the Technical and Vocational Educational Initiative (TVEI), the School Curriculum Industry Project (formerly Schools Council Industry Project (SCIP), and City Technology Colleges. The schools–industry movement has been described 'as a diverse collection of employer and trade union groupings; specially constructed educational or quasi educational ''projects''; government agencies and government statements and exhortations—all designed to put pressure on the education system to change the content of what is taught, how it is taught, and how it is assessed and examined' (Jamieson, 1985, p. 27).

In general, Jamieson notes that the schools–industry movement has had much greater impact in some areas than others. This depends on the economic and civic history and present labour market of the locality. The traditional industrial towns of the north, such as Barnsley and Wakefield, exhibit the greatest amount of activity. Here there is a strong sense of community and a feeling of civic ownership of schools. Industrial capital and labour are both strong local forces and both are actively involved. Such activity is also well developed in the suburban rings of large cities, where there is less sense of community and less trade union involvement but plenty of industrial and commercial activity on which to draw. The schools in shire towns have much more activity than their rural neighbours, which compete with inner cities for the least involvement with the movement. Even though there is all-party support for such schemes, less commitment from Labour councils may contribute to this lack of involvement in inner cities, as they rightly perceive trade unions as poor relations to business in the majority of schemes (Jamieson, 1985). The decline of manufacturing industry in inner cities is likely to be a much more important factor, although the presence of commercial activity in the nearby central business districts might have been expected somewhat to offset this. According to Jamieson the least activity, in general, seems to be in one of the areas where youth unemployment is greatest, the inner cities.

Unlike many of the above schemes, TVEI has been centrally initiated and funded. Moon and Richardson (1984) believe that the government's motivation for the initiative derives from their view that the failure of technical education has been a significant factor in British industry's declining competitiveness. TVEI is monitored by a unit within the Manpower Services Commission (MSC) and directed by local steering groups consisting of participating schools, LEAs, the MSC and both sides of industry. It is aimed at fourteen-to-eighteen-year-olds. It was announced in November 1982 from outside the education system, and pilot schemes were instituted in September 1983 in fourteen of the sixty-six LEAs that bid for them. Forty-four more authorities were included the following year, and others were included in succeeding years. It has represented rapid external change which has provided unprecedentedly large amounts of money at a time of general financial cutbacks. It has tried to redirect and restructure the school experience of a large proportion of pupils, bringing the school closer to the world outside, particularly the 'world of work'.

Neither the applications nor the awarded contracts for the scheme have been geographically uniform. All authorities were initially suspicious of its political, extra-educational origins, but some were undoubtedly attracted by the money, while others remained out of the initiative because they feared it would narrow the curriculum or reintroduce some form of selection into comprehensive education. Many Labour-controlled authorities, including inner city ones, did not apply. The differential geographical impact between authorities has been matched *within* many of the participating authorities. Different criteria have been used to select schools within authorities, producing varying social effects in different localities. In some cases the scheme has been used to equalize provision across the authority by bringing resources to the worst-off schools (Dale, 1985). In others it has been used to smooth school amalgamation and thus enabled the contraction process. Yet in a number of other areas, the differences in school resources have been accentuated, as powerful councillors win more resources for 'their' schools, and the 'better' schools are even more advantaged. Differential pupil access to the scheme within schools, and its beneficial or detrimental effects vary greatly between schools, depending on the degree of integration and penetration into the rest of the curriculum. Even though this initiative has spread rapidly, in the short term at both scales, it has, in many cases, increased the inequalities between schools and in the life chances of their pupils.

Given Jamieson's view of the lack of school–industry activity in inner cities, and Labour's initial opposition to TVEI, it is easy to see why central government would want to improve links with industry in these areas through their proposal for City Technology Colleges (CTCs) with their vocationally oriented curriculum (DES, 1986). The CTCs will have separate status outside LEA control, and be partly publicly and partly industrially financed. This proposal has met considerable opposition from the Association of Metropolitan Authorities (AMA, 1987), and from what a government minister has called the 'ed biz'. The removal of local power is part of a wider movement which extends into areas such as finance, housing, and development, and will be discussed later under community control. The potential educational and social effects of this careerist innovation which is targeted at cities will be taken up here.

Whether the trusts that will be set up to run them will manage these schools better than LEAs which, through economies of scale, can at least provide central resources, services, and advice, remains to be seen, as does industry's willingness to provide finance for more than a few CTCs. Contributing companies, such as the Hanson Trust, will be paying twice for education, once indirectly through their taxes and once directly to establish and run the colleges. Their returns may be variously interpreted: satisfaction from extra civic duties, promotional gains, indirect political advantage, means of influencing educational change, or trained labour. If they are large employers in the local area, they run the risk of souring their relationship with the local authority and local schools for any existing industry–school links, which, despite the general conclusion on their geographical distribution, are strong in some metropolitan authorities. They may also increase their dominance of the local labour market, access to which may be increasingly difficult for non-CTC pupils. There is then a danger of greater divisiveness both in school–industry links and in school–labour market links.

Given that the colleges will not be local-authority run, it is likely that politically opposed authorities will make it difficult for them to obtain planning permission. More welcoming authorities, such as Conservative-run Solihull, where the first college will open in 1988 (although, incidentally, it was not one of the possible twenty-six areas listed in the original proposal (DES, 1986)), will often lie outside the areas in greatest need. Paradoxically their best chance of early establishment in terms of sites is in closed local authority schools. Local authorities would then be even more aware of the savings from secondary-level rationalization and reorganization for sixteen-to-nineteen-year-olds being threatened, as CTCs attract pupils from remaining schools and colleges, so reproducing the under-utilization of capacity, that under central government pressure they had sought to reduce. This may affect neighbouring local authorities too; the Solihull CTC is located so that just over half of its catchment area extends into Birmingham, whose education committee fears that the best pupils and teachers will be attracted from its schools by the extra resources and marketing of the CTC (*Guardian*, 1987).

The possibility of higher teacher salaries or better promotional opportunities may also attract teachers away from the maintained sector, which will be particularly serious in the subjects where there are national supply shortages, the very ones which the maths-, science-, and technology-based curriculum of CTCs emphasizes. It is difficult to see how the education of the pupils remaining in LEA schools both within and outside the CTC catchment areas will be in any way enhanced by this initiative. It will not 'help *all* our children and young people [my emphasis—MB] to bring enterprise, versatility and application to their employment', part of the quotation from *Better Schools* with which the DES begins its *City Technology Colleges: A New Choice of School* (1986). It is likely to introduce questionable criteria of selection: of the pupil at the age of eleven, which most educational thinking suggests is inappropriate; and of the 'parents' commitment to full-time education or training up to the age of eighteen, to the distinctive characteristic of the CTC curriculum, and to the ethos of the CTC'. It seems likely that such commitment will not be distributed equally across the social classes and that therefore 'the composition of their intake will' *not* 'be representative of the community they serve', as is proposed. They are then likely to increase inequalities between schools and pupils' access to educational chances, and produce further need to rationalize LEA provision. They will probably both strengthen and weaken local industry's relations with different sections of the community, and, where the contributing industry is locally dominant, accentuate differential access to the youth labour market.

The MSC has also threatened local authority control over education, and some would say deflected funds from local authorities. It has reinforced the careerism movement, with its emphasis on 'social and life skills' and 'work socialization' which has permeated the wider school system (Horne, 1986). It has also had a profound impact on the transition from school to work through the one—and later two-year Youth Training Schemes (YTS). Although many of the MSC administrators aimed to effect a redistribution of jobs by race and gender, the mechanisms of the schemes have tended to reinforce previously unequal distributions, and indeed compound the effect of pre-market forces, most importantly the unequal school attainment levels of different social groups. The effects vary from locality to locality, partly through the structure and the working of their segmented labour markets (Peck, forthcoming).

The effects are felt within cities too. Premium funded YTS places (related to the old 'mode B' scheme) need the endorsement of the Careers Service. Some of the criteria used for this endorsement have been shown to be educational sub-normality, frequent truancy, and area of residence. The last is a further example of 'red-lining', in this case of the inner city and peripheral council estates, which often have their own schemes which are seen as 'natural' places to go. Future employment prospects are likely to be much reduced for premium-endorsed trainees, just as they have been previously for 'mode B' as against 'mode A' people. Inequalities from school are reinforced by YTS. Cynically, its effect has been to enable unequal access to employment to operate more effectively, through the one- or two-year screening of trainees by employers.

The various aspects of careerism have and will obviously bias the curriculum towards a training for work than for life, and contribute to a return to subject- rather than child-centred learning, both of which reduce the social input to schooling. They also appear to increase and reinforce social inequalities.

Commodification

The predominance of the economic imperative in the last decade has not only been reflected in careerism. More people have been attracted to private education, some undoubtedly to purchase better qualifications and chances for their children. Geographically, that growth has been most evident in Greater London, East Anglia, and the South East, so that the spatial polarization of the country has increased. Similar polarization has occurred within Greater London, where areas with low incidence of private education have declined and many with high take-up have relatively and absolutely increased (Bradford *et al.*, forthcoming). The educational consumption cleavage is becoming more spatially marked.

Commodification is also occurring elsewhere in the system. As resources become scarce, competition becomes more prevalent. The growth in demand by schools for work experience for their pupils and the decline in supply has led to a growing practice of 'poaching' placements from other schools (Shilling, 1987). The extra energy expended in attempts to gain placements has meant that they have become 'positional goods' (Hirsch, 1977). This is one example of a general tendency for commodification and associated competition leading not only to divisiveness but also to redirection and waste of, in this case, human resources.

Choice

Although educational vouchers have not yet been introduced, the proposals for parental choice and, less directly, 'opting out', are clearly designed to bring market forces into the system in a similar way. Commodification and choice are highly related. Market forces nearly always give greater choice to the better-off and more informed. Equality of opportunity, let alone of outcome, is unlikely to increase.

For choice to operate effectively there must be a wide variety of schooling presented to parents, but the proposed simultaneous introduction of a national curriculum will immediately standardize and reduce variety. Choice will then be based more narrowly on reputation.

The intended dynamic equilibrium processes whereby the attraction of pupils away from unpopular schools to popular ones is supposed to give the necessary incentives for unpopular ones to improve, are unlikely to occur because the unpopular schools will have less resources with which to improve their standards or to change their image (not at all the same thing, but one which will absorb resources and time in a competitive situation). Their standards may not have actually been any different in the first place. Reputations and indeed outcomes are affected by the social mix within the school. Choice mechanisms are likely to lead to increased social and indeed racial segregation between schools (the 1987 Dewsbury case in West Yorkshire of white parents not wanting to send their children to a primary school with 85 per cent Asian children presented an early warning of this). The inability of schools to respond immediately and accurately to changes in demand means both some form of selection being used for popular schools, in many cases accentuating social divisions, and under-use of resources for unpopular ones. Again the rationalization plans of LEAs would have been completely wasted. Choice and competition will in some cases lead to school closure and thus reduced choice, particularly in poorer areas where the more unpopular schools will probably emerge. Even in many areas of the market-oriented USA, allocation mechanisms operate within education in order to desegregate the schools (but need amending to maintain desegregation as housing areas change) (Lord and Catau, 1981). Market forces in such a service will waste resources as well as favour social outcomes completely at variance with those of the sixties. There are both strong economic and strong social arguments against such moves.

Community Control

Opting out of LEA control by schools and of ILEA by boroughs have also been proposed. As with CTCs, which may eventually form the model for opting-out schools, there are serious doubts about the availability of governors to manage the school trusts. Their ability and available time are one aspect of the problem. The degree to which they are representative of the community is another.

For other social arguments the American experience is revealing. In the USA one move for community control came from black groups who were dissatisfied with the education system. The white liberal response to this strategy to improve education for blacks was that groups formed around ethnic, racial, religious, or local ties tend to do so for irrational, affective reasons. The liberals considered the blacks to be deserting their joint commitment to rationality and universalism as alternatives to prejudice in American society, returning instead to the irrational, emotional community loyalty which, according to liberal ideology, helped to create prejudice (Church, 1976). The British initiative has not emanated from the local scale but from the national one, though that does not prevent it from being affected by local prejudice, as the Dewsbury case forewarns. Opting out, for example by Asian or white communities, may intensify racial differences. Already too many schools in all-white areas see little need for multicultural education. Opting out may well hinder its adoption, even though it is one of the centrally set priorities of in-service training (INSET). The backlash, even among left-wing groups, to anti-racist and anti-sexist educational initiatives by a few local authorities, particularly in Greater London, demonstrates both the need for such initiatives and at the same time the sensitivity required in their operation and promotion in order for them to achieve their ends. Opting out can be interpreted as a policy designed to curb local-authority power and to limit such initiatives, but in itself, it may intensify the very need for them.

Opting out by predominantly Conservative areas within Labour local authorities makes political differences more manifest. In all cases social divisions are made more spatially explicit and will probably be increased through the housing market. This refers to limited opting out. If the Thatcher comparison with council house sales becomes a reality, then social divisions will be even more obvious, with at one extreme residualized LEA schools sitting in the middle of residualized council estates.

The motives for the policy may be interpreted as either an increase in central powers relative to local government for political reasons, or a genuine decentralization of power to the community level. Since the national curriculum leaves little choice over local education, and centralization has been occurring through the MSC and in other spheres, the former seems more probable. Indeed centralization under-lies many of the six Cs, and should be included as a covert seventh.

The consequences of opting out, and indeed CTCs, commodifica-tion, and choice, would seem to be greater segmentation, segregation, and separatism. The integrative tendencies of the sixties appear to be waning.

The possibility of opting out has already made rationalization plans much more difficult, as schools designated for closure, amalgamation, or loss of sixth form threaten to opt out, as in Warminster and Ongar. This policy contradicts and impedes the aim of better financial management by LEAs. The lack of such future improvement may then give further credibility to national government's attack on local powers and produce even greater centralization.

Conclusion

Social change, in demographic terms, has provided a different context to education in the city. The fiscal policy of successive national govern-ments has restricted the responses to that changing context by reducing resources and by setting an economically oriented agenda both for the organization of schools and for their curriculum. The overall effects of these changes, although varying in detail with locality, have generally been to increase and sustain social inequalities in access to resources, and to educational and employment opportunities.

Recent proposals to introduce parental choice and opting out seem set to reinforce social, economic, and political differences within cities, and to give them an extra spatial manifestation. The increasing spatial polar-ization at the national scale of the cleavage between maintained and non-maintained education, which reflects and reinforces other socio-economic and political change, may then be reproduced in a different form within cities.

Recent and proposed changes in the education system, in their own economic terms, are contradictory and wasteful of resources. These new initiatives, which offer a 'solution' to economic and educational prob-lems, arguably mark the beginning of a repeat of the educational cycle 'from saviour to scapegoat' (CCCS, 1981). This time, though, the cycle threatens to have consequences that are much more socially divisive.

References

AMA (Association of Metropolitan Authorities (1987), *City Technology Colleges: A Speculative Investment* (AMA: London).

Bondi, L. (1986), 'The geography and politics of contraction in local education provision: A case study of Manchester primary schools', unpublished Ph. D. thesis, University of Manchester.

—— (1988), 'Political participation and school closures: an investigation of bias in local authority decision-making', *Policy and Politics*, 16 (1): 41–54.

—— (1989), 'Variations within education authorities: the politics of school closure', in M. G. Bradford, L. Bondi, F. Burdett, J. Peck, and B. Quirk, *Education, Space and Locality* (Routledge: London).

M. G. Bradford, L. Bondi, F. Burdett, J. Peck and B. Quirk (1989), *Education, Space and Locality* (Routledge: London).

—— and F. Burdett (1989), 'The spatial polarization of private education' *Area*, in press.

Briault, E., and F. Smith (1980), *Falling Rolls in Secondary Schools* (NFER: Windsor).

Brown, P., and S. S. Ferguson (1982), 'Schools and population change in Liverpool', in W. T. S. Gould and A. G. Hodgkiss (eds.), *The Resources of Merseyside* (Liverpool University Press: Liverpool), 77–90.

Carnoy, M., and H. M. Levin (1985), *Schooling and Work in the Democratic State* (Stanford University Press: Stanford).

CCCS (Centre for Contemporary Cultural Studies), University of Birmingham (1981), *Unpopular Education* (Hutchinson: London).

Church, R. L. (1976), *Education in the USA* (Free Press: New York).

Cox, C. B., and A. E. Dyson (eds.) (1969a), *Fight for Education: A Black Paper* (Critical Quarterly Society: London).

—— and —— (eds.) (1969b), *Black Paper 2: The Crisis in Education* (CQS: London).

—— and —— (eds.) (1971), *Black Paper 3* (CQS: London).

—— and R. Boyson (eds.) (1975), *Black Paper 1975: The Fight for Education* (Dent: London).

Dale, R. (1985), 'The background and inception of the technical and vocational education initiative', in R. Dale (ed.), *Education, Training and Employment: Towards a New Vocationalism* (Pergamon Press: Oxford), 41–56.

—— (1986), 'Examining the gift horse's teeth: a tentative analysis of TVEI', in L. Barton and S. Walker (eds.), *Youth Unemployment and Schooling* (Open University Press: Milton Keynes), 29–45.

DES (Department of Education and Science) (1977), *Falling Numbers and School Closures*, Circular 5/77 (HMSO: London).

—— (1978), *School Population in the 1980s*, Report on Education 92 (HMSO: London).

—— (1979), *Trends in School Population*, Report on Education 96 (HMSO: London).

—— (1986), *City Technology Colleges: A New Choice of School* (HMSO: London).

Guardian (1987), 'Heads told to snub city college launch', 27 October, p. 2.

Hirsch, F. (1977), *Social Limits to Growth* (Routledge and Kegan Paul: London).

Horne, J. (1986), 'Continuity and change in the state regulation and schooling of unemployed youth', in L. Barton and S. Walker (eds.), *Youth Unemployment and Schooling* (Open University Press: Milton Keynes), 9–28.

Jamieson, I. (1985), 'Corporate hegemony or peagogic liberation: the schools-industry movement in England and Wales', in R. Dale (ed.), *Education, Training and Employment: Towards a New Vocationalism* (Pergamon Press: Oxford), 23–40.

Lord, J. D., and J. C. Catau (1981), 'The school desegregation–resegregation scenario: Charlotte Mecklenburg's experience', *Urban Affairs Quarterly*, 16(3): 369–76.

Moon, J., and J. J. Richardson (1984), 'Policy-making with a difference?', *Public Administration*, 62(1): 23–33.

Peck J. (1989), 'Restructuring the transition from school to work: the impact of the Youth Training Scheme', in M. G. Bradford, L. Bondi, F. Burdett, J. Peck and B. Quirk, *Education, Space and Locality* (Routledge: London).

Saunders, P. (1981), *Social Theory and the Urban Question* (Hutchinson: London).

Shilling, C. (1987), 'Work-experience and schools: factors influencing the participation of industry', *Journal of Educational Policy*, 2(2): 131–47.

Williamson, B., and D. S. Byrne (1979), 'Educational disadvantage in an urban setting', in D. T. Herbert and D. M. Smith (eds.), *Social Problems and the City: Geographical Perspectives* (Oxford University Press: Oxford), 186–200.

9

The Housing Question

Peter Kemp

'The housing problem' emerged in Britain during the mid-nineteenth century and has been present ever since. The nature of this issue has in fact changed over time as individual problems were ameliorated and others came into focus. For as Donnison and Ungerson (1982, pp. 13–14) have remarked, '*The* housing problem is never solved: it only changes. That may nevertheless constitute progress. Some problems are nicer to have than others.' What this helps to remind us is that social problems such as 'the housing question' are social constructs rather than some necessarily objective reality that exists independently of our perceptions. In order for social phenomena to become 'problems' they must first be identified or defined as such. Indeed, what was once considered to be socially acceptable, normal, and inevitable may subsequently come to be regarded as a social problem to which the energies of the state should be directed. Moreover, policy solutions to particular problems may themselves come to be seen as problems at a later date. One current example of this is what Dunleavy (1981) has referred to as 'mass housing'. By mass housing, Dunleavy means the high-rise flats and large-scale housing estates (often located on the city periphery) that were built between the mid-1950s and the mid-1970s. These are now widely viewed as problems, but, when originally developed, they were seen as solutions to the problem of inner-city (pre-1919) slum housing.

While the housing problem, as a social construct, is always with us, this is not simply because absolute improvements in housing conditions have been accompanied by rising expectations about what is acceptable. It is true that housing problems in the modern city are much nicer ones to have than those of the Victorian city. But the definition of the housing problem cannot simply be reduced to technological and social progress. Although that progress is important, the social construction of the housing question—who defines it, how it is defined, and the solutions which that definition may imply—is essentially a political matter, and, consequently, a question of ideology.

The Housing Question in the Victorian City

Although the British state did not turn its attention to housing provision until the mid-nineteenth century, it is apparent that appalling housing conditions were not a new phenomenon, but had existed well before then (Burnett, 1986). To some extent, therefore, the emergence of 'the housing question', as it became known at the time, was a reflection of a change in attitudes towards conditions that had existed for decades, both in rural villages and in towns (see Holmans, 1987). Yet in part it was also a response to a material change in the *urban* housing situation, and, in particular, to the sheer scale and concentration of inadequate housing. For the rapid urbanization that occurred during the late eighteenth and early nineteenth centuries brought with it the development of appalling housing conditions on a wide scale (Ashworth, 1954; Gauldie, 1974; Wohl, 1977).

Many dwellings in the new and growing towns and cities were poorly designed or constructed and were built with shoddy materials. All too often space standards, natural lighting, and ventilation were very poor. Sewerage and water supply in many cases were inadequate if not wholly lacking. Individual dwellings were sometimes overcrowded and sharing of accommodation was widespread. And in central city locations, where land costs were very high, dwellings were often packed closely together in confined spaces (Ashworth, 1954). This urbanization was a product of the operation of market forces unfettered by government regulation.

From around 1840 onwards, a stream of official and unofficial reports was published, highlighting the urban housing question. These included, for example, Chadwick's Health of Towns report, Andrew Mean's *The Bitter Cry of Outcast London*, and the Royal Commission on the Housing of the Working Classes which reported in 1885. But despite the growing awareness of appalling housing conditions, the state at central and local level responded only slowly and with considerable reluctance. The reasons for this tardy response have been discussed elsewhere (see Gauldie, 1974; Wohl, 1977). However, it is worth stressing here that state intervention in the housing market did not fit in with the prevailing Victorian ideology of *laissez-faire* and self-help (see Fraser, 1981). Housing problems were seen as individual failures, even pathological in origin, which could (and should) only be solved by individual and private endeavour, not by the state.

Such intervention as there was during the nineteenth century mainly involved providing local authorities with discretionary rather than mandatory powers. Hence the adoption of these powers and the vigour with which they were used varied considerably between different local authorities. Most of these powers were regulatory in form and they generally had a public health orientation. For example, the Public Health Act, 1875, gave all local authorities the powers to lay down by-laws governing minimum standards for new housebuilding. The Artisans' and Labourers' Dwellings Act, 1868 (the Torrens Act), gave local authorities powers to demolish individual unfit dwellings. And the Artisans' and Labourers' Dwellings Improvement Act, 1875 (the Cross Act), allowed authorities to demolish groups of unfit dwellings and to build replacement dwellings (Yelling, 1986).

Housing Problems in the Twentieth Century

Thus the state's response to the urban housing question in the nineteenth century was limited and partial. And poor housing conditions were conceived essentially as a public health problem that could largely be tackled by the regulation of private provision rather than by subsidies or the provision of housing itself by the state. It was not until the First World War that housing (as opposed to public health) policy became established in Britain. In 1915 the war-time government reluctantly introduced rent controls in the privately rented sector in response to rent strikes that had followed rising rents in Glasgow and in other areas of acute housing shortage. In 1919 the post-war coalition government, having promised the nation during the 1918 general election 'homes fit for heroes' to live in, introduced Exchequer subsidies for council housebuilding. Subsidies were also introduced to encourage a revival of building for the private sector. The slump in housebuilding before 1914 and the cessation of construction during the war had left a severe housing shortage in most British cities, and widespread public demands for government action to deal with it. Swenarton (1981) and others (e.g. Merrett, 1979) have shown that the urgency with which the government introduced, and exhorted local authorities to implement, the homes for heroes' building programme was the result of a belief that social unrest over the housing question could develop into something much worse, possibly threatening the social order.

Rent controls and Exchequer subsidies for house-building were initially seen as temporary expedients which could be removed once 'normality' had returned. But far from withdrawing from housing provision, since 1919 the state has become ever more deeply involved, even if reluctantly. Although the precise extent and form of such intervention has varied over time, it has remained of central importance in housing provision.

Malpass (1986) has argued that the housing problem as it was understood by governments from the First World War up until the late 1960s was 'essentially about quantity, quality and price'. In consequence, housing policy was designed very largely to tackle these three elements of the problem. The balance of emphasis between the components varied over time. Particularly in the decade after the two world wars, the main thrust was geared towards achieving high levels of construction, to reduce the severe shortage that had developed during the hostilities. Then, when the urban housing shortage had abated, attention turned (in the 1930s and in the mid-1950s) to tackling the Victorian legacy of inner-city slum housing. This generally took the form of relatively large-scale clearance schemes, followed by redevelopment by local authorities on the cleared site or at peripheral urban locations.

The problem of price was a function of the relatively high production cost of housing compared with incomes, and was a recurrent theme throughout this period. For the most part, it was tackled on the supply side, by reducing the price of housing to the consumer (by means of subsidies, tax exemptions, and rent controls) to below its cost of provision. The alternative, but less used, mechanism was to boost demand by providing income supplements (such as rent rebates and allowances) which enabled households to pay the economic cost of their accommodation. In these ways, the state attempted to reduce the price that households had to pay for their housing to a level that they could reasonably be expected to afford.

Redefining the Housing Problem

Partly because of this extensive state intervention in housing provision, housing conditions have improved very considerably since the nineteenth century. Much of the worst housing constructed during the nineteenth century urbanization has now been demolished in slum-clearance schemes. Overcrowding has also been substantially reduced. As table 9.1 shows, the number of households living at more than 1.5 persons per room has fallen from 1,174,000 in 1931 to 109,000 in 1981. Similarly, the number of households lacking basic amenities (WC, hot and cold water, a bath, etc.) has also fallen considerably. For example, in 1947 5.2m. dwellings lacked a wash-hand basin, but by 1981 this had been reduced to 567,000. Again, the proportion of households in Great Britain lacking a fixed bath fell from 37.6 per cent in 1951 to 1.9 per cent in 1981. Internal standards have also improved. For example, in 1971 one-third of households had central heating and by 1981 this had risen to two-thirds.

Thus there is no doubt that, compared with the nineteenth century or even with the 1950s and 1960s, housing conditions have improved very

TABLE 9.1. Households living in crowded accommodation in England and Wales, 1931–1981 (thousands)

	Sharing households	Households not sharing	Total
1931	439	735	1,174
1951	233	431	664
1961	107	308	415
1971	47	179	226
1981	9	100	109

Note: 'crowded' includes all households living at more than 1.5 persons per room.

Source: Holmans, 1987, p. 135.

much in an absolute sense. Indeed, by 1971 there was even, for the first time, a crude surplus of dwellings over households. Some authors have detected a corresponding change of emphasis in official attitudes to the housing question during the late 1960s and early 1970s. Malpass (1986), for example, has argued that both Conservative and Labour governments began to present an optimistic, even complacent, interpretation of the housing situation. The twin problems of quantity and quality were now seen as substantially ameliorated, while the third component, the price of housing, was seen in a different light. From the late-1960s the emphasis in policy for dealing with poor housing conditions was switched away from slum clearance and rebuilding by councils to rehabilitation of the existing stock. Owner-occupation was increasingly seen, by both main parties, as the normal and natural tenure to which all households should aspire, while council housing had come to be regarded as an important but residual component of provision. Housing finance emerged during the 1970s as perhaps the most important policy issue in housing. But whereas previously the focus had been on the high cost of housing, the new emphasis was upon it being too low. As Malpass has put it, 'Whereas in the past it has been generally accepted that subsidies in the public sector were necessary to produce decent dwellings at rents that working class tenants could afford, in the early 1970s the government took a very different line. Now, apparently, far from housing being too expensive, tenants as a whole . . . were not paying enough' (Malpass, 1986, p. 7).

In 1972 the Conservative government passed the Housing Finance Act. This aimed simultaneously to reduce subsidies and increase rents in the council sector, while leaving subsidies to the owner-occupied sector untouched. Although the Act was repealed by the incoming Labour government in 1974, Labour set up a Housing Finance Review in 1975. Perhaps because it was wary of the electoral implications that a fundamental reform of housing finance would have, this review was subsequently diluted by widening it to an examination of housing policy as a whole. The resultant Green Paper was published in 1977 as the *Housing Policy Review* (DoE, 1977). According to Ball (1983, p. 3), the publication of this document marked 'the high point of post-war complacency over housing provision'. The government pronounced itself broadly satisfied with housing policy and proposed no major changes:

. . . it is a commentary on our times that housing is often discussed as though things were getting worse, when the facts do not support this view. We are better housed as a nation than ever before; and our standards of housing seem to compare well with those of similar and more prosperous countries. This should give pause to critics who start with an assumption that present arrangements have served and are serving badly (DoE, 1977, p. iv).

The conception of the housing problem which the *Housing Policy Review* outlined was not one of a nationwide phenomenon, but rather a series of small, localized problems. Further, such problems or difficulties were seen as essentially residual in nature and confined to the poor and to categories of 'special need' such as the elderly or the handicapped. The new consensus over housing tenure was confirmed, with the promotion of home ownership as the ideal and council housing as a second-best form of provision.

A New Housing Crisis?

The election of the Thatcher administration in 1979 marked a further readjustment of housing policy, and an altered presentation of the housing question. The newly elected Conservative government stressed the (crude) surplus of dwellings over households, refused to make projections of future housing need, and introduced substantial cuts in public sector housebuilding. The dominant thrust of housing policy between 1979 and 1986, however, was the promotion of home ownership (Booth and Crook, 1986). This policy was largely implemented by introducing, in the Housing Act 1980, a 'right to buy' for council tenants combined with generous discounts from the market value of houses thus sold. Between 1979 and 1986 one million council houses were sold, two-thirds of them under the right to buy legislation.

While the Conservative government was presenting home ownership as the answer to virtually all housing problems, some critics began to detect signs of a new 'housing crisis' (Ball, 1983; Harloe, 1987; Malpass, 1986). These authors argued that while substantial housing progress had undoubtedly been made over the decades, in the 1980s conditions had begun to deteriorate. Further, it was argued that many of these emerging problems were developing in the very sector of the market, owner-occupied housing, that the government was presenting as the holy grail. But the main problem, as these authors saw it, was the growing shortage of rented housing and the need to reform housing finance, which was biased in favour of home ownership. In the mid-1980s numerous reports (e.g. National Federation of Housing Associations, 1985; Archbishop of Canterbury, 1985) were published calling for a reform of housing finance and increased investment in housing to rent.

An examination of the empirical evidence does tend to support the view that in some respects the housing situation is deteriorating, although whether this amounts to a 'crisis' is debatable. As Malpass (1986) and others have pointed out, a significant housing shortage still exists. Once second homes, vacant properties and dwellings undergoing repair and improvement are deducted from the crude total, the surplus of dwellings over households turns into a deficit. Inevitably there are regional variations in the degree of housing pressure that exists. London has a particularly acute housing shortage, but the pressure of demand for housing is also a problem in the so-called British sun-belt, 'that swathe of tamed rurality which stretches between Bristol, Southampton and round and up to Cambridge' (Massey, 1983, p. 24). In this area of relative affluence, above average economic growth and low unemployment, house prices are rising at rates well above the increase in average earnings. Employers report particular difficulty in recruiting certain types of workers from other parts of the country because of the growing differential in house prices between the north and the south of the country (Conway and Ramsay, 1986). And the Department of the Environment

TABLE 9.2. Homeless households rehoused by local authorities in England, 1978–1986

	Number of households
1978	53,110
1979	57,200
1980	69,920
1981	70,010
1982	74,800
1983	78,240
1984	83,190
1985	93,980
1986	102,980

Source: DoE, 'Quarterly Homelessness Returns', 1979–87.

is under pressure from developers to release more land for house-building in London and the outer south-east in the face of opposition from the planners and the conservationist lobby.

Homelessness is also growing. The number of households accepted for rehousing by local authorities under the 1977 Homeless Persons Act has increased from 53,110 in 1978 to 102,980 in 1986 (table 9.2). This rise in 'official' homelessness has had an important effect upon access to local authority housing. Less households are being housed directly off the housing waiting list and an increasing proportion of all new council tenancies is being accounted for by the rehousing of homeless families. Thus the proportion of all new secure council tenancies in England accounted for by the homeless rose from one in eight in 1978/79 to one in five in 1984/85. The homelessness route into council housing is especially important in London, where it increased from one quarter to almost one half of all new secure tenancies over the same period (Central Statistical Office, 1986).

A further consequence of this rise in official homelessness is that many local authorities are placing homeless families in temporary accommodation such as bed and breakfast establishments, hostels and short-life dwellings prior to permanent rehousing. At 30 June 1986 there were 23,050 households placed in temporary accommodation by local authorities under the homelessness provisions of the Housing Act (DoE, 1987a). Of these, about half were in bed and breakfast establishments, a form of temporary accommodation that has been criticized as both unsuitable and expensive (Conway and Kemp, 1985; Audit Commission, 1986). Particularly in London, it is not uncommon for homeless households to spend over a year and sometimes several years in such 'temporary' accommodation before being permanently rehoused. Apart from the acknowledged health and fire risks that living in unsatisfactory bed and breakfast hostels can involve, lengthy stays can considerably disrupt the schooling of homeless families and make the provision of health services difficult. Diet can also be affected because of the lack of suitable cooking facilities (Conway and Kemp, 1985; Bonnerjea, 1986).

At the same time, there is growing evidence of what has been called an 'access crisis' (Kleinman and Whitehead, 1988). That is to say, a growing number of households, particularly unemployed single people and childless couples who do not qualify for help under the Homeless Persons Act, are finding it impossible to gain access to the formal housing market. Instead, they are having to resort to bed and breakfast accommodation, hostels, short-life housing and squats (Conway and Kemp, 1985). Evidence of the growing use of these forms of 'non-tenured' accommodation is partial but does tend to confirm it. For example, the number of supplementary benefit claimants living in what the Department of Health and Social Security calls 'ordinary board and lodging' accommodation increased from 49,000 in December 1979 to 139,000 in December 1984 (Conway and Kemp, 1985).

In some respects the condition of the housing stock is deteriorating. Although there has been a significant decrease in the incidence of dwellings lacking basic amenities and the number of unfit dwellings has also declined, the incidence of disrepair is growing. In the five-year period from 1976 to 1981 the number of dwellings in England that needed repairs costing in excess of £7,000 (in 1981 prices) increased by one-fifth (Gibson, 1986). Much of this increase took place in the owner-occupied sector and resulted from inadequate repair and maintenance activity on the part of home owners. This is a phenomenon that particularly affects low-income—or 'marginal'—home owners living in pre-1919 houses in the inner city and northern industrial towns. Many of these households are elderly or from ethnic communities, and their income is too low adequately to maintain their houses or deal with the problems of disrepair. The reality of marginal home ownership can thus contrast markedly with the comfortable image often attached to this tenure. Karn *et al.* (1985) found that house prices in inner Birmingham were increasing much more slowly than in the suburbs, thus effectively trapping inner-city marginal home owners at the bottom of the home ownership 'ladder'.

Disrepair in the council house sector is also growing, but there is an additional problem of design and construction faults in much of the system-built and other non-traditionally built stock owned by local authorities (Cantle, 1986). The total outstanding repair bill for English local authority housing in 1985 was estimated to be around £19b. (DoE, 1985). Local authorities estimated that 84 per cent of their stock needed some kind of renovation, with an average bill of £4,900 per dwelling.

Since 1979 there has been a rise in the number of households in arrears with their mortgage repayments as well as in the number of borrowers who have had their houses repossessed by the lender. For example, the number of repossessions by building societies increased more than four-fold between 1979 and 1984. And over the same period the number of borrowers who were between six and twelve months in arrears on their building society loan increased nearly five-fold (Karn *et al.*, 1985). The rise in unemployment since 1979 and the growing incidence of relationship breakdown appear to be two of the main reasons for this rise in mortgage arrears. Relationship breakdown (19 per cent) and mortgage arrears (10 per cent) were the immediate reasons for homelessness of nearly three out of every ten households accepted for rehousing under the homeless persons legislation in 1986 (DoE, 1987*a*).

Finally, over the past decade and more the problem of rundown and often difficult to let council estates has emerged. In a recent report, for example, the Audit Commission (1986, p. 5) stated that ' "Crisis" is a heavily over-worked word. Yet it is difficult to think of a more appropriate way to describe the state of much of the stock of 4.8 million council-owned dwellings in England and Wales . . . A combination of short-sighted national housing policies since the 1960s and shortcomings in local administration has produced a major management challenge . . .'. It is with the mass housing estates owned by some of the larger urban authorities that problems exist. These estates are located for the most part either in the inner city or on the suburban periphery and contain large numbers of deck access and high-rise flats (see Dunleavy, 1981). Apart from the disrepair and the design and construction faults that we have already mentioned, these estates often have few amenities such as shops and recreational facilities. They tend to suffer from high levels of empty properties and of rent arrears. Such 'problem estates' also often have high rates of unemployment and an above-average incidence of crime, vandalism, graffiti, and other indicators of alienation (Reynolds, 1986; Coleman, 1985).

Some critics have argued that the problems of council housing have been exacerbated by the introduction of the right to buy in 1980. Since the better-off tenants living in the most desirable properties are the most likely to buy their council house, the sector will take on, it is argued, a residual function, housing mainly low-income households in poor quality accommodation (English, 1982; Forrest and Murie, 1983). Even before 1980, council housing was beginning to house an increasing proportion of the very poor, but the evidence does support the view that sales will accelerate this trend. Thus, two out of five council-house buyers were skilled manual workers, compared with only one in five council tenants as a whole. And while more than eight out of ten buyers were in employment, this was true of less than one half of council tenants (Kleinman and Whitehead, 1987). While about one quarter of the council stock consists of flats, less than four per cent of all sales are in this category. Forrest and Murie have emphasized the geographical dimension to the pattern of sales. They found that 'Sales have in fact proceeded most rapidly in comfortable, affluent, less urbanised areas on the edges of cities. They are proceeding less rapidly in . . . areas . . . of inner-city deprivation or stigmatized council housing or in areas where the existing rates of home ownership are lowest' (Forrest and Murie, 1986, pp. 52, 54).

In addition to selling individual dwellings, some councils have privatized whole estates, often against the wishes of those living there. Unable to improve estates themselves because of government spending restrictions, or otherwise unwilling to do so, some councils such as Salford and Wandsworth have decanted the existing tenants to other council accommodation and sold the empty estate to a developer for improvement (often with the aid of government grants) and subsequent sale to owner-occupiers. Often the displaced residents have been unable to afford to purchase the improved houses which have sold at prices well above that which locals could afford. This has been the experience not only in London examples of privatization such as Wandsworth but also of the Trinity and Regents Road estates in Salford. This is therefore a late 1980s council sector example of 'gentrification', a process, usually associated with the private sector, which came to prominence in the early 1970s (Hamnett, 1973; Williams, 1976).

Combined with the continuing decline of the privately rented sector, the sale of council houses has led, according to some authors, to an increasing social polarization between an affluent majority of home owners and a immiserated and stigmatized minority of council tenants (Forrest and Murie, 1984). Saunders (1984) has taken this argument further in his critique of the housing classes thesis developed originally by Rex and Moore (1967) and to which he himself contributed (Saunders, 1978). Saunders (1984) now argues that the polarization of housing tenure is part of an emerging social cleavage in British society centred around the division between public and private modes of consumption. He argued that the privatization of welfare provisions, including housing, is intensifying this cleavage so much that consumption sector location may begin to become more important than class position as defined by the labour market. He further agues that housing tenure is the single most important aspect of consumption sector alignment. This is not only because of the psychological importance to the individual of owning her house but also because of the accumulative potential of home ownership (Saunders, 1984). Saunders's thesis has been criticized, not least by those who prefer to accord primacy to class structuration as determined by the labour market rather than consumption location (Forrest and Murie, 1986). Nevertheless, his argument is important because it emphasizes the need to see the current housing situation and housing policy in the light of the wider restructuring of the welfare state in Britain in the 1980s.

Public Attitudes to 'the Housing Crisis'

In the early 1980s, while the government presented a relatively complacent view of the housing outlook and paraded the growth of home ownership as a major policy success, an alternative image of incipient crisis was presented by a range of authors and bodies. Although the analysis and policy prescriptions of these critical reports and commentaries differed, the growing shortage of rented housing and (to a lesser extent) the management difficulties of rented housing were highlighted as the main problem areas.

Having outlined these two contrasting images of the housing situation and shown that, in some respects, conditions are deteriorating, it is interesting to examine public attitudes as revealed by the British Social Attitudes surveys. The 1985 survey certainly did not reveal any widespread perception of an emerging housing crisis (cf. Harloe, 1987). Only 9 per cent of respondents interviewed said that they were either 'very' or 'quite' dissatisfied with their own accommodation. And when shown a list of items of government expenditure, only 8 per cent cited 'housing' as their first priority for extra spending, while 15 per cent said it was their second priority. The overall conclusion of the survey in respect of housing was that it was a relatively low-profile subject generating fairly stable attitudes: 'in contrast to the position in the 1960s when housing was near the top of the political agenda, it is now a fairly uncontroversial area of social policy, exciting few strong views or major fluctuations in attitudes.' (Bosanquet, 1986, p. 146). Notwithstanding this overall conclusion, a significant minority of households were discontented with their housing circumstances, including 14 per cent of private tenants and 17 per cent of council tenants. Moreover, the 1985 survey, and that of 1983 which also explored the issue, did find 'strong evidence of pessimism' about conditions for council tenants (Bosanquet, 1986, p. 143). As table 9.3 shows, only about one-half of council tenants agreed with the statement that 'Council estates are generally pleasant places to live in.' And more than two-thirds agreed with the view that councils provide a poor standard of repairs and maintenance. These responses may

TABLE 9.3.   Council tenants' attitudes to council housing

	1983 (%)	1985 (%)
Councils give a poor standard of repair and maintenance:		
True	70	68
False	25	27
Council estates are generally pleasant places to live in:		
True	50	47
False	44	45

Source: Bosanquet, 1986, p. 143.

not add up to a 'crisis', but they certainly indicate considerable dissatis-faction with council renting. The Thatcher administration has been able to draw on this discontent to present a critique of council housing as part of its attempt to restructure the provision of rented housing more closely in line with its New Right ideology.

The Delegitimation of Council Housing

During its first two terms of office the over-riding goal of the Thatcher administration's housing policy was the extension of home ownership. The main policy instrument for achieving this was the right to buy for council tenants, though a number of other low-cost home ownership initiatives were also pursued (Booth and Crook, 1986). However, during 1986 the government began to turn its attention more closely to the pro-vision of rented housing. And following the Conservatives' re-election in 1987 a radical reform of housing policy was set in train. While the promotion of home ownership was still an important goal, the need to address the perceived problems of rented housing was seen as the most urgent issue.

The Thatcher administration thus began to present a revised inter-pretation of housing problems, not least in that it acknowledged that serious difficulties did exist in the provision of rented housing. But the analysis of the problem (and, therefore, also the policy prescriptions) as presented in its White Paper, *Housing: The Government's Proposals* (DoE, 1987b) was rather different from that of authors such as Malpass (1986) and Cantle (1986). For the critics, many of the problems of rented housing were a consequence of a lack of public investment. Public spending cuts had reduced public sector housebuilding considerably, from 132,000 in 1977 to 32,000 in 1986, and had reduced the local authorities' ability adequately to repair and maintain the existing stock.

For the Conservative government, the shortage of rented housing and the problems of housing management had two main causes. First, the shortage of rented housing was largely attributed to excessive controls. The main culprit here was seen to be rent regulation in the private sector. This had reduced profits from private renting, with the result that investors were unwilling to construct new rental housing and were unable to maintain their existing stock properly. Second, many of the problems of rented housing were presented as a consequence of the virtual monopoly of such housing enjoyed by local authorities. In a series of speeches (e.g. Waldegrave, 1987) and official documents (e.g. DoE, 1987b), municipal landlordism was presented as being excessively large in scale, remote from the tenants, insensitive to consumer wishes, and inefficient. Taken together, these factors were said to have reduced competition and also, therefore, tenant choice in the rental housing market.

The solution which followed from the Thatcher administration's analysis of the housing problem, therefore, was to deregulate the rented housing market and to reduce the ownership and control of rented housing by local authorities. Council housing was to be hived off to other owners, such as co-operatives, housing associations, and private landlords. The aim was presented as the creation of a pluralist, more market-oriented approach instead of the monopolistic, administrative system of rental housing provision that prevailed (DoE, 1987*b*). Taken together these changes represent the most fundamental reform of housing policy since the Second World War.

Concluding Remarks

This chapter has attempted to show that 'the housing problem' is not just a question of material conditions, whether in absolute or in relative terms. Of course, material conditions such as the ratio of dwellings to households, the provision of standard amenities, and the number of houses repossessed by the building societies, are important in determining the nature of the housing problem. But the way in which such factors are interpreted or presented and the policy 'solutions' to them which are proposed, are social constructs. Different interest groups, such a the Small Landlords Association, Shelter, or the National Association of Local Government Officers, will attempt to press their analyses and proposals for the problems and opportunities which they identify in housing. Similarly, the state at central and local level does not simply respond to housing problems in a neutral or benevolent way. Rather, the state is intimately connected with the social construction of the housing question.

These points are illustrated by the current policy debates over the future of council housing. The physical conditions and management difficulties of many large council housing estates are widely acknowledged. Yet analyses of the causes of these problems differ considerably, as do the proposed solutions. For the Left, the solutions include more resources and reform of the way in which council housing is managed, particularly through increased tenant involvement and decentralization of management from town hall to local estates. For the Right, including the present government, the solution is privatization. By mining a rich seam of discontent about paternalistic and inefficient council housing management, the Thatcher administration has been able to present the problem as the very existence of municipal landlordism. At the same time as attempting to delegitimate the public ownership of rented housing, the government has also striven to rehabilitate the image of the private landlord and to divest it of its associations with 'Rachmanism' (Kemp, 1987, 1988). It is worth recalling that one of the factors behind the introduction of subsidized local authority housing in the first place was the very failure of private landlords to provide adequate accommodation at rents working people could afford (Merrett, 1979). It is too early to say whether or not material improvements will result from the current reform of housing policy. What is clear is that the way in which rented housing is organized is set to change quite considerably. This will have important consequences not only for those who rent, or wish to rent, their home, but also for those who supply or wish to supply rented housing. It will also have implications for the way in which the housing question is perceived and debated.

References

Ashworth, W. (1954), *The Genesis of Modern British Town Planning* (Routledge and Kegan Paul: London).

Audit Commission (1986), *Managing the Crisis in Council Housing* (HMSO: London).

Ball, M. (1983), *Housing Policy and Economic Power* (Methuen: London).

Bonnerjea, L. (1986), *Homelessness in Brent* (Policy Studies Institute: London).

Booth, P., and T. Crook (eds.) (1986), *Low Cost Home Ownership* (Gower: Aldershot).

Bosanquet, N. (1986), 'Interim report: housing', in R. Jowell *et al.* (eds.), *British Social Attitudes: The 1986 Report* (Gower: Aldershot), 141–8.

Burnett, J. (1986), *A Social History of Housing* (2nd edn., Methuen: London).

Canterbury, Archbishop of (1985), *Faith in the City* (London: Church House Publishing).

Cantle, T. (1986), 'The deterioration of public sector housing', in P. Malpass (ed.), *The Housing Crisis* (Croom Helm: London), 57–85.

Central Statistical Office (1986), *Social Trends 1986* (HMSO: London).

Coleman, A. (1985), *Utopia on Trial* (Hilary Shipman: London).

Conway, J., and P. Kemp (1985), *Bed and Breakfast: Slum Housing of the Eighties* (SHAC: London).

—— and E. Ramsay, *A Job To Move* (SHAC: London).

DoE (Department of the Environment) (1977), *Housing Policy Review* (HMSO: London).

—— (1985), *An Inquiry into the Condition of Local Authority Housing Stock in England* (DoE: London).

—— (1987a), 'Quarterly Homelessness Returns: Results for Second Quarter 1987' (DoE: London).

DoE (Department of the Environment) (1987*b*), *Housing: The Government's Proposals* (HMSO: London).

Donnison, D., and C. Ungerson (1962), *Housing Policy* (Penguin: Harmondsworth).

Dunleavy, P. (1981), *The Politics of Mass Housing in Britain, 1945–1975* (Clarendon Press: Oxford).

English, J. (ed.) (1982) *The Future of Council Housing* (Croom Helm: London).

Forrest, R., and A. Murie (1983), 'Residualisation and council housing', *Journal of Social Policy*, 12: 453–68.

—— and A. Murie (1984), *Right to Buy? Issues of Need, Equity and Polarisation in the Sale of Council Houses*, Working Paper no. 39, School for Advanced Urban Studies (University of Bristol: Bristol).

—— and A. Murie (1986), 'Marginalization and subsidised individualism', *International Journal of Urban and Regional Research*, 10: 46–66.

Fraser, D. (1981), *The Evolution of the British Welfare State* (2nd edn., Macmillan: London).

Gauldie, E. (1974), *Cruel Habitations: A History of Working Class Housing 1780–1918* (Allen and Unwin: London).

Gibson, M. (1986), 'Housing renewal: privatisation and beyond', in P. Malpass (ed.), *The Housing Crisis* (Croom Helm: London), 86–124.

Hamnett, C. (1973), 'Improvement grants as an indicator of gentrification in inner London', *Area*, 5: 252–61.

Harloe, M. (1987), 'Manifestos for change', in M. Brenton and C. Ungerson (eds.), *Year Book of Social Policy 1986–7*, (Longman: Harlow), 196–224.

Holmans, A. E. (1987), *Housing Policy in Britain* (Croom Helm: London).

Karn, V., J. Kemeny, and P. Williams (1985) *Home Ownership in the Inner City* (Gower: Aldershot).

Kemp, P. (1987), 'The ghost of Rachman', *New Society*, 6 Nov., 13–15.

—— (1988), 'New policies for private renting', in P. Kemp (ed.), *The Private Provision of Rented Housing* (Gower: Aldershot), 175–85.

Kleinman, M. and C. M. E. Whitehead (1987), 'Local variations in the sale of council houses in England, 1979–1984', *Regional Studies*, 21:1–11.

—— and C. M. E. Whitehead (1988), 'The prospects for private renting in the 1990s', in P. Kemp (ed.), *The Private Provision of Rented Housing* (Gower: Aldershot), 96–123.

Malpass, P. (1986), 'From complacency to crisis', in P. Malpass (ed.), *The Housing Crisis* (Croom Helm: London), 1–23.

Massey, D. (1983), 'The shape of things to come', *Marxism Today*, Apr., 18–27.

Merrett, S. (1979), *State Housing in Britain* (Routledge and Kegan Paul: London).

NFHA (National Federation of Housing Associations) (1985), *Inquiry into British Housing* (NFHA: London).

Rex, J., and R. Moore (1967), *Race, Community, and Conflict* (Oxford University Press: London).

Reynolds, F. (1986), *The Problem Housing Estate* (Gower: Aldershot).

Saunders, P. (1978), 'Domestic property and social class', *International Journal of Urban and Regional Research*, 2: 233–51.

—— (1984), 'Beyond housing classes', *International Journal of Urban and Regional Research*, 8: 202–27.

Swenarton, M. (1981), *Homes Fit for Heroes* (Heineman: London).

Waldegrave, W. (1987), *Some Reflections on Housing Policy* (Conservative Party News Service: London).

Williams, P. (1976), 'The role of institutions in the inner London housing market', *Transactions of the Institute of British Geographers*, NS 1: 72–86.

Wohl, A. S. (1977), *The Eternal Slum* (Edward Arnold: London).

Yelling, J. A. (1986), *Slums and Slum Clearance in Victorian London* (Allen and Unwin: London).

10

Community Welfare Services in the Inner City

Sarah Curtis

This chapter is concerned with the special problems of providing community welfare services to the populations of the inner city. To some extent, similar issues confront health and social service agencies everywhere in the country, but they apply with particular force in highly urban areas. The cases taken as examples here are from inner London, whose characteristics are not all typical of other major urban areas in Britain. (Indeed, there are some features which make inner London a unique case.) However, in general the problems discussed here are most likely to occur in highly urbanized social and physical environments, and are relevant to the inner cities of all our major conurbations.

The welfare services given particular attention in this chapter are community health care provided by the National Health Service (NHS), and social services provided by the social service departments (SSDs) of local authorities. The focus is particularly on the interface between community health and social services, rather than the hospital sector, which is discussed in more detail in chapter 7. Although this represents a rather restricted definition of welfare services, there are important links with other services, such as local authority education and housing, and the voluntary and private sectors, and the challenges presented to health and social services in the inner city, which cannot be disassociated from those facing other parts of the welfare system, discussed elsewhere in this volume.

Themes in Urban Welfare Service Provision

The issues discussed in this chapter should not be interpreted purely as *social* problems. In fact, several may be better viewed as *institutional* problems, since they arise from the failure of the health and social services to adapt adequately to the particular requirements of inner-city populations. This is important, since it is more difficult to provide acceptable and appropriate services to those living in the inner city if they are persistently treated by the service agencies as problematic and deviant, simply by virtue of their special characteristics. This is especially true of ethnic minorities, who should be considered as a challenge inviting innovative response, rather than a problem to be somehow smoothed away. The discussion which follows distinguishes two particular features of inner-city populations: (a) the severity of social disadvantage for deprived urban residents, and (b) the diversity of the population. These have rather different implications for welfare service needs, although they often occur in combination.

Several forms of social and material disadvantage of a peculiar intensity coincide among deprived inner-city populations. The welfare services feel the impact in terms of a higher level of need and uptake of the care provided. No single theory of the roots of disadvantage is sufficiently broad to explain fully the causes of inner urban deprivation, which makes it all the more difficult to find an effective way to combat it.

There is also a great heterogeneity of urban populations which can result in highly differentiated service needs within quite small areas. Furthermore, populations are variable through time, because of their high spatial mobility, so that needs are constantly changing. Inner urban populations are not universally deprived, and it may be all the more difficult to tackle deprivation occurring in close juxtaposition with very privileged populations.

To be set against these features of the population are certain institutional aspects of the community health and welfare services in the inner city. The following discussion focuses especially on the lack of co-ordination between the various agencies responsible for health and welfare service provision, and with other agencies whose activities are relevant to welfare. Although the need for greater integration has long been recognized, it still remains in many respects a distant goal.

Two Case Studies

The following discussion uses two particular parts of inner London to illustrate the points outlined above. One of these is Tower Hamlets, located in London's East End. It corresponds to the district health authority (DHA) of Tower Hamlets, which is coterminous with the London borough (local authority) of Tower Hamlets. The other area is part of the Riverside district health authority in the West End of Central London, referred to here as the Victoria area. It was established in 1982 as a DHA in its own right, but since incorporated with parts of Hammersmith and Fulham to form a larger district. One of its features during recent years has therefore been a series of administrative changes in the NHS sector. The Victoria area covers the southern parts of two local authorities: Kensington and Chelsea, and Westminster. In Victoria, geographical areas of responsibility for health and for social services do not coincide, a point taken up below.

Different aspects of social disadvantage in the city

The two areas chosen as examples here are in some respècts unique, but at the same time they typify two rather different types of inner-city community recognized by Jarman (1981) in a review of health and social indicators in London. London's West End was characterized by highly mobile populations, with a high proportion of young adults, especially women, and large numbers of people in privately rented accommodation. The East End was distinguished by high proportions of households renting council homes, workers in unskilled or semi-skilled occupations, and various indicators reflecting poor health status.

The Victoria district corresponds to the West End type of area. Table 10.1 shows the demographic structure, with a high proportion of younger women. A high proportion of people present on census night were not living in private households or not resident in the district. The area also receives a large daily influx of commuters and visitors, numbering an estimated 350,000 people, considerably more than the resident population. The immigrant population born outside the UK was relatively large. No single group was especially predominant among these foreign-born populations, which included people from North America and European countries, as well as New Commonwealth countries, Bangladesh, and the Far East.

The housing tenure pattern was typical of London's West End, with a relatively high proportion of residents living in privately rented accommodation. Council rented accommodation was less common than elsewhere in London, although in parts of the district, large council estates provided homes for up to 30 per cent of the population of certain electoral wards. Housing conditions were variable, and quite a high proportion of the population lived in housing that lacked basic amenities. Also notable in this area was the high proportion of elderly living alone, and of single-person households generally. The occupational structure reflected a high proportion of professional and managerial grades, but a significant minority of the population were in unskilled or semi-skilled occupations or unemployed in 1981. The socio-economic structure may be summarized by the Underprivileged Area Score (Jarman, 1983), which combines eight census variables. When this composite score is standardized against an average value of zero for England and Wales, Victoria scores + 19, indicating a somewhat deprived population.

TABLE 10.1. Demographic and socio-economic statistics for Tower Hamlets and Victoria in the early 1980s (%)

	Tower Hamlets	Victoria
Population over 16		
males 16–29	16	14
30–44	10	12
45–64	16	12
65 +	7	10
females 16–29	15	17
30–44	10	13
45–64	15	10
65 +	11	15
Usually resident population not living in private households	3	9
Adult population born outside UK	20	22
Adult population who were		
owner occupiers	5	33
council tenants	82	16
privately renting or other	13	50
Households lacking sole use of bath and inside WC	4	10
Population living with more than one person per room	10	6
Household heads in		
non-manual occupations	24	73
manual occupations	76	26
Households with use of[a]		
central heating	56	71
washing machines	52	92
telephone	66	92
car	32	55
Households living above 3rd floor[a]	22	20

Note: Totals may not èqual 100 due to rounding.

Sources: Office of Population Censuses and Surveys, 1981; [a]Curtis, 1983, 1985.

By comparison, Tower Hamlets in 1981 was a more generally non-professional community, with higher proportions of manual workers. The housing tenure was predominantly council rented, and much of the housing was constructed to local authority standards, so that the proportion of homes lacking basic amenities was comparatively low. However, these figures disguise other deficiencies in the housing. Over one-fifth of the population live in high-rise flats above the third floor. The proportion having central heating is low and problems of cold, dampness, and condensation are common. Tower Hamlets households were less likely than those in Victoria to have use of facilities such as washing machines and telephones. In areas of privately rented housing, conditions were in many cases very poor. The average level of overcrowding in Tower Hamlets was also high.

The situation in Tower Hamlets is changing rapidly, owing to the explosion of private housing construction for owner-occupation in London's Dockland development zone. The occupants of this new housing are very different from the traditional East End community, being predominantly young professional people. For example, the Isle of Dogs had a population of 15,000 in 1981 and is expected to receive a large number of new residents by the end of the decade (variously estimated between 4,600 and 7,700). The contrasts between the occupants of the expensive new owner-occupied homes and those in the older council dwellings are stark.

Demographically, Tower Hamlets has a relatively high proportion of young men. The birth-rate is also very high, especially among the immigrant community. In 1985 the crude birth-rate was 19.4, compared with 13.1 in the country as a whole. In Tower Hamlets, as in Victoria, many ethnic groups are represented. Both districts have a Bangladeshi community, although this is much larger in Tower Hamlets, predominating in terms of absolute numbers over other immigrant groups in the district. In some parts of the district, over 75 per cent of the population may be classed as Bangladeshi by birth or ethnic background (Curtis and Ogden, 1986). The Underprivileged Areas Score for Tower Hamlets is + 55 when standardized against the rest of the country, which indicates that, according to this measure, the district is one of the most deprived in the country.

The two areas therefore show social disadvantage in the inner city to be a complex, multi-dimensional phenomenon. While some observers might wish to argue for a single over-arching explanation for social disadvantage in terms of material deprivation, we may draw on several models of disadvantage to express the processes at work, and the ways in which they influence the health of local populations. These include the cycle of deprivation, the operation of the labour market, differential access to housing, social and spatial segregation, relative poverty and alienation.

It is difficult to formulate effective social policies and programmes in dealing with this complexity of processes producing social disadvantage, in order to improve the health and welfare of inner-city populations. Programmes targetted at one part of the problem are unlikely to have much impact on the overall situation, but yet a co-ordinated attack on the combined forces leading to social inequality seems very hard to achieve.

Social Disadvantage and Health and Welfare

The processes which produce socio-economic differences have implications for health inequalities and the health and welfare needs of the populations of the two districts. In several respects, the population of Tower Hamlets has a relatively poor level of health and well-being. The overall standardized mortality ratio (SMR) in this district in 1985 was 113, the highest for district health authorities in London. People also experience more illness here than in other parts of London. Mortality from conditions such as respiratory disease, lung cancer and infectious diseases is comparatively high, especially among males (OPCS, 1981; Alderson, 1987). A survey in 1982 showed that adult residents have a relatively high propensity to report long-standing and recently restricting illness, and they report a higher than average prevalence of distress expressed in terms of pain, physical immobility, tiredness, sleep disturbance, emotional distress, and social isolation (Curtis, 1983) (table 10.2). The poor environmental and economic conditions experienced by many residents in this area imply higher than average needs for illness prevention and health promotion, as well as for curative health care.

In Victoria the resident population in general shows a rather better level of well-being. The mortality rate is similar to that for the country as a whole. The proportions of the population reporting morbidity and distress are lower than in Tower Hamlets. However, those from less

TABLE 10.2. Measures of ill-health and distress in Tower Hamlets and Victoria (%)

Survey respondents reporting	Tower Hamlets	Victoria
Long-standing illness	45	33
Recently restricting illness	16	14
Lack of energy	29	22
Pain	22	15
Emotional distress	46	32
Sleep disturbance	46	35
Social isolation	23	13
Physical immobility	25	19
Total no. of respondents	360	441

Note: long-standing illness covers 'long-standing illness, disability or infirmity'; recently restricting illness is morbidity which restricted activities in the two weeks before interview. The questions used were those also asked in the General Household Survey. The other data on different dimensions of distress were obtained using the Nottingham Health Profile.

Sources: Curtis, 1983, 1985.

privileged social groups (manual workers, council tenants, people without a household car) report more illness than wealthier residents. As already noted, the district is variable in terms of social profile, and areas which are relatively deprived include more residents reporting health problems such as pain and emotional distress and have higher mortality rates (Curtis, 1985). The health and social agencies providing for the Victoria population are therefore faced with a complex pattern of needs. Among the generally rather affluent population there is a significant number of less privileged and socially isolated residents who are not very 'visible' but to whom it may be necessary to provide outreach services (e.g. the large numbers of elderly living alone). Certain types of socio-medical pathology are particularly common among the Victoria population, for example drug abuse, venereal diseases and suicide or para-suicide. There is a relatively high need for some specialized forms of care for problems such as psychiatric disorders, drug abuse, sexually transmitted diseases, and AIDS. At the same time, the highly transient population, including commuters and tourists not resident locally, may need to use facilities such as accident and emergency services.

Welfare needs and service activity

Although a considerable amount of information exists about service activity by health and local authorities, it is difficult to determine the extent to which patterns of provision are a true reflection of local population needs. This is partly because levels of service provision are governed by local policy as well as by demands made by clients, and because the resources for health and welfare care are always finite and less than the amount of care which is required. Also, it is often difficult to determine whether services are used by people living locally or other clients. This is especially true of hospital patients, since the teaching hospitals such as the London Hospital in Tower Hamlets, and the Westminster Hospital in Victoria, draw patients from far beyond the district to make use of specialized medical services.

Furthermore, 'health behaviour' (behaviour intended to protect, promote, or maintain health) (Harris and Guten, 1979) varies between social groups. Those who are less privileged typically have rather low expectations for health and welfare, and may to some extent accept ill-health as part of normal life rather than a problem to be acted upon (Cornwell, 1984; Blaxter and Paterson, 1982; Pill and Stott, 1982). There is also evidence that the less privileged clients of health and social services may not always receive the same treatment or quality of care as others more able to communicate with service professionals (Cartwright and Anderson, 1981; Boulton *et al.*, 1986). Thus if higher levels of service use are recorded among disadvantaged populations, this may not fully reflect the greater burden of morbidity they experience.

Nevertheless, services are to some extent sensitive to local needs, and we can distinguish certain features about health and welfare provision which reflect the special needs of the populations in the two areas considered here. Studies in both North-east Thames (Bates, 1983) and North-west Thames regions indicate that inner-London populations with higher levels of mortality and social deprivation also have higher local hospitalization rates (see also Golding *et al.*, 1986). This is partly, but not entirely, explained by the fact that in inner-city communities, which are generally well served with hospitals, access to hospital beds is higher than average.

Studies of social service clients have also shown that social and economic deprivation are associated with an increased propensity to use personal social services (Curtis, 1981). Children living in socio-economically deprived families are more likely to come into the care of the local authority. Elderly people living alone are more likely to require home help provision.

The high levels of ill-health in Tower Hamlets are partly reflected in relatively high rates of use of some health and social services, as indicated by the statistics in tables 10.3 and 10.4. The community health survey in 1982 showed that while the proportion who had been hospitalized over the last year was similar to that recorded for other areas, the percentage who reported they had used outpatients services over the

TABLE 10.3. Some measures of health-care use in Tower Hamlets and Victoria

	Tower Hamlets	Victoria	Britain[a]
Survey respondents over 16 (%) who had consulted an NHS GP in the last 2 weeks	16	8[a]	12
been a hospital outpatient in the last 3 months	19	14	12
been an inpatient in the last year	13	12	9[c]
Total no. of respondents	370	450	32,042

[a]3% of respondents in Victoria had consulted a doctor privately.

Sources: Curtis, 1983, 1985; [b]data from the *General Household Survey 1981*; [c]data from the *General Household Survey 1984* (OPCS, 1986).

TABLE 10.4.   Expenditure and provision by local authority personal social
services departments in 1985/86

	Tower Hamlets	Kensington and Chelsea[a]	Westminster[a]	England and Wales[b]
Total expenditure (£000s)	20,866	19,193	29,949	3,029,453
% total expenditure on:				
Fieldwork	12	13	12	11
Children	27	24	23	18
Elderly	35	27	25	38
Physically handicapped	5	2	3	4
Mentally handicapped	5	6	6	10
Mentally ill	2	3	3	1
Total population (000s)	147.1	137.6	179.1	49923.5
% population under 18	24	15	15	24
% population over 65	15	14	17	15
Expenditure on social services (£ per capita)	142	139	167	61
Expenditure on children (£ per capita under 18)	160	224	256	46
Expenditure on elderly (£ per capita over 65)	330	264	245	154

[a]Kensington and Chelsea, and Westminster, are the boroughs responsible for the population of Victoria district, although their responsibilities also stretch outside this area.
[b]based on data for 112 of the 116 authorities.

Source: CIPFA, 1986.

three months preceding the survey was higher. The proportion who
recorded recent consultations with a general practitioner was also relatively high in Tower Hamlets.

The total per caput expenditure on personal social services in Tower
Hamlets was high compared with the country as a whole (see table 10.4),
and was above the average for inner London authorities generally
(£131 per capita in 1985/86). The borough spent a high proportion of

its social services budget in 1983/84 on children and the elderly. The higher expenditure reflects both the relatively high level of provision of care and the higher cost of providing services in inner London.

In Victoria, a smaller proportion of survey respondents reported use of hospital outpatient services than in Tower Hamlets, although there is some evidence that the total number of attendances reported was rather similar, because patients made more return visits. As in Tower Hamlets, a high proportion of outpatient attendances were to accident and emergency departments, rather than specialist clinics. It is therefore likely that in both areas, the pressure on outpatient services, especially accident and emergency, is comparatively high, and this may reflect difficulty of access to alternative forms of health care. Overall, fewer people in Victoria reported recent GP consultations on the NHS, although 3 per cent reported private consultations. The Victoria area is known to have rather high proportions of people not registered with a doctor under the NHS (about 9 per cent of adults generally, and as much as 30 per cent in some areas; Bone, 1984). This has implications for the accessibility of general practitioners' care, and may in part explain the lower consultation rate and the high rate of use of accident and emergency departments in the District.

Two different authorities are responsible for social services provision in the Victoria district, and these authorities also provide services for people living outside Victoria. Thus it is difficult to estimate precisely the input to the Victoria population. Expenditure on social services in the two boroughs of Kensington and Chelsea and Westminster are shown in table 10.4. As in Tower Hamlets, provision and expenditure are above average for the country as a whole. A smaller proportion of total expenditure was on service provided to the elderly than in Tower Hamlets, but expenditure on children and the mentally ill was comparatively high. In these boroughs, especially in Westminster, there was also a relatively high level of expenditure on grants to voluntary organizations and community groups. Westminster has a policy of encouraging voluntary organizations to provide services such as home help to the elderly which are normally provided by the authority itself, and is considering extending this practice to other services.

Heterogeneity and change: implications for welfare provision

Perhaps the most striking feature of the diversity in inner London's population is its varied ethnic composition. The needs of ethnic minorities for health and social care are distinctive because of cultural factors influencing ideas about health and welfare, because they are often subject to social and economic deprivation detrimental to health, and because factors such as language barriers and racial discrimination can limit their access to services.

Some ethnic minorities are highly concentrated in parts of the inner city, and present a particular challenge to the welfare services. In Tower Hamlets, for example, a good deal of effort is focused on attempts to adapt services to the special needs of Bangladeshis, who form the largest ethnic group, and have received attention nationally as well as locally (Silverstone, 1978; Curtis and Ogden, 1986). More scattered minority groups tend to receive less specific attention. Nevertheless, there are pressing needs among such minority groups as Chinese, Afro-Caribbeans and Africans in inner London (Tower Hamlets Health Inquiry, 1987; Francis, 1985). These small ethnic groups often depend on voluntary and community self-help groups for health and welfare support, rather than statutory agencies. It seems likely that by the time the health and welfare services have adjusted their activities to the current needs of ethnic minorities, circumstances and requirements will have changed. For example, much of current effort is directed toward provision for women and children. (Tower Hamlets currently has one of the highest birth-rates in the country, largely due to the high rates among the immigrant communities.) However, health and social services are already having to give thought to the provision of care for elderly people, who will be a rapidly growing group in the years to come (Tower Hamlets Health Inquiry, 1987; Blakemore, 1983; Norman, 1985).

Rapid demographic change is also a feature of other population groups in the districts considered here. In Victoria, for example, the total population has been declining quite rapidly (by a third over the period 1971–81). While the downward trend resulting from out-migration is expected to continue, the population predictions are variable, and have not been sufficiently reliable for forward planning purposes. Furthermore, not all groups in the population are dwindling at the same rate. For example, the number of men over sixty-five fell by only 5 per cent during 1971–81. As the general exodus of the population continues, certain 'residual' groups, such as the elderly living alone, and ethnic minority populations, increase in relative importance (Ingram, 1983; Warnes and Law, 1983). These changes have implications for the nature of needs of local residents and influence the ways in which resources need to be used.

This dynamic character of inner cities in terms of demographic trends and ethnic structure is compounded by the variable socio-economic profiles of the population over time. The 'yuppification' of London's East End by a young, upwardly mobile incoming population is a new trend which transforms the traditional picture of universal deprivation and carries implications for health and social services. Little attention has been given hitherto by the London Docklands Development Corporation to the impact of the newcomers on welfare services (Church and Curtis, 1989), who are likely to be more demanding and articulate than the present population, and may expect modern, high quality health centres and hospital facilities. It is also possible that these new residents may exert pressure for improved environmental conditions, community centres, etc.

For the present, the typical incomers can be appropriately dubbed 'DINKS' (dual income, no kids). This very mobile group might move on to other areas before having children, to be replaced by other young childless households. Thus, at least in the short term, the newcomers would not be expected to make immediate demands for nurseries, playgroups, or facilities for the elderly. On the one hand, the new residents will be competing with existing residents for some of the best of the local services provided, and on the other hand, they may have priorities for welfare resource expenditure which are different from those of the present inhabitants. It has been shown that often the more privileged members of society are particularly adept in gaining from the welfare system (Le Grand, 1982) and it would not be surprising if the newcomers to Tower Hamlets prove to be successful in deriving the greatest benefits from local public provision at the expense of the older, less privileged community.

Institutional Barriers to Change

The preceding discussion has illustrated how certain characteristics of inner-city populations such as deprivation, heterogeneity, and rapid change influence the pattern of need for welfare services. The overall effect is to produce generally high levels of need for care in these areas, and some needs which are rather peculiar to the inner city. Against this background, we may note some institutional characteristics which restrict the capacity of the system to provide adequately for local population needs. These are considered here under two headings: problems of resource allocation and problems of organization and co-ordination.

Resources for care in the inner city

A number of factors combine to make the resources of inner London welfare agencies inadequate for the task they face. These factors include the difficulty of staff recruitment and the need to offer particular incentives to those working in the inner city, and the national and regional processes of resource redistribution in the public sector which tend to shift resources away from inner London, in spite of the relatively high costs of meeting local needs in the capital.

Health and social services departments face considerable problems of staff recruitment, especially into nursing, health visiting, and social work. This partly reflects what is seen as a particularly intense and difficult workload for the caring professions in inner cities. The Joint Working Party on the Primary Health Care Team (JWPPHCT, 1981) identified the problems for members of these teams working in Britain's inner cities as unpleasant and threatening urban environments and difficulties of contacting clients and coping with their very challenging health and welfare problems. Work by Jarman (1983) and colleagues and a British Medical Association report (BMA, 1987) show that doctors also feel that inner-city deprivation has an effect on their potential workload.

Additional factors which contribute to these problems are relatively poor pay compared with other professions, the lack of affordable accommodation for employees moving to London, and the competing opportunities in the private sector, which is particularly well developed in the London area (Griffiths, Raynor, and Mohan, 1985). The failure to recruit staff from among ethnic minority populations living locally is a particular aspect of recruitment in the inner city.

The response of the health and welfare services to the needs of ethnic minorities has been slow and rather limited in scope. For Bangladeshis in Tower Hamlets there has been some progress in the provision of interpreters, the dissemination of public information literature in Bengali script, and the provision of more suitable hospital diets for Muslim requirements. The Maternity Services Liaison Scheme has helped to improve the care of mothers and young children. However, the induction of Bangladeshi staff into the services has progressed more slowly.

Even for longer established ethnic minorities such as West Indians, Indians, and Pakistanis it is apparent that there is a failure to respond to minority needs which amounts to institutionalized racism in health and social services. This is likely to persist as long as recruitment of personnel from among these minorities is so small (Hughes *et al.*, 1984).

In the field of personal social services, many of London's inner-city local authorities also have policies for recruitment of more staff from the ethnic minorities. However, Pilkington (1987) has commented that the mere existence of policies of equal opportunities for employment, of the type adopted by Westminster council, cannot ensure the desired pattern of employment. Westminster has no system to monitor the ethnic profile of its workforce. This is contrasted with the position in Brent, where a race equality unit is able to evaluate progress towards a more proportionate representation of the local black population. In Tower Hamlets, recruitment is organized through the social service divisions, and although there is some central monitoring of the ethnic background of applicants for social service posts, there are limits to the degree to which central intervention in recruitment is possible.

Campaigns to take into account the cultural background of children in the care of inner-city authorities in placement represent another aspect of the recruitment problem (Cheetham, 1982). In Tower Hamlets, for example, placement with racially matched foster families is considered desirable, but suitable families are often unavailable locally. In some cases, children must be placed with families living outside the area. The Social Service Department seeks to provide a family placement for children in care in preference to a lengthy residential placement, and will generally give this objective priority over considerations of ethnic matching.

More innovative approaches to recruitment are necessary to facilitate the induction of more black people into the caring professions, especially at the more senior levels. In Tower Hamlets, for example, an access-to-nursing course, providing preliminary bilingual training, is an example of the type of scheme which may have success in recruiting more Bangladeshis into the nursing service. However, in the short term, these schemes require some additional resources, or at least redeployment of expenditure in order to be effective. Thus the problems of recruitment are among the factors which may make health and welfare provision in inner London relatively costly.

With respect to health care, other factors which contribute to higher costs include the difficulties of maintaining an efficient operation in facilities which are old and outmoded. These problems have been graphically described in the context of hospital services in Haringey by Davidson (1986). In areas where institutional care is costly, it is more difficult to release funds for redeployment to the community, especially in a general climate of budgetary constraint. Detailed study of social service establishments shows that the factors influencing the wide variations in costs of providing care are complex (Knapp, 1984), but in the case of children's homes (Knapp and Smith, 1985) or of residential homes for the elderly (Darton and Knapp, 1984) it does appear that factors such as variations in wage levels, the type of client being cared for and the scale and design of the institution all play some part. Thus the problems experienced in the institutional sector of welfare provision have implications for care in the community.

Although the factors considered above imply a need for relatively generous resources for health and welfare, the systems of resource allocation are tending to produce a reduction of resources in real terms available in inner London. One contributory factor has been the national and regional systems for allocating NHS resources, the effects of which are described in chapter 7. In 1984/85, for example, Tower Hamlets DHA faced a cut in real revenue income of 0.7 per cent and Victoria lost 1.5 per cent (Wiles, 1984). Tower Hamlets is currently looking for ways of cutting £2m. from its budget 1987/88, and Riverside is seeking ways to reduce the district health budget by £3m. by 1994.

The budgets for personal social services and for other local authority services for deprived and minority populations in inner London have also been reduced in real terms. This is a result in some cases of central government policies enforced through rate capping, but also of changes in local borough policy. Added to these reductions are the withdrawal of funds previously provided by the Greater London Council, which are particularly important for voluntary groups catering for minorities in London (Hinton, 1984). Urban Programme funding once contributed significantly to welfare service provision, but more recent policy for the inner-city partnership scheme has been to direct funds towards projects stimulating economic regeneration (Higgins *et al.*, 1983).

Organization and co-ordination of welfare services

The division of responsibilities between health and local authorities, and between different departments within these two agencies, is an important institutional factor affecting the local response to population welfare needs, because of the persistent failure to co-ordinate health and welfare functions locally to ensure appropriate policies and service provision. This is particularly problematic in view of the processes of de-institutionalization and decentralization of welfare provision that are now taking place.

The 'new public health movement' currently gathering force in Britain (Smith, 1987) looks to the processes leading to social deprivation and social inequalities in health discussed above, and draws attention to the fact that housing, education, and youth training are all activities of local authorities which can have significant health and welfare outcomes. Concentration only on reactive health and welfare provision will not do much to ameliorate the processes leading to social deprivation. However, the present administrative system presents barriers to a more integrated response to public health problems.

The lack of liaison channels between housing and education departments and health authorities is an obstacle to initiatives to improve environmental and public health. Although the Association of

Metropolitan Authorities is encouraging the establishment of health committees in many local authorities of inner-city areas, the scope of their activities is very varied. Tower Hamlets, for example, has only recently constituted such a committee, which will have less than full committee status.

Even the links between health and social service departments are too weak to permit good co-ordinated planning of community care for the frail and sick. Community health and social services became fully separate in the wake of the Seebohm proposals. The principles underlying these recommendations were a clear differentiation between the social and medical professions, as well as a greater degree of variety in social work. The new 'generic' social worker was supposed to bring a more holistic approach to care of families with social difficulties, rather than specializing in certain types of individuals, such as children in care.

However, there has always been some uneasiness about the distinction between community health and social care. The Merrison report drew attention to the debate, and rehearsed once more the various arguments for and against different combinations of responsibility. Possibilities considered included the provision of social services by health authorities or the provision of health services through local government. These solutions presented difficulties in terms of the equity of geographical provision, local accountability of statutory agencies, and the working relationships of social and medical professionals.

Another strategy considered was the separate allocation of responsibility for different client groups to health and social services. The Merrison report pointed out the difficulty of retaining a holistic approach to welfare provision under such a system. However, more recently the Audit Commission report (Audit Commission, 1986) raised again the possibility of reallocation of responsibility for the elderly, disabled, and mentally ill (Millar, 1987). Under these proposals, provision to the elderly would be through a joint management board co-ordinating health and social services. The mentally ill would be the responsibility of the health authorities, while it has been suggested that the handicapped should be provided for by local authorities.

Some attempts have been made to forge links between health and local authorities by means of joint consultative committees and joint care planning teams responsible for initiatives which would make a co-ordinated response to the challenges of providing community care. The rather gradual growth of joint planning documented, for example, by the DHSS (1985) (see also Wistow and Fuller, 1983, 1986). The National Audit Office identified three factors hindering joint planning: the different planning timescales operating in DHAs and local authorities; the accountability and management structures of local authorities which do not allow sufficient power to local authority officers; and disparities in geographical coverage. The last problem is well illustrated in the two study areas considered here by the lack of correspondence in jurisdictional partitioning for health and welfare activities.

Victoria health district after the 1982 boundary revisions represented a typical example of dislocation in jurisdictional partitioning, since it covered the southern part of two separate London boroughs. The subsequent creation of the Riverside Health District has caused further administrative upheaval and brought a third borough, Hammersmith and Fulham, into the picture. Joint planning by the health authority with so many different authorities is a formidable task.

Tower Hamlets exemplifies the problem of the parallel processes of decentralization of welfare responsibility. The health district and local authority boundaries correspond, but the recent process of sub-division of these into neighbourhoods for local government functions and into localities for health-care planning raised further questions about co-ordination of services at the very local level. The local authority is devolving to seven neighbourhoods, while for health-care purposes a division into four 'patches' was proposed. This reflects the difficulty of identifying multi-purpose geographical partitions for the organization of different services, given that the appropriate scale for organizing local welfare services will vary to some extent according to the nature of the activity.

The next stage in the decentralization process should include liaison to co-ordinate points of access to health and other welfare services, perhaps at joint centres used by the health and local authority, which might also house key management personnel for both agencies. The decentralization of services therefore requires spatial as well as bureaucratic co-ordination, and the application of geographical techniques for administrative partitioning and facility location are relevant to the process.

In the future, as we move towards a national policy climate favouring greater privatization of welfare production, and, as in the case of Westminster, more dependency on the voluntary and informal sectors, the respective roles of health and social service departments may change again from providers of care to contractors responsible only for the commissioning and co-ordinating of services supplied by private organizations. In the case of residential care for the elderly this is already a reality: 47 per cent of elderly people supported by the local authorities of Kensington and Chelsea and Westminster in 1983/84 were in homes provided by other local authorities, or voluntary or private homes. It seems likely that the division of public sector responsibilities for health and social care will continue to be a problem, and that joint planning will need to involve a wider range of participants in the voluntary and private sector than hitherto (Harding, 1986).

Conclusions; Widening the Debate on Welfare Policy

The diversity and dynamic character of inner-city populations in Britain have always made them the focus of social, political, and bureaucratic change and reform in the quest for a better level of welfare for all members of society. However, the preceding discussion has shown that in spite of the progress which has been made, social deprivation in the inner city persists, and the public sector institutions have not succeeded in developing sufficiently flexible and sensitive responses to the special needs of local populations in the inner city. Recent national policy reactions to the 'problem' of the inner cities have abandoned investment in welfare services as a means to better welfare in favour of a strategy of economic regeneration. This seems too simplistic to have a real impact on what has been described here as a very complex set of processes producing disadvantage for some people living in the inner city. Therefore the results do not appear likely to be very satisfactory for those with the lowest levels of well-being.

We can only expect to see real improvements in public health and welfare if these become priority objectives for social and economic policies. Even within agencies such as the NHS, and local authority social service departments, which have welfare as their main aim, institutional rigidities and the exigencies of crisis management make it difficult to pursue welfare objectives single-mindedly. In the case of Tower Hamlets, this was clearly demonstrated in the report of the Tower Hamlets Health Inquiry (1987). Increased public participation in the planning process for community welfare services may help to redress this problem by shifting the balance of priorities towards policies designed to have a more direct impact on local needs. In Tower Hamlets, the Tower Hamlets Health Strategy Group has been established as a broad alliance of representatives from the statutory agencies, voluntary and community bodies and the public, with a remit to pursue the recommendations of the Health Inquiry. In Pimlico, Victoria, a committee was set up comprising local residents, voluntary sector representatives and health and social service professionals. In both cases part of the objective was to provide a forum to discuss local health and welfare needs. It is to be hoped that by widening the debate, the welfare of inner London's population will begin to receive the priority attention it deserves. Given the severity of the public health and welfare problems considered here, it makes social, economic, and political sense to place the public health and welfare issue much higher on the policy agenda, both locally and nationally.

References

Alderson, M. (1987), 'The use of area mortality', *Population Trends*, 47: 24–33.

Audit Commission (1986), *Making a Reality of Community Care* (HMSO: London).

Bates, T. (1983), *Patient Census Study: Social Factor Analysis*, Report 1249 (Northeast Thames Regional Health Authority Management Services: London).

Blakemore, K. (1983), 'The state, the voluntary sector and new developments in provision for the old of minority racial groups', *Ageing and Society*, 5(2): 175–90.

Blaxter, M. and E. Paterson (1982), *Mothers and Daughters: A Three-Generational Study of Health Attitudes and Behaviour* (Heinemann Educational: London).

BMA (British Medical Association) (1987), *Deprivation and Ill-Health*, BMA Board of Science and Education Discussion Paper (BMA: London).

Bone, M. (1984), *Registration with General Medical Practitioners in Inner London* (HMSO: London).

Boulton, M., D. Tuckett, C. Olson, and A. Williams (1986), 'Social class and the general practice consultation', *Sociology of Health and Illness*, 8(4): 325–50.

Bourne, L. (1980), *The Geography of Housing* (Edward Arnold: London).

Bramley, G. (1979), 'The inner city labour market', in C. Jones (ed.) *Urban Deprivation and the Inner City* (Croom Helm: Beckenham), 63–91.

Cartwright, A., and J. Anderson (1981), *General Practice Revisited* (Tavistock: London).

CIPFA (Chartered Institute of Public Finance Accountants) (1984), *Personal Social Services Statistics, 1983–1984 Actuals* (CIPFA: London).

Cheetham, J. (ed.) (1982), *Social Work and Ethnicity* (George Allen and Unwin: London).

Church, A., and S. Curtis (1989), 'London Docklands and health care planning', *London Journal*, forthcoming.

Cornwell, J. (1983), *Hard Earned Lives: Accounts of Health and Illness from East London* (Tavistock: London).

Curtis, S. (1981), 'Review notes on factors relating to risk of admission to care among children in the community', PSSRU discussion paper 1, Personal Social Services Research Unit (University of Kent: Canterbury).

—— (1983), 'Intra-urban variations in health and health care: the comparative need for health care survey of Tower Hamlet and Redbridge' (Queen Mary College: London).

—— (1985), *Community Health Survey of Victoria District: Final Report* (Queen Mary College: London).

—— and P. Ogden (1986), 'Bangladeshis in London: a challenge to welfare', *Revue européene des migrations internationales*, 2:136–49.

Darton, R., and M. Knapp (1984), 'The cost of residential care for the elderly:

the effects of dependency, design and social environment', *Ageing and Society*, 4(2): 157–83.

Davidson, N. (1987), *A Question of Care: The Changing Face of the National Health Service* (Michael Joseph: London).

DHSS (Department of Health and Social Security) (1985), *Progress in Partnership* (HMSO: London).

—— (1986), *Primary Health Care: An Agenda for Discussion*, Cmnd. 9771 (HMSO: London).

Edwards, J., and R. Batley (1978), *The Politics of Positive Discrimination: An Evaluation of the Urban Programme 1967–1977* (Tavistock: London).

Francis, W. (1985), 'Do not let their quietness deceive', *Community Care*, 564: 23 May, 22–4.

Golding, A., S. Hunt, J. McEwen (1986), 'Health needs in a London district', *Health Policy*, 6: 175–84.

Home Affairs Committee (1986), *Bangladeshis in Britain* (HMSO: London).

Griffiths, B., G. Raynor, and J. Mohan (1985), *Commercial Medicine in London* (Greater London Council: London).

Harding, T. (1986), 'More progress needed in the partnership', *Health Service Journal*, 11 Dec., 614.

Harris, D., and S. Guten (1979), 'Health-protective behaviour: an exploratory study', *Journal of Health and Social Behaviour*, 20(1): 17–29.

Higgins, J., N. Deakin, J. Edwards, and M. Wicks (1983), *Government and Urban Poverty: Inside the Urban Policy-making Process* (Basic Blackwell: Oxford).

Hinton, N. (1984), 'The role of the voluntary sector', *London Journal*, 10 Jan., 55–8.

Hughes, J., A. McNaught and I. Pennell (eds.) (1984), *Race and Employment in the NHS* (King Edward's Hospital Fund: London).

Hunter D. and Wistow G. (1987) *Community Care in Britain: Variations on a Theme* (King Edward's Hospital Fund: London).

Ingram, D. (1983), 'Changes in the size and age structure of London's population, 1971–1981', *Geography*, 68: 56–60.

Jarman, B. (1981), *A Survey of Primary Care in London*, Occasional Paper 16 (Royal College of General Practitioners: London).

—— (1983), 'Identification of underprivileged areas', *British Medical Journal*, 286: 1705–9.

JWPPHCT (Joint Working Party on the Primary Health Care Team) (1981), *The Primary Health Care Team* (DHSS: London).

Kings Fund Centre (1987), *Planned Health Services for Inner London: Back-to-Back Planning: Report on the Regional Plans for Inner London's Health Authorities* (King Edward's Hospital Fund: London).

Knapp, M. (1984), *The Economics of Social Care* (Macmillan: London).

—— and J. Smith (1985), 'The costs of residential child care: explaining variations in the public sector, *Policy and Politics*, 13(2): 127–54.

Le Grand, J. (1982), *The Strategy of Equality: Redistribution and the Social Services* (Allen and Unwin: London).

Millar, B. (1987), 'Options in community care', *Health Service Journal*, 27 Aug., 984.

Nocon A. (1987), 'Where there's a will, there's a way', *Health Service Journal* 4 June 1987, 640–1.

Norman, A. (1985), *A Triple Jeopardy: Growing Old in a Second Homeland* (Centre for Policy on Ageing: London).

OPCS (Office of Population Censuses and Surveys) (1981), *Area Mortality Decennial Supplement 1969–1973* (HMSO: London).

Osborn A. (1975), 'The day care of children under 5 in the city of Westminster'. Summary of a report of a survey conducted in March/April 1974 (Clearing House for Local Authority Social Services Research).

Pilkington, E. (1987) 'Race Equality Units at Work', *New Society*, Nov., special supplement, p. 2.

Pill, R., and N. Stott (1982), 'Concepts of illness causation and responsibility: some preliminary data from a sample of working class mothers', *Science and Medicine*, 16(1): 43–52.

Rhodes, G., U. Prashar, and K. Young (1986), *After Acheson* (Policy Studies Institute: London).

Silverstone D. (1978), 'The Bengali community in Tower Hamlets' (London Borough of Tower Hamlets, Directorate of Social Services).

Smith, J. (1987), 'Detecting a health care revival', *Health Service Journal*, 23 Apr.

Staltmeir, A. (1981), 'Services for elderly people in Tower Hamlets' (London Borough of Tower Hamlets, Directorate of Social Services).

Tower Hamlets Health Inquiry (1987), 'Tower Hamlets Health Inquiry Report' (Community Health Council: London).

Victoria Health Authority (1983), 'Evaluation of health services in Victoria: a strategic framework for the future' (Victoria District Health Authority: London).

Warnes, A., and C. Law (1984), 'The elderly population of Great Britain: locational trends and policy implications', *Transactions of the Institute of British Geographers*, 9: 37–59.

Wiles, R. (1984), *A Critical Guide to Health Service Resource Allocation in London* (Greater London Council: London).

Wistow, G., and S. Fuller (1983), *Joint Planning in Perspective: The NAHA Survey of Collaboration 1976–1982* (Centre for Research in Social Policy and National Association of Health Authorities: Loughborough).

—— and S. Fuller (1986), *Collaboration since Restructuring: The 1984 Survey of Joint Planning and Joint Finance* (Centre for Research in Social Policy and National Association of Health Authorities: Loughborough).

11

Social Problems of Elderly People in Cities

Anthony M. Warnes

Elderly people in aggregate constitute no more a social problem than the middle-aged or people with brown eyes. The reason for their appearance as a target group in this collection is that among the elderly population are many materially, socially, physically, or mentally disadvantaged people who tend to concentrate in large cities. Secondly, there is a widespread tendency to regard the ageing of our populations as a disturbing problem with economic and welfare dimensions. The 'economic burden of elderly people' is simplistically and alarmingly described, often on the basis of uncritical projections of age structures and the future costs of income support and health and social services. Similarly, prognoses of a mounting welfare problem among elderly people are commonly based on an exaggerated view of the prevalence in the age-group of disease, social isolation, and mental ill-health. It will be of value therefore to identify, briefly but with some precision, the actual nature of social problems asociated with elderly people, and to attack false stereotypes and analyses concerning them.

The description and assessment of the social problems of elderly people reflect the commentator's perspective, as illustrated by a physician's three answers to the question, 'What is a social problem in geriatrics?': the inappropriately passive acceptance by both professionals and patients of disease as an inevitable condition of later life; the elusiveness of consistent and close liaison between medical and social welfare agencies in the assessment and care of frail elderly people; and the pervasive nature of families' and professionals' responses to elderly people's incapacities which undermine their autonomy, e.g. by encouraging them to give up their own homes (Boyd, 1981). In contrast, a social science appraisal would describe the social problems of old age as ranging from their societal roles and material support to the mental and material circumstances of individuals. From another perspective, ill or deviant elderly people cause problems for their spouses and relatives, for welfare institutions, and even for the police but, expressed in this harsh way, they are seen as neither distinctive to the elderly nor solely a consequence of great age. Only a small minority fit the stereotypes of the most incapacitated, disadvantaged, and problematic group. This chapter opens with a summary review of demographic ageing, with particular reference to urban populations, and then discusses the nature of social problems connected with old people in urban areas. These sections support an examination with increased policy emphasis of three fundamental problems related to income, housing, and health services.

Demographic Ageing and Elderly Urban Populations

The populations of Western countries have aged substantially since the early decades of this century, with the share aged sixty over characteristically increasing from around 5 to 13–17 per cent. Far from being a phenomenon new to recent decades, the process has been under way since the eighteenth century in France (where fertility fell exceptionally early) and since the late nineteenth century in north-west Europe. Much has recently been published on the mechanisms of demographic ageing, but in summary the process is a lagged adjustment to the low mortality and fertility following the demographic transition (Clark and Spengler, 1980; Myers, 1985; Warnes, 1987*a*). The process has slowed markedly in north-west European countries in this half of the century and virtually ceased, or at least paused, in Britain and Scandinavia. In north America and Australia, where recent decades have seen higher fertility and net in-migration, the population is younger and the ageing process remains vigorous (Hugo, 1986; Siegel, 1980).

Generalizations about the age structure of urban areas in comparison to their containing countries or regions are difficult to sustain. There is great diversity in the relative presence of elderly people, partly because the characteristic is sensitive to the territorial definition of an urban area. Normally peripheral suburbs contain over-representations of new housing, young adults, and children. When these are excluded, the urban population appears to be relatively aged. Comparisons over time and between cities are therefore susceptible to artificial effects, particularly in regions of rapid urbanization or extensive labour markets, as can be seen in an account of Pittsburg's increasingly elderly population from 1940 to 1970 (Kory, 1980). A corrective methodology would be longitudinal analysis by a set of annular zones, and the most substantial of these is the study of Paris by Rhein (1987). She shows that from 1954 to 1982 the population of the inner city (Paris-ville of 20 arrondisements) altered from being relatively youthful in comparison to the whole of France to having a 32 per cent excess of the over-sixty-five age-group (table 11.1). The intermediate suburbs, developed largely during the first half of this century, aged slightly more rapidly than the populations of France and

TABLE 11.1. The changing representation of the population aged over 65 in zones of the Paris agglomeration, 1954–1982

Urban zone	Ratio of the zone share to that of France					
	Males			Females		
	1954	1975	1982	1954	1975	1982
Paris-ville	0.85	1.22	1.17	0.92	1.35	1.33
Seine-banlieue	0.65	0.75	0.74	0.77	0.85	0.83
Remainder	0.74	0.57	0.55	0.83	0.63	0.61
Agglomeration	0.80	0.80	0.79	0.85	0.91	0.89
France (% 65 +)	9.8	11.3	10.9	14.3	16.2	15.7

Source: recalculated from Rhein, 1987, table 1.

the agglomeration but remained relatively youthful. The outer ring of the metropolitan area (which has been given expanded territory at the more recent dates) has become markedly more youthful from 1954 to 1982, when the deficit of elderly males and females approached 40 per cent.

During the industrial revolution and until approximately the middle of this century, urban areas in Western countries were noted for high mortality (particularly among infants) and had relatively few elderly people. Both environmental and socio-economic factors were responsible. By the 1980s in Britain, however, urban–rural differentials were negligible in comparison to the regional variations in mortality: for example, the 1984 death-rate per 1,000 among females aged 75–84 years in Scotland (68.3) and in the Northern Region (69.1) was approximately 20 per cent higher than the rate for the South-west Region (57.2), while the rates for Greater London (57.0) and for Tyne and Wear (68.9) were actually slightly lower than for their containing regions (OPCS 1985; for further details see Warnes, 1988). Social class variations in age- and cause-specific mortality remain pronounced, however, and those cities with exceptional over-representations of unskilled workers do continue to report low life expectancy, e.g. Newcastle-upon-Tyne, Greater Manchester, and Glasgow (Howe, 1986). These variations may be significant in generating spatial variations in the relative presence of elderly people within the city.

If unfavourable mortality has declined as an influence on urban age structures, other factors continue to generate variations, such as a city's economic and occupational character, its recent rate of economic growth, and its long-term migration history. Large capital cities in Western countries with a concentration of office, personal service, and further educational functions attract a high net inflow of adolescents and very young adults·and, as has been shown for Amsterdam, Brussels, London, Paris, and New York, have exceptionally high rates of out-migration among the population reaching retirement (Rees and Warnes, 1986; Vergoossen and Warnes, 1986). They tend to have over-representations of the working population but slight under-representations of the elderly. In contrast, towns with a strong manufac-turing base and a recent history of recession or plant closure have lost the rejuvenating effect of the inflow of young workers. Urban areas with atypically high elderly populations tend to be either small, declining mining or industrial towns or are attractive places for retirement. While some large cities have a retirement function, few retain a highly dis-tinctive age structure, for they become diversified in function, like Brighton and Bournemouth in England or Nice in France, or acquire new specialist functions and populations dissonant to the retirement role, like Miami. Smaller urban areas share in a third effect, the declining attractiveness of the town for retirement, sometimes asso-ciated with actual or perceived obsolescence of housing and amenities, e.g. St. Petersburg, Florida, and Scarborough, Llandudno, Hastings, and many other small resorts in England and Wales.

Great variability characterizes not only the aggregate age structure of urban areas but also the internal geography of age profiles. While the density of the elderly population normally correlates with the density of the total population, and therefore follows the exponential decline with increasing distance from a city centre, except in a few rapid-growth cities it is not the case that there is an inverse relationship between distance from the centre and the elderly population share (Forrest and Johnston, 1981; Hiltner and Smith, 1974). In longer-established and larger cities, many variables influence the age dimensions of urban ecology, and they produce a far from simple or consistent pattern. The influential factors have not been fully evaluated, but can be enumerated as: the high mor-tality in low socio-economic status inner-city populations; the differential retention of retired people among low- or high-status and inner or outer suburbs; idiosyncratic influences upon the location of dedicated housing and institutions for elderly people; and the differential impact on various residential areas of both commercial and municipal redevelopment schemes.

In Greater London, for example, the areas with the highest elderly shares in 1981 formed an extensive south-western belt of relatively pros-perous and attractive residential suburbs from Richmond and Merton to the Surrey commuter settlements of Dorking, Leatherhead, and Guildford (Warnes, 1987*b*). While inner-city boroughs had the highest densities of elderly people, only Camden and Westminster had over-representations. London illustrates well the effects of political and developmental history on the intra-urban distribution of elderly people. From 1945 until the mid-1960s, little of the considerable public sector housing investment in inner-city redevelopment schemes, peripheral estates, or new towns was devoted to specialized or small dwellings intended for elderly people, and the affected areas had relatively few elderly. By the late 1970s, however, over 30 per cent of new local authority dwellings were dedicated to the age-group and this construction reinforced strong *in situ* ageing effects on the ex-London County Council peripheral estates and in the designated new towns. Different spatial effects have arisen from the history of private sector attention to dwellings for elderly people: only during the 1980s have builders turned in any number to this market, and they have concentrated in the more affluent retirement towns and outer suburbs (Warnes and Law, 1985).

Social Problems of Elderly People

A curious paradox exists between the recognition that increasing life expectancy is an achievement of rational science and modern social systems, and negative and alarmist assessments of the societal implications of ageing. The alleged problem of the 'burden' of the elderly is socially constructed and a superficial issue: it is founded in the partly volitional and partly imposed withdrawal of people from gainful employment at an arbitrary age. In most countries neither pensions rules nor taxation laws encourage part-time employment or a gradual transition from work to retirement (Markides and Cooper, 1987). The relative decline of gainful earnings as a source of retirement income has meant that the material support of elderly people, whether from state or private pensions, investment income, or direct transfers from younger people, has become more reliant upon the productivity of the younger (working) population (Townsend, 1979). Analyses of current trends in late-age economic dependency are used to generate concern about the economic consequences of ageing, but as the recent actions of governments in France, Great Britain, Japan, and the United States have shown, both pension funds and national social security accounts can be brought into balance with relatively minor adjustments in contributions, entitlement ages, or secondary benefits for dependants (Burtless, 1987).

The statutory age of retirement eligibility is a technical matter of social administration, and is not a grave issue of economic dependency and burden. Such allegations are falsely conceived, for they require a timeless world in which the interests of the young, middle-aged, and elderly are competing. Individuals are concerned for their welfare at all stages of life and do not seek to maximize comfort during the peak earning years at the expense of destitution while a child, raising children, or in old age: the interests of the working and the elderly populations are not opposed. A second argument is that few people are isolated or narrowly self-centered. Their well-being is a function of their social integration. Not only are parents actively concerned with the welfare of their descendants, but a willing commitment to the welfare of one's parents is normal. Intergenerational linkages are maintained for their emotional and social value and for reasons of lineage. Even beyond the familial sphere, each member of society is bound by numerous ties to others of many ages, and only the narrowest of pecuniary views could suggest that elderly people are unproductive in society.

Profound macrosocietal problems associated with the extension of retirement exist, but have been neglected (Phillipson, 1982). As it is a relatively new mass phenomenon, we have yet to elaborate diverse and satisfying roles for people in the 'third age of life'. Also required is a theoretical basis for and a means of applying a model for the life-time distribution of material and welfare benefits. Remarkably little attention has been given in political and social theory to these problems, although the debate has begun (Esposito, 1987; Kingson *et al.*, 1986). A derivative problem is to overcome, in nations experiencing inflation and long-term economic growth, the in-built disadvantage to the older population of the difference between their level of living in retirement and the economic expectations and productivity of the following generation. To alleviate poverty and comparative disadvantage, we need to arrange a large transfer of resources towards the older age-groups. Associated fiscal and policy problems are those of promoting the most effective mix of private and public insurances to achieve two goals: the upgrading of the safety net for the poorest members and casualties among the elderly population, and the highest possible level of retirement living for the majority consistent with personal choice and determination.

In most Western nations, the evolution of late-age income support arrangements has produced a system which magnifies the differentials of working ages. Basic state retirement pensions were normally introduced to remove indigence and were set at minimal or subsistence levels. Their later evolution has seen real growth of the basic benefit and the addition of means-tested supplements, as with social security and housing benefits in the United Kingdom, which however are not claimed by large fractions of the eligible groups. State retirement benefits of whatever kind provide only low income. For a fortunate minority, payments from occupational and private pensions are also received, and the strategy adopted in Britain during the 1970s under the State Earnings-Related

Pension Scheme (SERPS) was to ensure that a large majority of future elderly generations would receive enhanced pensions based on their own or their spouse's best twenty years of earnings. The present Conservative administration has challenged and diluted the SERPS approach for fiscal reasons, but there are more fundamental objections. Should those individuals with incomplete histories of paid employment, including a large majority of women and those with lengthy periods of unemployment (even if these are a consequence of recession or sickness), receive such differential advantage in retirement? An alternative approach would be to establish for all a social wage of retirement at a level which allowed the older population a greater share in the nation's prosperity (Midwinter, 1985).

Elderly people of course face problems as individuals and as members of intimate groups. These have bases in both the physiology and the social construction of ageing. Later life is associated with a decline in physical function, as with hearing, sight, and lung-capacity, and with an increasing susceptibility to disabling diseases such as arthritis, cardiovascular disorders, and dementia, but except among the population of advanced age (eighty-five or over), the most dysfunctional diseases such as blindness or severe dementia are rare. Much more pervasive are the socially and psychologically based problems of adjustment to retirement, the associated constriction of roles and opportunities for social contact, coping with bereavement among near relatives, the contraction of the domestic unit, and the attenuation of familial and friendship networks. A person's ability to adjust to the losses of work, good health, and family members, and to develop new activities and roles, is related to their previous experiences, character, and material position. There are interrelationships between the structurally based problems and the expression of personal difficulties, and some of these have qualitative or quantitative urban dimensions.

Poverty

The pioneer studies of poverty in Britain by Charles Booth (1894) and Seebohm Rowntree (1901) focused upon urban populations and found a concentration among older age-groups. Rowntree's investigation in York suggested that most manual workers' families were in poverty when they were raising dependent children and in old age: the intervening interval of comparative prosperity was too short for many to accumulate savings with which to enter late life. It has been estimated that average adult working-class wealth in 1906 was £10, and in 1936, £41 (in 1985 prices), 'so there is little evidence of large-scale life-cycle planning among this section of the population before the Second World War . . . the real problem of old age was (and is) poverty.' Nor is it the case that this century's economic growth has ended the poverty cycle or the possibility of ending a working life with no accumulated capital (Johnson, 1985, pp. 17–18).

In 1978 nearly two-thirds of the elderly in Great Britain lived in or on the margins of poverty, i.e. with an income no higher than 140 per cent of the supplementary benefit rate for an equivalent family unit (Layard, Piachaud, and Stewart, 1978). Townsend's (1979, p. 819) intricate analyses of 1968 survey data came to very similar conclusions: 'nearly 20 per cent (of the pensionable population), representing 1.7 million, were found to be in poverty, and 44 per cent, representing 3.7 million, on the margins of poverty according to the state's definition. The elderly poor comprised 36 per cent of the poor.' Johnson (1985, p. 30) argues that the shift away from earnings as a source of income and the increased duration of retirement has increased the probability of relative poverty among those of advanced old age.

There are strong interrelationships between age, sex, marital status, social class, and location in the distribution of wealth and poverty in old age. Inflation and expenditure deplete savings and income with age, among other things making it increasingly difficult to replace durables and maintain dwellings. These effects are compounded by the loss of household members and their income entitlements. In 1981 in Great Britain, 67 per cent of 65-9-year-olds were married, but only 17 per cent of those aged 85-9 years (OPCS, 1983, table 1). The relationships of social and marital status with income were indicated by the 1981 Family Expenditure Survey: among pensioners drawing more than three-quarters of their income from state benefits, those living alone had a mean weekly income of just under £40 and those living in two-person households just under £60; among others (with significant non-state income), single-person households had a mean weekly income of £62 and two-persons households, £103 (Midwinter, 1985, pp. 104–5).

In the elderly population reliance upon state benefits is concentrated among widows and the lower socio-economic groups, the latter tending particularly to concentrate in inner and industrial cities. One vulnerable group comprises migrants to Britain: a study of the West Indian born elderly people in Leicester in the late 1970s found that most were ineligible for a full retirement pension (Cooper, 1979). They were able to draw a supplementary benefit 'pension' of equivalent amount, but remained disadvantaged. Whereas a person receiving a retirement pension could then earn up to £45 per week in the first five years after statutory retirement age and any amount thereafter without any loss of pension, those on supplementary benefits could earn only £4 per week.

In 1983, the equivalent 'disregards' were £65 and still £4 (Bradshaw, 1985). While this specific example of differential treatment will recede as a higher proportion of the British ethnic minority population reaching retirement has a full contributions record, the same effects apply to the disabled, long-term sick, and women who opted out of full contributions.

The degree to which the elderly poor are concentrated in cities and their constituent districts needs further research. A simple dichotomy between metropolitan deprivation and rural affluence is not found, but some urban areas have exceptional concentrations of the poor: in a district of Salford 38 per cent were poor, in a Glasgow area 48 per cent, and in a Belfast area 50 per cent (Townsend, 1979). All these neighbourhoods had concentrations of one-parent families, of unemployed males, and of unskilled manual workers. Other studies confirmed that spatial variations were less pronounced than the heterogeneity within each urban and rural district (Holtermann, 1975; for a review see Hall and Laurence, 1981). The confused spatial picture is in part a consequence of factors of little cross-sectional relevance to the elderly's income, such as the low wages of the remoter western counties of Great Britain, high unemployment rates in northern Britain and Northern Ireland, and low unemployment and high wages in London. No London supplement or urban–rural differential applies to the state retirement pension (although housing benefits will reflect local costs), and it is possible that the elderly poor are more concentrated in cities than the working-age poor.

Some disadvantaged groups of elderly people are heavily concentrated in urban areas and in their districts of poorest housing and environment, as with black elderly in the United States and the rapidly growing elderly population in the ethnic minorities of Britain. Elderly people living alone, the registered disabled, and the mentally ill elderly populations are also over-represented in cities, but in each case the social problem of poverty is manifest in urban areas but not demonstrably a problem of the city. Amelioration or solution of these problems is not a matter of improved urban government, management, or services, but a matter of national policy for retirement incomes.

Housing and the Home Support of Elderly People

Most people move infrequently after their early adult years and the establishment of their marital homes. The 'cohort effect' is that few elderly people occupy the newest housing and their housing amenities reflect the conditions of the past. While urban housing standards have enormously improved during the last four decades, there remain considerable numbers of housing difficulties for elderly people, some in the remaining pre-First World War stock, but many in more modern dwellings. Recent abrupt changes in housing improvement and new construction budgets in the public sector have delayed the time when basic structural difficulties are rare, but the more common problems today are deficient or malfunctioning amenities, inappropriate design for an incapacitated elderly person, and inconvenient location. It is a truism that as the prosperity of Western nations has increased, the benefits expected from a dwelling have diversified far beyond shelter. Housing problems are now discerned through comparative judgements of the occupier's ability to sustain a comfortable, satisfying, and socially integrated life. The number of households occupied by elderly people has increased much more rapidly than the age-group, partly reflecting demographic factors but also the increasing financial ability of the population to express its preference for independent living (Dale, Evandrou, and Arber, 1987; Ermisch and Overton, 1985). When controlled for age and sex, there is a positive relationship among elderly people between their income and the likelihood of a person either living in an independent household or being a household-head.

In the United States a great diversity of dedicated housing arrangements for elderly people have arisen in response to market demands for small, cheap dwellings, congregate settings, and 'sheltered' or care facilities. They range from the converted, obsolescent commercial hotel and low-grade mobile home parks to sumptuous and self-consciously medicalized life-care facilities (Mangum, 1982). In Britain, responses to the demands for small and well-equipped dwellings in retirement and recognition that a minority have special housing needs have seen a mixture of segmented and partial measures. There has been a progressive elaboration of the forms of specialist and supported housing and vigorous development of sheltered housing schemes, first in the voluntary and public sectors and latterly in the private sector (Butler, Oldman, and Greve, 1983). During the 1980s the emphasis has moved towards adapting general housing for smaller households and for individuals with mild disabilities. These have included improvements to heating, kitchen, sanitary, and electrical services, the occasional installation of chair lifts and other special equipment, the provision of alarm and communication systems, and the employment of peripatetic wardens and domiciliary carers (Tinker, 1984). There has also been encouragement of the private sector's role in specialized housing, residential-care, nursing, and medical service provision, and severe restraint of further expansion of the public sector's role in housing and residential care.

The principles underlying recent policy changes have been common to many Western countries, but in each their articulation has been distinctive. Theorists and practitioners in social welfare have successfully criticized institutional policies for their damaging effects on individual mental health and well being, because many people are inappropriately placed, and because there are intractable problems of achieving long-term flexibility of care management and delivery. An insistent aim has been to restrain expenditure and raise cost-effectiveness. In comparison to the more prosperous and collectivized nations of Scandinavia, Britain's success in achieving 'de-institutionalization' has been handicapped by the endemic problems of liaison between the health, personal social service, and housing authorities, by inadequate budgets, and by dilatoriness in the necessary redistribution of funds among the responsible agencies (Cumberledge, 1986). Recently, however, there has been a spate of innovation and experiment in domiciliary social and nursing support services to frail elderly people in their own homes (Davies and Challies, 1987). The 1980s have seen ramifying problems associated with the support of physically and mentally frail elderly people, but the direct cause of these is less the increase in the number of such people than it is the government's failure to resolve the policy, practice, and funding issues associated with de-institutionalization. Two important government-commissioned reports, the Griffiths report on community care, and the Wagner review of residential care were published in mid-1988: it must be hoped that these stimulate more positive and determined action than has been characteristic this decade (Department of Health and Social Security, 1988; National Institute for Social Work, 1988).

A recent review of the British public's attitudes to various aspects of the welfare state found little enthusiasm for care by the community or residential care (except in specific circumstances), but support for a range of community-based services which best serve the interests of dependency groups and which alleviate the burden of private carers (Taylor-Gooby, 1985). It is not that families are unwilling to support their elderly relatives, but that (*a*) all parties seek to preserve autonomy; (*b*) sometimes external help as for example to a spouse, is essential if the independent household is to be sustained; and (*c*) there are many people of advanced old age without close relatives. The last quarter of the century is seeing and will see difficult and novel adjustments in the societal suport of dependent elderly people and their relatives. In broad terms we are abandonding the 'medical model' of institutionally based care and the early post-war ambition to universalize and upgrade a range of residential and domiciliary services that had been developed as a safety net for the weakest members of society. In their place are seen chaotic, pragmatic and hesitant experiments to find effective mixtures of individual, market, and state support services. To achieve the best combination of assistance in terms of preserving the dignity of elderly people, minimizing cost, and ensuring the dependability and speed of response to domestic crises, is a demanding agenda for social administrative policy and practice. In detailed respects, as in the deployment of paid carers or the establishment of neighbourhood alarm systems, solutions will be easier in urban areas than in areas of low population density, but the defects of urban housing contribute an extra dimension to the problems.

Urban Health Services

There are few statistics on the health status of the population aside from surrogates such as life expectancy or the prevalence of severe disabilities, but such evidence as exists suggests that health in old age has improved during the last few decades and that health expectations have risen faster. Today's health problems in and of the city are less epidemiological than related to deficiencies in medical services and facilities, particularly in primary care. Elderly people have high rates of acute events and prevalence of chronic conditions, and make correspondingly high demands for treatment. Apart from the systemic problems of cost and finance, the most frequently recognized problems of medical care are often at their most severe in cities: it is widely accepted that many disorders are diagnosed and treated much later than is desirable, that the assessment and long-term management of multiple chronic conditions is inadequate, and that communication and co-ordination is poor between the primary and acute services.

A common characteristic of many large cities is their possession of regional acute and teaching hospitals as well as many old, small hospitals with accident and emergency departments. The latter have served an important primary care function for the low-income population of the inner city, but the declining population of these areas has led health authorities to reduce provision of acute beds and emergency departments which, along with cut-backs in local authority social services and the delays in implementing community care, have raised concern about the quality and effectiveness of primary care. In inner London a low proportion of general practitioners work in group practices; they are relatively difficult to contact and place high reliance on deputies (table 11.2). Many are of pensionable age (a retirement age of seventy is now proposed for GPs), and they have low and contracting lists with little incentive to take on new patients; but unlike other inner cities, London is not 'under-doctored'. Low list-size generally means there is capacity to care for additional patients, so the entry of new GPs has been restricted. Other problems specific to inner-city areas are the high cost of surgery premises (more fully discussed in Chapter 7), the tendency for doctors to live remote from their practices, the high turnover of community nurses and paramedical staff, and, in London, the availability of more highly remunerated private work. The results give strong support to the thesis that in areas with major social problems the primary care services are less well organised to cope with the extra burdens involved in caring for patients in the community and many more people end up being treated in hospital (London Health Planning Consortium, 1981, p. 19). Many similarities have been found in the organization and practice of primary dental health services in inner south London (Gelbier and Fiske, 1987).

TABLE 11.2.   Characteristics of general practitioners in London, *c.* 1980

Area	% in group practice	% aged 65 +	% in practices with nurse	% with lists of < 1,000
Kensington, Chelsea and				
Westminster	21	22	17	15
Camden and Islington	40	22	15	6
City and East London	46	18	30	1
Lambeth, Southwark and				
Lewisham	49	13	32	3
Inner London	41	18	25	6
Outer London	52	11	59	3
England and Wales	72	6	68	1

Source: London Health Planning Consortium, 1981, tables 3–9.

The Elderly *or* the City as a Social Problem

Social gerontology is a rapidly growing field of research, and invest-igations into many other topics with an urban dimension have been conducted. Limited space precludes detailed treatments of the problems associated with transport, mobility, vulnerability to crime, perception of crime hazards, or the reactions of elderly residents to population turn-over, gentrification, or racial succession. Attention has instead concen-trated on three fundamental problems: income, housing, and health. Deficiency of resources is foremost, partly because state-organized arrangements for transferring resources from the working to the retired populations are still founded on preventing indigence and on earnings-related social insurance, and therefore perpetuate into retirement the income differentials of working age. The social problem of low income in late life, while manifest in cities, is not their creation, and the required radical approach is an issue of macroeconomic and social but *not* specifically urban policy. The problem of substandard, expensive, and inconvenient dwellings has a more direct urban dimension. The interaction of low income with the high cost and poor quality of much urban housing produces demoralizing and disabling problems for elderly people. It is therefore lamentable that both client- and property-based programmes for improving, adapting, and constructing general and special-purpose housing have received such capricious support in recent years. Of the three basic issues considered in this review, the urban dimensions of primary health care problems have been given most emphasis. The interactions between the exceptional needs of the age-group, the characteristics of the inner city, and administrative foibles have generated exceptional weaknesses in the service.

Cities are not uniformly hostile environments for elderly people. They offer a wide range of accessible activities and facilities, often have comparatively frequent (if declining) public transport services, well-developed personal social services, residential care, and acute medical facilities, and active voluntary organizations concerned with the welfare of elderly people. Many elderly residents in towns and cities still live exceptionally proximate to their relatives and friends, and the large population brings extensive social opportunities. In cities, as elsewhere, most elderly people live self-reliant, active, purposeful, and satisfying lives. Their individual problems are little different to those of other age-groups, and handled tolerably within intimate and family groups. The social problems of disadvantage, discrimination, and dysfunction among elderly people are only in part intrinsic to age and some of their facets are amenable to reform: they deserve a higher priority than they presently receive.

References

Booth, C. (1894), *The Aged Poor* (Macmillan: Basingstoke).

Boyd, R. V. (1981), 'What is a "social problem" in geriatrics?', in T. Arie (ed.) *Health Care of the Elderly* (Croom Helm: Beckenham), 143–57.

Bradshaw, J. (1985), 'Social security policy and assumptions about patterns of work', in R. Klein and M. O'Higgins (eds.), *The Future of Welfare* (Basil Blackwell: Oxford), 204–15.

Burtless, G. (ed.) (1987), *Work, Health and Income among the Elderly* (Brookings Institution: Washington, DC).

Butler, A., C. Oldman, and J. Greve (1983), *Sheltered Housing for the Elderly* (Allen and Unwin: London).

Clark, R. L., and J. J. Spengler (1980), *The Economics of Individual and Population Ageing* (Cambridge University Press: Cambridge).

Cooper, J. (1979), 'West Indian elderly in Leicester: a case study', in F. Glendenning (ed.), *The Elders in Ethnic Minorities* (Beth Johnson Foundation: Stoke on Trent), 20–41.

Cumberledge, J. (1986), *Neighbourhood Nursing: A Focus for Care*, Report of the Community Nursing Review (HMSO: London).

Dale, A., M. Evandrou, and S. Arber (1987), 'The household structure of elderly population in Britain', *Ageing and Society*, 7: 37–56.

Davies, B. P., and D. Challis (1987), *Matching Resources to Needs in Community Care* (Gower: Aldershot).

Department for Health and Social Security (1988), *Community Care: An Agenda for Action* (HMSO: London).

Ermisch, J., and E. Overton (1985), 'Minimal household units: a new approach to the analysis of household formation', *Population Studies*, 39: 33–54.

Esposito, J. L. (1987), *The Obsolete Self: Philosophical Dimensions of Aging* (University of California Press: Berkeley).

Forrest, J., and R. J. Johnston (1981), 'On the characteristics of urban sub-areas according to their age structure', *Urban Geography*, 2: 31–40.

Gelbier, S., and J. Fiske (1987), 'Dental health and elderly people', Working Paper 1 (Age Concern Institute of Gerontology, King's College: London).

Hall, P. G., and S. Laurence (1981), 'British policy responses', in P. G. Hall (ed.), *The Inner City in Context* (Heinemann: London), 52–63.

Hiltner, J., and B. W. Smith (1974), 'Intra-urban residential location of the elderly', *Journal of Geography*, 73: 23–33.

Holtermann, S. (1975), 'Areas of urban deprivation in Great Britain: an analysis of 1971 census data', *Social Trends*, 6: 33–47.

Howe, G. M. (1986), 'Does it matter where I live?', *Transactions of the Institute of British Geographers*, NS 11: 387–414.

Hugo, G. (1986), *Population Aging in Australia*, Papers of the East–West Population Institute 98 (Honolulu, Hawaii).

Johnson, P. (1985), *The Economics of Old Age in Britain: A Long-Run View 1881-1981*, Discussion Paper 47 (Centre for Economic Policy Research: London).

Kingson, E. R., B. A. Hirshorn, and J. M. Cornman (1986), *Ties That Bind: The Interdependence of Generations* (Seven Locks Press: Washington, DC).

Kory, W. B. (1980), 'Spatial distribution of the elderly in Pittsburgh, Pennsylvania', *Pennsylvania Geographer*, 18: 25–44.

Layard, R., D. Piachaud, and M. Stewart (1978), *The Causes of Poverty*, Paper 5, Royal Commission on the Distribution of Income and Wealth (HMSO: London).

London Health Planning Consortium (1981), *Primary Health Care in Inner London* (LHPC: London).

Mangum, W. (1982), 'Housing for the elderly in the USA', in A. M. Warnes (ed.), *Geographical Perspectives on the Elderly* (Wiley: Chichester), 191–222.

Markides, K. S., and C. L. Cooper (eds.), (1987), *Retirement in Industrialized Societies: Social, Psychological and Health Factors* (Wiley: Chichester).

Midwinter, E. (1985), *The Wage of Retirement: The Case for a New Pensions Policy*, Policy Studies in Ageing 4 (Centre for Policy on Ageing: London).

Myers, G. C. (1985), 'Aging and worldwide population change', in R. H. Binstock and E. Shanas (eds.), *Handbook of Aging and the Social Sciences* (Van Nostrand Reinhold: New York), 173–98.

National Institute for Social Work (1988), *Residential Care* (HMSO: London).

OPCS (Office of Population Censuses and Surveys) (1983), *Great Britain Census 1981: Sex, Age and Marital Status* (HMSO: London).

—— (1985) *1984 Mortality Statistics: Area* (HMSO: London).

Phillipson, C. (1982), *Capitalism and the Construction of Old Age* (Macmillan: London).

Rees, P. H., and A. M. Warnes (1986), *Migration of the Elderly in the United Kingdom*, Working Paper 473 (School of Geography, University of Leeds).

Rhein, C. (1987), 'Transformations des structures urbaines et vieillissement démographique dans l'agglomération parisienne, 1954-1982', *Espace Populations Sociétés*, 1987(1): 153–70.

Rowntree, B. S. (1901), *Poverty: A Study of Town Life* (Macmillan: London).

Siegel, J. S. (1980), 'On the demography of ageing', *Demography*, 17: 345–64.

Taylor-Gooby, P. (1985), 'The politics of welfare: public attitudes and behaviour', in R. Klein and M. O'Higgins (eds.), *The Future of Welfare* (Basil Blackwell: Oxford), 204–15.

Tinker, A. (1984), *Staying at Home: Helping Elderly People* (HMSO: London).

Townsend, P. (1979), *Poverty in the United Kingdom* (Penguin: Harmondsworth).

Vergoossen, T. W. M., and A. M. Warnes (1986), 'Mobility of the elderly', paper presented at the conference on Comparative Population Geography of the United Kingdom and The Netherlands, Oxford.

—— and C. M. Law (1985), 'Elderly populations and housing prospects in Britain', *Town Planning Review*, 56: 292–314.

Warnes, A. M. (1987a), 'Geographical locations and social relationships among the elderly in developing and developed nations', in M. Pacione (ed.), *Progress in Social Geography* (Croom Helm: London), 252–94.

—— (1987b), 'The distribution of the elderly population of Great Britain', *Espace populations sociétés*, 1987(1): 41–56.

—— (1988) 'The demography of ageing', in A. Davenport (ed.), (*Anaesthesia and the Aged Patient* (Blackwell Scientific: Oxford) 9–26.

12

Women's Inequality in Urban Britain

Jane Lewis and Sophie Bowlby

This chapter examines the changing role and position of women in urban Britain in the 1980s. During this period, women's employment in both outer and inner urban areas has declined significantly, women's unemployment has increased dramatically, and women's access to public housing, health care, transport, child-care, and other public services has been diminished by government policies aimed at reducing public sector ownerhip and expenditure.

Within the broad area of geographical research, very little has been written documenting these recent trends in women's position and role in urban areas. In this chapter, therefore, after briefly reviewing the current understanding of the relationship between the organization of urban environments and women's position in society, we examine some of the general trends in women's employment and women's access to facilities. We finish by discussing recent policy initiatives aimed at changing women's social position in urban Britain.

The Background: Theoretical Approaches to Women's Inequality

This section covers briefly the range of current approaches to understanding women's subordinate position in society. First, however, we will explain to what kinds of inequality we are referring when we speak of 'women's subordinate position in society'.

Women are clearly not a 'minority' group, since at present they make up about 52 per cent of the population (*Social Trends*, 1987). But although women are numerically dominant, they are economically and socially unequal to men. Within the labour market women are concentrated in low-skilled and low-paid jobs, with full-time women workers earning, on average, only two-thirds of full-time male workers' pay (DE, 1987). In the home women continue to do the majority of the work, even when they do paid work as well. For example, women who are in paid work do 300 per cent more hours of housework and 84 per cent of the hours of paid work that men do (Seager and Olsen, 1986). Furthermore, women make up the overwhelming majority of the victims of domestic violence (Pahl, 1985).

A wide range of theories attempt to explain this gender inequality and the basis of 'patriarchy' or male power (Walby, 1986). For example, some theories focus on women's reproductive role (e.g. Firestone, 1974); some on the nature or construction of female and male sexuality (Foord and Gregson, 1986); and some emphasize the economic and social role played by domestic labour or a domestic mode of production (Walby, 1986). There is also considerable debate over the relationship between the systems of patriarchy and of capitalism. Some argue that they are autonomous systems, and others argue either that capitalism or that patriarchy is the dominant system of inequality. Although it is clear that women's inequality is not unique to capitalist economies, the nature of the relationship between capitalism and patriarchy remains an issue of both theoretical and practical importance (Walby, 1986; McDowell, 1987). A further difference between theorists, one that has been of particular significance within geography, is the relative importance assigned to social relations within the home and within the workplace in accounting for women's inequality.

Whichever theoretical approach is adopted it remains true, in our view, that the unequal distribution of power between women and men exists as a central feature of our society that both structures and can induce social change. It is important, therefore, that we research the ways in which patriarchal relations and social change are linked. Our particular concern here is to examine how changes currently occurring in urban life and the built environment reflect or affect the nature of the opportunities open to women. We start by discussing the small but expanding body of work which is concerned with the relationships between gender inequality and urban life and the built environment. This work falls into three broad categories: research on urban structure; research on women's access to urban services and workplaces; and research on women's employment.

The structure and design of the built environment

A number of feminist scholars have shown how the built environments of the home and the city that exist today have reflected and helped to create the ideal of a way of life for women centred on husband and children and based firmly in the home. Much of this work looks at the nineteenth and early twentieth century and focuses on British or American cities (Mackenzie and Rose, 1983; McDowell, 1983; WGSG, 1984). It shows how the form of the city with which we are now familiar—with home and workplace separate, and with specialized residential, commercial, and industrial areas, is a product not only of capitalist development but also of the development of a particular division of labour between men and women (Matrix Book Group, 1984; Foord and Lewis, 1984; Bowlby *et al.*, forthcoming). These studies show how both ideological and material pressures, stemming from the changing organization of capital and patriarchal relations at home, at work, and in the design professions, have structured the nature of the built environment at different periods in ways that have stereotyped women as 'housewives and mothers' and made it difficult for women to combine domestic and paid work.

A particular aspect of the design of the urban environment to which both researchers and policy-makers have addressed themselves is that of women's safety from attack. Many women avoid being alone in public space, especially at night, since they fear attack or rape by men (Hall, 1985; Hanmer and Saunders, 1984). The design of the environment is held by many both to affect the real possibilities of attack (Newman, 1972) and to affect women's perception of the risk of being alone (Haringey Borough Council, 1986; LSPU, 1986*b*). The lack of involvement by women in urban design is pointed out as an important factor in its inappropriateness for women's safety (Wekerle *et al.*, 1980; Matrix Book Group, 1984). This area of research has great potential for providing further insights into the links between patriarchal relations and the form of the built environment.

Access to facilities: variation in women's needs

Much of the early research on issues of gender within geography, planning, and urban and regional studies was concerned with issues of access (Bowlby *et al.*, forthcoming). This includes both physical access to particular facilities, and economic and social access to services such as housing or health-care. One of the major messages of this research is that women have particular problems of access which stem from their subordinate position. For example, it shows that the majority of women are dependent upon public transport during the day, since only a third of women own cars and only about half of women in car-owning households have everyday access to a car (WEG, 1987; Pickup, 1984). This situation arises because few women earn enough to buy and run their own car; because husbands monopolize the 'household' car for their journey to work; and because of the existence of gender stereotypes which suggest that maintaining and driving cars is a 'masculine' activity.

A number of studies concentrate on physical access and women's time budgets to show how the social expectations that women should care for children and do the bulk of domestic work *interact* with the lack of adequate physical access to facilities to create problems for women and to limit their ability to do well-paid or full-time work. Studies by Tivers of women with young children (1985) and by Pickup of women's access to paid work in Reading (1984) illustrate the interaction of social structures and expectations with the physical separation of homes from workplaces and other social facilities. They show how women's access to work, shops, leisure, and social contacts are more circumscribed than men's. This work complements the research discussed in the previous section and shows how unsuitable most suburban residential environments are for women.

This work on access has tended to concentrate on the 'typical' woman—married and with children. Other research, however, has focused on women's unequal access to particular services, including housing (Watson and Austerberry, 1986; Drake *et al.*, 1982; Trenchard and Warren, 1983), transport (GLC, 1985/86), and health-care (WGSG, 1984), or on the access problems of particular groups of women. These include women suffering domestic violence, black and ethnic minority women, elderly women, single women, and lesbian women. In general, work on the problems of access to services faced by such women, done by geographers and planners in Britain and published in mainstream academic journals is conspicuous by its absence. However, a variety of work on these issues is being done by pressure groups and by particular local planning authorities.

The existing research on access problems has provided clear empirical evidence of the difficulties faced by many women. However, much of the early work used an inadequate conceptualization of the basis of women's social and economic inequality. It assumed implicitly that women's inequality derived from the acceptance, by men and women, of particular stereotyped gender roles. However, used in this way, gender role theory, though providing some useful insights, draws attention away from the active and changing social relationships through which role models alter and develop. It also draws attention away from the unequal power of men and women to change or create particular gender roles (Foord and Gregson, 1986). A further problem is that this approach implied that women's inequality in the labour market and their difficulties of access derived solely from their lack of power in the home. As we shall explain below, recent research on the workplace has shown this to be an oversimplified picture.

Much of the research on the access problems of particular groups is 'action research', and in many cases it does not, therefore, draw out the theoretical implications of the analyses it provides. However, it offers both a source of empirical data and insights into the mechanisms by which women's access to services is limited.

Women in the labour market: an overview

Although women's share of total employment has steadily increased throughout the post-war period, so that women now represent 45 per cent of the workforce, the inequalities women experience relative to men in the labour market remain acute. Women are heavily, in fact increasingly, concentrated in a relatively small number of industries, particularly in the education, health, retail, personal, and financial service sectors, and throughout all industries are concentrated in low-grade and low-paid jobs (Hakim, 1981; Lewis, 1984; WGSG, 1984).

There have been many attempts to explain why women experience such inequality in the labour market (Lewis, 1984; Walby, 1986). In much of this literature, although written from very different theoretical perspectives—including neo-classical labour market theory, labour market segmentation theory, Marxist theory and much feminist theory—women's inequality in the labour market is seen to originate from the unequal domestic division of labour. Women's position in the family, caring for husband, children, and home, is therefore seen as the primary factor determining their subordinate position in the labour market. More recently, however, a number of feminist researchers have identified the determinates of women's unequality in paid work within the labour market itself (Beechey, 1983; Cockburn, 1985; Walby, 1986). Their studies have identified how management and trade union strategies have sought to create and reinforce gender inequalities within the workplace as a means of either reducing labour costs or of maintaining or increasing the skill-levels, pay, and conditions of male workers (Cockburn, 1985).

While these studies provide a detailed understanding of some of the mechanisms producing women's inequality in the labour market, they do not consider the reasons for the large spatial variations which exist in both the proportion of women who work and in the types of job available to women. There is a considerable body of work in industrial and regional geography which explains these variations as resulting from the processes of industrial restructuring that took place during the 1960s and early 1970s (Hudson, 1980; Meegan, 1982; Elson and Pearson, 1981; Lewis, 1984; Massey, 1984). These involved the decentralization of semi-skilled production work in major sectors of manufacturing during the 1960s and early 1970s, especially in the electrical engineering, food and drink processing, and clothing industries. Routine, labour-intensive production processes for standardized, mass-produced goods were established in the suburbs and new towns, frequently in the 'development areas'. Companies were attracted by the availability of potentially large numbers of women workers living on the new, predominantly public sector, housing estates recently constructed on the peripheries of major cities such as Liverpool or in new towns such as Peterlee and Washington New Town in the north-east (Lewis, 1984; Foord and Lewis, 1984).

Most of the existing published work on the spatial variations in women's employment is written with the assumption that it was social relations in the home that led to women being a cheap, inexperienced, and attractive labour force. The newer work by feminists referred to above suggests that this assumption must be re-examined, and also that we should explore the ways in which changes in women's and men's opportunities at work impinge on relations in the home. The research findings of the locality research initiative funded by the ESRC, entitled 'Changing Urban and Regional Systems' (Cooke, 1986), which examines recent economic, social, and political change in seven predominantly urban localities throughout England, may provide some evidence on the impacts of work experience on domestic relations. The findings should also provide more detailed evidence of both what has been happening to women's employment during the 1980s and of the processes behind recent changes.

Women's Inequality in the 1980s

In this section we will outline some of the changes that have occurred in women's lives in relation to: the changing spatial structure of our cities; changes in the provision of public and private services, in particular housing; and changes in the labour market. Firstly, however, we provide a general context by outlining some of the changes in women's position in the family.

The changing family and household

During the 1980s there have been changes in both the nature of and people's expectations about family life. Indeed, the nature of 'the family' and 'family life' have become significant political issues. However, it is important to remember that the changes in family life during the 1980s are a continuation of changes that have been taking place for some time.

One change, much discussed in the media, has been the growth of household types other than the nuclear family. Single-parent families, divorced families, and cohabitation, although in no sense new, are now more commonplace (*Social Trends*, 1987).

Despite such developments, the overwhelming majority of women in Britain are married. Ninety per cent of both women and men marry at least once, and the average woman spends 75 per cent of her adult life in marriage (Open University, 1983). Although the divorce rate has risen very considerably since the Divorce Reform Act 1969, which made obtaining a divorce easier, this does not imply that a life-style involving marriage and children has become unpopular. A survey of couples divorcing in 1973 found that 56 per cent of men and 48 per cent of women had remarried within five years (Leete and Anthony, 1979). Thus, although at present only 29 per cent of households consist of a couple with one or more dependent children (United Kingdom, 1987), most women live in such a family as a wife and mother at some time during their lives. Nevertheless, the 'traditional' nuclear family with a male 'head of household' and non-working wife, and the patterns of life which characterize it, have changed significantly.

One development encouraging change is that the majority of women now go out of the home to do paid work, either full- or part-time (60 per cent of married women aged between eighteen and sixty now do paid work (Martin and Roberts, 1984). It is also important to remember that a sizeable minority of women do low-paid work in the home, doing 'traditional' homeworking jobs such as sewing, or 'new' homeworking jobs such as word processing (Huws, 1984). For most women, this has resulted in playing a dual role, as both paid worker and domestic worker. A recent report shows that there has been little change in the division of domestic labour. Few men do very much housework, whether or not their wives do paid work (Henwood *et al.*, 1987). However, the view that men *should* take an equal share in domestic work, particularly in child-care, has become much more popularly accepted, and this is especially true among younger women. For women in relatively highly paid professional or managerial work there is the possibility of reducing the problems of their dual role by paying for child-care or housework to be done by other, less well paid, women. But for the majority of women this is not an option.

Another important change is the increase in the numbers of elderly women. Large numbers of elderly women live in the household of, and are cared for by, a female relative—usually their daughter or daughter-in-law. Many others live alone, while others live in residential homes. In Britain today about a third of women over sixty and about half of all women over seventy live alone (*Social Trends*, 1987). A high proportion are on low incomes and in poor health, and are therefore dependent on state benefits or on their children to provide them with care either in their own homes or in institutions (Ungerson, 1985).

Although there has been a significant increase in the number of 'non-family' and single-parent households, for most households the important changes in family life lie in the activities and expectations of women and of men. A point of considerable importance, but one not yet adequately explored by researchers, is that these general trends of change in domestic life have not occurred evenly over space, nor have they affected working-class women in the same way as middle-class women, or Asian or Afro-Caribbean women in the same way as white women. Thus the outcomes of the general patterns of social change vary from place to place and city to city and, within each locality, between women in different class and racial groups.

Although most women's lives no longer conform to the pattern of the unpaid married woman working at home caring for children and doing the housework while the man goes out to earn the money, this is not reflected in the physical structure of our cities. There have been no significant developments, in response to the growth of women's paid work, in the pattern of urban land use. The response continues to come from women in the shape of part-time work and time spent travelling. There has been some move in the private market to increase the provision of housing for young single and for elderly people, but, as we will see in the following section, many women are prevented from taking advantage of this provision by their low incomes.

Cutbacks in public services: the case of housing

The 1980s have seen major changes in the assumptions underlying the supply of public services and widespread cutbacks in their provision. During the 1980s there have been major changes in government policy in relation to the provision of public services. In general there has been an attempt to reduce public expenditure and increase the involvement of the private sector. For example, public transport has been opened up to further private sector competition, and public subsidies to transport operators have been limited. In the Health Service, despite increases in the money spent in real terms, the costs of medical care have risen faster than government funding and questions about the feasibility of continuing to fund the NHS on the present basis are being raised by many politicians, while the quality of health-care provision has declined significantly. In education, major changes in the organization and funding of secondary, further, and higher education are under way. All these changes in the provision of public services will impinge strongly on women, since they form a high proportion of public sector workers—especially in education and health-care—and also are more frequently in contact with these services as consumers than are men. For example, it is usually women rather than men who take children to school, and children and elderly people to the doctor or hospital. Many women also visit doctors more regularly than men, for gynaecological care, and women are more dependent than men on public transport. We have not space here to discuss all these services, and we have therefore chosen to concentrate on housing, and to examine the problem of access to housing faced by particular groups of women.

Single parents are often dependent on state income. The majority (88 per cent) of single-parent families are headed by women, and most such women are not able to take paid work because of the need to look after their children, the lack of public-sector child-care provision, and the costs of private child-care services. The result is that most single women with children have very low incomes and are reliant on either council housing, housing associations, or very cheap private rental housing. Fifty per cent of divorced or separated women are council tenants (compared with 37 per cent of divorced and separated men), and female-headed households make up 36 per cent of council tenants—a figure which has increased by 6 per cent between 1978 and 1984 (Forrest and Murie, 1987; OPCS, 1984). Black single parents are even more likely to be council tenants. In a study carried out in 1984, Brown (1984) found that 55 per cent of white single parents were in council housing compared to 74 per cent of West Indian single parents. The cutbacks in council housing have meant increasing problems for single-parent families. Many have been forced into either a still shrinking private rental sector or into homelessness. Such homeless families are normally accommodated in highly unsuitable bed and breakfast accommodation.

Because so many women earn low wages, few are able to enter owner-occupation independently (in 1981, 54 per cent of male household heads but only 32 per cent of women household heads were owner-occupiers, and many of the latter had inherited their houses from their husbands (WEG, 1987). As a result women who are forced to leave their parental or marital home because of family tensions, violence, or divorce have great difficulty in finding adequate accommodation—especially single women without children, who are not normally eligible for council housing. Nine out of ten places in statutory hostels are for men, and there is very little provision for the particular needs of single Asian or black homeless women (WEG, 1987). Refuges for battered women are well below the one place per 10,000 population recommended by the Select Committee on Violence in Marriage (United Kingdom, 1975).

The incidence of housing problems specific to women also varies from area to area—not only because of variations in current and past local housing provision and policy, but also because the proportion of single women and single-parent families varies. In general there are more such families in the inner areas of large cities than elsewhere. For example, 30 per cent of households in Greater London are headed by women and 19 per cent of families in London are single-parent ones. Although in some urban areas there is a substantial proportion of women earning relatively high wages, who are able to enter owner occupation (for example, in a number of inner London boroughs, such as Hackney and Islington, women now account for about 40 per cent of people to whom building society mortgage loans have been made), the general trends in the provision of housing are working to the disadvantage of people with little independent economic power, most of whom are women. Such difficulties in obtaining housing can keep women living in household relationships in which they are unhappy or abused.

Employment in British cities in the 1980s

During the 1980s, the large urban areas have suffered major job losses and the economic decline and dereliction of the inner cities has again been high on the political agenda. The Conservative government has responded by setting up new area-based initiatives in many urban areas, with the aim of regenerating inner urban economies. Both inner and outer city areas have, however, continued to suffer dramatic job loss and an equally dramatic growth in unemployment. At the same time, employment growth in the service sector has slowed down—in large part because of the government's commitment to reducing public ownership and expenditure, which has involved substantial job losses throughout the public sector transport, health, education, and local government services.

While these recent trends in employment and government policy are both familiar and well documented (Hamnett, 1983; Cooke, 1986; Martin and Rowthorn, 1986), their impact on women's employment is much less well known. The literature on women's paid work tends either to be concerned with trends in women's employment during the 1960s and 1970s (Hudson, 1980; Lewis, 1984; Massey, 1984), or focuses on specific aspects of more recent changes in women's employment such as the impact of new technology on women's jobs in particular sectors (Cockburn, 1985; Wernerke, 1983; Huws, 1984) and the increasing casualization of women's employment (Coyle, 1985; Mitter, 1986). In the following paragraphs we therefore provide a brief outline of the general trends which have taken place in women's employment during the 1980s.

Throughout the economic recession of the 1980s, women have continued to account for an increasing proportion of total employment in Britain. By 1985, women accounted for 45 per cent of employment nationally as compared with 42 per cent in 1979 (DE, 1980, 1987). However, this continued feminization of the workforce as a whole does not reflect any absolute growth in the number of women in employment, resulting largely from a fall in the number of employed men.

TABLE 12.1. Female and male employment, 1979–1986

Region	Employees in employment				Employment change	
	1979		1986		No. (000s)	%
	No. (000s)	%	No. (000s)	(%)		
Female						
South East	3,187	34	3,342	35	155	5
East Anglia	289	3	324	3	35	12
South West	667	7	703	7	26	4
Total South	4,153	44	4,369	46	216	5
W. Midlands	906	10	879	9	− 27	− 3
E. Midlands	645	7	659	7	14	2
Yorks & Humberside	813	9	787	8	− 26	− 3
North West	1,137	12	1,058	11	− 79	− 7
North	506	5	480	5	− 26	− 5
Wales	414	4	378	4	− 36	− 9
Scotland	902	10	865	9	− 37	− 4
Total North	5,323	56	5,106	54	− 217	− 4
Great Britain	9,476	100	9,475	100	− 1	0
Male						
South East	4,326	33	4,028	34	− 298	− 7
East Anglia	425	3	452	4	27	6
South West	928	7	878	8	− 50	− 5
Total South	5,679	43	5,358	46	− 321	− 6
W. Midlands	1,342	10	1,161	10	− 181	− 13
E. Midlands	920	7	855	7	− 65	− 7
Yorks & Humberside	1,200	9	990	8	− 210	− 18
North West	1,541	12	1,218	10	− 323	− 21
North	743	6	602	5	− 141	− 19
Wales	623	5	482	4	− 141	− 23
Scotland	1,205	9	1,020	9	− 185	− 15
Total North	7,574	57	6,328	54	− 1,246	− 16
Great Britain	13,253	100	11,686	100	− 1,567	− 12

Source: Department of Employment, 1980, 1986.

Underlying the overall stability in women's employment, there are substantial sectoral and spatial variations (see table 12.1). In Greater London, for example, the number of women in employment has increased by 2 per cent or by 31,000 (LSPU, 1986*a*). In terms of sectoral trends, women's employment in the service sector has continued to increase, albeit at a lower rate than during the 1970s. Within the manufacturing sector, however, women's employment has fallen dramatically. Since 1979, more than one in every four of women's manufacturing jobs has disappeared, a decline of 27 per cent (DE, 1987). Those industries in which women have experienced particularly severe job losses, of between 25 and 35 per cent since 1979, are the electrical and electronic engineering industries, the food, drink, and tobacco processing industries and the clothing, footwear, and textile industries. Overall, only 16 per cent of women workers are now employed in the manufacturing sector in Great Britain, as compared with 22 per cent in 1979.

It now seems that the feminization and spatial decentralization of major sectors of manufacturing industry were trends which were more or less specific to the 1960s and early 1970s. The evidence suggests that there is now a trend to the *de-feminization* of manufacturing industry which goes back to the mid-1970s at least. Since then many of the plants located in the outer estates and new towns have closed down, while many others have substantially reduced the size of their workforce (Lewis and Meegan, 1986). In these areas women are heavily concentrated in semi- and unskilled production jobs, such as in assembly work, testing, and packing, which have proved and seem likely to continue to prove particularly vulnerable, with the introduction of increasingly automated production technology (SPRU, 1982).

The opportunity for women to find employment in manufacturing has therefore further diminished during recent years in both inner and outer urban areas throughout the country. This has had a particularly serious impact on women's employment in northern cities where employment growth in the service sector has been far less than in London, the South East and Midlands. Much of the growth in women's service-sector employment in the latter areas has, however, been of part-time jobs. The growth in women's employment in London, for example, was composed of an increase of 12 per cent in women's part-time employment and a decline of 3 per cent in women's full-time jobs (LSPU, 1986). This move to part-time work is part of a general trend towards a more flexible workforce (Cooke, 1986; Mitter, 1986). The term 'flexible workforce' has been used to refer to people who work part-time, on temporary contracts, as homeworkers or who are self-employed. The results of the 1985 Labour Force Survey suggest that by this definition the flexible workforce in Britain had increased by 16 per cent, or over one million workers, between 1981 and 1985, and accounted for over one-third of the total workforce by 1985. It was estimated that this 'flexible workforce' was composed of five million women and three million men. In other words, over one half of all women in employment now form part of this flexible workforce. While the growth of part-time work accounts for some of the increasing casualization of women's employment, the growth of temporary work has been particularly significant (Meager, 1986). Recent evidence also points to a further growth in numbers of women homeworkers (GLC, 1986; Mitter, 1986).

Not only have women suffered significant job losses over recent years, but the nature of many remaining jobs is being changed, particularly by new technology. (SPRU, 1982; Werneke, 1983; GLC, 1986). For example, new technology is transforming, and many would argue de-skilling, women's jobs in the retail sector, with the increasing introduction of electronic-point-of-sales equipment linked to automated stock-control systems. The restructuring of the retail industry has also involved a shift in the location of retail jobs from existing high streets to new surburban locations, and a trend towards employing a small core of full-time staff with the remainder of the workforce, predominantly women, employed on a part-time basis.

Such changes in employment structure have also led to recent changes in trade union policy. A number of the major trade unions, the Transport and General Workers Union (TGWU) and the General Municipal Boilermakers and Allied Trades Union (GMBATU) in particular, have recently mounted campaigns aimed at increasing trade union membership among and improving the rights and conditions of part-time and temporary workers, the majority of whom are women. The TGWU's 'Link-Up' and GMBATU's 'Fair Law and Rights in Employment' campaigns, for example, are both aimed at improving the condition of this rapidly increasing group of workers.

Perhaps one of the major influences on both the availability and the terms and conditions of many women's jobs in urban areas, is the Conservative government's commitment to reducing public ownership and expenditure. Since the early 1960s, when employment in the public health, education, and other local government services expanded rapidly, women have been heavily concentrated in these sectors. Women's employment has fallen in public administration and education since 1979, and such trends seem likely to continue throughout the public sector. In particular, the government's privatization legislation, in the form of the forthcoming Local Government Act, will severely affect women's employment, as it proposes that cleaning and catering, among other local government services, must be put out to competitive tender by private contractors.

Alongside the changes we have mentioned which affect the majority of working women, there has been a continued growth of a new group of middle-class professional and managerial women workers in major urban areas, particularly in London, over recent years. In itself the growth of this middle-class group of women workers is having implications for working-class women, as many middle-class women employ other women, as cleaners and child-carers, to allow them to cope with the dual role of paid and unpaid work (Hanson, 1987*a*, 1987*b*).

So far the growth of women's unemployment during the 1980s has not been mentioned. This is mainly because the official figures of those registered as unemployed are well known to be a poor guide to the number of women either 'seeking' or 'wanting' paid work, as they seriously undercount women's, and particularly married women's, unemployment. Despite this, even the official unemployment figures indicate that women's unemployment in Britain increased dramatically between 1979 and 1986. As table 12.2 also shows, in Greater London the rate of increase was much larger than the national rate.

TABLE 12.2. Women's unemployment in London and Great Britain, 1979–1986

	October 1979		March 1986		Increase	
	No.	% total	No.	% total	No.	%
Great Britain	357,400	29.6	992,300	31.0	634,900	178
Greater London	30,300	24.9	124,048	30.5	93,748	292

Source: LSPU, 1986*a*.

By comparing the 1985 Population Census figures for women's unemployment with the Department of Employment's figures for London, a recent report estimates that women's unemployment was undercounted by 38 per cent in the official DE statistics. This compares with an undercounting of only 1 per cent in men's unemployment (LSPU, 1986*a*). As the report states 'Applying this level of undercounting to the . . . 1986 figures . . . (and the problem has undoubtedly increased following the 1982 changes to counting methods), we can make a conservative estimate that there are about 172,000 unemployed women in London' (p. 14).

If this figure is correct, than the increase in women's unemployment in London between 1979 and 1986 has been almost 475 per cent.

During the 1980s major changes have obviously been taking place in women's employment and unemployment. Women's employment in manufacturing has seen a major decline, while unemployment has increased sharply. The vast majority of women now work in the service sector. However, there have been job losses within a number of public and private service sector industries, while the reorganization of others has changed the content and conditions of significant numbers of women's jobs. The majority of women in both inner and outer city areas have seen their employment opportunities significantly reduced during the 1980s.

Policy Initiatives in Urban Areas

Feminist politics aim to change the unequal power relations between women and men, some aspects of which have been examined in this chapter. Differences between feminist theorists as to where the cause of the inequality between women and men lies have resulted in different emphases within feminist politics. Some of these differences have been identified earlier in the chapter, for example, betwen those who attribute the causes of gender inequality to women's reproductive role, to the construction of female and male sexuality, to the unequal division of domestic labour, or to unequal gender relations in the waged workplace.

In our view, the unequal power relations between women and men cannot be attributed solely to any one of these elements of patriarchy. Inequality between women and men is created and recreated throughout all spheres of activity. Policies to eradicate such inequality therefore need to challenge and transform gender inequality in all of these spheres. However, when we examine current policies we find their implementation is patchy and that they focus on only two principal areas: first, on easing the burdens of domestic labour and child-care carried by women, without directly challenging the gender division of domestic work; and, secondly, on attempting to achieve equal opportunities for women in the workplace. There has been relatively little policy action concerned with the social construction of sexuality, and such action as has occurred has provoked strong oppositon from many political and religious groups. There is, therefore, still a gap between feminist analyses of the reasons for women's inequality and the nature and extensiveness of the policies aimed at reducing it.

Women's initiatives in the voluntary and local government sectors

Despite the gap between theory and practice noted above, recent years have seen the emergence and proliferation of a large number of important initiatives concerned with tackling the inequalities women face in employment, training, housing, transport, and access to other services, together with initiatives around women's safety and violence against women. These initiatives have taken place both within the voluntary sector and, more recently, in a number of Labour-controlled local authorities in major urban areas, as well as within some trade unions and workplaces. Many of these initiatives have their origins in voluntary-sector groups, with women organizing themselves to provide, for example, refuges for women suffering domestic violence and rape-crisis centres. Since the late 1970s and early 1980s a number of Labour-controlled local authorities in urban areas have either set up 'women's committees' and 'women's units' or established 'women's equalities' posts within specific departments such as planning and housing, with the aim of tackling the inequalities faced by women within these areas (Halford, 1988; Goss, 1985).

These recent initiatives are all attempting to increase awareness of women's needs with respect to council service provision, to make service provision more relevant to women's needs, and to overcome some of the inequalities women face on the labour market. Within planning, for example, attempts are being made to increase women's safety by improving street and estate lighting, to ensure child-care and baby changing facilities are provided in shopping centres, and to ensure transport routes and frequencies reflect women's needs for non-rush-hour travel.

Women's initiatives within local authority economic development policies are also being formed. In particular, emphasis has been placed on improving women's access to training facilities and providing specific training courses for women in traditional as well as non-traditional skills. Other developments include funding child-care provision, both as a source of new jobs and to enable women to re-enter employment; funding women's employment projects; and attempting to improve the pay, conditions, and career structures of the large numbers of women employed by the local authorities themselves, which are very often by far the largest local employers in many urban areas (Mackintosh and Wainwright, 1987). In many cases these local authority initiatives have built on and helped to fund projects which were initiated by women's groups within the local community.

Conclusion

As we stated in the introduction, too little research is being done on the ways in which women's lives are changing in the cities of Britain. This is not because there are no important questions to be answered, nor because of a lack of adequate theoretical or methodological tools with which to do the needed research. More researchers should recognize the need to study the impact that recent economic, social, and political changes in Britain's urban areas are having on women of different classes and races.

References

Beechey, V. (1983), 'What's so special about women's employment? A review of some recent studies of women's paid work', *Feminist Review*, 15: 23–45.

Bowlby, S. R., J. Foord, J. Lewis, and L. McDowell (forthcoming), 'The geography of gender', in R. Peet and N. Thrift (eds.), *New Models in Geography* (Edward Arnold: London).

Brown, C. (1984) *Black and White Britain: The Third PSI Survey* (Heinemann: London).

—— (1985), *Machinery of Dominance: Women, Men and Technical Know-How* (Pluto Press: London).

Cooke, P. (ed.) (1986), *Global Restructuring: Local Response* (ESRC: London).

Coyle, A. (1985), 'Going private: the implications of privatisation for women's work', *Feminist Review*, 21: 5–22.

DE (Department of Employment) (1980), *Employment Gazette*, May (HMSO: London).

—— *Employment Gazette*, May (HMSO: London).

Drake, M., M. O'Brien, and T. Biebuych (1982), *Single and Homeless* (HMSO: London).

Elson, S., and R. Pearson (1981), ' "Nimble fingers make cheap workers": an analysis of women's employment in Third World export manufacturing', *Feminist Review*, 7: 87–107.

Firestone, S. (1974), *The Dialectic of Sex: The Case for Feminist Revolution* (Morrow: New York).

Foord, J., and J. Lewis (1984), 'New towns and new gender relations in old industrial regions: women's employment in Peterlee and East Kilbride', *Built Environment*, 10 (1): 42–52.

—— and N. Gregson (1986), 'Patriarchy: towards a reconceptualisation', *Antipode*, 18(2): 181–211.

Forest, R., and A. Murie (1987), 'Social polarisation and housing tenure polarisation: associations and dislocations', paper presented to the Urban Change and Conflict Conference, University of Kent, Canterbury, 20–3 Sept.

Goss, S. (1985), 'Women's initiatives in local government', in M. Boddy and C. Fudge (eds.), *Local Socialism* (Macmillan: London).

GLC (Greater London Council) (1985/6), *Women on the Move: GLC Survey on Women and Transport* (GLC: London).

—— (1986), *The London Labour Plan* (GLC: London).

Hakim, C. (1981), 'Job segregation: trends in the 1970s', *Employment Gazette*, Dec., 521–9.

Halford, S. (1988), 'Women's committees in local authorities', paper presented at the Institute of British Geographers Conference, Loughborough, Jan.

Hall, R. E. (1985), *Ask Any Woman* (Falling Wall Press: Bristol).

Hamnett, C. (1983), 'The conditions in England's inner cities on the eve of the 1981 riots', *Area*, 15: 7–13.

Hanmer, J., and S. Saunders (1984), *Well-founded Fear* (Hutchinson: London).

Hanson, M. (1987*a*), 'Nanny's biggest byte', *Guardian*, 3 Nov., p. 24.

—— (1987*b*), 'Reach out I should be there', *Guardian*, 4 Nov., p. 29.

Haringey Borough Council (1986), *What Makes Women Feel Safe: A Survey of Housing Safety in Haringey* (Haringey Borough Council: London).

Henwood, M., L. Rimmer, and M. Wicks (1987), 'Inside the family: changing roles of men and women', Occasional Paper No. 6 (Family Policy Studies Centre: London).

Hudson, R. (1980), *Women and Work: A study of Washington New Town*, Occasional Publications NS, 16 (Department of Geography, University of Durham).

Huws, U. (1984), *The New Homeworkers* (Low Pay Unit: London).

Leete, R., and S. Anthony (1979), 'Divorce and remarriage: a record linkage study', *Population Trends*, 16: (HMSO: London).

Lewis, J. (1984), 'Post-war regional development in Britain: the role of women in the labour market', Ph.D. thesis, University of London.

—— and R. Meegan (1986), in P. Cooke (eds.), *Global Restructuring* (ESRC: London).

LSPU (London Strategic Policy Unit) (1986), *A City Divided: London's Economy since 1979*, Economic Policy Group Strategy Papers (LSPU: London).

—— Transport Group (1986), *Community Safety and Transport* (LSPU: London).

McDowell, L. (1983), 'Towards an understanding of the gender division of urban space', *Environment and Planning D: Society and Space*, 1(1): 59–72.

—— (1987), 'Beyond patriarchy: a class-based explanation of women's subordination', *Antipode*, 18(4): 311–21.

Mackenzie, S., and D. Rose (1983), 'Industrial change, the domestic economy and home life', in J. Anderson, S. Duncan, and R. Hudson (eds.), *Redundant Spaces and Industrial Decline in Cities and Regions* (Academic Press: London).

Mackintosh, M., and H. Wainwright (eds.) (1987), *A Taste of Power: The Politics of Local Economics* (Verso: London).

Martin, J., and C. Roberts (1984), *Women and Employment: A Lifetime Perspective*, Department of Employment/Office of Population Censuses and Surveys, (HMSO: London).

Martin, R., and B. Rowthorn (1986), *The Geography of Deindustrialisation* (Macmillan: London).

Massey, D. (1984), *Spatial Divisions of Labour: Social Structures and the Geography of Production* (Macmillan: London).

Matrix Book Group (1984), *Making Space: Women and the Man-made Environment* (Pluto Press: London).

Meager, N. (1986), 'Temporary Work in Britain', *Employment Gazette*, Jan., 7–15.

Meegan, R. (1982), *Telecommunications, Technology and Older Industrial Regions* (CES Ltd.: London).

Mitter, S. (1986), *Common Fate: Common Bond: Women in the Global Economy* (Pluto Press: London).

Newman, O. (1972), *Defensible Space: People and Design in the Violent City* (Architectural Press: London).

OPCS (Office of Population Censuses and Surveys) (1984), *The General Household Survey* (HMSO: London).

Open University (1983), *The Family: Daughters, Wives and Mothers, Unit 9, The Changing Experience of Women* (Open University: Milton Keynes).

Pahl, J. (1985), *Private Violence and Public Policy* (Routledge and Kegan Paul: London).

Pickup, L. (1984), 'Women's gender role and its influence on their travel behaviour', *Built Environment* 10(1): 61–8.

Seager, J., and A. Olsen (1986), *Women in the World: An International Atlas* (Pluto Press: London).

SPRU (Science Policy Research Unit) (1982), 'Microelectronics and women's employment in Britain', SPRU Women and Technology Studies, (University of Sussex: Brighton).

Tivers, J. (1985), *Women Attached* (Croom Helm: London).

Trenchard L. and H. Warren (1983), *Something to Tell You* (Trojan Press: London).

Ungerson, C. (1985), 'Paid and unpaid caring: a problem for women or the state?', in P. Close and R. Collins (eds.), *Family and Economy in Modern Society* (Macmillan: London).

United Kingdom (1975), *Report of Select Committee on Violence in Marriage, 1974–1975* (553-II) xxxv. 73 (HMSO: London).

—— (1987), 'Households and families', *Social Trends*, 17: 45–6, Tables 2. 10–12 (HMSO: London).

Walby, S., (1986), *Patriarchy at Work* (Polity Press: Cambridge).

Watson, S., and H. Austerberry (1986), *Housing and Homelessness: A Feminist Perspective* (Routledge and Kegan Paul: London).

WEG (Women's Equality Group) (1987), *London Women in the 1980s* (London Strategic Policy Unit: London).

Wekerle, G., R. Peterson, and D. Morley (eds.) (1980), *New Space for Women* (Westview Press: Boulder, Colo.).

Werneke, D. (1983), *Microelectronics and Office Jobs: The Impact of the Chip on Women's Employment* (International Labour Office: Geneva).

WGSG (Women and Geography Study Group) (1984), *Geography and Gender* (Hutchinson: London).

13

Urban Unemployment

Ian R. Gordon

Unemployment appears to be a characteristically urban phenomenon. The modern concept of unemployment, as the deprivation of access to full-time employment, has its roots in the experience of ports and industrial cities in the last decades of the nineteenth century (Treble, 1979). Cities then, although growing in employment, had a particularly marked incidence of unemployment because of their close links with a volatile trading economy, the scale of their consumer and labour markets, which supported activities with highly unstable patterns of demand, and (so it was said) because of the physical and moral degeneration which turned sturdy and employable migrants from the country into an enfeebled or truculent mass (Stedman Jones, 1971).

In the contemporary Third World, where a similar process of rapid urbanization is under way, high rates of unemployment have also been seen as an essentially urban phenomenon, with inflated wage rates (Harris and Todaro, 1970), or an exaggerated perception of the availability of well paid employment opportunities (Harris and Sabot, 1982), being held responsible for an over-supply of urban labour.

In Britain in the 1980s urban unemployment is more readily associated with the current decline of the cities than with their period of growth, which in most cases is long past. Hence for politicians both of Left and Right the key to its solution has been seen as urban regeneration. Yet some striking parallels with the experience of the economically successful Victorian cities—not least the concentration of high rates of unemployment in 'inner city' areas such as London's East End—suggest that this analysis may be too crude. It is true that urban concentrations of unemployment (and other forms of deprivation) are no longer confined to the traditional inner-city 'black spots', with some of the highest levels of unemployment now being found in public sector housing estates at the periphery of cities such as Liverpool and Glasgow (Lever and Moore, 1986). Indeed London is almost exceptional now in retaining the classic 'ring' structure in which the poor are housed immediately around the central business district. But even the changes apparent in the geography of unemployment within other cities reflect a more significant social continuity, since for the most part the communities in the outer estates of the 1980s had been removed from inner-city areas redeveloped in the 'planning' hey day of the 1960s and 1970s.

At the same time, then, there tends to be both a strong spatial patterning to urban unemployment, and substantial ambiguity as to whether high levels of unemployment are associated with particular *areas*, requiring essentially spatial explanations, or particular *populations*, requiring social or psychological explanations. This descriptive issue, of how unemployment is actually distributed in the city, has considerable significance both in terms of what the answer may imply about appropriate policy responses *and* because of its relevance to long-standing theoretical debates about the causes of unemployment, and whether these should be seen in *aggregative* or *individualistic* terms. The debate has a very strong ideological element to it, centred around the question of who or what is to be held 'responsible' for unemployment, but it nevertheless involves a number of substantive causal questions, to which the close examination of geographical patterns can help provide an answer. But this empirical analysis has itself to be based on a careful consideration of what the various theoretical models would imply in a spatial market.

In the remainder of this chapter we shall pursue this line of enquiry, firstly through a discussion of the geographical dimension to some of the key theories of unemployment and labour market behaviour, and then by an attempt to discriminate between four specific hypotheses about the causes of concentrations of unemployment in inner London.

Explanations of Urban Unemployment

In capitalist societies (and for that matter in the state capitalist economies of Eastern Europe) the tendency is to treat labour power as a commodity like any other commodity. In the free market case this means that individuals compete with each other to sell their labour to employers, who are expected to carry on purchasing extra units of it up to the point where its wage cost is only just covered by the extra value of output produced. Changing conditions in product markets will alter the value of that marginal output, and hence both the wage that employers are willing to pay and the amount of labour which they purchase. If the labour market operates like a competitive market for commodities, however, price (i.e. wage) adjustments should ensure that everybody is selling as much of their labour as they would want to, given the currently available wage. The only unemployment then would be 'voluntary', in the sense that all those outside paid employment preferred the options of leisure, study, unpaid domestic employment, *or* prolonged search for a job, to employment at the currently available wage. This would remain the case even if there were differences between workers in their (expected) productivity, since these should be reflected simply in varying wage offers according to the market's perceptions of their abilities. In this so-called 'price–auction' model of the labour market (Thurow, 1983) everybody is employable at an appropriate wage. Hence for neo-classical economists who take this as the norm, either all unemployment is 'voluntary' (in this sense) or there is something defective in the operation of the labour market. These defects may take the form either of a general inflexibility of wages, allowing the emergence of 'demand-deficient' unemployment; inflexibility in relative wages, allowing the emergence of 'structural unemployment' (when demand is deficient only in some submarkets); or delays in market adjustment processes, leading to 'frictional unemployment.'

As Thurow (1983) and others have pointed out, however, labour is an odd, and somewhat recalcitrant, commodity, and different forms of employment relationship may be necessary to ensure its productivity. Employers may have good (i.e. profitable) reasons for offering a reasonably stable wage to their existing workforce, if they need its commitment and specific skills, rather than allowing 'outsiders' to price themselves into these jobs by undercutting the established rate. In this case, the market operates on what Thurow calls a 'job-competition' basis (as distinct from 'wage competition'), with selection being make among those willing to work at this fixed rate on the basis of their perceived capacities. If demand for labour falls, the unemployed can then only 'price themselves back' into jobs by 'bumping down' the skills hierarchy, with skilled workers taking semi-skilled jobs, and so on. Unemployment thus becomes concentrated among those who are seen as least skilled, unless there is a substantial pool of more casual jobs available for them in which wages *are* flexible downwards. Even if there is, the level of wages at which they all could be profitably employed in this relatively small sector of the economy may well be unacceptable in relation to the 'floor' of support offered by state benefits to the unemployed. In terms of the traditional categories those out of work might well be seen as voluntarily unemployed then, although the principal causes of their unemployment lay firstly in the rigidity of wage rates in skilled jobs, and secondarily in those individual characteristics which counted against them in the process of competition for the limited pool of more stable jobs. Others who are willing to work at the going rate in this marginal and insecure sector of employment may be out of work between jobs for a significant proportion of the year and fall into the 'frictionally unemployed' category.

From this necessarily brief review of labour market processes affecting unemployment, we can identify three principal types of explanation which have a bearing on its spatial distribution. These are:

1. a broadly Keynesian explanation which emphasizes the role of 'demand deficiency' in a situation of generally inflexible wages, and thus focuses on the *aggregate* 'gap' between labour supply and demand;
2. an *individualist* explanation which focuses on factors keeping particular members of the labour force out of employment, whether these are disadvantageous personal characteristics or situational influences on their willingness to accept, hold on to, or search for available jobs;
3. *structural* explanations, in which the effects of deficient demand and individuals' characteristics each depend on the particular way in which labour market processes are structured, with the two sets of effects interacting strongly with each other.

Within each of these sets of explanations variants can be found which come from very different theoretical positions. The 'aggregative' category, for example, would include not only orthodox Keynesians but also Marxists who see the state acting to maintain a 'reserve army of labour' for capitalist interests, and 'new classical' economists who believe that state action could not alter the 'natural rate' of unemployment. Moreover, at an urban level, where flows of labour migrants are substantial, no real distinction can be drawn between demand-deficiency and excess supply in the labour market. Hence this category also includes those, such as Minford (1985), who see the level of unemployment in declining areas as substantially attributable to constraints on the mobility of council tenants and other 'sitting tenants' in the protected private rental sector. Indeed any characteristics of an area which encourage an excess of in-over out-migration will add to its level of demand-deficient unemployment (Burridge and Gordon, 1981). From this perspective a greater risk of unemployment may be part of the price to be paid for living in an area with an attractive environment, above-average wage rates, or the greater range of choice offered by large urban labour markets.

What adherents to the *aggregative* view have in common is the belief that an individual's chances of being unemployed depend largely on the overall balance between labour supply and demand in his or her local labour market. In fact, because people are generally free to change their place of work, and if necessary to move house as well, in response to shifting patterns of employment opportunity, local (or even regional) labour markets cannot be seen as closed entities. Induced migration and commuting changes lead over time to a spatial diffusion of the effects of supply or demand changes in any particular area, so that the chances of being unemployed will depend on developments in its regional and national hinterland as well as within the immediate local labour market. Thus when there is a severe national recession, as in 1979–82, considerable increases in unemployment are experienced across the whole country, even in areas (such as London) where employment trends were scarcely affected by the recession (Buck *et al.*, 1986). Broadly speaking, it is only *differences* in rates of unemployment (not their level) which are to be explained in terms of conditions in urban labour markets, and it is *differences* in the pressure of demand for labour between areas that are relevant in explaining them.

Another inference which has been drawn from this line of argument is that if, as seems to be the case in Britain, labour migrants are influenced by differences between areas in the risk of unemployment, a once-for-all employment change will eventually be entirely absorbed by migration (or commuting changes) with no permanent effect on local unemployment. In the long run then, higher *levels* of unemployment are only expected where there is a persistent tendency for employment *growth* to be slower (or decline to be more rapid)—or factors, such as high birthrates, boosting the natural increase in labour supply. How strong this relationship is would depend upon levels of mobility in the labour force and the accessibility of the particular area to potential migrants and commuters from elsewhere. In the case of highly qualified white-collar workers, operating effectively in a national labour market, or of relatively small and centrally located areas, local employment changes (or demographic factors) may have a minimal impact on local unemployment levels. On the other hand, among manual workers, or at the level of a large peripheral region (such as Scotland), the impact would be much stronger. Hence, from the aggregative perspective at least, it seems that spatial variations in unemployment rates ought to be more important at lower levels in the occupational hierarchy, and at a regional rather than an urban level of analysis. Similarly, if mobility is inhibited by a slack labour market, high national unemployment will lead to wider spatial differentials in unemployment rates, as has been the case since the late 1970s (Gordon, 1985).

From this aggregative perspective, attempts to reduce unemployment within an area have to work on the balance between supply and demand, most obviously by promoting job creation, but possibly also by encouraging or facilitating out-migration. The effects of a once-for-all job loss could be offset by creation of an equivalent number of new jobs; in the case of persistently high unemployment caused by a relatively slow employment growth rate, a *continuing* boost to the rate of job creation (or emigration) would be required to keep unemployment down, not just a once-for-all injection of jobs.

The *individualist* explanations of urban unemployment turn this logic on its head by treating the overall unemployment rate in an area as a consequence, rather than a cause, of the specific chances of being unemployed of the various members of its population. From this perspective, high rates of unemployment in some urban areas are to be explained in terms of a population structure containing an above average share of those experiencing disadvantage in the labour market, those particularly prone to instability in their work patterns, or possibly of those who have a weaker incentive to work rather than to subsist on benefits. Casual empiricism and more systematic studies (Nickell, 1980; Buck and Gordon, 1987) both indicate substantial variations in individuals' chances of being unemployed, which are systematically associated with such characteristics as being young and single, unskilled and of black or Asian ethnic origins. Unemployment rates are thus likely to be correlated with the proportion of the working population of an area belonging to these vulnerable groups. And, if the influence of migration and commuting flows is so strong that there are no real variations between areas in the pressure of demand for labour, concentrations of unemployment would be entirely attributable to such 'personal characteristics' of areas' workforces. Such differences in unemployment rates would not be smoothed out by migration and commuting, since individuals could not alter disadvantages associated with their personal characteristics by moving to another area. In practice, where there are also variations in the pressure of demand for labour, the consequences of disadvantage will tend to be more serious in the weaker labour markets. Buck and Gordon (1987), for example, show that characteristics such as lack of formal qualifications or black ethnic origins have similar *multiplicative* effects on the chances of unemployment in both declining northern conurbations and in southern growth areas (roughly doubling risk in these cases), but this means that the simple differences in unemployment rates are much more marked in the high unemployment areas.

Two basic questions are raised by the personal characteristics approach: why should there be spatial concentrations of disadvantaged, or uncompetitive, groups of workers; and, secondly, why should labour market disadvantage be expressed in the form of unemployment rather than simply low wages, or poor conditions? At an intra-urban level, within particular labour market areas, the first question has a simple answer in terms of familiar processes of residential segregation. Those at a disadvantage in the labour market tend to be at a disadvantage in the housing market also. Within the private sector they are more likely to be found in low rent or low price areas, typically in or around the urban core. The majority, however, will tend to be concentrated in the lower-status estates of the public sector, which, according to local political and planning circumstance, may also be in the inner city (as in the London case discussed by Metcalf and Richardson (1980)) or out on the periphery. Underlying this explanation is the fact that almost all urban labour markets encompass sufficient diversity in occupational mix, life-cycle stage, and housing opportunities to generate and retain a significant minority of disadvantaged workers.

Why and how this proportion varies between labour market areas is less simply explained. In the case of ethnic minorities, we should have to look at the attractions which areas offered in terms of housing and employment opportunities (as well as distance from ports of entry) during the post-war period of Commonwealth immigration. This group of the disadvantaged may thus be more heavily represented in areas which have (or had) a relatively strong pressure of demand for labour (Metcalf, 1975). Other mobile groups with a high propensity to unemployment, such as young single males, may also be attracted to city areas (such as inner west London) with a stock of rentable accommodation and good access to job vacancies. The key question, however, concerns the distribution of unskilled and unqualified workers, who are both particularly exposed to periods of unemployment throughout the life-cycle and relatively immobile. Because of this immobility it has long been argued that these disadvantaged groups form an increasing share of the working population in areas of employment decline which more competitive groups have left. Such a process of selective migration is well documented, but its effects are relatively limited, since to double the proportion represented by even a perfectly immobile group requires a halving of the total working population. Where there are substantial disparities in the composition of the labour force, we need also to look at internal processes within the labour markets of declining areas to find an explanation for slower rates of decline in their *numbers* of unskilled, relative to the standards set in the growth areas (Buck and Gordon, 1987).

There is also the question of why labour market disadvantage should take the form of periods of unemployment, rather than simply low pay. That it need not is indicated by the case of women. Despite equal opportunities and equal pay legislation, various forms of discrimination against women persist within the labour market, while career interruptions for family raising also place many married women at a disadvantage. As a consequence, female hourly earnings remain about a third lower than those of males; but, when full allowance is made for concealed unemployment among apparently inactive married women, male and female unemployment rates are very similar.

The *structural* approach to urban unemployment really starts from these questions, and from the observation by Norris (1978) that the most crucial individual characteristics associated with unemployment were not 'personal' at all but the *outcome* of labour market experience. Conventional measures of 'skill', for example, only relate to the most recent job (or Job Centres' view of the most likely next job), not to either potential, or to the highest status achieved by a worker. Unemployment, particularly involuntary unemployment in a slack labour market, is liable to produce a downgrading of 'skill' on this criterion, as Norris shows with case studies of Greenwich and Sunderland.

The whole concept of 'skill' is in any case problematic, with employers' perceptions of likely responsibility, stability, and compliance being at least as important as specific manual or mental abilities (Oliver and Turton, 1982). Jobs differ crucially in terms of their stability, with quite different conditions, requirements, and recruitment criteria being applied to stable jobs and to those in which a high turnover is anticipated. Screening criteria, particularly for the more stable jobs, tend to include not only qualifications and various personal characteristics for which there are stereotypes, but also past work histories including job durations, spells of unemployment, and the stability characteristics of recent jobs. Employment in unstable 'secondary sector' jobs can thus become self-perpetuating, and involuntary job loss carries with it the risk of a downward spiral to underemployment (Norris, 1978), particularly if the pressure of demand for labour in the area is low.

The implications of this type of argument are that, while individuals' characteristics may have an important part to play in accounting for local, and even regional, levels of unemployment (Gordon, 1987), they are not the end of the story, and have to be related to the structure and processes of the labour markets concerned. Persistent decline which leads to demand-deficient unemployment within an area is liable to produce an increasing proportion of workers who are (individually) at a disadvantage in competition both with other local workers and with migrants or commuters from outside. Thus Elias and Blanchflower (1987) have shown that occupational attainment among young workers in areas of high unemployment is significantly reduced by their more frequent job changing and by breaks in their work history. Equally we should expect to find that a concentration of employment in small-scale competitive enterprises in activities such as private consumer services, offering relatively unstable jobs, will also tend to produce and reproduce a relatively uncompetitive labour force. Incentives to acquire formal qualifications, for example, are likely to be weaker where such secondary sector jobs predominate. In this case the areas involved might include places such as seaside resorts, as well as the larger urban labour markets where firms with high turnover rates can fill vacancies quickly and adjust their employment levels to fluctuating demand. Classic cases of this sort include the casual labour market of nineteenth century

London (Stedman Jones, 1971), which is showing signs of re-emergence in the wake of manufacturing decline, and many Third World cities.

Discriminating between Explanations: A Case Study

The three sets of explanations operate at different levels and require different sorts of evidence. For some hypotheses it is data about individuals (or about their jobs) which is most relevant; in other cases it would be ecological data (relating to average characteristics) at a particular geographical level; for some, cross-sectional comparisons are crucial; in other cases time-series or, ideally, longitudinal analyses (of changes in individuals' situations) are required. What this means is that no one study can stand on its own as an arbiter of the explanations. But, as we shall try to show, it is possible to learn a great deal from a single cross-sectional study with ecological data if some care is applied in setting it up.

The case study outlined here relates to London, which is obviously not entirely typical of British labour markets. Its advantages as a case are, however, its size and geographical extent, which offer a large number of observations (both of individuals and areas) for analysis, together with the body of previous research by various authors which can be drawn on for comparisons (e.g. Evans, 1980; Metcalf and Richardson, 1980; Bramley, 1979). Comparison could also be drawn with two studies carried out as part of the same project which made use, in the first case, of individual level data from the London sub-sample of the national Labour Force Survey for 1981, and, in the second, of time series data on employment and unemployment in London over the past three decades (Gordon, 1988). The main analysis, however, was undertaken with cross-sectional data on unemployment rates and other ecological variables derived from the 1981 Census Small Area Statistics for the 754 wards of Greater London.

The broad geographical pattern to unemployment in Greater London is fairly simple, and its main features are long established, notably the peak in the inner city, particularly the East End, and the decline in all directions towards the outer suburbs. For Greater London as a whole, the rate of unemployment among residents has tended to be at or below the national level (e.g. 9.7 against 9.8 per cent in October 1987), but for most of the inner boroughs it is about half as high again, while in Hackney and Tower Hamlets it is double the national and London averages.

On the basis of the general analyses of urban unemployment considered above, four possible explanations of the inner–outer pattern to London unemployment suggest themselves, focusing on:

1. contrasts in the pressure of demand for labour as a result of the much faster rate of employment decline in inner London;
2. the concentration in inner London housing, particularly in the crescent of public sector estates east of Charing Cross, of groups of workers whose personal characteristics place them at a competitive disadvantage;
3. a concentration in the same areas of individuals working in the unstable sector of the labour market;
4. discrimination by employers against residents of stigmatized inner areas.

Sets of variables relevant to each of these hypotheses were specified from the basic data available at small area level from the Census. In the case of the pressure of demand variables, relevant factors were not merely the local rates of employment growth or natural change, but rather weighted averages across the areas in which local residents work. Measures of this type have been successfully operationalized at London borough level (Gordon and Lamont, 1982), where they display a relatively smooth pattern of variation across the city, but are not readily computed for areas as small as wards. In their place a fourth order trend surface (a function of the eastings and northings of each area) was included in the regression analyses to pick up the contours of relative growth and decline in employment potential. The underlying assumption here was that, because of the overlapping character of travel to work areas in London, there should be no sharp discontinuities in the effective pressure of demand for labour and only a limited number of peaks, troughs, and valleys in the demand surface. In fact the major element in the trend surface tended to be simply an inner–outer slope from a peak around Tower Hamlets in inner north-east London, where employment has been declining most rapidly.

The personal characteristics measures were operationalized ecologically as the proportion of the relevant population possessing a particular characteristic identified as significant in individual level analyses. The major omission in this case was the lack of an indicator of the proportion of the population without qualifications, a very strong influence on individuals' chances of unemployment, but not recorded in the Census.

Also lacking from the Census is any work history information which might allow a clear distinction between individuals' characteristics and those of their jobs. All that is available is the most recent occupation (or socio-economic group) and industry. As a starting-point, the industry was treated as a job characteristic (which is reasonable), and the socio-economic group as a personal characteristic, although the latter assumption is clearly open to question. Finally, the hypothesis about

TABLE 13.1. Regression of unemployment rates across wards in Greater London 1981

Independent variable	Males	SWD females	Married females	16–19-year-olds
Local authority tenure	0.077	0.057	0.014	0.072
	(15.9)**	(9.3)**	(3.9)**	(5.1)**
Housing Association tenure	0.062	0.050	0.014	0.038
	(5.8)**	(3.8)**	(2.0)*	(1.2)
Unfurnished rented tenure	0.017	0.022	– 0.012	0.094
	(1.4)	(1.4)	(1.4)	(2.8)**
Furnished rented tenure	0.020	0.013	0.016	0.069
	(1.3)	(0.7)	(1.6)	(1.5)
Owner-occupied tenure	—	—	—	—
Local Authority housing areas	0.008	0.006	0.004	0.008
	(5.1)**	(3.4)**	(3.6)**	(1.8)
SEG 1, 2, 13 (employers, managers	– 0.005	0.014	0.025	– 0.010
	(0.4)	(0.6)	(1.9)	(0.2)
SEG 3, 5 (professionals)	– 0.006	0.004	– 0.035	0.015
	(0.3)	(0.1)	(1.4)	(0.2)
SEG 5, 6 (inter/junior non-manual)	– 0.015	—	—	– 0.060
	(1.0)			(1.3)
SEG 12, 14 (own account)	0.004	0.055	0.051	– 0.078
	(0.2)	(1.1)	(1.8)	(1.1)
SEG 8, 9 (skilled manual)	—	– 0.030	0.016	—
		(0.9)	(0.8)	
SEG 7, 10, 15 (semi-skilled)	0.001	0.043	0.032	0.033
	(0.0)	(3.3)**	(4.3)**	(0.6)
SEG 11 (unskilled manual)	0.082	– 0.002	– 0.037	0.004
	(3.4)**	(0.1)	(2.6)*	(0.1)
SEG 17 (unclassified)	0.100	0.205	0.103	0.155
	(4.5)**	(7.6)**	(6.8)**	(2.3)*
Black working age population	0.108	0.112	0.023	0.274
	(10.2)**	(8.1)**	(2.9)**	(9.5)**
Asian working age population	0.033	0.018	0.082	0.070
	(4.1)**	(1.7)	(14.1)**	(2.9)**
Other NCWP working age population	0.010	– 0.046	– 0.042	0.087
	(0.4)	(1.6)	(2.6)**	(1.3)
'Excess' 16–29 age NCWP	0.253	0.311	0.273	1.039
	(2.9)**	(2.8)**	(4.3)**	(4.2)**
Irish 16–29	0.162	– 0.093	– 0.111	– 0.077
	(1.2)	(0.5)	(1.1)	(0.2)
Irish 30-retirement age	– 0.067	0.022	0.122	—
	(0.8)	(0.2)	(2.0)*	—
16–19 age in working age population	0.278	0.377	0.040	—
	(5.6)**	(6.0)**	(1.1)	

Independent variable	Males	SWD females	Married females	16–19-year-olds
Age balance in 16–19 population (older ages)	—	—	—	– 0.062 (7.2)
20–4 age in working age population	0.120 (3.4)**	– 0.090 (1.9)	0.138 (5.2)**	—
25–44 age in working age population	0.123 (7.4)**	0.111 (5.2)	0.071 (5.9)**	—
45-retirement age in working age population	—	—	—	—
Over retirement age: working age	– 0.008 (0.8)	– 0.042 (3.0)**	– 0.009 (1.1)	—
Production industries employment	0.020 (1.7)	– 0.001 (0.1)	– 0.007 (1.0)	– 0.095 (2.8)**
Construction industries employment	0.051 (2.9)**	0.015 (0.7)	– 0.025 (2.1)*	0.047 (0.9)
Transport industries employment	– 0.023 (1.7)	– 0.021 (1.3)	– 0.032 (3.4)**	– 0.066 (1.6)
Distribution industries employment	0.006 (0.4)	– 0.001 (0.1)	– 0.011 (1.2)	– 0.057 (1.4)
Services industries employment	—	—	—	—
Married males (or females)	– 0.099 (5.1)**	– 0.001 (0.0)	– 0.008 (0.6)	– 0.275 (4.7)**
Trend surface	1.0 (3.2)**	1.0 (2.5)**	1.0 (1.9)**	1.0 (2.4)**
$\overline{R}^2$	0.934	0.841	0.782	0.773

Note: * = significant at 5 % level; ** = significant at 1 % level; N = 754; t values are shown in brackets.

discrimination by residence was operationalized on the basis of the tenure characteristics of groups of wards centred around the observation and similar in scale to a London postal district. After considerable experiment this was finally expressed as a dummy variable, distinguishing groups of areas (all around the Thames in inner east London) in which local authority housing was the dominant tenure.

On this basis a set of thirty-two variables was defined, plus the trend surface, for inclusion in regressions with male, female, and youth unemployment rates as the dependent variable. The detailed results, presented in table 13.1, offer some support for each of the hypotheses, but it is the personal characteristics of residents which emerge as the crucial influences on ward unemployment rates. In particular, the ethnic origin and housing tenure variables stand out as the strongest influences on local variations in unemployment rates, followed by the proportion of very young workers and of individuals with unclassifiable occupations. The trend surfaces, representing pressure of demand factors, are always significant and reflect a clear tendency for unemployment rates to be higher in and around the inner areas where employment decline has been most rapid. But when other influences are controlled for, it appears that less than a fifth of the overall gradients found in the raw data are directly attributable to locational factors, as distinct from the social ecology of disadvantaged groups and areas. Industry of employment is also a significant factor for all except unmarried females, despite the very broad groupings to which the Census tabulations limit us. Male jobs in construction appear to be particularly unstable, while for young workers it is construction and services which stand out. For married females only transport stands out as a source of stable jobs. Together with the importance of the 'unclassified' last occupation, these results indicate that the jobs occupied by inner area workers have a direct influence on their vulnerability to unemployment, as well as indirectly through their acquired characteristics of 'skill', housing tenure, etc. The significance of the 'local authority housing areas' variable, even when the tenure pattern of households has been controlled for, provides some evidence that the stigmatization of areas may also be an important source of disadvantage in the labour market, although comparison with individual level studies confirms that its effect is much weaker than the direct impact of public sector tenure.

The two main conclusions which should be drawn from this particular case study are that local demand deficiency is not the principal cause of inner-city concentrations of unemployment, but that these cannot simply be attributed to lack of skill either, or any other single indicator of poor employability. Many factors are involved, of which the racial one is both very important and symptomatic. The general problem, however, is that inner-city residents for various reasons have come to occupy relatively weak positions in the competition for jobs, particularly those offering prospects of security and advancement. The prime requirement of an effective urban employment policy is that it acts to improve the *relative* competitive position of those disadvantaged by conventional labour market practices and judgements.

Conclusion

A final question to ask is whether the urban dimension to unemployment really matters. Is it only a matter of *how* the deck-chairs are arranged on the *Titanic*—or do urban concentrations of unemployment make a real difference to its overall level and/or the social costs it imposes? Surprisingly, in view of all that is written about urban unemployment, there is little hard evidence on which to base an answer to this question, and a substantial element of value judgement is involved.

So far as possible effects on the general level of unemployment are concerned, the main issue is whether spatial concentration makes the unemployed less effective as a potential labour supply, increasing the chances of labour shortages being experienced before unemployment has been substantially reduced. If housing arrangements are an important constraint on inter-urban (or inter-regional) mobility, unemployment in Glasgow or on Merseyside may be quite irrelevant to the inflationary potential of expanison in southern England. Similar considerations apply if inner-city populations come to be seen as consisting of 'unemployables'. In practice, however, we know that substantial mobility can be induced by employment growth, and that standards of employability vary with demand; the question is one of speed of adjustment and the extent to which spatial concentration impedes this.

As to whether the psychological costs of unemployment, or the effect on social order, are greater or less when unemployment is concentrated, this remains completely unknown. All that is clear is that the problems are less readily ignored by the political élite when they are shared by more than a small minority of a community. Similarly, in academic studies the importance of urban analyses of unemployment is not that locational factors are central to an explanation, but that at this level it becomes harder to ignore the specific labour market processes through which groups of workers are disadvantaged and consigned to a state of unemployment.

References

Bramley, G. (1979), 'The inner city labour market', in C. Jones (ed.), *Urban Deprivation and the Inner City* (Croom Helm: Beckenham), 63–91.

Buck, N., and I. Gordon (1987), 'The beneficiaries of employment growth: an analysis of the experience of disadvantaged groups in expanding labour markets', in V. A. Hausner (ed.), *Critical Issues in Urban Economic Development*, ii (Clarendon Press: Oxford), 77–115.

—— I. Gordon, and K. Young (1986), *The London Employment Problem* (Clarendon Press: Oxford).

Burridge, P. and I. R. Gordon (1981), 'Unemployment in the British metropolitan labour areas', *Oxford Economic Papers*, 33: 274–97.

Elias, D., and P. Blanchflower (1987), 'Local labour market influences on early occupational attainment', in I. Gordon (ed.), *Unemployment, Regions and Labour Markets* (Pion: London), 154–67.

Evans, A. (1980), 'A portrait of the London labour market', in A. Evans and D. Eversley (eds.), *The Inner City: Employment and Industry* (Heinemann: London), 204–31.

Gordon, I. R. (1985), 'The cyclical sensitivity of regional employment and unemployment differentials', *Regional Studies*, 19: 95–110.

—— (1987), 'The structural element in regional unemployment', in I. Gordon (ed.), *Unemployment: The Regions and Labour Markets* (Pion: London), 67–88.

—— (1988), 'Evaluating the effect of employment change on local unemployment', *Regional Studies*, 22: 135–47.

—— and D. Lamont (1982), 'A model of labour market interdependencies in the London region', *Environment and Planning A*, 14: 237–64.

Harris, J. R., and R. H. Sabot (1982), 'Urban unemployment in the LDCs: towards a more general search model', in R. H. Sabot (ed.), *Migration and the Labour Market in Developing Countries* (Westview Press: Boulder, Colo.), 65–89.

—— and M. Todaro (1970), 'Migration, unemployment and development: a two sector analysis', *American Economic Review*, 60: 126–42.

Lever, W., and C. Moore (eds.) (1986), *The City in Transition: Policies and Agendas for the Economic Regeneration of Clydeside* (Clarendon Press: Oxford).

Metcalf, D. (1975), 'Urban unemployment in England', *Economic Journal*, 85: 578–89.

—— and R. Richardson (1980), 'Unemployment in London', in A. Evans and D. Eversley (eds.), *The Inner City: Employment and Industry* (Heinemann: London), 193–203.

Minford, P. (1985), *Unemployment: Cause and Cure* (2nd edn. Basil Blackwell: Oxford).

Nickell, S. J. (1980), 'A picture of male unemployment in Britain', *Economic Journal*, 90: 776–94.

Norris, G. M. (1978), 'Unemployment, subemployment and personal characteristics: (B) Job separation and work histories: the alternative approach', *Sociological Review*, 25: 327–47.

Oliver, J. M., and J. R. Turton (1982), 'Is there a shortage of skilled labour', *British Journal of Industrial Relations*, 20: 195–200.

Stedman Jones, G. (1971), *Outcast London* (Oxford University Press: Oxford).

Thurow, L. C. (1983), *Dangerous Currents: The State of Economics* (Oxford University Press: Oxford).

Treble, J. H. (1979), *Urban Poverty in Britain* (Batsford: London).

14

Economic Restructuring, the Urban Crisis and Britain's Black Population

Vaughan Robinson

Black people have lived in Britain for almost three centuries, but they did not really become a significant element in the nation's population until the mass labour migration of the 1950s (Fryer, 1984; Visram, 1986). Employers in post-war Britain soon exhausted the pool of dislocated European refugees, and turned instead to the Commonwealth, where persistent underemployment and unemployment ensured a steady supply of eager volunteers keen to migrate to the 'motherland'. Labour migration from the Caribbean consequently increased sharply from 1954 onwards, to be followed at the end of the decade by immigration from the Indian subcontinent (Peach, 1979; Robinson, 1980). Despite the 1962 Commonwealth Immigrants Act which severely curtailed further primary migration, the continued arrival of dependants throughout the 1960s ensured that Britain's black population grew from 75,000 in 1951 to approximately 1.4m. in 1971. The youthful age structure of the main black groups and their higher fertility rates have been responsible for the sustained growth of the non-white population to the point where it numbers 2.38m. in 1985. Within this overall total, those of Indian ethnicity are the most numerous (689,000), followed by West Indians (547,000), Pakistanis (406,000), Africans (102,000), and Bangladeshis (99,000). The Chinese and Arabs are also significant non-white groups, but they are excluded from the present discussion, which concerns itself only with the black population defined as those of West Indian and South Asian ethnicity. Definitions aside, it is of some importance to note that all the non-white groups are ceasing to be *immigrant* populations, since an increasing proportion of their numbers have been born and raised in Britain. This is the case for over half those individuals of Afro-Caribbean ethnicity.

The Role of Black Labour in the British Economy

The conventional account of black labour migration to the UK stresses that it was the very success of the British economy which attracted West Indians and Asians. The relatively rapid expansion of the economy produced labour shortages of two kinds: in certain industries which were enjoying particular success, the demand for labour simply exceeded the local indigenous supply; in other industries, labour shortages were brought about by successful industries poaching employees from sectors where the work was unpleasant, hard, or poorly paid. In both cases, though, black labour was simply sucked into the vacuum created by success (Peach, 1968).

Work by Cohen and Jenner (1968) and Fevre (1984) suggests that there was a further dimension to black recruitment not captured by the replacement labour thesis. They demonstrated that black labour was not only used where there was an *absolute* shortage of white labour, but in two other circumstances: either where limited capital investment had radically altered the labour process and degraded certain occupations to the point where blacks were the only workers who would consider these jobs; or where companies were attempting to reduce their unit labour costs rather then engage in the capital investment that would restore their competitiveness. In the former, companies were using black labour to make capital investment possible, while in the latter black labour acted as a substitute for restructuring and modernization. In both cases, though, black labour was viewed as a temporary measure by companies and industrial sectors which were failing to remain competitive in changed market conditions.

As a result, by 1971 black labour was entrenched in many of those sectors of the economy which were the most vulnerable to competition and technological change. West Indians were concentrated in engineering and metal goods, public transport, chemicals and metal manufacture, and vehicle building. Indians were found in the same sectors, as well as in textiles and clothing. Pakistanis were employed in textiles, engineering, and metal goods, chemicals and metal manufacture, and again public transport.

While contemporary accounts stressed the value of black labour as a short-term cost-cutting initiative (both for state and employer), it is now clear that insufficient thought was given to two critical aspects of this economic palliative. First, because of her colonial past, Britain almost coincidentally had a residual legal obligation to black members of the Commonwealth which gave them the right to permanent settlement in the United Kingdom. Although this was rescinded by the 1962 Commonwealth Immigrants Act, it was too late to prevent what were seen by many as temporary labour migrants from becoming permanent settlers. Secondly, little thought was given to the likely consequences of introducing black labour into factories and neighbourhoods alongside members of the white working class who had been socialized into regarding black people as inferior. Status insecurity was an almost inevitable result, and latent prejudice was fanned by competition and perceived threat. White Britons closed ranks and erected a ring of exclusionary barriers around the black population.

Britain in the late 1980s therefore has a black population of approximately two million who form a permanent, significant, and excluded part of the nation and the workforce. However, in the thirty-year period during which the black population has become established and then grown, there has also been a parallel economic and demographic restructuring of the country on a scale not seen since the industrial revolution. The purpose of this chapter is to consider the extent to which Britain's black population, which had been introduced to forestall and ease economic change, found itself the unwitting victim of that change.

The Urban Crisis as a Product of Economic and Demographic Change

Britain's current urban crisis flows directly from the broader changes in the national space-economy which began in the post-war period and which have since gathered momentum. These can be summarized under five points.

(1) As Britain has moved into a post-industrial phase, major sections of the manufacturing base have withered and the number of manufacturing jobs has fallen by 35 per cent between 1971 and 1986. In total 2.8m. jobs were lost, but certain industries suffered disproportionately: 333,000 jobs disappeared in the textile and clothing industry between 1975 and 1986 alone, and the engineering sector shrank by almost one million jobs over the same period.

(2) The selective closure of manufacturing plants has instigated a wholesale spatial redistribution of employment opportunities. There has been massive job loss in regions such as the North West (– 16 per cent 1979–86), Yorkshire (– 12 per cent), Wales (– 17 per cent), and the West Midlands (– 10 per cent), while other areas such as East Anglia (+ 9 per cent), the South West (– 2 per cent), and the South East (– 2 per cent) have maintained or even expanded their employment base. Overlaid on this regional dimension has been differential job loss between the conurbations, major cities, small towns, and rural areas. Conurbations, and more particularly their cores, were especially vulnerable.

Manchester, for example, lost 67,000 manufacturing jobs over the period 1971–6. In contrast, new jobs have been created elsewhere, particularly in the small and medium-sized towns of the South East.

(3) As industry has belatedly introduced capital-intensive production technology, there has been a combination of labour-shedding and increasing 'technologization' of the remaining workforce. The latter is reflected in falling demand for highly skilled and unskilled labour relative to that for semi-skilled machine minders (Green and Owen, 1985). In the inner city, the jobs which have survived are therefore increasingly available only to non-local labour which commutes from the suburbs, or for local female labour.

(4) Britain was one of the first nations to industrialize and is therefore one of the first to face the problem of obsolescent urban fabric. The housing stock is a prime example of this problem: recent figures indicate that the average age of British housing is now 55 years, and around one-quarter of English households live in dwellings erected before the First World War. Essential repairs and renovations have been costed at £54 billion.

(5) Britain has experienced a process of selective counter-urbanization. Major conurbations have been losing population since 1951 to small and medium-sized free-standing towns and indeed to rural areas. Again, though, it has been the conurban cores that have suffered most. Tower Hamlets in east central London, for example, was home to 601,000 people in 1901, half a million people in 1931, but only 147,000 people in 1985. Evidence demonstrates that it is the young, the white-collar workers and the decision-makers who have abandoned the inner areas, leaving the elderly, the unskilled, and the welfare-dependent in spatial, social, and economic marginality.

Britain has undergone a radical economic restucturing over the last twenty-five years which has been beneficial to certain regions of the country and to certain types of town. This redistribution of economic opportunity has been largely at the expense of major conurbations and more particularly their cores (Champion *et al.*, 1987). Moreover, the indigenous economic and social base of the urban cores has been weakened during a period of major world recession and increasing constraints on public expenditure. The mechanisms and resources which might previously have been expected to cushion economic change have themselves been reduced, and have been unable to provide the same strength of countervailing or ameliorative influence.

Britain's Black Population: Disadvantage and Spatial Location

All black people in Britain face handicaps aside from those imposed by economic restructuring. These include racial discrimination and racial disadvantage. The former can be direct or indirect, intentional or unintentional, but regardless of its type it is both widespread and a serious barrier to fair treatment. Accounts describe how discrimination occurs in the appointment of employees, their working conditions and salary, the speed of their promotion, and the decision to lay off labour (see Jenkins, 1986, for recent case-study evidence). It also takes place in the housing market, where private individuals and gatekeepers use black skin as a way of differentiating the 'deserving' and the 'undeserving', and therefore as a way of allocating mortgages, rented accommodation, public housing, and grants (see Phillips, 1987 for a review of the contemporary literature). Research indicates that, despite the Race Relations Acts of 1965, 1968, and 1976, discrimination persists, albeit in covert form. The attitudes which underlie discrimination have also persisted over the last twenty years, with blacks still seen as 'problems' and 'trouble-makers' (Robinson, 1987a). Racial disadvantage is a more complex phenomenon, which includes disadvantages brought about by newness to a country, cultural and linguistic differences, past discrimination, overconcentration in environmentally deprived areas, and educational difficulties. Discrimination and disadvantage ensure that black people are operating with additional imposed handicaps even in times of economic growth and success.

Neither has economic restructuring been equitable in its impact. Certain industries have been particularly hard hit, with sectors such as textiles, engineering, and vehicle manufacture suffering more than others. However, work on economic restructuring suggests that the industrial profiles of places is insufficient in itself to explain why certain places have survived restructuring unscathed while others have been decimated. Regional location and type of place seem to have been of equal importance, such that conurbations have suffered more than small towns, and northern conurbations have suffered more than southern ones. These factors of space and place are also crucial to an understanding of the impact of restructuring on Britain's black population. If blacks are not only concentrated in vulnerable industries, but also in vulnerable regions and vulnerable types of settlement, then it is clear that restructuring will have a particularly profound effect on them.

All the groups which together make up the black population *are* indeed concentrated (see Robinson, 1987b for a review of the geographical literature on this issue). Table 14.1 reveals that large tracts of Britain are almost devoid of blacks. In the case of Bangladeshis, for example, almost

TABLE 14.1. Proportional distribution of blacks in England and Wales, by enumeration district and selected countries of origin

% of ED's population born in countries 1–5	% of English and Welsh ED's having population born in countries 1–5				
	1. NCWP	2. West Indies	3. India	4. Pakistan	5. Bangladesh
0–0.99	51.0[a]	84.5	88.0	91.5	96.9
1–5	38.8	12.9	9.8	7.4	2.7
6–10	4.5	1.7	1.2	0.5	0.2
11–20	3.6	0.8	0.6	0.5	0.1
21–40	1.8	0.1	0.3	0.2	0.0
40 +	0.2	0.0	0.0	0.0	0.0
TOTAL	100.0	100.0	100.0	100.0	100.0
Maximum recorded in any ED	100	42	100	56	86

[a]*Example*: Of all EDs in England and Wales, 51% have between 0–0.99% of their population of NCWP birth.

Notes: All figures rounded. NCWP = New Commonwealth and Pakistan.

Source: Calculated from aggregations of unpublished data for all 140,431 EDs in England and Wales.

97 per cent of Enumeration Districts (EDs) have less than 1 in 200 of their population of Bangladeshi birth. At the other extreme, EDs do exist which have a majority of their population born in either India, Pakistan, East Africa, or Bangladesh.

Of more relevance, though, is the location of these concentrations. Table 14.2 indicates the major regional concentrations for three groups, and the extent to which they changed over the decade 1971–81. West Indians are heavily concentrated in the South East, with a smaller proportion in the West Midlands: this is true of both 1971 and 1981. Indians are found in the South East and both the West and East Midlands, and their pattern of distribution has become more diversified since 1971. Pakistanis are also concentrated in the South East, albeit with major settlement in the West Midlands, Yorkshire, and the North West. Their regional profile has also become more diversified.

Important as the regional dimension is, economic regions are really too large to provide precise conclusions. This is particularly true for the black population, which is often concentrated into one conurbation or city within an economic region. Table 14.3 shows how—over a period when the population as a whole was leaving the conurbations in large numbers—six conurbations retained a disproportionate importance for

TABLE 14.2.   Regional concentration of the black population in the UK (%)

Region	Place of birth							
	UK Whites		American NCW		India		Pakistan	
	1971	1981	1971	1981	1971	1981	1971	1981
North	7.1	6.3	0.3	0.2	0.8	1.3	2.0	2.2
Yorkshire and Humberside	10.1	9.9	5.0	4.9	5.9	6.5	19.7	21.1
North West	14.2	13.1	4.6	4.8	6.6	8.3	14.6	15.7
East Midlands	7.1	7.8	4.9	5.2	7.4	9.4	3.5	4.2
West Midlands	10.5	10.5	15.2	15.6	20.9	20.8	20.9	21.7
East Anglia	3.5	3.8	1.1	1.0	1.0	1.2	1.2	1.4
South East	33.8	34.1	65.3	64.9	53.8	48.4	35.6	31.1
South West	7.9	8.8	3.0	2.7	3.3	3.0	1.4	1.6
Wales	5.8	5.7	0.6	0.6	0.4	1.0	1.1	1.1

Notes: 1971 data exclude whites born in the American NCW, India, or Pakistan.
1981 data relate to all members of households headed by a person born in . . . These data will include some whites but they also include British-born blacks.
American NCW includes the British West Indies, Guyana, and Belize.

Sources: 1971 data from GBG Lomas (1973).
1981 data from Commission for Racial Equality (1985).

TABLE 14.3.   New Commonwealth and Pakistani population in the conurbations, 1961–1981 (%)

	West Indians			Indians			Pakistanis		
	1961	1971	1981	1961	1971	1981	1961	1971	1981
Greater London	57.3	55.2	57.0	33.5	33.5	36.3	21.7	22.0	19.6
West Midlands	14.4	13.0	12.8	11.0	14.0	16.5	24.1	16.9	18.6
SE Lancashire	3.2	3.4	3.4	3.2	3.9	3.9	4.0	9.0	9.3
Merseyside	0.6	0.5	0.4	1.7	0.7	0.6	0.8	0.3	0.2
Tyneside	0.2	0.1	0.1	1.4	0.6	0.6	1.6	0.6	0.7
West Yorkshire	3.0	3.4	3.0	3.7	5.0	4.6	19.3	15.9	17.3
Total, six conurbations	78.7	75.6	76.7	54.5	57.7	62.5	71.5	64.7	65.7
Rest of England and Wales	21.3	24.4	23.3	45.5	42.3	37.5	28.5	35.3	34.3

Sources: 1961 data: Census England and Wales, 1961. *Birthplace and Nationality* Tables, HMSO, 1964; 1971 data: Census Great Britain, 1971. *Age, Marital Condition and General* Tables, HMSO, 1974; 1981 data: Census Great Britain, 1981. *Country of Birth*, HMSO, 1983.

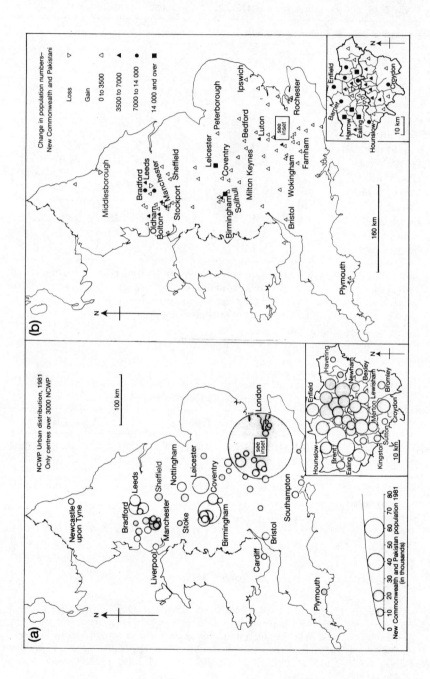

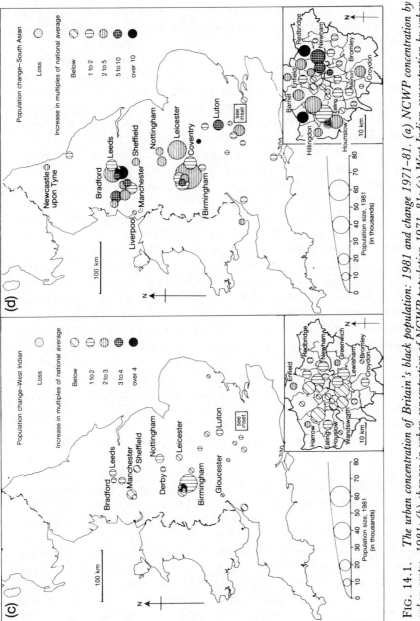
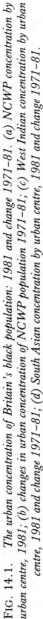

FIG. 14.1.   *The urban concentration of Britain's black population: 1981 and change 1971–81. (a) NCWP concentration by urban centre, 1981; (b) changes in urban concentration of NCWP population 1971–81; (c) West Indian concentration by urban centre, 1981 and change 1971–81; (d) South Asian concentration by urban centre, 1981 and change 1971–81.*

Source: Original research from Census data.

all three of the major black populations. Indeed the proportion of Indians living in the conurbations actually increased between 1961 and 1981. Table 14.3 also indicates how these totals are made up, and how Greater London and the West Midlands have a disproportionate significance for all the groups.

Despite these strong conurban concentrations, between 25 and 40 per cent of the three main groups live outside Britain's largest cities, and it is important that they are not excluded from any analysis (see Robinson, 1986 and Jones, 1978 for a discussion of the black urban system). Figure 14.1 looks at the entire urban hierarchy both for the black population as a whole and for its two main ethnic groups. The maps reveal a number of points of importance. Figure 14.1(*a*) shows that the black population is concentrated into a relatively small number of cities and towns and that these settlements are almost exclusively within Britain's industrial 'coffin', which stretches from London in the south to Lancashire in the north. Settlement is very limited within the new growth areas of East Anglia, the M4 corridor, the Hampshire basin, and the new towns. Figure 14.1(*b*) demonstrates that population growth over the period 1971–81 has largely been in the form of incremental additions to existing centres such as Leicester, Birmingham, London, Bradford, Huddersfield, and the Lancashire textile towns. Figure 14.1(*c*) indicates the sparse nature of West Indian settlement outside the two largest conurbations as well as the lack of intercensal growth, particularly in the free-standing towns of the South East. And Figure 14.1(*d*) shows the importance of the Pennine textile towns and the settlements of the East Midlands for the South Asian population. It also highlights the impact of family reunion on growth rates, with relatively large increases recorded in a number of settlements including those in the North West, parts of London, and centres in the Midlands.

Leaving aside the detail revealed by these maps, all four point to the same conclusion: the black population and its constituent groups are heavily concentrated within Britain's urban system into London, the provincial conurbations, industrial cities and towns north of a line between the Severn and Huntingdon, and to a lesser degree in provincial service centres. The Centre for Urban and Regional Development Studies (C U R D S) at Newcastle University has recently completed an analysis of which categories of settlement have gained from restructuring and which appear to have lost (Champion and Green, 1985). Its findings are that the most successful places are found in an arc around London stretching from Chelmsford through St Albans, Aylesbury, the M4 and M3 corridors into Surrey. Those places which have suffered badly from restructuring are the conurbations and manufacturing towns north of a Severn–Lincolnshire line. It is these very categories of settlements which house most of the black population. Indeed in 1981, approximately 65 per cent of all Asians lived either in industrial conurbations, in textile and engineering cities, or in the inner industrial zones of London (Robinson, 1986).

However, the plight of the black population in the late 1980s is exacerbated by a further locational twist, namely intra-urban concentration. Several factors conspired to ensure that on arrival black immigrants received only the poorest housing in the least desirable parts of the city: they were employed in industries which could no longer afford to pay an economic rate for their labour; they arrived at a time of acute housing shortage; they were categorized as undeserving by urban gatekeepers because of the colonial legacy; they faced open and legal racial discrimination; and they entered British cities during an era of wholesale clearance and therefore planning blight. As a result, black people initially rented rooms in lodging houses in the zone in transition. Later, West Indians moved into the public sector, but received properties largely on inner-city dump estates unwanted by whites (Henderson and Karn, 1984). Asians bought their way into owner-occupation by purchasing unimproved artisans' cottages in areas that had escaped the threat of demolition (Robinson, 1981). Figure 14.2 reveals the patterns of intra-urban concentration which developed in several cities as a result, and shows how black residents were unduly concentrated in core areas and relatively absent from the suburbs. Recent suburbanization, by Asians in particular (Werbner, 1979; Ward *et al.*, 1982), has been insufficient seriously to challenge the spatial isolation of the black population in the inner city, since whites are continuing to leave in greater numbers.

It is clear that Britain's black population *is* concentrated into some of those areas which are suffering most from the economic restructuring that has taken place since the 1950s. They are found in the cores of those major cities which are suffering from job loss, selective population loss, obsolete infrastructure, and inadequate investment. They are found mainly in those cities which have traditionally depended upon manufacturing industry for their wealth and employment. And they are concentrated into some of the regions experiencing the greatest shake-out of labour because of their reliance upon branch plants and their loss of the control function through merger and rationalization.

Location and Life-chances

The black population is likely to be one of the groups which most clearly demonstrates the impact of economic restructuring. Several indicators can be used to demonstrate this.

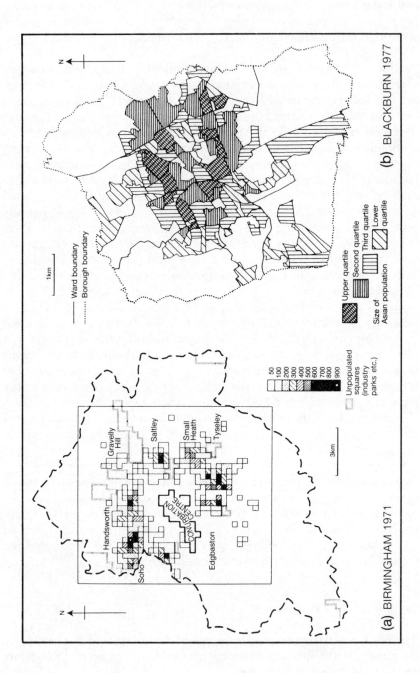

(a) BIRMINGHAM 1971

(b) BLACKBURN 1977

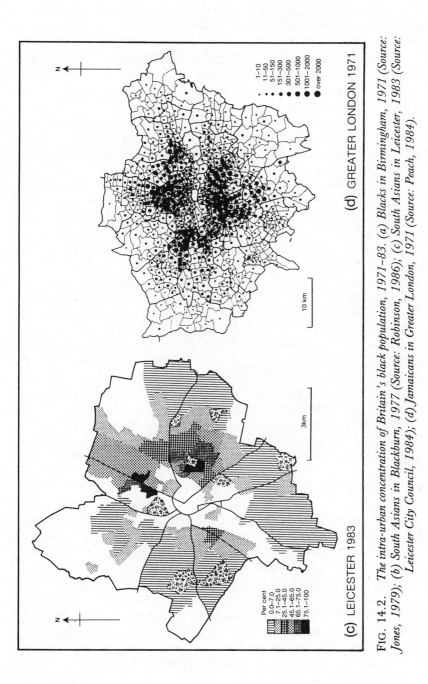

FIG. 14.2. *The intra-urban concentration of Britain's black population, 1971–83. (a) Blacks in Birmingham, 1971 (Source: Jones, 1979); (b) South Asians in Blackburn, 1977 (Source: Robinson, 1986); (c) South Asians in Leicester, 1983 (Source: Leicester City Council, 1984); (d) Jamaicans in Greater London, 1971 (Source: Peach, 1984).*

Researchers at CURDS have recently completed a project which allocates each one of England and Wales' Census EDs to one of twenty-two types of neighbourhood (see Charlton *et al.*, 1985, for a discussion of the general methodology). These neighbourhood types or 'superprofiles' provide a standardized summary of socio-residential characteristics across the country and therefore offer an overview of the life-chances enjoyed by people who live in such EDs. For this chapter, the super-profile typology has been used in conjunction with unpublished birth-place data from the Census for each ED. Birthplace is not an ideal surrogate for ethnicity, but it is the only viable alternative available at present. By way of comparison, data were also analysed for all persons living in a household headed by an NCWP-born individual: such a categorization provides a more accurate if undifferentiated measure of the total black population. Table 14.4 contains a summary of the results of the analysis. It reveals the extent to which Britain's blacks are under-represented in certain types of areas. These include: middle-class neighbourhoods; long-established areas of owner-occupied and improved terraces; more desirable council estates; and rural areas. Conversely, they are over-represented in the poorer parts of our cities, namely areas of unimproved terraces and less popular council estates with flatted accommodation. Table 14.4 also reveals that discrepancies exist between West Indians and South Asians. The former have moved from privately rented accommodation into the public sector, while the latter have turned instead to owner-occupation of cheaper terraces. Nevertheless both groups still reside in neighbourhoods which are object-ively inferior and which offer more limited life-chances.

The superprofile analysis is useful, but it provides only an overview and one which is potentially flawed by the ecological fallacy. It is there-fore necessary to use more precise and direct measures of the impact of disadvantage and restructuring. Unemployment is one such measure. Even when differing levels of qualifications are controlled for, ethnic unemployment is consistently higher than white unemployment, occa-sionally by as much as 300 per cent (DE 1987: Brennan and McGeevor, 1987). Other evidence suggests that blacks are also over-represented among the long-term unemployed. Table 14.5 looks at ethnic unem-ployment by region, and indicates how blacks living in those areas most affected by economic restructuring have suffered most from unemploy-ment, as inefficient sectors of the economy have tackled their historic weaknesses. In these areas, black unemployment is often twice or three times the already high rate for whites. Clearly, as industry has finally accepted the need for comprehensive restructuring, it has in parallel abandoned the temporary strategy of reducing unit labour costs by employing black labour.

TABLE 14.4.   Summary of superprofile analysis of Enumeration Districts in England and Wales (%)

Neighbourhood type to which ED allocated	Total population	NCWP	West Indian	Indian	Pakistani
1. White-collar families in suburban or semi-rural detached or semi-detached properties; owner occupation; high car ownership.	37.1	16.7	10.5	21.5	9.0
2. Skilled and semi-skilled families in improved terrace housing; average unemployment.	7.8	3.9	2.7	4.0	4.4
3. Semi-skilled and unskilled families in cramped owner-occupied terraces.	2.0	24.1	10.8	32.6	54.2
4. Flats in converted properties; unskilled families; high unemployment.	2.6	3.5	2.8	2.7	5.3
5. Council properties; low residential turnover; skilled and unskilled families.	25.9	9.3	10.5	8.1	5.2
6. Council properties, especially flats; unskilled families; high unemployment; very low car ownership.	7.0	14.6	27.4	5.8	5.6
7. Rural areas.	8.6	1.4	1.3	1.0	0.4

Note: NCWP = all persons (regardless of birthplace) living in a household headed by an individual born in the New Commonwealth or Pakistan. As only main neighbourhood types are given, columns do not sum to 100.

Source: calculated from unpublished Census data using Openshaw's ED typology.

TABLE 14.5. Ethnic male unemployment by region, spring 1985

Region	Whites	W. Indians	Indians	Pakistanis
South East	100	287	125	312
West Midlands	100	300	192	308
North West	100	293	200	236
Yorkshire	100	250	208	292
East Midlands	100	267	211	278

Note: All ethnic figures are expressed as an index value related to white unemployment in the same region.

Source: Calculated from DE 1987, 1985 Labour Force Survey.

Housing provides an alternative measure of the opportunities offered to blacks in post-industrial Britain. However, interpretation of data can be hazardous because ethnic groups have adopted different strategies towards life in Britain, and housing has not always been allocated the same priority by all groups (Robinson, 1984). Housing preferences are culturally determined (Dahya, 1974), and housing opportunities vary greatly across the country. Despite these difficulties, evidence exists at all scales, from national to intra-urban, to demonstrate that black households gain access to inferior accommodation to their white counterparts. Several examples illustrate the point: The Department of Environment's (1979) National Dwelling and Household Survey found that only 14 per cent of West Indians and 17 per cent of Asians were 'very satisfied' with their accomodation, while this was true of 38 per cent of whites. Brown's (1984) national survey of racial disadvantage in 1982 demonstrated that Asians and West Indians were housed in poorer accommodation than whites regardless of tenure or the precise index of housing quality employed (see table 14.6). The House of Commons Select Committee on Home Affairs revealed during their investigations of the Bangladeshi community in Britain (1986) that although the group forms only 9 per cent of the population of Tower Hamlets, it represents some 90 per cent of the borough's homeless and 80 per cent of all households in bed and breakfast accommodation. And, lastly, extensive research into the allocation of public housing has shown that black applicants are more likely to be given older, flatted accommodation on unpopular inner-city estates (e.g. CRE, 1984; Phillips, 1986). A combination of economic marginalization, racial disadvantage and discrimination, and historic patterns of settlement, have thus consigned Britain's blacks to a residual position in relation to housing markets. Given the importance of residence and residential location for status, access to services, and proximity to employment, disadvantage is likely to be self-perpetuating. Indeed the Swann report (1985) on ethnic

TABLE 14.6.   Housing conditions of white, West Indian, and Asian households

	% in flats	% in detached or semi-detached houses	% in dwellings built pre-1945	% lacking basic amenities	% with more than 1 person per room
All tenure groups					
Whites	15	54	50	5	3
West Indians	32	23	60	5	16
Asians	16	26	74	7	35
Owner-occupiers					
Whites	5	67	56	3	2
West Indians	1	37	84	3	13
Asians	4	29	81	5	33
Council tenants					
Whites	27	39	27	3	5
West Indians	54	9	34	3	20
Asians	54	11	35	7	43
Private tenants					
Whites	32	33	87	27	2
West Indians/Asians	24	21	83	32	22

Source: Brown, 1984, table 35.

education pointed to the link between the social and economic circumstances of West Indian parents and the educational achievement of their children.

The spatial concentration of Britain's black population into the cores of declining conurbations and industrial cities has thus imposed upon that population enormous economic and social costs. Concentration has not, however, been without some advantages. Anwar (1986) has calculated that black electors now constitute a significant proportion of the electorate in around 100 constituencies. Their ability to influence the outcome of elections was an important factor behind the increased number of black candidates put forward by the major parties in the 1987 General Election, and their votes were certainly responsible for returning the first black MPs for some time. Concentration has also ensured a protected market for ethnic entrepreneurs (see Ward and Jenkins, 1984), who in the case of the Indian population now form 23.7 per cent of the male workforce (cf. 14 per cent for white males). In addition, it has allowed the reconstruction of island- or village-kin social networks, with the emotional and economic support which these provide; it has provided the territorial basis for the development of community institutions; and it has given limited protection from racial attacks and harassment. Concentration can therefore provide certain benefits, but in the case of Britain's black population these have to be set against the fact that those concentrations which do exist are found on the social, economic, and environmental margins of the wider society.

Blacks, Targeted Policy, and Inner-city Regeneration

Government policy towards black people has been remarkably constant over the last twenty years, and has had four major dimensions: the reduction of immigration, supposedly to improve race relations for black people already in Britain; the provision of a statutory framework and appropriate institutions to eradicate overt manifestations of discrimination; the combating of racial disadvantage through non-specific social policy wherever possible, with only limited assistance given to programmes aimed specifically at ethnic minorities; and the expansion of the role local authorities are expected to play in bringing about equal opportunities. Most commentators regard these steps as necessary, but also as little more than a minimal response. Policy has more often been guided by political expediency, and in particular a desire not to provoke a much-feared white backlash, than by any sense of sustained moral commitment. Each of these dimensions of policy will be discussed in turn.

Immigration policy is of only indirect relevance to the concerns of this chapter, but it cannot nevertheless be ignored (see Brown, 1983, for a fuller discussion). The period since 1961 has seen a series of immigration acts, which became effective in 1962, 1968, and 1971. There has also been a new Nationality Act in 1981. Without exception, this legislation sought to reduce the immigration of new primary labour migrants, except where individuals had skills which were in short supply in the British labour market (see Robinson, 1988). In a number of cases, they have also curtailed the right of dependants to join those already admitted for settlement. It would appear that, once the strategy of using black labour as a palliative for inherent economic weaknesses was seen to be ineffective it was abandoned, and the rights which colonial Britain had unthinkingly granted all its citizens were progressively withdrawn. Blacks were tolerated only as long as they served a purpose. It is also interesting that the legislation designed to end immigration was not presented in its real light, but rather as a way of helping black people who were already here.

Parallel legislation in 1965, 1968, and 1976 sought to outlaw overt discrimination, and later also indirect discrimination. It was, however, left to the aggrieved individual to complain, and it was then necessary to make a case either at an industrial tribunal or in a county court. The formalities involved in either procedure, and the difficulty of proving discrimination, particularly when indirect, have conspired to limit the number of complaints which are actually pursued (McCrudden, 1983). The Commission for Racial Equality (CRE), established in 1976 to promote racial harmony, itself describes the number of cases as insignificant in relation to the scale of discrimination: 213 cases were completed in 1987, for example. The CRE was also given wider strategic powers to identify discriminatory practices and deal with these outside the law. Two avenues have been pursued in relation to this: first, formal investigations prompted and undertaken by the Commission (Sanders, 1983) and, secondly, promotional work to encourage good practice and adherence to voluntary codes on equal opportunities (Ollerearnshaw, 1983). Twenty-seven of the 39 formal investigations published so far have been into employment and housing, and in 11 of the first 14 discrimination was found to have occurred and non-discrimination notices were issued. The Commission's report on the allocation of public housing in Hackney (1984) is a good example of these investigations, and has been used extensively in promotional work. In reality though, the work of the CRE is hampered by limited resources and also by the absence of an effective means of imposing penalties.

Successive governments have chosen to tackle the problem of racial disadvantage primarily through colour-blind inner-city policy. The thinking behind this strategy is that since the black population is disproportionately concentrated in the inner city, it will benefit disproportionately from any such initiatives. The £500m. per annum currently spent on the inner cities has undoubtedly benefited the black population to a degree, but Inner City Partnerships, Urban Development Corporations, enterprise zones, YTS, the Community Programme, the Restart scheme, and Enterprise Allowance do not address racial disadvantage directly. Moreover, despite substantially increased spending on ethnic projects after the 1981 disturbances, combined expenditure under the traditional Urban Programme and the Inner Areas Programme on specifically ethnic schemes was only £35m. in 1986/87: this represented 11 per cent of Programme expenditure. Even where race was a determining factor in developing a new initiative, this was not always apparent in the end results, as the Merseyside Task Force demonstrated (House of Commons Environment Committee, 1983). Indeed, only one policy instrument has been used specifically to assist ethnic minorities in an open way: Section 11 of the 1966 Local Government Act. Expenditure on this will rise from its 1986/7 level of

£91m. to a forecast £100m. in 1987/8, but because it can be used for staffing costs alone, 75–80 per cent is used for educational purposes (e.g. ESL teachers). Despite relaxation of certain of the regulations in January 1982, Section 11 is still widely criticized for being too restrictive and inflexible. Had it not been for the 1979 General Election, it would have been replaced under the Ethnic Groups (Grants) Act by a more general grant designed to alleviate racial disadvantage directly. This might have allowed scope for more imaginative policies such as those suggested by Cross (1987).

The final plank of public policy has been to elevate local authorities to the front line of the attack on racial discrimination and disadvantage. The 1976 Race Relations Act required local authorities to review their own operations and procedures in order to eliminate any factor standing in the way of equality of opportunity. Having done this, they were also to promote the general principle, using themselves as examples of good practice. Few local authorities have embraced these responsibilities wholeheartedly; Young (1982) thinks the number may be as few as one in ten even of those authorites in multi-racial areas. He went on to develop a typology of authorities, from the 'pioneers' through the 'learners' and 'waverers' to the 'resisters'. Those local authorities which did take action, however, succeeded in creating a significant impact. The Greater London Council's decision to commission an independent investigation into the allocation of council accommodation in Tower Hamlets was one good example of timely intervention (Phillips, 1986). Their policy of 'contract compliance' was another, despite the adverse publicity it generated (Carr, 1987). However, not all local authority intervention in the field of race has been either helpful or well-conceived: Birmingham's enforced dispersal policy between 1969 and 1975 would fall into this category (Flett *et al.* 1979).

Although Lord Scarman's report on the Brixton disturbances (1981) has been rightly criticized on a number of fronts, it *was* successful in bringing to a much wider audience the flaws in Britain's policy towards ethnic minorities in the city. It also stimulated discussion into the whole question of race and the inner city, and lent weight to a higher-profile approach to the issue. The disturbances themselves, and their repetition elsewhere throughout the early 1980s, did much to add a sense of urgency to the policy process, but commentators feel that little of substance was actually achieved between 1982 and 1987 outside the arena of policing (Benyon, 1984; Scarman, 1986). Indeed it was only when it became apparent that the Tories were electorally vulnerable on the associated issues of the inner city, 'two nations', and 'caring', that the inner city was elevated to become a leading priority on the political agenda. It is still too early to know whether this change in emphasis will materially address the issue and consequences of black settlement and economic restructuring, but the early signs do not appear promising. There is no mention of extra resource or candidly racial policy, and the continuing onslaught on the independence of local authorities may even undermine the gains which have already been made by the pioneers. Policy towards race is likely to remain deceitfully covert, and will continue to take the form of *ad hoc* crisis management devoid of clearly defined goals.

Conclusion

This chapter has shown how the migration of black labour to Britain in the late 1950s needs to be seen in the context of the contemporary state of large sections of the British economy. Black labour was introduced in an unsuccessful effort to forestall or ease the restructuring of significant parts of the British space-economy. When that restructuring did finally take place, it was against a backdrop of world recession, obsolete Victorian urban infrastructure, and severely constrained public expenditure. Moreover, unlike in West Germany, Britain's migrant labour retained residual colonial rights to permanent settlement, which it opted to exercise. In so doing, it also became the chief victim of the restructuring it was so optimistically 'imported' to forestall. Sadly, while some argue that Britain is now emerging into a healthy and profitable post-industrial dawn, this appears to be irrelevant to the fate of many of Britain's blacks who find themselves continuing to bear the economic and social costs of an economic experiment which was not of their making. Even more ironically, having used them when it suited our purpose, Britain's governments and indeed British society have systematically denied black people any resources to cushion the impact of restructuring or offered them any alternative role within mainstream British life. Certain groups within the black population will survive despite this, and will find their own roles and routes to success (Robinson, 1989). Others will not.

Acknowledgements

I wish to thank the ESRC Data Archive for supplying data for this chapter. The analysis and interpretation are, however, the responsibility of the author.

References

Anwar, M. (1986), *Race and Politics: Ethnic Minorities and the British Political System* (Tavistock: London).

Benyon, J. (1984), *Scarman and After: Essays Reflecting on Lord Scarman's Report, the Riots and their Aftermath* (Pergamon: Oxford).

Brennan, J., and McGeevor, P. (1987), *Employment of Graduates from Ethnic Minorities* (Commission for Racial Equality: London).

Brown, C. (1983), 'Ethnic pluralism in Britain: the demographic and legal background', in N. Glazer and K. Young (eds.), *Ethnic Pluralism and Public Policy* (Heinemann: London), 32–54.

—— (1984), *Black and White Britain: The Third PSI Survey* (Heinemann: London).

Carr, J. (1987), *New Roads to Equality: Contract Compliance for the UK?*, Fabian Society Tract 517 (Fabian Society: London).

Champion, A. G. and A. E. Green (1985), *In Search of Britain's Booming Towns*, CURDS Discussion Paper 72 (Centre for Urban and Regional Development Studies, Newcastle University: Newcastle).

—— D. W. Owen, D. J. Ellin, and M. G. Coombes (1987), *Changing Places: Britain's Demographic, Economic and Social Complexion* (Edward Arnold: London).

Charlton, M., S. Openshaw, and C. Wymer (1985), 'Some new classifications of census enumeration districts in Britain', *Journal of Economic and Social Measurement*, 13: 69–96.

Cohen, B. G., and P. J. Jenner (1968), 'The employment of immigrants: a case-study within the wool industry', *Race*, 10: 41–56.

CRE (Commission for Racial Equality) (1984), *Race and Council Housing in Hackney*, (CRE: London).

—— (1985), *Ethnic Minorities in Britain* (CRE: London).

Cross, M. (1987), 'The black economy', *New Society*, 24 July, 16–19.

Dahya, B. (1974), 'The nature of Pakistani ethnicity in industrial cities in Britain', in A. Cohen (ed.), *Urban Ethnicity* (Tavistock: London), 77–118.

DE (Department of Employment) (1987), 'Ethnic origin and economic status', *Employment Gazette*, Jan., 18–29.

Department of Environment (1977), *National Dwelling and Housing Survey* (HMSO: London).

Fevre, R. (1984), *Cheap Labour and Racial Discrimination* (Gower: Aldershot).

Flett, H., J. Henderson, and B. Brown (1979), 'The practice of racial dispersal in Birmingham, 1969-75', *Journal of Social Policy*, 8: 289–309.

Fryer, P. (1984), *Staying Power: The History of Black People in Britain* (Pluto Press: London).

Green A. E., and D. W. Owen (1985), 'The changing spatial distribution of socio-economic groups employed in manufacturing in Great Britain, 1971-81', *Geoforum*, 16: 387–402.

Henderson, J., and V. A. Karn (1984), 'Race, class and the allocation of public housing in Britain', *Urban Studies*, 21: 115–28.

House of Commons Environment Committee (1983), *The Problems of Manage-*

ment of Urban Renewal (Appraisal of the Recent Initiatives in Merseyside) (HMSO: London).

House of Commons Home Affairs Committee (1986), *Bangladeshis in Britain* (HMSO: London).

Jenkins, R. (1986), *Racism and Recruitment* (Cambridge University Press: Cambridge).

Jones, P. N. (1978), 'The distribution and diffusion of the coloured population in England and Wales, 1961-71', *Transactions, Institute of British Geographers*, 3: 515–33.

—— (1979) 'Ethnic areas in British cities'. In D. T. Herbert and D. M. Smith (eds.) *Social Problems and the City: Geographical Perspectives* (Oxford University Press: Oxford), 158–85.

Leicester City Council (1984) *Survey of Leicester, 1983. Initial Report of Survey* (City Council: Leicester).

Lomas, G. B. G. (1973), *Census 1971: The Coloured Population of Great Britain, Preliminary Report* (Runnymede Trust: London).

McCrudden, C. (1983), 'Anti-discrimination goals and the legal process', in N. Glazer and K. Young (eds.), *Ethnic Pluralism and Public Policy* (Heinemann: London), 55–74.

Ollerearnshaw, S. (1983), 'The promotion of employment equality in Britain', in N. Glazer and K. Young (eds.), *Ethnic Pluralism and Public Policy* (Heinemann: London), 145–61.

Peach, C. (1968), *West Indian Migration to Britain* (Oxford University Press: London).

—— (1979), 'British unemployment cycles and West Indian immigration 1955-74', *New Community*, 7: 40–4.

—— (1984) 'The force of West Indian island identity in Britain' in C. Clarke, D. Ley and C. Peach (eds.), *Geography and Ethnic Pluralism* (Allen and Unwin: London), 214–31.

Phillips, D. (1986), *What Price Equality?*, Housing Research and Policy Report 9, (Greater London Council: London).

—— (1987), 'Searching for a decent home: ethnic minority progress in the post-war housing market', *New Community*, 14: 105–18.

Robinson, V. (1980), 'Correlates of Asian immigration to Britain', *New Community*, 8: 115–23.

—— (1981), 'The development of South Asian settlement in Britain and the Myth of Return', in C. Peach, V. Robinson and S. Smith (eds.), *Ethnic Segregation in Cities* (Croom Helm: London), 149–70.

—— (1984), 'Asians in Britain: a study in encapsulation and marginality', in C. Clarke, D. Ley, and C. Peach (eds.), *Geography and Ethnic Pluralism* (Allen and Unwin: London), 231–58.

—— (1986), *Transients, Settlers and Refugees: Asians in Britain* (Clarendon Press: Oxford).

—— (1987*a*) 'Spatial variability in attitudes towards race in the UK', in P. A. Jackson (ed.), *Race and Racism* (Allen and Unwin: London), 161–89.

—— (1987*b*) 'Race, space and place: the geographical study of UK ethnic relations 1957-87', *New Community*, 14: 186–98.

—— (1988), 'Who's Who, Who's What and Who's Where: an Indian elite in Britain', in G. Pande (ed.), *Who's Who Indians in Britain* (Computers and Geotechnics: Swansea), 282–91.

—— (1989), 'Boom and gloom: the success and failure of Britain's South Asians', in C. Clarke, A. Mayer, C. Peach, and S. Vertovec (eds.), *South Asians Overseas: Contexts and Communities* (Cambridge University Press: Cambridge), in press.

Sanders P. (1983), 'Anti-discrimination law enforcement in Britain', in N. Glazer and K. Young (eds.), *Ethnic Pluralism and Public Policy* (Heinemann: London), 75–82.

Scarman, Lord (1981), *The Scarman Report: The Brixton disorders 10–12 April 1981* (HMSO: London).

—— (1986) 'Preface', *The Scarman Report* (Penguin: Harmondsworth).

Swann, Lord (1985), *Education for All: the Report of the Committee of Inquiry into the Education of Children from Ethnic Minority Groups* (HMSO: London).

Visram, R. (1986), *Ayahs, Lascars and Princes: Indians in Britain 1700–1947* (Pluto Press: London).

Ward, R., S. Nowikoski, and R. Sims (1982), 'Middle class Asians and their settlement in Britain', in J. Solomos (ed.), *Migrant Workers in Metropolitan Cities* (European Science Foundation: Strasbourg), 155–73.

Ward, R., and R. Jenkins (1984), *Ethnic Communities in Business* (Cambridge University Press: Cambridge).

Werbner, P. (1979), 'Avoiding the ghetto: Pakistani migrants and settlement shifts in Manchester', *New Community*, 7: 376–89.

Young, K. (1982), 'An agenda for Sir George: local authorities and the promotion of racial equality', *Policy Studies*, 3: 54–70.

15

The Challenge of Urban Crime

Susan J. Smith

The streets of Britain are getting meaner. The demise of law and order seems inevitable, and by almost all accounts the problem of urban crime has changed dramatically in recent years. Since 1960 recorded crime in England and Wales has risen by more than 6 per cent per year, increasing by 63 per cent between 1975 and 1985. The latest figures confirm the trend: between 1985 and 1986 theft, criminal damage, and robbery increased by 6, 8 and 9 per cent respectively (Home Office, 1987). The prison population is more than 8,000 in excess of prison capacity; and public expenditure on law and order is already more than one and a half times greater than in 1979.

At the same time, the capacity of society to cope with crime appears to have diminished. The 'clear-up rate' (the proportion of crimes 'solved' by the police) has fallen steadily since 1970 (when it stood at 45 per cent) to a mere 31 per cent in 1986; and fully 60 per cent of the British public worry about the prospect that they or members of their household might become victims of crime (see Smith, 1988). Law and order has, as a consequence, become one of the most pressing problems of current times. Nevertheless, the new-found prominence of urban crime often has as much to do with developments in politics as with trends in delinquency. In this chapter, therefore, I describe how recent changes pose a conceptual and analytical challenge as well as a problem for the agents of social control.

In recent years, the politicization of crime in Britain has gathered unprecedented momentum. This partly reflects growing public concern about the steady rise in official crime rates, but it symbolizes too the huge political rewards that follow when parties succeed in defining themselves as the champions of law and order. A turning-point came in the run-up to the 1979 General Election when a resurgence of popular authoritarianism (one strand of what was to become a distinctively British version of the 'New Right') swept the Conservative party to victory on a law-and-order platform. Since then, there has been massive and well-publicized expenditure on crime control and law enforcement, despite efforts to curb public spending on a range of other social services.

Although this strategy reflects a broader ideological preference within neo-Conservatism for investment into what Dunleavy and O'Leary (1987) term the 'first' sphere of state intervention (shaping the legal infrastructure, defending the nation and upholding moral values, rather than disturbing the market to redistribute wealth and meet social needs), the strategy proved so successful (in political, if not crime-preventive, terms) that the remaining parties are now making a concerted bid to appropriate the Conservative monopoly on 'law and order' (Morison, 1987) outlines some of the issues involved).

By the General Election of 1987, crime prevention had achieved prominence on the manifestos of all the major parties. Apart from some asides about the nature of police accountability, there were few obvious partisan differences. Law and order did not become a campaign issue, but none dared to ignore its centrality. The Alliance announced its plans to tackle 'Crime Crisis Areas'; Labour introduced its 'Crimometer' to illustrate the magnitude of the problem it would solve with its 'Safe Estates', 'Safer Streets', and 'Safer Transport' policies; and the Conservatives promised continuing priority for an already quite massive 'fight against crime'. These strategies are outlined in the relevant party manifestos for the June 1987 election. They differ in the balance of responsibilities assigned to the police, local authorities, and the public at large, but all pledge commitment to crime prevention in the event of electoral success.

At one level, increasing political interest in the problem of urban crime can be understood in terms of increasing public concern about safety and security. Marplan polls conducted for the *Guardian* show a steady increase in public anxiety during the early 1980s, and by the middle of the decade, a quarter of those surveyed regarded 'law and order' as today's most important political issue. At another, perhaps more cynical level, the politicization of crime can be seen as an important pre-requisite for securing the popular legitimacy of strategies which, although they appear (and, of course, are intended) to tackle the problem of deviance, simultaneously expand the forces for social control at a time when recession and unemployment have provided a significant catalyst for civil unrest. (Policing, as Reiner (1985) shows, has always been more notable for its role in relation to public order than for its efficacy as an instrument of crime prevention.) The incompatibility of these twin goals (of responding to crime and maintaining public order) will be more obviously apparent below.

A Framework for Research

Whatever its cause, the politicization of law and order in modern Britain mirrors events which occurred more than a decade earlier in the USA (Cronin *et al.*, 1981). North American experience suggests that this poses difficulties for conventional analyses of the problem of urban crime, and that it makes new demands—empirical, theoretical, and ethical—on the research community. In Britain, the struggle to disentangle policy-relevant fact from political (and mass media) rhetoric adds new impetus to at least three traditional concerns of urban criminology.

First, it is hard to overstate the truism that many of the most widely canvassed 'facts' about crime are equivocal, and often particularly poorly documented in the UK. The problems and pitfalls of 'official' statistics are well rehearsed elsewhere (most standard textbooks carry a section on this; Lea and Young (1984) provide a brief and accessible critique of the key issues.) It is now largely accepted that statistics of crimes known to the police provide primarily an index of police practice and citizen reporting behaviour (and even then, definitional and legal changes undermine the validity of all but the crudest attempts to monitor long-term trends). It is less widely appreciated among students of distinctively *urban* crime that there is no comprehensive, routinely issued publication which provides official figures allowing cities and conurbations to be studied separately from their rural hinterlands.

Crime surveys[1] are now routinely used to provide a fuller measure of crime than that contained in 'official' statistics—at least with respect to the victimization of private individuals and households. (These surveys are not, of course, without their own range of theoretical and methodological difficulties.[2]) The British Crime Survey (BCS), however, is relatively small by international standards and has only a short history; consequently, neither spatial nor temporal trends can be discerned without reservation. So far, only three sweeps of the BCS have been completed in England and Wales (1982, 1984, and 1988), two in Scotland (1982, 1988) and none in Northern Ireland (the key findings of the first

---

[1] Crime surveys are primarily designed to elicit the incidence and experience of victimization among a random sample of the population. One aim is to provide a measure of crime that is independent of police practice. Such surveys also typically provide information on the predictors of vulnerability to crime, the effects of crime, attitudes towards the police, and so on.

[2] The main drawbacks of crime surveys are that they cannot monitor 'victimless' or corporate crime; and, because they rely on human memory, they are subject to the errors of forgetfulness, and of the forward and backward 'telescoping' of incidents into or out of the survey reference period.

two surveys are summarized in Chambers and Tombs, 1984; Hough and Mayhew, 1983, 1985). Complementary and supplementary information is available from a range of local surveys (some of which are discussed by Bottoms *et al.*, 1987; Kinsey, 1984; Smith, 1982; Sparks *et al.*, 1977; Young *et al.*, 1986), but firm evidence on time series and trends cannot yet be pieced together. In short, no amount of political rhetoric or elaborate policy-making can overcome the fact that, empirically, there are major gaps in our knowledge of just what the problem of urban crime *is*.

Secondly, developments in the 1980s urge analysts to adopt a more critical perspective, challenging rather than accepting 'top down' definitions of criminality and recognizing the authenticity of public experiences and opinion. This seems crucial if responses to the problem of crime are to be sensitive to the needs of the public rather than to the demands of political expediency. Most research in the more traditional areas of offender behaviour (see, for instance, Bennett and Wright, 1984; Carter and Hill, 1980), environments of crime (an approach best summarized in Brantingham and Brantingham, 1981), and urban design (a tradition at its most controversial in the work of Newman (1972) and Coleman (1985)) seems willing to take the legal context and police-led definition of crime for granted. This perspective has been challenged by the so-called critical criminologists (see, for instance, Taylor *et al.*, 1975), but this school has been preoccupied with class bias in the labelling of crime and criminals. Critical criminology has had little to say about the aspirations and demands of actual and potential victims (who comprise the majority of the population). This has begun to change with the advent of a 'New Left realism' (see Kinsey *et al.*, 1986; Lea and Young, 1984; Matthews and Young, 1986), but there remains ample scope for analysts across the political spectrum to explore the critical implications of their research.

Finally, the politicization of law and order is a process which inevitably draws increasingly rigid boundaries between criminals and victims. Support for the fight against crime is best mobilized where there are clear symbolic distinctions between the deviant few and the law-abiding majority. In this context, criminology's well-rehearsed dictum that the problem of crime cannot be divorced from the society which produces, defines, and reacts to it acquires a new significance. To develop a balanced critique of the character and extent of urban criminality, the essential normality of much that is considered deviant must be appreciated. There is often an overlap and interchangeability between offender and victim populations, and 'crime' is frequently just one point on a continuum of everyday behaviours and encounters. If both social theory and public policy are to tackle crime adequately, criminological research will be subject to a wider range of disciplinary influences than has been usual; deviance must be regarded as part of a wider structure of social, political, and economic organization, not as an element that stands outside these structures.

By addressing these three sets of concerns, it should be possible to glean a clearer idea about how and why the problem of urban crime has been transformed in the last decade. Current trends obviously reflect, in part, an abundance of new opportunities for criminals (increased property ownership, social status acquired through conspicuous consumption, trends in life-style and activity patterns, and so on) as well as the changed circumstances of potential offenders (such as increased unemployment and benefit dependency). They also express new political priorities and ideologies which have successfully exploited the problem of crime for electoral gain. In seeking further to disentangle crime as the public experiences it from crime as the politicians construct it (and without denying that these categories overlap), I shall examine three poorly understood facets of this enduring urban problem. My foci will be the plight of the victim, the *effects* of crime (including fear), and the organization of social control. I aim to show how research on these themes has contributed to the tasks (outlined above) of (a) establishing what, and how extensive, the problem of urban crime is; (b) drawing out the political implications of the character of this problem; and (c) conceptualizing and coping with the experience of crime by drawing on more general strategies for the management of urban life.

Victimization and Urban Deprivation

Challenging the offender-centred orientation of Britain's criminal justice system, crime surveys have drawn welcome attention to the plight of the victim. These surveys show that victimization is much more extensive than official statistics suggest. They indicate that between two-thirds and three-quarters of all crimes experienced by the public never come to the notice of the police (Chambers and Tombs, 1984; Hough and Mayhew, 1985). Although these unrecorded offences are often relatively trivial,[3] a minority, including rape and domestic violence, are very serious (less than 10 per cent of known rapes are reported to the police), and even crime surveys cannot capture their full extent.

From a potential victim's perspective, the probability of experiencing crime is neither evenly nor randomly distributed. Cities are always less

---

[3] More than half those who fail to report offences to the police claim that the crime was too trivial to bother with.

safe than their rural surroundings, and inner cities are consistently more risky than suburbs. Some crimes, however, notably burglary, robbery, and thefts from the person, have a more distinctly urban dimension than others. In 1981, for instance, 27 per cent of inner city households, but only 16 per cent of their rural counterparts, experienced at least one property offence (the patterns are discussed in detail by Gottfredson, 1984). There are equally striking variations *within* cities in rates of victimization. In 1983, in England and Wales, actual or attempted burglaries affected 12 per cent of households on the poorest council estates, 10 per cent of those living in 'multi-racial' transition zones, just 3 per cent of respondents in the more affluent suburbs, and 4 per cent of those living in council estates with intermediate socio-economic status (Hough and Mayhew, 1985, p. 37)[4]. Even within high-risk zones, small area variations in individual and household vulnerability have been measured; they reflect the diverse structural and social character of different housing environments (Smith, 1986a). This patterning indicates clearly that crime is one of a number of hazards which disproportionately afflict those living in the more run-down, less well serviced, areas of the major cities.

Socially structured variations in the distribution of risks also give cause for concern. (These social factors interact with location, but, as Gottfredson (1984) shows, neither subsumes the other.) The young are more vulnerable than the elderly to a range of personal and property crimes; males are more at risk than females from violent crimes (with the exceptions of rape and domestic violence); and black people are more vulnerable than whites to racial attack (Home Office, 1981; Smith and Gray, 1983). Demographic characteristics alone, however, do not account fully for these differences in vulnerability. Exposure to risk, as controlled by life-style and activity patterns, is at least as important.

The significance of life-style was first explored in relation to the changing character of North American society. The increased separation of workplace from residence, increasing female participation in the labour force, and a preference for leisure activities located outside the home, all facilitate crime simply because these trends ensure that (a) property is more often left unguarded and (b) there is a greater intensity of routine mixing between potential offenders and potential victims. Tests of this 'life-style–exposure to risk' thesis show it works well in the

---

[4] The first BCS relied on a classification of parliamentary constituencies to define inner-city, suburban, and rural areas. Subsequently the ACORN classification of enumeration districts into 38 neighbourhood types (usually grouped into 11 classes) has also been added. These conventions are outlined in the main reports of the two surveys (Hough and Mayhew, 1983, 1985).

United States (Cohen and Cantor, 1980; Cohen and Felson, 1979). More recently, its relevance to Britain has become apparent.

Within one inner-city zone, 70–90 per cent of residents engaging in leisure activities outside the home once a week or less, compared with only 60 per cent of those whose activities are more frequent, escape victimization in any one year (Smith, 1986a). Throughout the country, people who go out on weekend evenings are two or three times more likely than those who stay in to suffer personal victimization (Gottfredson, 1984). Variations in activity patterns rather than demography *per se* might therefore account, for instance, for low victimization rates among the elderly, who tend to be less active than the young.

In sum, victim studies suggest not only that crime is spatially coincident with the most common indicators of urban deprivation, but also that socially, the incidence of victimization is ultimately connected with the routine practices of an urban life-style. The plight of the victim, when couched in these terms, has political as well as policy implications, and I shall mention them in turn.

Victimization studies represent, potentially at least, a democratization of concern for law and order. Already, such surveys have been used to draw attention to victims' opinions about the crime-preventive role of the police. Kinsey (1984), for instance, drawing on the Merseyside crime survey, claims that those most at risk demand a comprehensive yet minimal amount of police service: comprehensive in responding to particular criminal incidents; minimal in its propensity to interfere in a range of other community activities. Shapland and Vagg (1987) also use actual and potential victims' testimonies to outline a role for the police, illuminating the importance of rapid response, a willingness to collate criminal evidence, and an ability to provide a *visible* service to deter offenders.

The use of surveys to articulate victims' demands may be regarded as one contribution to a growing victims' movement in Britain. At the moment this movement is primarily concerned to define and meet victims' needs. This is an area of social policy where the servicing of emotional needs is at least as important as providing practical assistance, and where demand is grossly under estimated (Maguire, 1985). The main policy instrument currently in place is the growing network of victim support schemes which are sponsored by government but rely largely on volunteers for operational success. Their problems and potential are assessed by Maguire and Corbett (1987). A second development within the victims' movement aims to secure victims' *rights* within the offender-oriented criminal justice systems which characterize Western democracy. In the USA, victims' rights groups have been relatively successful in pressing for legislative change (their achievements are reviewed by B. L. Smith, 1985), and in articulating demands to redefine criminal victimization in terms of a violation of human rights (see Elias, 1985). The British response is less well developed, but the importance of securing a rights-based perspective in providing victims' services cannot be in doubt.

Increasing political, legal, and social sensitivity to the experience, needs, and demands of actual and potential victims sheds new light on traditional crime-prevention policy. For over a decade, governments' over-riding concern in Britain has been to bring the crime rate down (or, at least, to stop it rising), principally by investing in policing and related services. A victim-oriented perspective suggests some qualifications to this strategy, demanding much greater interplay between crime control and more general approaches to urban management.

The 'life-style–exposure to risk' thesis suggests that part of the rise in crime is a contingent effect of essentially desirable facets of the changing life-styles of the late twentieth century. This implies that a blanket reduction in crime could involve restrictions on life-style which might be unacceptable when judged by other criteria. A fair distribution of risks rather than a (probably unachievable) reduction in crime may therefore be the most appropriate goal to pursue. This seemingly modest aim is more able than national campaigns to recognize that, at an intra-urban level, the distribution of victimization coincides with other aspects of urban deprivation. For the public, crime is just one of many hazards associated with urban life; for those most at risk, it is one indicator among many of the disadvantage they experience by virtue of who they are and where they live.

The risks of victimization are spread differentially across cities in much the same way, and by many of the same processes, as the risks of other urban problems. Empirically, as well as theoretically, there are strong grounds for linking crime-prevention policy with a range of related urban, housing, and social policies, all of which now converge on the principle of neighbourhood revitalization as the leading edge of urban regeneration. Such locally sensitive schemes achieve less promin-ence than national law and order campaigns, but the relevance of linking crime-prevention policy with mainstream public policy is increasingly apparent (see Bottoms and Wiles, 1986, 1987; Smith, 1986a). Because law and order is the sphere of the Home Office while housing policy rests with the Department of the Environment and urban policy seems increasingly the domain of the Departments of Industry and Employment the required co-ordination might be hard to achieve. It is, nevertheless, a recommendation to which we shall repeatedly return.

The Effects of Crime on Urban Life and Culture

Crime is not only a problem for those who experience it directly. The *prospect* as much as the 'reality' of crime is ever-present in the major cities, and this alone is sufficient to impair the quality of life of individuals and communities. Indeed, the impact of crime is often greatest among those it seems least likely to affect. Women and the elderly, for instance (two ostensibly low-risk groups) are more fearful than men or youths (who are much more likely to be the victims of violence). Fear has a geography as well as a sociology (described in more detail in Smith, 1987), and though this is not unrelated to the geography of crime (as demonstrated by Hope and Hough, 1987; Warr, 1982), there are other factors which may be as (or more) important in determining the extent and distribution of anxiety (a counter-intuitive discovery which is discussed at greater length by Maxfield, 1984, 1987; Smith, 1983; Warr, 1984).

British crime surveys, national and local, show clearly that in the most deprived urban areas, public fears are accurately grounded in local risks: the poor suffer most both from crime and from the anxiety it generates (see Kinsey, 1984). On the other hand, the facts that, within any one community, fear is more widespread than recent victimization, and that it affects a different portion of the local population, have prompted analysts to examine the variety of social and environmental cues which appear to operate independently of objective risk to translate local events and experiences into the potential threat of crime. I have reviewed this literature elsewhere (Smith, 1987, 1988), and noted the importance of a sensationalist provincial press (S. J. Smith, 1985), repressive styles of policing (Lewis and Maxfield, 1980), a decaying physical environment (Lewis and Maxfield, 1980); and incomplete social support networks (Merry, 1981; Skogan and Maxfield, 1981). Likewise, Taylor and Hale (1986) find that neighbourhood 'disorder', community concern, and 'indirect victimization' (i.e. knowing about rather than directly experiencing local criminal incidents) all tend to inflate individuals' fears. Most thought-provoking, however, is the discovery that fear is most acute, and most likely to be debilitating, where communities feel a sense of powerlessness in the face of unpredictable local change.

Fear, it seems, is bound not only into sociology and psychology, but also into local politics. Lewis and Salem (1981), for instance, link high levels of anxiety in the USA with urban residents' limited capacity to control their lives and environment. According to Taylor et al. (1986), fear of crime is one of a range of emotions triggered when communities have insufficient resources to resolve the uncertainties associated with urban degeneration. High anxiety is an expression of the inability of local institutions to control the 'social disorganization' perceived by residents: it is 'a reaction to the decline of an area' where local publics are unable to mobilize the political and economic force they need to begin a process of revitalization (Lewis, 1980, p. 22).

At root, then, fear seems to have as much to do with loss of authority over space as with actual vulnerability to crime. The political implications are clear: while tackling crime must be an important pre-requisite for managing fear, so, too, must the task of increasing the extent of effective local control over local affairs (this means affording local publics the resources both to define their problems and develop solutions). Lewis and Salem (1981) found in North America that not only do communities who succeed in winning political power develop the ability effectively to address local problems, but also that this capacity itself often contributes to diminishing fear. In Britain, too, it seems possible that local democratic control in respect of a variety of governmental issues might be effective in reducing anxiety about crime (see, for instance, a range of evidence discussed by Lea and Young, 1984).

The effects of urban crime may, however, be more far-reaching than even the analysis of fear suggests. Increasingly researchers are probing beyond emotional and attitudinal responses, focusing instead on the implications of reactions to crime for the organization of urban life and the conduct of public policy. Most commonly, such work provides an account of the range of protective and avoidance strategies routinely implemented by the public. In a survey in inner Birmingham, for instance, fully two-thirds of respondents admitted to making some tangible response to the threat of crime. Only one-third of these actions could be described as protective 'target hardening'; the remainder involved strategies of avoidance or evasion—practices which inevitably contributed to mutual suspicion between different social groups (Smith, 1986a). Nationally, too, the BCS indicates that over a quarter of the population always or usually avoids certain types of people or neighbourhoods as a precaution against crime, and 14 per cent say the risk of crime discourages their participation in otherwise desirable events and activities. Moreover, among those who feel very unsafe and who we know are disproportionately clustered within 'multi-racial' inner-city areas and the poorest council estates, over two-thirds avoid going out on foot at night, and just over a quarter claim never to go out at all *solely* because of their concern about crime. Women and the elderly are particularly adversely affected, often effectively living under curfew in parts of the major urban areas like Islington and Merseyside (Kinsey, 1984; Young *et al.*, 1986).

Notwithstanding the social and psychological significance of these individual behavioural reactions, it is increasingly recognized that the effects of crime might affect behaviour at the level of *household* decision-making, and so carry important implications for the processes of neighbourhood decline or revitalization. Katzman (1980), for instance, has shown that high central city crime rates in the USA tend to inhibit in-movement by the upwardly mobile professionals who are most likely to act as a catalyst for urban regeneration. Taub *et al.* (1984) show in more detail how the perceived threat of crime affects people's evaluations of economic opportunities in the housing market, how it affects public willingness to invest in neighbourhood upkeep, and how it increases the probability of outmigration from declining urban areas. Skogan (1986) has recently developed a more formal schema to link fear of crime with residential change in urban neighbourhoods. He demonstrates, in fact, that the effects of a range of factors traditionally associated with urban decline—including disinvestment, demolition and deindustrialization—are mediated through, and exacerbated by, fear (the fullest account of this is given in Skogan, 1987).

The effects of crime must therefore be viewed as one among a variety of influences on urban development. As such they impinge directly on mainstream housing and urban policy. At a time when neighbourhood- or area-based initiatives are becoming the centre-piece of governments' strategy for urban revitalization, North American experience warns that the constraints on urban development introduced by fear of crime cannot be ignored. Like crime itself, fear impinges on a wide range of social, political, and economic processes; its impact reaches well beyond the traditional mandate for law enforcement; and its effective management might depend on extending the remit for urban policy. This broadening of responsibility for the management of fear directly parallels the broadening of responsibility for crime prevention outlined above. This kind of strategy requires a redefinition of the role of the police and, more urgently, a clarification of the increasingly blurred distinction between the problem of crime and the problem of policing.

Urban Crime and the Politics of Policing

Until recently, policing in Britain was examined primarily with a view to establishing its effects on the social and spatial distribution of 'official' criminality. It has long been suspected that police practice not only determines which crimes and criminals are most likely to enter the official statistics, but also introduces systematic bias into these statistics. Discretionary decisions in the pursuit of law and order may, for instance, contribute to the over-representation of black people in the arrest statistics of the Metropolitan Police (House of Commons Select Committee on Home Affairs, 1980; Smith and Gray, 1983), and account for social bias in the decision to prosecute rather than caution juveniles (Farrington and Bennett, 1981; Landau and Nathan, 1983). It seems less likely that variations in the deployment and organization of officers accounts for spatial variations in the incidence of the most common crimes (a possibility examined and rejected by Mawby, 1979), largely because six in seven of these offences are drawn to the attention of the police at the initiative of the public (Chatterton, 1976). Nevertheless, some authors, such as Huff and Stahura (1980) and Jacob and Rich (1980), maintain that an increase in the size of police forces and in the intensity of policing can significantly inflate the official crime rate (if only because there are more officers to discover and record offences which might otherwise have become part of the elusive 'dark figure' of crime). Lowman (1982) shows further that among offences whose discovery depends almost exclusively on police observations (particularly 'victimless' crimes such as drugs offences and soliciting for prostitution), discretionary policing can significantly affect crime rates and distributions. The nature and organization of policing is, therefore, an important component of any attempt to specify the extent and character of urban criminality. However, the debate about official statistics is the least of the controversies raised when the organization of policing impinges on the problem of urban crime.

Since the late 1970s, policing has become the centre-piece of the fight against crime. Spending on the police more than doubled during the first five years of the present Conservative government, and funding for the service increased by 38 per cent in real terms between 1979 and 1985. The police forces of England and Wales enlarged by more than 50 per cent between 1971 and 1981, and numbers climbed from 111,754 in 1979 to 121,550 in 1986 (an increase of almost 9 per cent). Police officers' salaries rose by 16 per cent in real terms between 1980 and 1984, and there are now more police per head of the British public than ever before, on salary scales that have improved significantly relative to those of employees elsewhere in the public sector.

Yet, in Britain, as in other Western democracies, this investment has had little demonstrable effect on the crime rate (a problem discussed in some detail by Heal, 1983). There is little evidence that larger, better equipped police forces are more efficient in detecting crime (Carr-Hill and Stern, 1979) or that greater police presence acts as a deterrent to potential offenders. Indeed, all the signs are that, above a certain minimum, there is little return in terms of crime control from increased investment in policing. In view of this, and because so many recent changes were initiated by governments' concern to maintain law and order, it seems reasonable to regard modern policing not so much as an influence on, as an effect *of*, crime—and one that is experienced unevenly within and between communities.

Lea and Young (1984) have argued that for policing purposes large cities are often tacitly divided into 'respectable' and 'non-respectable' parts, reflecting differences in social structure and the extent of urban decay. They argue that this has shaped two distinctive styles of policing, 'one in the inner city based on force and coercion, the other in the suburbs and the smart part of town based on consensus' (p. 65). This kind of analysis confirms that in some areas at least the problems caused by crime have become entangled by those caused by the way the law is enforced.

To an extent, the more problematic aspects of urban policing are, as Reiner (1985) points out, the inadvertent by-product of an otherwise laudable attempt to inject greater professionalization, specialization, and technical sophistication into the policing process. Unfortunately all these trends have been associated with a centralization of authority and power which has distanced key decision-makers from the public, and contributed to a decline in the local sensitivity (and, as we shall see, accountability) of the service. Policing has shifted from being a locally based, loosely co-ordinated operation to becoming 'a tightly integrated, national network of highly professionalized, autonomous police bureaucracies' (Baldwin and Kinsey, 1982, p. 104). The problems this introduces have been more pressing in some areas than others; the gap between the police and the public seems widest in the 'inner cities' and amongst racial and cultural minorities. Gordon (1984), Lea and Young (1984) and Kinsey and Young (1985) show that, ironically, it is these heavily policed, most severely victimized communities that are least well serviced in terms of crime prevention and law enforcement. More than any other factor, these systematic intra-urban differences in police practice have brought the politics of policing to the forefront of public debate.

It is frequently argued that the balance of interests influencing chief constables' operational and organizational decisions has, in the last twenty years, tipped away from local communities and in favour of the Home Office. Brogden (1982) and Rhind (1981) both describe this process, pointing out that when national and local conceptions of police powers conflict, the views of central government prevail. This lack of accountability to local communities is frequently blamed for the strained and deteriorating quality of police—community relations and for violent confrontations between the police and local pressure groups in some working-class areas. Demands for greater local accountability have led police authorities to clash with their chief constables throughout the country (especially in Labour-controlled areas). (Scraton's (1984) case study of Merseyside is particularly illuminating, and Boateng (1982) discusses the special problem of local sensitivity in London.) A crisis of accountability now divides those striving for the ideal of an independent, non-partisan police force from those demanding greater public partici- pation in policing at the level of policy and organizational strategy. The dispute has reached a stalemate which threatens to undermine the popu- lar legitimacy of the police; and because so many other traditional claims to legitimacy are now in doubt, local accountability is, as Baldwin (1987, p. 105) demonstrates, 'not a peripheral issue or merely a useful way to increase responsiveness, it is where hope has come to lie.'

In popular and political wisdom, the problem of accountability is usually regarded as a symptom of the extent of the problem of crime and lawlessness. Solutions are therefore sought within the conventional channels for managing law and order. So far, this has failed to resolve an increasingly bitter debate over the politics of policing, and has brought little comfort to those most at risk of crime. An alternative strategy (Smith, 1986*b*) removes the accountability debate from the ambit of law and order and inserts it into a wider debate on the balance of central– local government relations. Viewed in this broader context, the diffi- culties associated with police accountability become just one facet of a more general problem of specifying the degree of local autonomy which is most appropriate in advanced capitalist states. To use Clark's (1984) terms, sufficient 'initiative' is needed to allow local democracies a role in defining and solving the problems they experience, while 'immunity' from centrally dispensed sanctions can only be preserved while agreed principles (relating, for instance, to the operation of democracy and the authority of the law) are adhered to.

Drawing on the literature of political geography and political science (which has traditionally ignored policing issues), there is considerable scope to construct a model of police accountability that is acceptable to chief constables and central government as well as endorsed by local con- sent. The problem, though, is only partly to do with law and order: it is primarily about the effective organization of liberal democracy. This broader specification does not provide an *easier* solution, but it does provide a sounder basis from which to approach the question. Once again, an effective response to the problem of crime may depend on its integration with, rather than abstraction from, more general themes in urban management.

Conclusion

Law and order is justifiably prominent on the political agenda in post-war Britain. High crime rates pose a real threat to thousands of citizens, and the material and psychological consequences of actual and potential victimization should not be underestimated. However, the character of the problem has changed in recent years. The newfound political salience of law and order has created a new urgency for research that is able both to specify the 'problem' and develop solutions that are practically as well as politically effective. I have identified three areas where problems seem acute and policies undeveloped. These concern the plight of crime victims, the complexities of managing fear, and the strategies required to disentangle the problem of crime from the problem of policing. Even a brief review of these issues draws attention to the empirical, political, and practical complexity of what is lightly termed *the* problem of urban crime. Most fundamentally, then, this chapter shows that we do not yet know just how mean the streets of Britain are. The immediate challenge is to specify the issues more precisely, respond to them more broadly, and demystify the rhetoric which so effectively diverts attention from the experiences and demands of those most at risk.

References

Baldwin, R. (1987), 'Why accountability?', *British Journal of Criminology*, 27: 97–105.

—— and R. Kinsey (1982), *Police Powers and Politics* (Quartet: London).

Bennett, T., and R. Wright (1984), *Burglars on Burglary* (Gower: Aldershot).

Boateng, P. (1982), 'Democratic accountability and the Metropolitan police', in T. Bennett (ed.), *The Future of Policing* (Institute of Criminology: Cambridge), 163–9.

Bottoms, A. E., R. I. Mawby, and M. A. Walker (1987), 'A localised crime survey in contrasting areas of a city', *British Journal of Criminology*, 27: 125–54.

—— and P. Wiles (1986), 'Housing tenure and residential community crime careers in Britain', in A. J. Reiss jun. and M. Tonry (eds.), *Communities and Crime* (University of Chicago Press: London and Chicago), 101–62.

—— —— (1987), 'Crime and housing policy: a framework for crime prevention analysis', in T. Hope and M. Shaw (eds.), *Communities and Crime Reduction* (HMSO: London), 84–98.

Brantingham, P. J., and P. L. Brantingham (1981), *Environmental Criminology* (Sage: Beverly Hills and London).

Brogden, M. (1983), *Policing: Autonomy and Consent* (Academic Press: London).

Carr-Hill, R. A., and N. H. Stern (1979), *Crime, the Police and Criminal Statistics* (Academic Press: London).

Carter, R. L., and K. O. Hill (1980), 'Area images and behaviour: an alternative perspective for understanding urban crime', in D. E. Georges-Abeyie and K. D. Harries (eds.), *Crime: A Spatial Perspective* (Columbia University Press: New York), 193–204.

Chambers, G., and J. Tombs (1984), *The British Crime Survey: Scotland* (HMSO: London).

Chatterton, M. (1976), 'Police in social control', in J. F. S. King (ed.), *Control without Custody* (Institute of Criminology: Cambridge), 104–22.

Clark, G. L. (1984), 'A theory of local autonomy', *Annals, Association of American Geographers,* 74: 195–208.

Cohen, L. E., and D. Cantor, (1980), 'The determinants of larceny: an empirical and theoretical study', *Journal of Research in Crime and Delinquency*, 17: 140–59.

—— and M. Felson (1979), 'Social change and crime rate trends: a routine activity approach', *American Sociological Review*, 44: 588–609.

Coleman, A. (1985), *Utopia on Trial* (Hilary Shipman: London).

Cronin, T. E., T. Z. Cronin, and M. E. Milakovich (1981), *US v Crime in the Streets* (Indiana University Press: Bloomington).

Dunleavy, P., and B. O'Leary (1987), *Theories of the State* (Macmillan: Basingstoke).

Elias, R. (1985), 'Transcending our social reality of victimization: towards a new victimology of human rights', *Victimology*, 10: 6–25.

Farrington, D. P., and T. Bennett, (1981), 'Police cautioning of juveniles in London', *British Journal of Criminology*, 21: 123–35.

Gordon, P. (1984), 'Community policing: towards the local police state', *Critical Social Policy*, Summer, 39–58.

Gottfredson, M. R. (1984), *Victims of Crime: The Dimensions of Risk* (HMSO: London).

Heal, K. (1983), 'The police, the public and the prevention of crime', *Howard Journal*, 22: 91–100.

Home Office (1981), *Racial Attacks* (HMSO: London).

—— (1987), *Statistical Bulletin on Notifiable Offences Recorded by the Police in England and Wales 1986* (Home Office: London).

Hope, T., and M. Hough (1987), 'Area crime and incivilities: a profile from the British Crime Survey', in T. Hope and M. Shaw (eds.), *Communities and Crime Reduction* (HMSO: London), 30–47.

Hough, M., and P. Mayhew (1983), *The British Crime Survey: First Report* (HMSO: London).

—— —— (1985), *Taking Account of Crime: Key Findings from the 1984 British Crime Survey* (HMSO: London).

House of Commons Select Committee on Home Affairs (1980), *Race Relations and the 'Sus' Law*, HC 559 (HMSO: London).

Huff, C. R., and J. M. Stahura (1980), 'Police employment and suburban crime', *Criminology*, 17: 461–70.

Jacob, H., and M. J. Rich (1980), 'The effects of the police on crime: a second look', *Law and Society Review*, 15: 109–22.

Katzman, M. T. (1980), 'The contribution of crime to urban decline', *Urban Studies*, 17: 277–86.

Kinsey, R. (1984), *Merseyside Crime Survey: First Report* (Merseyside County Council: Liverpool).

—— J. Lea, and J. Young (1986), *Losing the Fight against Crime* (Basil Blackwell: Oxford).

—— and J. Young (1985), 'Crime is a class issue', *New Statesman*, 109: 16–17.

Landau, S. F., and G. Nathan (1983), 'Selecting delinquents for cautioning in the London Metropolitan area', *British Journal of Criminology*, 23: 128–49.

Lea, J., and J. Young (1984), *What is to be Done about Law and Order* (Penguin: Harmondsworth).

Lewis, D. A. (1980), *Sociological Theory and the Production of a Social Problem: The Case of Fear of Crime* (Reactions to Crime Project, Northwestern University Center for Urban Affairs: Evanston, Ill.).

—— and M. G. Maxfield (1980), 'Fear in the neighbourhoods: an investigation of the impact of crime', *Journal of Research in Crime and Delinquency*, 17: 140–59.

—— and G. Salem (1981), 'Community crime prevention: an analysis of a developing strategy', *Crime and Delinquency*, 27: 405–21.

Lowman, J. (1982), 'Crime, criminal justice policy and the urban environment', in D. T. Herbert and R. J. Johnston (eds.), *Geography and the Urban Environment*, v (Wiley: London), 307–41.

Maguire, M. (1985), 'Victims' needs and victim services', *Victimology*, 10: 539–59.

—— and C. Corbett (1987), *The Effects of Crime and the Work of Victim Support Schemes* (Gower: Aldershot).

Matthews, R. and J. Young (1986), *Confronting Crime* (Sage: London).

Mawby, R. I. (1979), *Policing the City* (Saxon House: Farnborough).

Maxfield, M. G. (1984), 'The limits of vulnerability in explaining crime: a comparative neighbourhood analysis', *Journal of Research in Crime and Delinquency*, 21: 233–50.

—— (1987), *Explaining Fear of Crime: Evidence from the 1984 British Crime Survey*, Home Office Research Paper 41 (Home Office: London).

Merry, S. E. (1981), *Urban Danger* (Temple University Press: Philadelphia).

Morison, J. (1987), 'New strategies in the politics of law and order', *Howard Journal*, 26: 203–6.

Newman, O. (1972), *Defensible Space* (Macmillan: New York).

Reiner, R. (1985), *The Politics of the Police* (Wheatsheaf: Brighton).

Rhind, J. A. (1981), 'The need for accountability', in D. Pope and N. L. Weiner (eds.), *Modern Policing* (Croom Helm: Beckenham), 42–52.

Scraton, P. (1984), 'Accountable to no-one: policing Merseyside', in P. Scraton and P. Gordon (eds.), *Causes for Concern: British Criminal Justice on Trial* (Penguin: Harmondsworth), 11–42.

Shapland, J., and J. Vagg (1987), 'Using the police', *British Journal of Criminology*, 27: 54–63.

Skogan, W. G. (1986), 'Fear of crime and neighbourhood change', in A. J. Reiss jun. and M. Tonry (eds.), *Communities and Crime* (University of Chicago Press: London and Chicago), 203–29.

—— (1987), *Disorder and Community Decline* (Center for Urban Affairs and Policy Research, Northwestern University: Evanston, Ill.).

—— and M. G. Maxfield (1981), *Coping with Crime* (Sage: Beverly Hills and London).

Smith, B. L. (1985), 'Trends in the victims' rights movement and implications for future research', *Victimology*, 10: 34–43.

Smith, D. J., and J. Gray (1983), *Police and People in London: The Police in Action* (Policy Studies Institute: London).

Smith, S. J. (1982), 'Victimization in the inner city—a British case study', *British Journal of Criminology*, 22: 386–402.

—— (1985), 'News and the dissemination of fear', in J. Burgess and J. Gold (eds.), *Geography, the Media and Popular Culture* (Croom Helm: London), 229–53.

—— (1986a), *Crime, Space and Society* (Cambridge University Press: Cambridge).

—— (1986b) 'Police accountability and local democracy', *Area*, 18: 99–107.

—— (1987), 'Fear of crime: beyond a geography of deviance', *Progress in Human Geography*, 11: 1–23.

—— (1988), 'Social relations, neighbourhood structure and the fear of crime in Britain', in D. T. Herbert, and D. Evans (eds.), *The Geography of Crime* (Routledge: London), in press.

Sparks, R. F., H. G. Genn, and D. J. Dodd (1977), *Surveying Victims* (Wiley: Chichester).

Taub, R. P., D. G. Taylor, and J. D. Dunham (1984), *Paths of Neighbourhood Change* (University of Chicago Press: Chicago).

Taylor, D. G., R. P. Taub, and B. L. Peterson (1986), 'Crime, community organization and causes of neighbourhood decline', in R. M. Figlio, S. Hakim, and G. F. Rengert (eds.), *Metropolitan Crime Patterns* (Criminal Justice Press: New York), 161–77.

Taylor, I., P. Walton, and J. Young (eds.) (1975), *Critical Criminology* (Routledge and Kegan Paul: London).

Taylor, R. B., and M. Hale (1986), 'Testing alternative models of fear of crime', *Journal of Criminal Law and Criminology*, 77: 151–89.

Warr, M. (1982), 'The accuracy of public beliefs about crime: further evidence', *Criminology*, 20: 185–204.

—— (1984), 'Fear of victimization: why are women and the elderly more afraid?', *Social Science Quarterly*, 65: 691–702.

Young, J., T. Jones, and B. Maclean (1986), *The Islington Crime Survey* (Gower: Aldershot).

16

Riots as a 'Social Problem' in British Cities

Michael Keith

The dramatic scenes of violence in Bristol in 1980, across the country in 1981, and in London and Birmingham in 1985 all shocked the national consciousness and firmly established the notion of 'the riot' on the political and popular agenda for the 1980s. These were scenes that in living memory had previously been confined to 'abroad', or at least the popular notion of that term which invoked the concept of 'mainland Britain', conveniently excluding recalcitrant Ulster. Yet did these riots constitute discrete problems in themselves; did the readily identifiable political issue of rioting correspond with a distinctive and specific form of popular mobilization in social reality, the phenomenon of rioting?

The central tenet of this chapter is that there is no separate problem of civil disorder as such, but rather a series of specific conflicts built into the structure of civil society, conflicts that may both surface in popular and violent mobilization and may be manipulated in the rhetorical symbolism of political discourse. Specifically, most urban riots in 1980s Britain must be understood primarily as grim moments in the evolution of a conflict between British black communities and the police, not as distinct events, nor indeed as repetitions of a single phenomenon.

The Academic Response

It has become part of received wisdom at times of rioting in British cities to make a straightforward, and usually unfavourable, comparison between the events on this side of the Atlantic and the American experience of the 1960s (Field, 1982; Killian, 1981; Kilson, 1987). While it would be foolish to ignore the lessons that can be learned from such comparison, there are dangers in the sometimes glib assumption that the disorders in the two countries are very similar.

The very many differences between the 'long hot summers' in the USA and the clashes seen in 1980s Britain cover many areas, ranging from the national economic and political situations of the two countries to the numerical black involvement in both ghetto residence and ghetto rioting. The disorders in the northern cities of the United States occurred after a transitory period in the black civil rights movement which had changed its emphasis from combating racism in the courts in the early 1950s to a stress on mass participation and grass-roots mobilization in (non-violent) sit-ins, freedom rides, public demonstrations, and campaigns of civil disobedience in the late 1950s and early 1960s. It was in this context that, while riots generally stemmed from conflict with white police forces in black ghettos, they could be much more easily tied to the politics of protest than could the British rioting.

This is not to say that policing was not a major issue in the American riots. Nevertheless, it is significant that in certain cities notorious for poor police–black relations (e.g. Chicago and Philadelphia) it was possible to raise the proportion of black police considerably and rapidly. In both Chicago and Philadelphia by 1970 more than 20 per cent of the police were black, whereas in the mid-1960s blacks constituted considerably less than 10 per cent of these forces (Sherman, 1983). Regardless of the measures taken, most black 'community leaders' and senior police officers would think it unlikely that such a change could be achieved so quickly in most British cities. If this is the case, it might well imply that poor police–black relations in the USA are considerably different in some way from poor police–black relations in the UK.

A second common error of comparisons with the USA stems from the opinion sometimes voiced in the media and at popular gatherings that the Americans found some panacea to stop the 1960s riots. The constrictions of space prohibit too detailed an analysis, and it is certainly not the intention here to denigrate the advances made in the fields of affirmative action and contract compliance in the USA, but it is worth noting that there is considerable debate in the American academic literature over whether these advances were produced by the civil rights movement or the ghetto riots. Nevertheless, it should be stressed that the levels of segregation are as high as ever in the American ghetto, that levels of deprivation are as high or even higher now than in the early sixties in several major black ghetto areas, and that in the 1980s a Chicago police chief is alleged to have threatened to resign if a black mayor was elected in the city.

However, the academic response to disorder in British cities, particularly in 1981, was not averse to borrowing explanatory frameworks from the American experience, in spite of Killian's (1981) warning that it is dangerous to say how alike two experiences of rioting were when even the Americans themselves are not sure of the causes or form of their own ghetto revolts.

Inevitably, analysis of civil disorder depends as much on the perspective taken and questions asked as on the nature of the disorders themselves. It is not the intention here to review all relevant literature, only to acknowledge that it is valuable to place rioting in its proper context in terms of the tradition of violent mobilization in British history (e.g. Gaskell and Benewick, 1987; Hobsbawm, 1959; Rude, 1964), the incidence of collective disorder generally (e.g. Taylor, 1984a, 1984b; Gurr, 1970; Berk, 1974), and the specific history of racial oppression and racially motivated violence in British society (e.g. Sivanandan, 1982; Joshua and Wallace, 1983; Fryer, 1984).

However, certain problems recur in analysis because of the competing notions of the riot as either an instinctive product of a particular set of social conditions or as a considered popular mobilization. Most major riots in 1980s Britain have certain superficial similarities that might suggest it is possible to deduce a list of causal elements which together constitute the 'ideal type' recipe for civil disorder. The people involved in such disturbances tended to be predominantly young, predominantly male, and predominantly black. Most riots have taken place in settings of economic depression and high umemployment. A constellation of 'social problems' gathers around the issue of civil disorder—'the inner city', 'youth', 'racial injustice'—implying connections without specifying causal links (e.g. Rex, 1981, 1984; Gough, 1982; Hamnett, 1983).

Yet it is not so easy to conceptualize the link between these material relations (economic structure) and one particular form of social action (the riot) without resorting to an attempted falsification/verification of the ecological fallacy. Specifically, the construction of an identikit 'average rioter' from such patterns (Southgate, 1982; Cashmore and Troyna, 1982; Lea and Young, 1982; Kettle and Hodges, 1982) tends to lead only to the explanation of implausible and stereotypical 'young, black, male, alienated' individuals, rather than to an explanation of real people's actions, depriving the act of riot of rationality (Keith, 1987).

The link is more profitably seen in terms of material causality. Just as a statue is causally linked, in the material sense, to the stone from which it is fashioned, life-style and position in relation to the means of production are similarly inseparable. The lifeworld (umwelt) or 'alternative reality' of black Britain (Bhavnani *et al.*, 1986) is fashioned out of the material relations of production, work, and worklessness, set against the exigencies of a racialized labour force and structured by the ideology of racism. Yet mobilization in riots is not an example of a class in itself becoming a movement for itself. Clashes between black people and the police are seen in the context of the blighted cities of twentieth century Britain; the existence of the latter does not necessitate the occurrence of the former.

Partly in recognition of the dehumanizing influence of emphasis on social pre-conditions, other writers have preferred to emphasize the

active role of participants in disorder, the riots seen as a social movement. Yet this classification covers subtle but significant variations in
the understanding of this movement, ranging from a conception of riots
as extemporized revolts, the flashpoint reactions to particular situations,
to a notion that has the riot as a form of deliberate political strategy. For
example, in 1981 Howe was keen to emphasize the revolutionary nature
of the disorders, and Verner (1981, p. 355) even suggests that Howe saw
the riots as 'an organized guerilla uprising against the police'. Certainly,
for Howe, the status of the rioting as a social movement of rebellion was
guaranteed by the shortcomings of Lord Scarman's inquiry into the
Brixton disturbances. He claimed that 'those forms which appeared in
embryo on the streets of Britain's cities must necessarily develop into full
blown manifestations in the not too distant future' (1981, p. 70).

Paradoxically, such description is not dissimilar to many conspiracy
theories proposed at the time of the rioting by some senior police officers
and newspapers (e.g. *Sun, Daily Mail*, July 1981, *passim*). In both cases the
riots are cast as orchestrated protests; only approbation or opprobrium
distinguishes the two conceptions of disorder. Yet for others (Gordon,
1983) the spontaneity of the uprisings is stressed and the rioting is seen
as an essentially disorganized activity.

The one writer to acknowledge this apparent contradiction was
Gilroy, who suggested that 'Understanding new political movements—
new class struggles—requires analytic concepts historically appropriate
to the new forms they take. These *spontaneous* struggles may sometimes
become violent, but this does not render them irreconcilable with a
strategic long-term war of position' (1981, p. 221; my emphasis). Prob-
lematically, violence is here legitimized in the cause of black resistance,
and rioting seen as contiguous with other forms of black mobilization.
Such a position has profound implications that are not only moral but
also relate to the sort of explanation suitable to rioting. Specifically, 'the
crowd' involved in disorder gains ontological status as a political actor.

The 'radical' historical provenance of the riots of 1981 is also at times
inconsistent. For some, 'In the summer of 1981 the British state went on
the attack against the people' (Bunyan, 1981, p. 153). Bunyan saw
street conflicts as the inevitable product of a shift away from consensus
politics produced by the late twentieth century crisis of British capitalism, and the police as the iron-fisted arm of the authoritarian state.
Consequently, the riots are not so much the property of any specific
racial division but belonged to the more general (and more abstract)
unit, 'the people'. Implicitly, black people were caught in the front line
of this conflict, almost by an accident of history. Explicitly, the
ostensibly multi-racial nature of rioting is stressed and 'a class dimension was added' (Bunyan, 1981, p. 153).

Conversely, the historical context for Fryer (1984) is the long history of repression suffered by black people in Britain in general, and the repression of black people in British cities by the police over the last thirty years in particular. The difference in emphasis is crucial. The sense of ownership that underlies this contrast is an important and recurrent theme. Whether or not the proprietorial claims on urban violence are age-specific (again the elusive notion of 'youth'), gender-specific or class-specific are similarly moot points. Riots may be 'the language of the unheard' (Martin Luther King), but who speaks this tongue? Black people, young people, working people (who are not work-ing), or is this merely the voice of the powerless? Many would bid for this powerful symbol, and it is in the clamour of the historical auction that it is easy to concur with Rushdie's point that 'History is natural selection. Mutant versions of the past struggle for dominance, new species of fact arise, and old saurian truths go to the wall, blindfolded and smoking last cigarettes. Only the mutations of the strong survive' (1983, p. 124). In this sense the bid to attach sympathetic interpretation to civil disorders, to define rioting as political action, is understandable, a legitimate exer-cise in political discourse. Yet it is perhaps wise to distinguish the *meaning* of disorder from its *genesis*. Contemporary perception differs, quite properly, from the significance of an event in hindsight. For the notion that the uprisings seen on British streets in the early 1980s should be explained as equivalent to an organized *social movement* (the rioters forming either an insurrectionary mob of 'extremists' or a scheming political actor) is as spurious as the discredited vision of the riot as a *social outcome*, an inevitable product of a recipe of preconditions.

Social Conflict as a 'Historical Product'

In their submission to Lord Scarman in 1981 the Commission for Racial Equality expressed surprise, not that serious rioting had occurred in Britain, but that it had taken so long to occur. For relations between the police and black communities in Britain did not suddenly deteriorate immediately before the Brixton disturbances; they had been marred by ill-feeling and confrontation for at least thirty years before hostility evolved into 'civil disorder' (Hunte, 1966; John, 1970; Lambert, 1970; Pullé, 1973; Howe, 1981; Fryer, 1984). Yet this conflict cannot be reduced to any simplistic monocausal explanation and instead must be understood in terms of the nature of *all* police work: 'the job' that society demands of its police force, the ubiquitous racial (and racist) categorization of social groups, and the long-term negotiation of the relationship between police and public which becomes built into the institutional practice and daily routine of both the police and the communities that are policed.

The ultimate sanction available to any police officer in dealing with members of the public is the legitimate use of force. In the final analysis this is the fundamental basis of 'police power', a resource that underwrites every single contact between police and public. Consequently 'It flows from the nature of police work that it is important for officers to keep control in any encounter' (Smith and Gray, 1983, p. 166). Ideally, the 'control' alluded to is sustained by the professional management of encounters, the sort of micro-sociology of *face engagements* analysed in detail by Goffman (1963, 1974), and confirmed in analysis of police behaviour (Skolnick, 1966; Cain, 1973; Manning, 1977; Holdaway, 1983; Smith and Gray, 1983).

Giddens (1979, 1984) has stressed the point that it is such mundane performances that subsume the whole process of social reproduction. Institutional forms, social rules and norms, power relations, and interpretative schema are all implicated in the *durée* (routine) of everyday life. In this way any single interaction involving a police officer can be seen to operate on at least two levels.

1. *Manifest content*: Functional policing (the 'purpose' of interaction: stop, arrest, caution, advise, etc.)
2. *Latent content*: (a) Social reproduction (defining and redefining the role of police in society); (b) reproduction of power relations (the 'internal' relation between police and the policed).

The manifest content will normally only produce conflict with individuals transgressing particular 'laws'. The latent content of police action may involve conflict with social groups. This phenomenon may involve potential as well as actual conflict (raising questions of the perception of the police by the policed, legitimation, hegemony), and covert as well as overt conflict (concerning the 'interests' of those groups involved, depending on the relation of the police institution to the state and changes in this relation). (For elaboration of these concepts see Lukes, 1974; Giddens, 1984; Foucault, 1986.) On the level of manifest content, a meeting may be purely functional but through the repetition of such practice the police–policed power relation is reproduced, reinforced, or even, in the process of structuration, redefined. In the policing of a democratic society this power relationship is in principle more complex than an exercise in coercion, resting ultimately on the institutionally embedded historical role of the police as both a social service and an agent of social control.

It is because the police must, paradoxically, be one of the principal institutions enforcing an unjust social order that the notional ideal of policing by consent is in its pure form unobtainable. Police find themselves in conflict with those groups in positions of structural disadvantage within society. The extent to which this conflict is expressed will depend on the extent of public support generated for the police by the community of interest in combating much crime, the visibility of social divisions in society, and the cultural perception of the police role. The British police force managed to win widespread acceptance by the second half of the twentieth century because of both the successful incorporation of the majority of the population in civil society and through their own success in legitimating police practices, successfully defining the role of 'the British bobby' (Reiner, 1985).

However, the legitimacy conferred on the police force by the combination of consensus politics, their social service role, genuine crime fighting, and the 'Dock Green' ideology was never relevant to those people who migrated from the New Commonwealth to Britain in the post-war period. In fact it could be argued that their very closeness to the society they served guaranteed that the hostility of that receiving society would be reflected by the police force—the reproduction of racism in the name of law and order.

This has evolved through three main stages, two of which have been well documented elsewhere. In the late 1950s and early 1960s the manifest racial prejudice of white society generally, openly displayed in racial attacks and ostentatious discrimination, was commonplace in the police force, evinced in such activities as 'nigger-hunting' expeditions in Brixton (Hunte, 1966) and the treatment of black social centres. From the late 1960s on, this overt prejudice was compounded by the even more invidious process of the criminalization of young black people through the combined influences of pervasive stereotypical (racist) images of the 'criminal classes' (Reiner, 1981, 1985; Lea, 1986), the moral panic which exaggerated the incidence and increased the fear of a diffuse form of street crime that became known as mugging (Hall *et al.*, 1978), through the manufacture of racist 'common sense' images of young black males (Lawrence, 1982*b*; Solomos, 1984), and through the self-fulfilling prophecy of the offence of SUS (Gilroy, 1982; Christian, 1983), whereby an individual could be charged on the suspicion that he was about to commit an arrestable offence. Prejudices justified themselves because guilt resided in divined 'intention' rather than observed action.

The third and less well documented trend was the increasingly pronounced hostility that marked even the most routine interaction between police and the black public. The police had found themselves confronting black communities both because of the contradiction built into their role as arbitrators of justice in an unjust society (a conflict of interests) and because the pervasive ideology of racism in British society *as a whole* rendered this contradiction impossible to conceal (overt rather than covert conflict). The reproduction of this conflict over time redefined the police–policed relation for black communities. This is not merely a question of attitudes or perceptions, not a cultural/subcultural facet of either group. Indeed it would be both conceptually and morally erroneous to suggest that at any one time there was or is a single black perception of the police; such a position would itself be racist. Instead, positions of opposition have become built into routine interaction, the daily realization of conflict, sometimes negotiated away peacefully, sometimes not (James, 1979; Smith and Gray, 1983; Keith, 1986*b*), frequently resulting in 'knock-on' offences after initial hostile inter-action (see Benyon, 1986, on 'contempt of cop').

It is only through understanding this, largely unreported, *historical depth* of conflict that it is possible to understand why large sections of British black communities (not just 'young alienated males') became increasingly prepared openly to oppose police actions in the late 1960s and early 1970s. Such opposition most often took the form of collective resistance of arrest, and was most likely in those places where there were both large numbers of sympathetic spectators (normally social centres) and where the history of antagonistic police–black relations formed part of 'local knowledge' (Geertz, 1982). Crucially, such resistance occurred (and occurs) not because of the 'manifest content' of any particular interaction but because of what that interaction has come to symbolize (at times rendering impossible routine police actions in good faith). In this sense these locationally specific challenges to police authority are most readily seen as challenges to the conventional power relation between police and public, the realization of a heritage of confrontation that has defined the meaning of any police action in the depressing vocabulary of oppression and resistance.

The locationally specific nature of these challenges was clearly seen again in the disorders of 1980 and 1981, when in St. Paul's, Bristol; Liverpool 8; Brixton; Stoke Newington; Southall, and other parts of London violent clashes were confined within very small areas. In such circumstances the severity of violence was not always a good indicator of the intensity of conflict—in All Saints Road, Notting Hill, violent dis-order was minimized by police reticence in challenging the barricades built across the road, a *de facto* recognition of the successful (if not permanent) inversion of conventional power relations achieved in the uprising. The most serious disorders of 1981 were thus not exceptional in their local context, representing the escalation of confrontations that predated any 'rioting', in nature similar to other challenges to police authority.

However, in many of the (often under-reported) clashes that have occurred since 1981 this defensive, almost parochial, dimension, has diminished. Most notably, in Brixton and Tottenham in 1985, disorder was much more closely linked to an articulated social protest over the shooting and the death (respectively) of black women as a direct result of police actions, the levels of violence were notably higher, the consequences (including the murder of one police constable) that much more gruesome.

The situation has changed in the 1980s in two important respects. Most obviously the contradiction built into the police role as law enforcers and representatives of one particular social order has grown more marked, as the racial inequalities in British cities have grown through the effects of structural, locational, demographic and racist influences (Cross, 1986; DE, 1987; ch. 15). Less obvious but equally significant, the internal relation between police and black communities has been reproduced and transformed so that the conflict between the two parties has been hammered into the institutional practice of the police force and the daily routine of black Britain. This is best illustrated by example in an examination of some of the specific policy responses to this conflict that have been replicated in other British cities.

Policy Responses: The Metropolitan Police Force

Since the Scarman report of 1981, genuine efforts have been made by the Metropolitan Police in the vague field known as 'community relations'. It is not intended here to examine in detail these changes, or to underestimate the considerable personal commitment behind much community involvement work. Attempts to improve community consultation and neighbourhood mobilization against crime have also been made (Morgan and Maggs 1984, 1985; Smith 1986). Nor is it the intention to comment on the argument that such reforms as community involvement and consultation might develop into community surveillance and co-optation (Christian, 1983; Gordon, 1983). Rather, it is suggested that alongside these reforms, less publicized and more significant changes in policing strategy in London have been implemented, changes that have incidentally, not deliberately, institutionalized the conflict between police and Black communities.

In particular, certain parts of London in which large-scale confrontations between the police and black communities are considered possible have been designated as 'symbolic locations' by senior management at Scotland Yard. Similarly, twenty London housing estates have been classified as having 'a similar potential for disorder as exhibited on

Broadwater Farm Estate, Tottenham . . .' They have been 'graded in their likelihood of spontaneous public disorder occurring' (Scotland Yard, internal document, 1986). The notion that the struggle over power relations in particular places formed a central theme in rioting is reinforced by the policing strategies adopted in such areas since 1981.

In spite of the importance of Scotland Yard, it is not the suggestion here that all such policies have been the successful product of centralized control, indeed a principal element of the Metropolitan Police reorganization of the early and mid 1980s has been to focus managerial power on the division, to decentralize policy-making, making it responsive to local needs. Rather, it is the contention that these changes have been the almost inevitable product of the localized collapse of policing by consent, united by the common goal (content) of reimposing the conventional power prerogative implied in the internal police–policed relation in those parts of London where police power has been most successfully challenged. Such strategies are of major significance for two reasons. One is because they recognize the *de facto* inversion of power relations within the context of the need to consider maintaining order as a higher priority to law enforcement on those occasions when the two are mutually irreconcilable. Secondly, they embody the *imposition* of social order on a particular place. The exigencies of policing without consent make this imposition of particular relevance to all police actions in such areas. Four of these strategies are highlighted here.

(1) *Immediate Response Units/District Support Units.* Immediate Response Units, normally eleven police constables and a sergeant in a van, were introduced in the immediate aftermath of the 1981 riots in order to provide quick support on occasions of spontaneous outbreaks of public disorder. Their name was later changed to District Support Units, before they were merged with the Special Patrol Groups in 1986. In part, these moveable squads represent a custom-made response to challenges to police authority, a presence that is often seen by junior officers as enforcing a form of symbolic control, which may or may not operate outside the management goals of senior officers. Brian Hilliard, editor of *Police Review*, has remarked:

There are areas in London which are recognized as potential trouble spots where serious disorders might break out at any time. The areas are almost fully manned, all the stations are up to strength, not only that but the District Support Units, which are supposed to patrol a wider area, tend to congregate there so you have a more visible presence of policemen. . . . also because there are more police about they feel they have to do more and so more people get stopped in the street, more motorists get checked, more roadblocks are held. (London Weekend Television, 11 July 1986)

(2) *Special Patrols, Special Orders*. In several parts of London a special patrol is assigned to a single road, or small area, where trouble is considered likely. It is not unusual for such patrols to be warned not to make 'inflammatory arrests'; it is common for minor offences (e.g. motoring and 'soft drugs') to be ignored, policies that frequently cause much resentment among junior officers who may have to spend a whole shift with both their discretion and area of patrol strictly circumscribed (Keith, 1986a). For though the common resistance to police actions in such locations does provide a severe handicap to police work, *the level of crime alone*, which may be higher than in other parts of the division, seldom if ever justifies the level of manpower commitment that these patrols involve. Quite clearly, the secondary function of police work, the latent content of interaction, is of singular importance in the deployment of the patrols; they again establish the police right to police all of London, an ostentatious refutation of 'no-go areas'.

(3) *Dog Patrols*. In his report on the Brixton disorders, Lord Scarman commented:

On two occasions . . . dogs were deployed in an undesirable way in the handling of a crowd. All officers who gave evidence to the Inquiry recognized that dogs are not appropriate instruments for dispersing crowds in sensitive situations. . . . Arrangements must be introduced to prevent the deployment of dogs in handling major crowd disorders in the future. (1981, 4.84)

In spite of this recommendation, dogs were deployed in disorders in Brixton in 1982 and 1985. Also in one particular 'symbolic location' in London, dogs were used in 1982 and 1983 on a daily patrol that was confined to a single road. In the micro-sociology of police patrols the implicit or latent resource of the legitimate use of force is normally hidden; with the dog patrol it is manifest. That it should be manifest in such a place was quite clearly a 'pre-emptive response' to possible challenges to police authority.

(4) *Surveillance*. Traditional policing by patrol and covert observation have at times in the 1980s been supplemented by high-powered surveillance methods. Most of the 'symbolic locations' in London have at some time been monitored in this way (Keith, 1986a). It must be acknowledged that a principal reason for the introduction of these techniques has been to replace the sort of disastrous operations like SWAMP 81 in Brixton, with its arbitrary stop and search tactics that brought such massive numbers into hostile contact with the police and reaped such little long-term reward in fighting crime. However, for the communities who live in such areas, who often spot the observation vehicles used by the police, who know the houses (and sometimes the owners of the houses) which are used for observation, and who occasionally see the

cameras and binoculars (Gifford, 1986), there is often a bitter resentment that their lives are monitored, scrutinized and spied on in this way.

In short, policy may take no account of the history which underwrites conflict. Organization becomes organization to *control* specific areas and 'win' in any confrontation. Similarly, at each stage in the escalation of conflict, dating back to the 1960s, police policy can be seen normally reacting to events rather than analysing them. In part this is no more than one facet of the precedence of 'reactive' over 'proactive' policing that has been debated within the police service itself (e.g. Alderson, 1979, 1984; Newman, 1983, 1986). One significant feature of this phenomenon is that the historical context of changes in the form of policing is not considered (cf. Reiner, 1980, 1985). Quite possibly this derives from the understandable concentration of management on present-day objectives, taking the worst incidents of yesterday as the worst possible case that might be handled today.

After the clashes in Notting Hill and Lewisham in the mid-seventies police 'trouble' with 'black youth' was considered as normal, and police were equipped with shields to deal with future incidents. With increased clashes at the scenes of arrest and the rioting of 1981, 'rioting' by 'black youth' was considered permanently on the managerial agenda, and the Immediate Response Units, protective clothing, and militaristic training were introduced to cope with this phenomenon. By 1986, following the armed insurrection on Broadwater Farm Estate and serious rioting in Brixton and Handsworth in 1985, the response was the use of 'riot cities' for more training, new truncheons for public order situations, and the mooted use of plastic bullets (baton rounds) and water canon. The police are seen to go hand in hand with the escalation of violence. At each level police take the new public order phenomenon as *given*, one of many *natural* phenomena of contemporary society, unaware or unwilling to be aware of their own causal role in this process. The anticipation of public order problems is obviously one essential part of police management. Yet it appears that the primary managerial goal is to ensure that in situations of public order conflict the police 'do not lose'. Incidental to this anticipation, in preparing this capacity to control disorder, police management build into the very structure of police practice the conflict between police and black people. The distinction between cause and effect is vital. It is the managerial task itself that, like the modern myth 'transforms history into nature' (Barthes, 1963, p. 129), treating riots (or civil disorder) as 'natural' phenomena, divorced from history, not cultural products of particular times and places.

In exactly the same sense it is important to understand the locational interplay of power relations that preceded the rioting of 1981 as part of this process of institutionalizing conflict. Personal racism among police officers was of only marginal significance in the immediate genesis of violent conflict, precisely because long before 1981, in those places which witnessed serious confrontations, the conflict between black people and the police had become part of the durée (daily routine) of police practice and black resistance, even before a majority of police constables had arrived at their respective police stations. The relative significance of personal racism in the inception of this conflict in the 1950s is a different issue. The effect of rioting has been to hammer the conflict yet further into this institutional structure. Rioting in 1980s Britain is about the whole history and social context of policing black Britain, not about a cultural pathology of racialist police officers (however many such officers there are), nor about a violent clash of personalities.

The process of stigmatizing outsider groups (Becker, 1963; Goffman, 1972, 1981; Young, 1974; Hall *et al.*, 1978) both precedes and is reinforced by the incidence of rioting. The 'common sense', racist image of the black man as mugger has been supplemented by the equally invidious portrayal of the black man as irrational rioter, pathologically violent, culturally disposed to disorder.

Exactly the same process operates at a spatial level. Areas of conflict between the police and the local community become stigmatized by both the police and many other groups as 'criminal' or 'undesirable' areas; the violent realization of this conflict (not necessarily full-scale 'riots') rapidly drives those residents who can to escape. Typically, clashes in Sandringham Road, Hackney, in 1981 led to a major exodus of people who lived there, according to the local residents' association; the resultant substantial increase in the number of vacant properties prompted a concomitant increase in the level of squatting and social/ petty crime problems that accompanied an itinerant population and reinforced the creation of a 'problem road'. Labelling and crimin-alization by area assume the nature of a self-fulfilling prophecy, a cumulative spiral of decline that callously victimizes the poorer and powerless groups in society. Almost inevitably, the introduction of special policing strategies in these areas lends an official seal to this stigmatization of space, institutionalizing conflict in practice.

Crucially, it is this process of institutionalization that might suggest much about the definition of 'social problems'. It is perfectly possible to see disorder itself rather than the roots of violence as 'the problem'. It may well be possible to combat this violence with repression, to contain discontent. Certainly, looking across the Atlantic the spectre of military tanks now used by police in the Watts ghetto of Los Angeles plays wicked parody to the much lauded liberal reforms of the 1960s. There is more than one solution to the 'problem' of civil disorder.

Only Connect

The notion of civil disorder as a social problem in its own right is reinforced by official attempts to inquire into individual 'riots'. Such public inquiries or commissioned reports can rarely be considered solely as forensic exercises in truth-seeking, but should instead be understood as part of the political process in their own right (Lipsky and Olsen, 1969), implicated in attempts by the national/local state or local police force at self-justification, allocating blame and buying political time. Not only can such inquiries echo the simplistic behaviourist explanations already criticized by producing a recipe of causes of 'a riot', but they may also reinforce the cultural stereotypes of the average rioter. Moreover, in the British experience there is already clear evidence that central government pronouncement on public disorder may not square with confidential diagnosis (Layton-Henry, 1986); the rioting may become a central term in a rhetorical glossary.

The very fact that there is no clear-cut 'problem' of civil disorder renders the subject ideal for manipulation in political discourse. The imagery of Hobbes can be used to illumine the rhetoric of the law-and-order lobby, that of Lenin to highlight a particular crisis of post-modern capitalism. For it is the fear of the real violence and the putative anarchy that underscores these images that undermines serious analysis. Rioting is on the political agenda, but more as a symbol of collective violence than as a tragic manifestation of social conflict.

But while the hyperbole and hypocrisy of Westminster may be easily derided, it is essential to understand the manner in which the specific conflict between the police and Britain's black communities has slipped into a wider social context. The very incidence of rioting in 1981 conditioned expectations for the forthcoming decade, and to an extent *normalized* perceptions of social conflict, altering perspectives on group violence. In this sense it is important to understand the processes by which street clashes in the inner city leak 'incidentally' into the coalfields of Nottingham. There is no need to resort to images of the prescient, authoritarian state to recognize the shadows of 1981 and 1985 not only on changes in police practice but also in popular discourse. There is no need to resort to conspiracy theory sociology to recognize that policing techniques fashioned in Ulster have now been exported to mainland Britain, not through the conscious ploys of police officers but through the task demanded of the police by the British state. Alarmingly, in 1987, in no small part through the incidence of civil disorder, the institution of the British police force has learnt military skills. It cannot so readily unlearn them.

Yet the roots of the conflict that prompted these changes remain. The reality of 'civil disorder' becomes dessicated and dehumanized in prose. Anger is real; violence hurts. The hatred is sincere, bot rhetorical; it is rooted in an unjust society. There is a social problem of injustice. There is an academic problem of clarifying the mechanisms by which this injustice is realized in violent confrontation. It is worth remembering that the two are not quite the same. It is worth keeping the significance of academic discourse in its proper perspective.

References

Alderson, J. (1979), *Policing Freedom* (Macdonald and Evans: London).
—— (1984), *Law and Disorder* (Hamish Hamilton: London).
Barthes, R. (1963), *Mythologies* (Paladin: London).
Becker, H. (1971), *Outsiders* (Free Press: New York).
Benyon, J. (1986), *A Tale of Failure: Race and Policing* (Centre for Research in Ethnic Relations: Warwick).
Berk, R. (1974), *Collective Behaviour* (Wm C. Brown: Dubuque, Iowa).
Bhavnani, R., J. Cooke, P. Gilroy, S. Hall, H. Ousley, and K. Vaz (1986), *A Different Reality* (West Midlands Council: Birmingham).
Bunyan, T. (1981), 'The police against the people', *Race and Class*, 23: 153–71.
Cain, M. (1973), *Society and the Policeman's Role* (Routledge and Kegan Paul: London).
Cashmore, E., and B. Troyna (1982), *Black Youth in Crisis* (Allen and Unwin: London).
Christian, L. (1983), *Policing by Coercion* (Greater London Council: London).
Cross, M. (1986), 'Migration and exclusion: Caribbean echoes and British realities', in C. Brock (ed.), *The Caribbean in Europe* (Frank Cass: London), 85–109.
DE (Department of Employment) (1987), *Employment Gazette*, Jan.
Field, S. (1982), *Urban Disorders in Britain and America* (HMSO: London).
Foucault, M. (1986), 'Disciplinary power and subjection', in S. Lukes (ed.), *Power* (Basil Blackwell: Oxford), 229–43.
Fryer, P. (1984), *Staying Power: The History of Black People in Britain* (Pluto Press: London).
Gaskell, R. and R. Benewick (1987), *Crowds and Collective Behaviour* (Sage: London).
Geertz, C. (1982), *Local Knowledge* (Hutchinson: London).
Giddens, A. (1979), *Central Problems in Social Theory* (Macmillan: London).
—— (1984), *The Constitution of Society* (Polity Press: Cambridge).
Gifford, A. (chair) (1986), *The Broadwater Farm Inquiry: Report* (Harringey Borough Council: London).
Gilroy, P. (1981), 'You can't fool the youths: race and class formation in the 1980s', *Race and Class*, 23: 112–20.
—— (1982), 'Police and thieves', in CCCS (Centre for Contemporary Cultural Studies), *The Empire Strikes Back* (Hutchinson: London), 143–82.

Goffman, E. (1963), *Behaviour in Public Places* (Macmillan: New York).
—— (1972), *Interaction Ritual* (Allen Lane: London).
—— (1974), *Frame Analysis* (Harper and Row: New York).
—— (1981), *Forms of Talk* (Basil Blackwell Oxford).
Gordon, P. (1983), *White Law* (Pluto Press: London).
Gough, I. (1982), 'The crisis of the British Welfare State', in N. I. Fainstein, and S. S. Fainstein (eds.), *Urban Policy under Capitalism* (Sage: London).
Gurr, T. R. (1970), *Why Men Rebel* (Princeton University Press: Princeton, NJ).
Hall, S., T. Critcher Jefferson, J. Clarke, and B. Roberts (1978), *Policing the Crisis* (Macmillan: London).
Hamnett, C. (1983), 'The conditions in England's inner cities on the eve of the 1981 riots', *Area*, 15: 7–13.
Hobsbawm, E. J. (1959), *Primitive Rebels* (Manchester University Press: Manchester).
Holdaway, S. (1983), *Inside the British Police* (Basil Blackwell: Oxford).
Howe, D. (1981), *From Bobby to Babylon* (Race Today Collective: London).
Hunte, J. (1966), *Nigger Hunting in England?* (Institute of Commonwealth Studies: London).
James, D. (1979), 'Police–black relations: the professional solution', in S. Holdaway (ed.), *The British Police* (Edward Arnold: London), 167–89.
John, A. (1970), *Race and the Inner City* (Runnymede Trust: London).
Joshua, H., and T. Wallace (1983), *To Ride the Storm* (Heinemann: London).
Keith, M. (1986a), ' "Something happened"—explanation of the 1981 riots', in P. Jackson (ed.), *Race and Racism* (Allen and Unwin: London), 275–303.
—— (1986b), 'The 1981 Riots in London', (D.Phil. thesis, University of Oxford).
—— (1987), 'Social conflict and the "No-Go Areas" of Britain', in D. M. Smith and J. Eyles (eds.), *Qualitative Methods in Human Geography*, (Polity Press: Cambridge), 39–48.
Kettle, M., and L. Hodges (1982), *Uprising!* (Pan: London).
Killian, L. (1981), 'The perils of race and racism as variables', *New Community*, 9: 378–80.
Kilson, M. (1987), 'Politics of race and urban crisis: the American case', in J. Benyon and J. Solomos (eds.), *The Roots of Urban Unrest* (Pergamon: Oxford), 51–60.
Lambert, J. (1970), *Crime, Police and Race Relations* (Oxford University Press: Oxford).
Lawrence, E. (1982a), 'In the abundance of water the fool is thirsty: sociology and black "pathology" ', in CCCS (Centre for Contemporary Cultural Studies), *The Empire Strikes Back* (Hutchinson: London) 95–143.
—— (1982b), 'Just plain common sense: the roots of racism,' in CCCS (Centre for Contemporary Studies) *The Empire Strikes Back* (Hutchinson: London) 47–94.
Layton-Henry, Z. (1986), 'Race and the Thatcher government', in Z. Layton-Henry, and P. B. Rich (eds.), *Race, Government and Politics in Britain* (Macmillan: London), 73–99.
Lea, J. (1986), 'Police racism: some theories and their policing implications',

in R. Matthews and J. Young (eds.), *Confronting Crime* (Sage: London) 145–65.

—— and J. Young (1982), 'The riots in Britain', in D. Cowell, T. Jones, and J. Young, (eds.), *Policing the Riots* (Junction Books: London), 5–20.

Lipsky, M., and D. J. Olsen (1969), 'Riot Commission Politics', in P. Rossi, D. J. Olsen, and P. H. Marsh (eds.), *Ghetto Revolts* (Aldine Press: Chicago), 109–41.

Lukes, S. (1974), *Power: A Radical View* (Macmillan: London).

Manning, P. (1977), *Police Work: The Social Organisation of Policing* (MIT Press: London).

Morgan, R., and C. Maggs (1984), *Following Scarman: A Survey of Formal Police/ Community Consultative Arrangements in Provincial Police Authorities in England and Wales* (University School of Social Policy: Bath).

—— (1985), *Setting the PAGE: Police Community Consultative Arrangements in England and Wales* (University School of Social Policy: Bath).

Newman, K. (1983), *Policing and Social Policy in Multi-Ethnic Areas in Europe* (Cropwood: Cambridge).

—— (1986), *Report of the Commissioner of the Metropolitan Police for the Year 1985* (HMSO: London).

Pullé, S. (1973), *Police/Immigrant Relations in Ealing* (Runnymede Trust: London).

Reiner, R. (1980), 'Fuzzy thoughts: the police and law and order politics', *Sociological Review*, 28: 377–423.

—— (1981), 'Black and blue: race and the police', *New Society*, 17, 17 Sept., 466–70.

—— (1985), *The Politics of the Police* (Wheatsheaf: Brighton).

Rex, J. (1981), 'The 1981 urban riots in Britain', *International Journal of Urban and Regional Research*, 6: 88–113.

—— (1984), 'Disadvantage and discrimination in cities', in J. Benyon (ed.) *Scarman and After* (Pergamon: Oxford).

Rudé, G. (1964), *The Crowd in History*, (Wiley: New York).

Rushdie, S. (1983), *Shame* (Picador: London).

Scarman, Lord (1981), *The Scarman Report: The Brixton Disorders 10–12 April 1981*, (HMSO: London).

Sherman, L. (1983), 'After the riots: police and minorities in the United States 1970–1980', in N. Glazer and K. Young (eds.), *Ethnic Pluralism and Public Policy* (Heinemann: London) 212–35.

Sivanandan, A. (1982), *A Different Hunger*, (Pluto Press: London).

Skolnick, J. (1966), *Justice Without Trial* (Wiley: New York).

Smith, D. J., and J. Gray (1983), *The Police in Action* (Policy Studies Institute: London).

Smith, S. (1986), 'Police accountability and local democracy', *Area*, 18: 99–107.

Solomos, J. (1984), *The Politics of Black Youth Unemployment: A Critical Analysis of Official Ideologies and Policies* (Research Unit in Ethnic Relations: Warwick).

Southgate, P. (1982), *The Disturbances of July 1981 in Handsworth, Birmingham*, Home Office Research Study 72 (HMSO: London).

Taylor, S. (1984*a*), 'The Scarman Report and explanations of riots', in J.
    Benyon (ed.), *Scarman and After* (Pergamon: Oxford), 20–36.
—— (1984*b*), *Social Science and Revolutions* (Macmillan: London).
Verner, M. (1981), 'What the papers said about Scarman', *New Community*,
    9(3): 354–63.
Young, J. (1974), 'New directions in sub-cultural theory', in J. Rex (ed.),
    Approaches to Sociology (Routledge and Kegan Paul: London).

17

Heroin Use in Its Social Context

Geoffrey Pearson

Drug misuse has been increasingly identified in recent years as a major urban problem in both Europe and North America. The aim of this chapter is to set this problem, and particularly that of heroin misuse, within in its social context.

This will involve reviewing a range of research evidence which often points to the connections between heroin misuse and a variety of social problems such as unemployment, poor housing, and other forms of urban deprivation. It is also, of course, a problem which is often associated with crimes such as burglary, shoplifting, and snatch thefts, as the means by which people who have become dependent on heroin support their drug habits. There is, however, no necessary connection between heroin use and these other social difficulties—otherwise, one would not find heroin problems in the social orbit of millionaire pop stars—and people with such wealth at their command obviously do not need to support their habits through crime, hustling, or prostitution. Nevertheless, heroin misuse tends to be most densely concentrated in areas of high social deprivation, so that it demonstrates its own distinctive social ecology. A principal aim of this chapter is to understand why this is so.

It is important to enter a few complications into this general picture at the outset. Drug misuse is by no means a new problem, for example, and drugs such as morphine and cocaine were regular features of late nineteenth-century diet, both in Europe and North America (Berridge and Edwards, 1981; Musto, 1973). Nor is it only an urban problem, although drug problems tend to assume their most serious dimensions in cities such as New York, Hamburg, Amsterdam, Karachi, Bangkok, and Hong Kong, whereas in Britain we associate major drug problems with Liverpool, Glasgow, Manchester, Edinburgh, and of course London, with its longer post-war involvement. Even so, forms of drug use have long been known in rural areas, examples being opium-eating in the Indian subcontinent (where it was introduced centuries ago by Arab travellers), opium-smoking (which was more specifically found in China and South East Asia), or the chewing of coca leaves in some parts of rural Latin America. Indeed, although it is in Europe and North America that most public concern has been generated about drug use, problems such as heroin misuse are now understood to assume global proportions (Trebach, 1982, ch. 1; Henman *et al.*, 1985). The USSR has only recently admitted as part of the new policy of *glasnost* that it has a serious opiate problem, and there is no reason to believe that any major quarter of the globe is exempt—with the possible exception of contemporary China, where extensive efforts were made to eradicate opium-smoking after the revolution of 1949.

Finally, it is always necessary to issue a few words of caution, in any discussion of heroin misuse in Britain and North America, about the comparative dimensions of the problem in relation to other forms of drug use and misuse. Heroin is a drug which excites fear and apprehension, commanding sensational news headlines in such a way that the preoccupation with heroin misuse could easily be described as a 'moral panic'. There have been, of course, any number of such 'moral panics' orchestrated by the news media in response to various kinds of crime, violence, deviant conduct, and drug misuse (Cohen, 1973; Cohen and Young, 1980; Young, 1971*a*, 1971*b*, 1974; Chibnall, 1977; Pearson, 1983; Kohn, 1987). Given the notoriety of heroin, the potential certainly exists for the problem to become over-enlarged in the public mind. Even so, all the evidence points to the fact that in the course of the 1980s heroin misuse has indeed become a more serious and difficult problem in Britain (Pearson, 1987*a*; Pearson *et al.*, 1986; Dorn and South, 1987). It nevertheless remains indisputable that socially sanctioned drugs such as alcohol and tobacco are far more damaging to the nation's health, and that innumerable people also experience serious problems with medically prescribed drugs such as 'tranquillizers' (Plant *et al.*, 1985; Plant, 1987).

Socio-historical Bearings: The 'Social Construction' of Drug Problems

Whenever the question of drugs is placed on the agenda, it seems invariable that it is discussed as a 'problem'. And yet, throughout known historical time and through all the subtle twists and turns of cultural diversity known to social anthropologists, it would seem that drug use is an entirely 'normal' feature of human societies. Throughout the world, for example, various kinds of drugs are integrated within different forms of religious ceremony and observance—whether we think of the Christian communion wine, the use since Aztec times of exotic hallucinogenic peyote mushrooms by Mexican Indians, or the reverence shown to the holy 'herb' marihuana (or ganja) within the Caribbean Rastafarian faith. Drugs are also used for commonplace recreational purposes— whether in the form of 'social drinking', the use of cannabis preparations in non-drinking Muslim cultures, or the habitual chewing of cola nuts in parts of West Africa and betel nuts in many parts of East Africa in much the same way that people smoke cigarettes in Europe and North America. Sometimes it is difficult to establish precisely where a drug fits into a pattern of cultural activity. When toasts are exchanged at a wedding, for example, is this ritual or recreation? And when the social anthropologist Evans-Pritchard (1956, pp. 36–7) recorded a seance among the North African Nuer people, intended to cast out the spirit *nai* from a sick youth, what was the significance of the fact that the prophet called for his pipe before he began to question the spirit? Was this part of the ritual, or force of habit?

Drug use is therefore an endemic feature of human conduct, and it is virtually impossible to identify any form of civilization or culture which does not resort to some form of drug use. Moreover, what might be counted as a 'dangerous' form of drug use in one culture will sometimes be found acceptable in another. The traditional chewing of coca leaves, which form the basis for cocaine extraction, in the mountainous regions of the Andes, is a case in point. The widespread use of opium in the Indian subcontinent, which had long been understood as a harmless pastime, is equally difficult to reconcile with the widespread abhorrence of opium preparations such as morphine and heroin. In the nineteenth century, opium, according to Fay (1976, p. 7), was 'the ordinary Indian's remedy for malaria, his rejuvenator in old age, the agent of his relief from fatigue and pain—no more to be frowned upon than bhang or hashish'. Indeed, the tolerance of the highly dangerous practice of tobacco-smoking in so many parts of the world only further deepens the confusion about what is held to be 'problematic' about drug use.

The simple point is, as with any social problem, that these problems are socially defined—rather than being in some way 'natural'. This is one aspect of the 'social construction of reality' (Berger and Luckmann, 1971). Different historical times and different cultures have correspondingly defined different boundaries by which the limits of 'acceptable' drug use are to be understood, sometimes involving massive shifts in perception. In the West it is only quite recently in historical terms that these boundaries, which are now so taken for granted, have entered into a settled and established usage. Coca-Cola, for example, actually contained cocaine until as recently as 1903, and in the late nineteenth century cocaine had traditionally been an active ingredient in any number of other popular North American preparations such as soda pop, wines, medicines, and coca-leaf cigarettes. Cocaine had even been proclaimed as the official remedy of the American Hay Fever Association, and the neurologist William Hammond, who was a former surgeon general of the army, 'swore by it and took a wineglass of it with each meal' (Musto, 1973, P. 7). The founder of psychoanalysis, Sigmund Freud, also appears to have flirted briefly with cocaine in the 1890s (Masson, 1985).

The various pick-me-ups and powders which entered into use in nineteenth-century Europe and North America often involved drugs which we would now regard with deep suspicion and place beyond the law. The use of opium-derivatives such as morphine and laudanum also formed part of any number of patent medicines, such as Collis Browne's 'chlorodyne' preparation or Godfrey's Cordial, which were marketed under trade-names such as 'Pennyworth of Peace'. These were both recommended and widely used as remedies for complaints such as sleeplessness, upset stomach, coughs and colds, and a variety of aches and pains (Berridge and Edwards, 1981). Indeed, in spite of vigorous campaigns and scandals about malpractices such as 'infant doping', it was not until the 1890s that a consensus began to form against the widely tolerated use of opium.

It would therefore be wrong to think of celebrated figures such as Thomas De Quincey and his *Confessions of an Opium Eater* as exceptional cases. De Quincey's mentor Samuel Coleridge Taylor struggled for many years with an addiction to opium, and the eminent prison reformer Elisabeth Fry was devoted to laudanum and opium use (Lindop, 1985; Rose, 1980). References to opium and laudanum are scattered throughout the English novels of nineteenth century, in ways that are not always disapproving—in Charles Dicken's final and unfinished novel *The Mystery of Edwin Drood*, Mrs Gaskell's story of Manchester factory life *Mary Barton*, or Wilkie Collins's detective novel *The Moonstone*. Nor was Sherlock Holmes's dedication to cocaine and the hypodermic needle in some of the Conan Doyle stories merely a fantastic aspect of the novelist's imagination. As Virginia Berridge and Griffiths Edwards have described in detail in their book *Opium and the People* (1981), such forms of drug use were endemic in Victorian Britain, and not confined to any walk of life.

A significant development within this history, however, was the way in which a distinction came to be made between the perfectly acceptable use of opium preparations for self-medication among the middle classes, as against what was known and feared as 'stimulant' use by working-class people. And it was this 'stimulant' use which became identified as a problematic form of opium misuse, in contrast with its legitimate use as a helpful medical tonic (Berridge and Edwards, 1981). In North America, disapproval of opium use became associated in a similar way with the persecution of the Chinese population on the West coast, targeted against the infamy of the 'opium den'. While in the Southern States of America the eventual prohibition of cocaine early in the new century was substantially organized around fears of crime-waves said to be the result of the 'cocaine-crazed Negro brain' which, as Musto (1973, p. 7) describes it, 'coincided with the peak of lynchings, legal segregation and voting laws all designed to remove political and social power' from the Black population. From the first awakening of social concern in the late nineteenth and early twentieth centuries, one might conclude that the social problem of drug misuse has been constructed as one which was centrally preoccupied with socially disadvantaged groups.

The Post-war Heroin Epidemics in Britain and North America

Having described how drugs such as opium and cocaine came to be identified as social problems, we can now trace the subsequent development of heroin misuse in Britain and North America. It was in the 1870s that heroin had first been chemically synthesized from morphine, with commercial production starting in Germany in 1898. Before the outbreak of the Second World War, however, heroin use was virtually unknown in Britain and still exceedingly uncommon in the USA. In North American cities its use in the 1930s was largely confined to small groups of people such as entertainers and musicians, as well as gangsters and racketeers, thieves, pimps, and prostitutes. The major ethnic groups involved were Italians, Irish, Jewish, and also black people in the entertainment industry, although heroin use was also known among the Chinese, with their history of opium-smoking. All in all, the extent of heroin use was extremely limited in the inter-war years and attracted little publicity (Preble and Casey, 1969, p. 4).

    This was to change when the war ended, and a number of North American cities experienced sharp increases in heroin use in the late 1940s and early 1950s. Some social scientists regard it as inappropriate to describe these changes as heroin 'epidemics', arguing that this implies a false analogy with contagious diseases. A 'contagious disease model' has nevertheless been usefully employed to research and illuminate the way in which heroin use can spread with great rapidity through friendship networks and neighbourhood contacts (Hughes and Crawford, 1972; Hughes *et al.*, 1971). It has been found repeatedly that it is through people being first introduced to heroin by friends, rather than through 'pushers', that the habit spreads within a community (Pearson *et al.*, 1986; Pearson, 1987*a*). This also ensures that the pattern of heroin misuse establishes a distinctively localized geographical profile—so that while friendship is the lubricant of a heroin epidemic, it also sets limits to its dispersal. Therefore, although public health models of 'contagion' and 'epidemic' *are* only analogies, they are ones which can nevertheless usefully be applied to the understanding of the social contexts of heroin misuse.

The first post-war North American heroin epidemic in Chicago peaked in 1949, and it is a further indication of the previous lack of attention to heroin as a potential problem that at this time the penalties for its possession were far less severe than those for the possession of marijuana. Heroin use had first started to become popular around the swinging 'night spots' of the city's Negro South Side, among what Hughes *et al.* (1972) describe as 'hip, street-wise non-delinquents', although by the early 1950s the heroin problem was increasingly identified with the lower-class delinquent 'dope fiend'.

In New York a somewhat different pattern emerged. New York was undergoing a major transformation during the 1940s, as a result of the large-scale migration to the city of Puerto Ricans and poor blacks from the southern states. In the late 1940s it was in the slum neighbourhoods in which these new immigrants had settled that heroin use first became established, largely as a social habit in a party atmosphere among friends who would gather together to inhale the drug. Heroin was in cheap and plentiful supply at this time, it was used mainly by young adults in their twenties and thirties, and it was not associated with any significant level of crime or other social problems. From around 1951, however, heroin began to become popular among younger people in the New York ghetto districts, especially, as Preble and Casey (1969, pp. 5–6) describe it, 'among street gang members who were tired of gang fighting and were looking for a new high'. The distribution of narcotics use among younger people, however, remained densely concentrated in the city's worst slums (Chein *et al.*, 1964). Moreover, as the price of heroin began to escalate through the 1950s and into the 1960s—resulting not only in the more likely adulteration of the drug in order to maximize the profits of dealers, but also increasing economic pressures on heroin addicts in order to support their habits—so heroin users increasingly began to resort to crime. The mould was now set. Heroin had become a notorious problem in New York and other cities, associated with crime waves of burglary and street robberies. By the 1980s, with the problem still most densely located in the ghetto districts of east and central Harlem, it has been estimated that a daily heroin user must generate an income of $25,000 per year in order to support a drug habit (Johnson *et al.*, 1985).

By contrast with the USA, Britain was a 'late developer' in establishing a heroin problem. Heroin use remained virtually unknown through the 1950s and early 1960s, except in the form of small numbers of registered addicts and in tiny pockets of illicit use around the London jazz scene (Spear, 1969). British policy since the 1920s had allowed medical practitioners to prescribe maintenance doses of pharmaceutically pure heroin to addicts under their treatment. In the 1950s and early 1960s these were largely people known as 'medical addicts', who had either become dependent on opiates in the course of medical treatment, or who were themselves members of the medical profession with professional access to dangerous drugs. The logic of the 'British system' was that it removed the need for heroin addicts to supply themselves with drugs from illicit sources, thus restricting the possibilities of a growth in the illicit 'black market' or 'street market', while also obviating the need for addicts to commit crimes in order to sustain their habits (Schur, 1964).

The subsequent change in British policy from the late 1960s onwards, which introduced tighter restrictions on the rights of medical practitioners to prescribe illicit drugs, remains an area of intense controversy (Trebach, 1982). A government committee (the first Brain Committee) which had reviewed the situation in 1961 concluded that there was no reason to change this policy, forming the view that the heroin problem was still of negligible proportions and that the majority of addicts were respectable citizens. However, the social climate was to change abruptly in the next few years, with a large amount of public attention given to drug problems such as the use of 'pep pills' by young people, the growth in cannabis use, and new drugs such as LSD. In this changing context the Brain Committee was hastily reconvened in 1964, reporting in the following year, when it recommended the introduction of a more stringent policy (Stimson and Oppenheimer, 1982, pp. 40–61). The most significant policy change, in terms of heroin use, was that doctors were to have their right to prescribe dangerous drugs removed from them, with the treatment of addicts confined to the newly created Drug Dependency Units or 'Cinics' which were opened in 1968.

This major shift in policy was partly in response to a sharp, but nevertheless small increase in an illicit heroin scene in London and also the abuse of the system by a small number of doctors who had been found to be prescribing dramatically large amounts of drugs to their patients. The late 1960s were, however, to witness a much wider set of concerns, when drug problems were firmly placed on the public agenda in Britain for what was, in effect, the first time. The unfolding 'moral panic' had any number of elements: the death by drug overdose in Oxford of the grandson of former Prime Minister Harold Macmillan in 1965; the imprisonment of the pop star Mick Jagger of the Rolling Stones in 1967 for the possession of amphetamie sulphate and the publicity given to hallucinogenic drugs by the Beatles; and the emergence of the 'psychedelic' drug culture and the 'hippie' phenomenon. The public reaction to these events was undoubtedly an over-reaction, suggesting that it was the control of youth rather than the control of drugs which fuelled the 'moral panics' (Cohen, 1973; Young, 1971*a*, 1971*b*, 1974; Pearson, 1975, pp. 59–60). Indeed, by the end of the 1960s there were still no more than 3,000 registered heroin addicts in the whole of Britain—still, on any reasonable estimate, a trifling problem.

Through the 1970s the heroin problem in Britain largely stabilized with no substantial increase in the number of notified addicts, and a marked tendency for the proportion of newly notified addicts under twenty-one years of age to decrease (Home Office, 1984). One vitally significant development, however, was the emergence of a more active 'street market' as addicts who became dissatisfied with the stringent controls of the clinics turned to illicit means of supplying their habits (Stimson and Oppenheimer, 1982). There was also the growth of a new style of 'poly-drug' use, whereby drug users began to experiment with the highly dangerous practice of injecting barbiturates often mixed in a 'cocktail' with other drugs. These dangerous practices excited little public concern, however, other than in specialist professional circles (Jamieson *et al.*, 1984). Indeed, this lack of public concern once more indicates that there is no necessary relationship between mass media activity and the actual seriousness of a drug problem. But although 'poly-drug' use went largely ignored, more generally a growing recognition of the dangers of barbiturates did nevertheless result in a steep decline in the level of prescribing, from approximately 12 million prescriptions per year in 1972 to less than 2 million in 1984 (Plant, 1987, p. 80).

By this time, however, Britain had been overtaken by a major and undeniable change in patterns of drug use, with the number of known addicts increasing three-fold between 1979 and 1983 (Home Office, 1984). The change first occurred between 1979 and 1981, when heroin began to become available in cheap and plentiful supply not only in London, but also in cities such as Liverpool, Manchester, and Glasgow which had never before experienced significant levels of heroin misuse. The question of supply was undoubtedly a crucial determinant of this shift, involving the import of heroin from regions of South West Asia such as Iran, Pakistan, and the north-west frontier with Afghanistan— reflecting social and political upheavals such as the fall of the shah and resistance to the Soviet supported Kabul regime in Afghanistan— whereas previously it had been the opium-poppy fields of the 'Golden Triangle' of South East Asia bordering on Thailand, Burma, and Laos which had dominated the global heroin market (Lewis, 1985). These new trade routes resulted not only in a sharp fall in the 'street price' of heroin in Britain, but the drug also became available in a form that could be smoked and did not need to be injected (Lewis *et al.*, 1985). The practice of smoking heroin, known in the Cantonese dialect of Hong Kong as 'Jüi Lüng' or 'Chasing the Dragon', was essentially new to Britain, and the removal of the major cultural taboo against self-injection was undoubtedly another factor which helped to encourage the spread of the new heroin problem (Pearson, 1987a; Pearson *et al.*, 1986).

Britain's heroin epidemic of the early 1980s involved a number of other important changes. It would perhaps be wrong to think of it as a 'national' problem, for example, in that it assumed a highly localized and scattered form—troubling some towns and cities much more than others (Pearson *et al.*, 1986). And whereas the London heroin scene of the 1960s had been largely confined to 'Bohemian' subcultures and lifestyles, the people who were more likely to become involved in the 1980s came from conventional backgrounds and intact families (Strang 1984). What was most significant, however, was the emphatic association between the new heroin problem and the return of mass unemployment. This was demonstrated in a variety of ways, including a review of national statistical trends (Peck and Plant, 1986), an examination of local and regional variations in heroin misuse undertaken on behalf of the Health Education Council (Pearson *et al.*, 1986), and detailed survey research on Merseyside which established a correlation between the local prevalence of heroin misuse and a range of social deprivation indicators (Parker *et al.*, 1988). Britain in the 1980s was thereby to repeat the earlier experience of North America, whereby heroin misuse tended to be most densely concentrated in the run-down housing estates which were already suffering from multiple forms of social deprivation (Pearson, 1987b).

Heroin Use and Social Deprivation: 'Escapism' or Active Life-styles?

The association between social deprivation and heroin misuse has been clearly demonstrated in the post-war heroin epidemics in both Britain and North America. It remains necessary to explain the nature of this connection. Perhaps the most common way of explaining why heroin misuse and social deprivation come to be linked is to invoke the notion of drug use as 'escapism'—a flight from the harsh realities of life into drug-induced fantasy. One of the pharmacological effects of opiate drugs is certainly that they provide a 'cushioning' effect against both physical and emotional pain, which is why they have been employed by medical practitioners in the treatment of chronic pain conditions and with patients such as those who are terminally ill. On the available evidence, however, this does not seem to be the best way of understanding the relationships between heroin use and unemployment. Rather, the sociological research tradition suggests that it is more useful to attend to the life-styles which emerge in socially deprived neighbourhoods.

The idea of drug use as 'escapism' is nevertheless one which has enjoyed a wide currency, not only in commonsense thinking but also within sociological theory. This was utterly explicit in Robert Merton's (1938, 1957) formulation of the social contexts of different forms of deviance: whereas theft was understood as an 'innovative' activity, whereby socially disadvantaged groups engaged in the illicit acquisition of wealth, drug misuse was defined as a 'retreatist' phenomenon to be classed along with the social disengagement of tramps and hobos. This view had been subsequently reinforced by Cloward and Ohlin (1960) in their theory of delinquent subcultures, which distinguished three different forms of neighbourhood gang activity: 'criminal' gangs which engaged largely in property theft, 'conflict' gangs for whom street fighting was the dominant life-style, and finally 'retreatist' subcultures who indulged in drug use. The 'retreatists' were defined by Cloward and Ohlin as 'double failures', who could compete successfully neither in the conventional world, nor in the 'criminal' and 'conflict' subcultural options. In their major study of delinquency and narcotics use in New York during the 1950s and early 1960s, Chein *et al.* (1964) had also adopted 'escapist' assumptions in order to explain why heroin use should be most densely concentrated in the socially and economically disadvantaged ghetto areas. Young people in these neighbourhoods, it was suggested, developed a 'sense of futility' which made them more susceptible to experimentation with narcotics because of the escapist attractions they promised.

However, this view of drug misuse as a passive, retreatist activity subsequently came under challenge from a significant body of North American sociological research. Primarily, what it had failed to acknowledge was that people who engaged in narcotics use often enjoyed high status within their neighbourhoods. Theirs was also a much more active life-style than was implied by the 'escapist' model, as was shown by both Finestone (1957) and Hughes *et al.* (1972) who described how the Chicago heroin epidemic had been associated with the 'cool' life-style adopted by young black 'cats' in the context of the jazz culture. From San Francisco, Sutter (1966) also failed to support the notion of a passive and retreatist drug subculture, pointing instead to the status enjoyed by the 'righteous dope fiend' who was a successful drug user rarely seen by either psychiatrists or law enforcement officers. Research in Boston and New York by Feldman (1968) confirmed the view that becoming involved in heroin was an important way in which 'action-seeking' youth in slum neighbourhoods could demonstrate their manhood and claim status as a 'stand up cat'. In Feldman's view, it was precisely the notoriety of heroin which attracted young men who aspired to a local reputation, thereby accepting a challenge as to whether they could control the drug, or whether it would control them. Heroin misuse in these terms was not so much a retreat from the subcultural challenges of thieving and fighting, which is how Cloward and Ohlin had described it, but an ultimate test of manhood in mortal combat with the 'demon drug'. In a rare account of heroin use by women, Rosenbaum (1981) also showed that getting involved in heroin was a means of engagement with the 'fast life', rather than a form of passive escape.

Undoubtedly the most explicit departure from the 'retreatist' view of heroin use was that offered by Preble and Casey (1969) in their analysis of the life-style of the New York street addict. Here, the heroin user was depicted as someone 'aggressively pursuing a career that is exacting, challenging, adventurous and rewarding', for which it was necessary to remain 'alert, flexible and resourceful' in order to remain successful in 'taking care of business':

Their behaviour is anything but an escape from life. They are actively engaged in meaningful activities and relationships seven days a week. The brief moments of euphoria after each administration of a small amount of heroin constitute a small fraction of their daily lives . . . The surest way to identify heroin users in a slum neighbourhood is to observe the way people walk. The heroin user walks with a fast, purposeful stride, as if he is late for an important appointment—indeed, he is. He is hustling (robbing or stealing), trying to sell stolen goods, avoiding the police, looking for a heroin dealer with a good bag (the street retail unit of heroin), coming back from copping (buying heroin), looking for a safe place to take the drug, or looking for someone who beat (cheated) him—among other things. He is, in short, *taking care of business* (Preble and Casey, 1969, p. 2).

It is necessary to contrast this hectic life-style with the more usual consequences of mass unemployed, in which people drift aimlessly through the day without effective time-routines and little purpose (Jahoda, 1982; Jahoda *et al.*, 1972). The rigorous time-routines which are imposed by the heroin user's life-style can then be seen as one of the ways by which the unemployed are more likely to be attracted to its risks and excitements (Pearson, 1987*b*). It has been repeatedly shown, moreover, that, whereas it might be expected that socially inadequate people would be most likely to be susceptible to involvement with drugs, it is more likely to be local opinion-leaders who will first introduce the heroin habit within friendship and neighbourhood networks (Hughes *et al.*, 1971; Hughes and Crawford, 1972; Hughes, 1977).

Low-level drug markets involving 'user-dealers' are also characterized by a flurry of economic exchanges and activities, which become one
more way in which local reputation and status can be achieved in poor
neighbourhoods, and which become closely integrated with the 'informal economy' of perks, fiddles, and crime (Auld *et al.*, 1986). When
these developments become more advanced, as within the ghetto districts of New York, then the street-level heroin distribution system and
heroin-related crime become in themselves a vast economic system.
Indeed, under such circumstances there is what Johnson *et al.* (1985,
p. 184) have described as a 'jarring realisation' that, viewed in purely
economic terms, more people stand to gain from heroin-user crime than
suffer by it. Stolen goods which are offered for sale at only a small
proportion of their normal market price enlarge the purchasing power of
poor families, thus helping to sustain a vigorous demand for stolen
property within ghetto economies. The prolific economic activity of the
heroin addict thereby becomes not only a means by which to sustain a
habit, nor even by which to achieve local status, but also a significant
contribution to the local economy of the entire community—a sobering
judgement which points to the complex social and economic realities
with which any attempt to contain and control local heroin epidemics
must contend (Moore, 1977).

Conclusion: The Social and Economic Constraints of Policy Formulation

Social policies relevant to drug problems have three different and distinct aims: to control and limit the production and distribution of drugs;
to treat and rehabilitate problem drug users; and to promote health
education in the wider community. Each aspect of policy has its own
social and economic constraints.

It should be clear from the foregoing discussion that the idea that
social policy might be directed towards the achievement of a 'drug-free'
society is quite simply nonsense. It is not only the evidence of history and
social anthropology which points to a universal tendency for human
beings to devise some form or another of intoxicant for recreational
purposes. There is also the global economic imperative which means
that not only are there vast profits to be made (and tax revenues collected) through the alcohol and tobacco industries, but also that the
production and distribution of illicit drugs (principally cannabis,
heroin, and cocaine) has become a huge economic venture (Henman *et
al.*, 1985; Johnson *et al.*, 1985; Wisotsky, 1986). A viewpoint which only
recognizes the economic gains within this traffic by the 'drugs barons'

(i.e. smugglers and major dealers) misses the point. Cannabis is now a major cash crop in a number of Third World countries, and also in some of the states of the USA. The cocaine industry has carved out a major share of the gross national product of nations such as Columbia, Bolivia, and Peru. Heroin is a currency which aids the Afghan rebellion from the border region with Pakistan, and possibly other forms of guerrilla war and terrorism. In these contexts, it is not irrelevant to consider how the production of dangerous drugs might be curbed at source. However, given the economic stakes, small-scale interventions such as 'crop substitution' programmes—under which peasants are given subsidies for eradicating opium, coca, or cannabis plantations in order to cultivate a more acceptable cash crop—are small beer. The substituted crops will often not be found acceptable in the free market, thus failing the test of economic competitiveness as against illicit drug harvests. Indeed, the challenge of the world trade in illicit drug commodities is that it has achieved such dimensions that what would be involved is the restructuring of the national economies of probably a dozen Third World countries, and possibly even more. But it is important to remember that even this is not an entirely new development, and that it was equally momentous economic forces which shaped the huge export of opium from India to China by British merchants in the nineteenth century, in an attempt to open up the Chinese economy to foreign trade, resulting in the Opium War of the 1840s (Fay, 1976).

Social and economic considerations such as these should also be brought to bear on medical controversies about whether heroin addicts should be treated by maintenance doses of pharmaceutically pure heroin or heroin-substitutes such as methadone. The arguments which resulted in the suspension of this 'British system' in the late 1960s have more recently been questioned, because of fears that the AIDS virus will spread through injecting addicts (Robertson, 1987). This is by no means an unimportant consideration, although there are other reasons for rethinking prescribing policies. More liberal prescribing policies are sometimes opposed on the grounds that they are 'soft' on addicts and condone drug misuse. Nevertheless, maintenance prescriptions might not only help drug users to refashion their lives, by reducing their need to resort to crime or prostitution in order to support their habits, but also reduce the burden of heroin-user crime on the wider community. In economic terms, maintenance policies might be thought of as ways of intervening in the market, offering addicts incentives to reduce their participation in the illicit 'street market', and thus restricting the competitiveness of the market in illicit drug commodities.

Finally, the social and economic contexts of health education and drug prevention campaigns are perhaps less obvious, but nevertheless possible to discern. On the available evidence it is undeniable (although it is sometimes regarded as morally scandalous even to hint at it), that relatively safe forms of drug use (including heroin use) are not only possible, but also achievable (cf. Zinberg, 1984; Peele, 1985). These possibilities are nevertheless shaped by a number of factors, including not only sound knowledge of the limits of 'safe' drug practices—for example, only using harmful drugs infrequently and *never* on consecutive days—but also the existence of valued commitments and activities which compete with the claims of heroin. One vitally important commitment is employment, which brings with it not only financial benefits but also a meaningful self-identity. Where these commitments are absent, as in areas of mass unemployment, the ground-work is laid for illicit drug problems on an epidemic scale. Government policies which tolerate high levels of unemployment cannot be blamed for directly causing heroin misuse. The principal cause of heroin misuse is the drug's availability. Nevertheless, such policies do contribute to the difficulty and make heroin problem more difficult to control. Schemes of health education and health promotion are equally difficult to sustain in the absence of viable social opportunities and life-styles. In these ways, the social and economic contexts of heroin misuse suggest that it is not only a problem for addicts and their families. It is a problem for us all. In other words, it is truly a 'social' problem.

References

Auld, J., N. Dorn and N. South (1986), 'Irregular work, irregular pleasures: heroin in the 1980s', in R. Matthews and J. Young (eds.), *Confronting Crime* (Sage: London), 166–87.

Berger, P. L. and T. Luckmann (1971), *The Social Construction of Reality* (Penguin: Harmondsworth).

Berridge, V. and G. Edwards (1981), *Opium and the People: Opiate Use in Nineteenth Century England* (Allen Lane: London).

Chein, I., D. Ferard, R. Lee, and F. Rosenfeld (1964), *The Road to H: Narcotics, Delinquency and Social Policy* (Tavistock: London).

Chibnall, S. (1977), *Law-and-Order News* (Tavistock: London).

Cloward, R., and L. Ohlin (1960), *Delinquency and Opportunity* (Free Press: New York).

Cohen, S. (1973), *Folk Devils and Moral Panics* (Paladin: London).

—— and J. Young (eds.) (1980), *The Manufacture of News* (Constable: London).

Dorn, N., and N. South (eds.) (1987), *A Land Fit for Heroin?* (Macmillan: London).

Evans-Pritchard, E. E. (1956), *Nuer Religion* (Oxford University Press: London).

Fay, P. W., (1976), *The Opium War 1840–1842* (Norton: New York).

Feldman, H. W., (1968), 'Ideological supports to becoming and remaining a heroin addict', *Journal of Health and Social Behaviour*, 9: 131–9.

Finestone, H. (1957), 'Cats, kicks and colour', *Social Problems*, 5(1): 3–13.

Henman, A., R. Lewis, and T. Malyon (1985), *Big Deal: The Politics of the Illicit Drugs Business* (Pluto Press: London).

Home Office (1984), 'Statistics of the misuse of drugs in the United Kingdom, 1983', *Home Office Statistical Bulletin*, 18/84.

Hughes, P. H. (1977), *Behind the Wall of Respect: Community Experiments in Heroin Addiction Control* (University of Chicago Press: Chicago).

—— and G. A. Crawford (1972), 'A contagious disease model for researching and intervening in heroin epidemics', *Archives of General Psychiatry*, 27: 189–205.

—— ——, N. W. Barker, S. Schumann, and J. H. Jaffee (1971), 'The social structure of a heroin copping community', *American Journal of Psychiatry*, 128(5): 551–8.

—— N. W. Barker, G. A. Crawford, and J. H. Jaffe (1972), 'The natural history of a heroin epidemic', *American Journal of Public Health*, 62(7): 995–1001.

Jahoda, M. (1982), *Employment and Unemployment: A Social-Psychological Analysis* (Cambridge University Press: Cambridge).

—— P. F. Lazarsfeld, and H. Zeisel (1972), *Marienthal: The Sociography of an Unemployed Community* (Tavistock: London).

Jamieson, A., A. Glanz, and S. MacGregor (1984), *Dealing with Drug Misuse: Crisis Intervention in the City* (Tavistock: London).

Johnson, B. D. P. J. Goldstein, E. Preble, J. Schmeiller, D. S. Lipton, B. Spont and T. Miller (1985), *Taking Care of Business: The Economics of Crime by Heroin Abusers* (Lexington Books: Lexington, Mass.).

Kohn, M. (1987), *Narcomania: On Heroin* (Faber: London).

Lewis, R. (1985), 'Serious business: the global heroin economy', in A. Henman *et al.*, *Big Deal: The Politics of the Illicit Drugs Business* (Pluto Press: London).

—— R. Hartnoll, S. Bryer, E. Daviaud, and M. Mitcheson (1985), 'Scoring smack: the illicit heroin market in London 1980–1983', *British Journal of Addiction*, 80: 281–90.

Lindop, G. (1985), *The Opium Eater: A Life of Thomas De Quincey* (Oxford University Press: Oxford).

Masson, J. F. (1985), *The Complete Letters of Sigmund Freud to Wilhelm Fliess, 1887–1904* (Harvard University Press: Cambridge, Mass.).

Merton, R. K. (1938), 'Social structure and anomie', *American Sociological Review*, 3: 672–82.

—— (1957), *Social Theory and Social Structure* (Free Press: New York).

Moore, M. H. (1977), *Buy and Bust: The Effective Regulation of an Illicit Market in Heroin* (Lexington Books: Lexington, Mass.).

Musto, D. (1973), *The American Disease: Origins of Narcotics Control* (Yale University Press: New Haven, Conn.).

Parker, H. J., K. Bakx and R. Newcombe (1988), *Living with Heroin: the Impact of a Drugs Epidemic on an English Community* (Open University Press: Milton Keynes).

Pearson, G. (1975), *The Deviant Imagination* (Macmillan: London).
—— (1983), *Hooligan: A History of Respectable Fears* (Macmillan: London).
—— (1987a), *The New Heroin Users* (Basil Blackwell: Oxford).
—— (1987b), 'Social deprivation, unemployment and patterns of heroin use', in N. Dorn and N. South (eds.), *A Land Fit for Heroin?* (Macmillan: London) 62–94.
——, M. Gilman, and S. McIver (1986), *Young People and the Heroin: An Examination of Heroin Use in the North of England* (Health Education Council and Gower: London and Aldershot).
Peck, D. F. and M. A. Plant (1986), 'Unemployment and illegal drug use: concordant evidence from a prospective study and from national trends', *British Medical Journal*, 293: 929–32.
Peele, S. (1985), *The Meaning of Addiction: Compulsive Experience and its Interpretation* (Lexington Books: Lexington, Mass.).
Plant, M. A., (1987), *Drugs in Perspective* (Hodder and Stoughton: London).
—— D. F. Peck and E. Samuel (1985), *Alcohol, Drugs and School-leavers* (Tavistock: London).
Preble, E. and J. J. Casey (1969), 'Taking care of business: the heroin user's life on the street', *International Journal of Addictions*, 4(1): 1–24.
Robertson, R. (1987), *Heroin, AIDS and Society* (Hodder and Stoughton: London).
Rose, J. (1980), *Elisabeth Fry: A Biography* (Macmillan: London).
Rosenbaum, M., (1981), *Women on Heroin* (Rutgers University Press: New Brunswick, NJ).
Schur, E. M. (1964), 'Drug addiction under British Policy', in H. S. Becker (ed.), *The Other Side: Perspectives on Deviance* (Free Press: New York), 67–83.
Spear H. B. (1969), 'The growth of heroin addiction in the United Kingdom', *British Journal of Addiction*, 64: 254–5.
Sutter, A. G. (1966), 'The world of the righteous dope fiend', *Issues in Criminology*, 2 (2): 177–222.
Stimson, G. V. and E. Oppenheimer (1982), *Heroin Addiction: Treatment and Control in Britain* (Tavistock: London).
Strang, J. (1984), 'Changing the image of the drug taker', *Health and Social Service Journal*, 11 Oct. 1202–4.
Trebach, A. S. (1982), *The Heroin Solution* (Yale University Press: New Haven, Conn.).
Wisotsky, S. (1986), *Breaking the Impasse in the War on Drugs* (Greenwood: New York).
Young, J. (1971a), *The Drugtakers* (Paladin: London).
—— (1971b), 'The role of the police as amplifiers of deviance, negotiators of reality and translators of fantasy', in S. Cohen (ed.), *Images of Deviance* (Penguin: London).
—— (1974), 'Mass media, drugs and deviance', in P. Rock and M. McIntosh (eds.), *Deviance and Social Control* (Tavistock: London).
Zinberg, N. E. (1984), *Drug, Set and Setting: The Basis for Controlled Intoxicant Use* (Yale University Press: New Haven, Conn.).

18

Alcoholism and Alcohol Control Policy in the American City

Christopher J. Smith

It has been popular for recent US residents to launch an all-out 'war' on drug abuse in the American city. Drugs, it is argued, have eroded the moral fabric of modern urban society, and the malaise is spreading from the inner city to the suburbs. The fear of death and disfigurement at the hands of crazed drug addicts, and the implied link between drugs and street crime, have helped to keep the drug issue in the political limelight for almost two decades (Wilson, 1975). A crackdown on drugs is a predictable event, but much less attention is given to beverage alcohol, which is surprising in light of what we know about the human costs associated with alcohol abuse (NIAAA, 1978, 1983; Smith and Hanham, 1982). It has been estimated that ten times more people die as a result of someone abusing alcohol than from the abuse of all the illegal drugs combined (NYSDAAA, 1986). In spite of this, beverage alcohol is easily available, relatively cheap, and widely advertised.

This chapter provides an account of the changes that have occurred in the development of alcohol policy in the United States in the latter half of the twentieth century. Because alcohol is bought and sold legally in the marketplace, there are some obvious entry points for policy inter-ventions. A commodity that is distributed legally can also be controlled legally, and it would seem to be both straightforward and sensible to insert some prevention goals into the local, state, and federal policies that regulate the production and distribution of alcoholic beverages.

Changes in alcohol policy occurred in a series of stages since the repeal of Prohibition in the early 1930s. This event signalled the ability of the alcoholic beverage industry to throw off the shackles of Prohibition once and for all (Clark, 1976). From the mid-1930s the industry would remain the dominant force in shaping the politics of alcohol, and as a result the availability of beverage alcohol increased as the controls over drinking were gradually liberalized (Aaron and Musto, 1981). Begin-ning in the 1950s, the industry started to make some concessions to other groups who had a professional and intellectual concern with the alcohol issue, most notably the medical profession and the academic social sciences. By the middle of the 1970s even more accommodations had been made and a new public health orientation had emerged.

In spite of the intensity of the debate, little real progress has yet been made. There has been a lot of research, both theoretical and applied, and much discussion, but not very much concerted action. At the present time further progress seems unlikely unless the alcohol industry accepts (or is forced to accept) a much greater responsibility for the creation and maintenance of alcoholism and problem drinking. It is doubtful, however, that the industry will make any dramatic moves to threaten its own livelihood, and equally doubtful that any significant attempts will be made to restrict the profitable operations of the business world. At least in the short run, it appears that we shall have to watch the futility of one arm of government generating revenues from the sale of beverage alcohol, while another arm of government has to plough most of it back to deal with alcohol-related problems of all types.

The Alcohol Problem in the United States

It is difficult to quantify the wide-ranging effects of alcohol abuse in a contemporary society. Much has been written about the adverse effects of heavy drinking on health; the damaged lives of the children of alcoholics; the carnage that results from drunken driving; the involvement of alcohol in acts of violence in the home and on the streets; and the loss of revenue that results from absenteeism and lowered productivity in the workplace. As indicated in table 18.1, the impact of alcohol consumption spreads beyond the drinkers themselves to the people who are intimately connected with or dependent on them, as well as a much broader segment of the general population (Moore and Gerstein, 1981).

The most recent attempts to quantify the overall economic costs associated with alcohol-related problems in the United States have put the annual cost at $116.7 billion (NIAAA, 1983). In the state of New York alone, with a population of about 17 million, this would have amounted to about $10 billion. In New York in 1983 there were more than 12,000 alcohol-related crashes, resulting in 876 fatalities and over 20,000 injuries, and these have resulted in costs to New Yorkers of over $1 billion in medical costs, insurance settlements, and property damage costs (NYSDAAA, 1986). Over 2,000 deaths in 1983 in New York were directly attributable to alcohol through either alcohol psychosis, alcoholism, alcohol abuse, or alcohol poisoning; in addition to the 3,000 plus deaths that were attributed to alcohol-induced liver cirrhosis. Alcohol-related admissions accounted for 750,000 patient days in New York general hospitals in 1983, with another 319,000 in Veterans

TABLE 18.1. Drinking outcomes on drinkers, intimates, and society

Effects on drinkers	Effects on intimates	Effects on society
Health	*Health*	*Health*
Medical effects (e.g. heart, brain, liver, etc.)	Medical effects (e.g. nutrition, development	Overall medical costs, insurance
Traumatic effects (accidents, assaults, suicide, etc.)	of infants)	
Traumatic effects accidents, assaults, etc.)	Traumatic (accidents, assaults)	
Psychological effects (mood, self-esteem, anxiety, etc.)	Pyschological effects (stress, anxiety)	
Economic independence/ security	*Economic independence/ security*	*Economic position*
Expenditures (on alcohol, damage repair)	Expenditures, loss of family income	Expenditures on law enforcement, medical care, education, welfare
Income (loss of earnings)	Work performance of drinker	
Dependency on others	Family working pattern	Changes in productivity
Social functioning	*Social functioning/ family*	*Social relations*
Discharge of duties	Family duties	Between government and individual
Development of social relationships	Family morale	Social morale
Personal reputation		

Source: Adapted from Gerstein and Moore, 1981, p. 22.

Administration hospitals. In addition to these estimates, there is a link between drinking and social problems such as divorce, child abuse, and neglect, suicide, homocide, rape, robberies, and thefts; and drinking is a major cause of accidents in the workplace and in the home, as well as of recreational accidents like drownings, fires, and falls. It is impossible to put dollar estimates to these relationships, but there is no doubt that they represent an enormous amount of waste in both human and economic terms.

As public concern with this problem mounts, the alcohol issue has once again returned to the stage of American politics, where it has not been a major force since the repeal of Prohibition in 1933. There have been some significant developments within the last decade, signalling a retreat from the gradual liberalization of alcohol controls that occurred throughout the 1960s and 1970s. The most important of these has been the return to the twenty-one year drinking age in many American states in the 1980s. This has been accompanied by a number of other trends which are not as significant but which have important symbolic value, such as the designation of certain college campuses as 'dry' areas; a move to exert greater control over alcohol advertising in the media; new guidelines for educating the public about drinking; and new proposals to regulate alcohol availability at the local level. In a recent speech, for example, a New York Senator outlined the upcoming agenda for the next few years of the Senate Committee on Mental Hygiene and Addiction Control; it contains some reasonably controversial legislation (Padavan, 1986):

expanding the provisions of mandated alcoholism health insurance to cover family;

generating funds for prevention programmes by dedicating 2.4 per cent of the states alcohol taxes;

banning promotions such as 'happy hours' that encourage excessive drinking;

facilitating community residences for alcoholics by removing restrictions on their locations in areas zoned for multiple families;

encouraging small businesses to participate in Employee Assistance Programmes for troubled employees by providing start-up grants, using a $1 million appropriation fund that would become self sufficient after five years.

All of this activity suggests that politicians are no longer shy of the alcohol issue, but there is still not a clear commitment among a majority of legislators to push ahead with aggressive measures. In New York State, for example, there are still some glaring inconsistencies in alcohol policies. In spite of the increase in the legal age for drinking in 1985, most bars in New York can still remain open until 4 a.m.; and in the same year that the drinking age was raised, the governor of the state signed a bill making it legal to sell wine coolers in grocery stores (wine coolers have a much higher alcohol content than beer, and wine is not available in New York's grocery stores).

This lack of consistency is not just a problem in New York. In the country as a whole the 'real' price of alcoholic beverages has fallen significantly in recent years as a result of successful lobbying efforts on behalf of the alcoholic beverage industry (Cook, 1981). This has effectively taken the sting out of most of the prevention measures that have been introduced. During the 1970s, prices for all consumer goods increased by 97 per cent, but the price of alcohol rose by only 54 per cent, making alcohol 45 per cent less expensive by the end of the decade. This helps to explain why sales of alcohol rose from $22 bn. to $45bn., an increase of 105 per cent. Americans bought more alcohol than ever before, but they spent proportionately less than ever to buy it. In fact by

1979 Americans were spending only 2.74 per cent of their disposable income on alcohol, compared to 3.18 per cent in 1970, a decline of 13.8 per cent (NYSDAAA, 1986). The largest increases in consumption have been in beer and wine, largely because the federal excise taxes on beer and wine have not been increased since 1950, and also because the prices of all alcoholic beverages have risen slower than the inflation rate (Smith and Hanham, 1984).

A consensus has slowly emerged in the literature and in government policy at both the federal and the state level about the desirability of adopting a prevention approach to the alcohol problem (Room, 1984). To begin to understand why this consensus has taken so long to emerge, and why it still has an uncertain future, it is necessary to look briefly at the way alcohol policy develops in a consensus-based system of politics.

Alcohol Politics in the United States since the 1930s

The alcohol issue is one on which people tend to hold strong views one way or another. Many different groups enter the political arena to make their presence felt, and to a large extent the policies that emerge can be seen as the outcome of the balance of power between the competing groups, and of the differential abilities of the parties involved to win political support for their own proposals. The outcome of the inter-actions between the competing groups varies over time and across space, which helps to explain the hodgepodge of rules and regulations that have always governed the use of alcohol across the United States (Smith and Hanham, 1982).

Drinking is currently legal in all of the States, but at the turn of the century the Anti-Saloon League was successful in combating the influ-ence of the alcohol lobby because it was able to follow through on the threat to ruin the career of politicians who did not vote for the 'dry' cause (Clark, 1976). As a result, in 1919, the industry was shocked to its foundations when the Prohibitionists were able to impose a fourteen-year dry spell on the entire country. It has been recognized that Prohibi-tion would never have come about, no matter how popular a movement it was, had it not been for the support it received from the highest echelons of America's business community (Aaron and Musto, 1981). The Eighteenth Amendment was ratified in large part because no sig-nificant elements of the existing corporate elite opposed it, and in fact a number of business leaders supported it. We can only speculate about their motives, but it is reasonable to suggest that they hoped Prohibition would reduce crime and other social problems, make workers more efficient and better disciplined, and replace the saloon with the home as the legitimate centre of working-class social life (Smith, 1987).

Ironically some of these same corporate leaders later came to see Prohibition as a threat to their economic and political interests. Many businessmen felt that the revenues not being generated as a result of Prohibition represented a serious drain on the economy. They also believed that Prohibition was turning the working classes against the government and the law, and was sowing the seeds for a much more radical uprising some time in the near future. All these fears were exacerbated in the early 1930s as the Great Depression advanced.

The repeal of Prohibition may seem to us a small and symbolic act, but it helped to remove a major source of public resentment. At the same time it provided a reward for the working classes, something they had not experienced in a long time—easy access to drink as a way of relieving some of the tension that was endemic in their lives. In this sense repeal was not only a way to keep the economy stimulated; it was also a sign of goodwill toward the working classes. Naturally, the alcoholic beverage industry was delighted to be back in business. Beer was once again to be widely available in restaurants and grocery stores, and this trend towards greater availability would continue almost unchecked until the 1970s. But during the next fifty years the industry had to respond to a series of challenges to its hegemony.

Alcohol and Consumption: The Privatization of Alcoholism

One of the major advances in the treatment of alcohol abuse in the first decades after Prohibition was the gradual acceptance of the *disease model* of alcoholism. Instead of being thought of as a sin or a crime, as had been the case before and during Prohibition, alcoholism came to be treated as a disease just like any other. Public opinion slowly shifted towards this view until it became dominant both in the treatment professions and in everyday speech (Beauchamp, 1980).

From the disease perspective, alcoholism could be understood as a set of personal characteristics, either physical or psychological, that make certain individuals quantitatively and qualitatively different from non-alcoholics in their drinking habits. In the *disease model* alcoholics can clearly be differentiated from the majority of people who drink moderately. Because their disease results from an addiction it makes no sense to try to reduce their level of consumption by any preventive strategies, such as making alcohol more expensive or less easily available. Not only would this be ineffective, it would needlessly penalize many moderate drinkers who are not alcoholics. In other words, the public policy implications of the disease model were quite explicit. It was a waste of time trying to get alcoholics to drink less alcohol; the only viable strategy was for each alcoholic to enter a programme of treatment based on complete abstinence (Armor *et al.*, 1976).

The disease or medical model represented a major advance over many of the previous conceptions of alcoholism. It made more funds available for treatment programmes, and it helped to remove the stigma associated with alcoholism by allowing the individual to think of his or her addiction as an illness rather than as a moral failing. Not surprisingly, the alcoholic beverage industry also viewed the disease model in a favourable light, even though alcoholism was recognized as a deadly affliction. The industry sought comfort in the evidence (or rather the belief) that only a small percentage of all drinkers would become alcoholics. It was a relief to the producers and distributors of alcohol to be told by respectable scientists that alcoholism was not contagious, and that one could not 'catch' it simply by drinking too much. The industry spokepersons could in all sincerity encourage people to drink, but to do so moderately. At the same time they could recommend that alcoholics and people in high risk categories should not drink at all.

In the 1960s social scientists started to argue for a shift away from the focus on a single concept of alcoholism to a much broader set of issues that would become known as 'alcohol-related problems' or 'problem drinking' (Smith and Hanham, 1982). A series of nation-wide drinking surveys had identified a range of public health and public order problems that were related to drinking but were not necessarily symptoms of alcoholism (Cahalan and Room, 1974). In the interests of prevention it was considered necessary to focus not just on the relatively small group of existing alcoholics in the population, but also on the much larger group of 'hidden' alcoholics and problem drinkers. The rigid adherence to the disease model of alcoholism had always made this difficult to achieve (Room, 1984).

The alcoholic beverage industry was not happy with the new expanded definition of the alcohol abuser, because it implied that far more people could potentially suffer as a result of their drinking habits. This clearly contradicted the industry's argument that alcohol was just another commodity like any other, and that it only became a problem in the hands of alcoholics.

At about the same time another perspective on alcoholism was being introduced into the policy debate, the so-called *social* or *cultural integration model* (Smith and Hanham, 1985). This model would also turn out to be largely acceptable to the alcoholic beverage industry, and its implications would be largely assimilated into public policy. This perspective originated from the social sciences, mainly sociology and anthropology, which are much less likely to be taken seriously in the business world than the medical sciences. As with the disease model, however, the distinctive feature of this perspective was that it focused on the way people drink alcohol, why they drink it, and with what effects—but this time the focus was on the social or cultural characteristics of the drinkers rather than their individual characteristics.

The *social integration model* begins with the assumption that a reasonable proportion of the problems associated with excessive consumption would disappear if drinking were more fully integrated into the prevailing culture. Proponents of this model suggest that if alcohol becomes more generally available within a locality, the overall prevalence of problems will be lower.

Evidence to support this position has been gathered by numerous cross-cultural observations. In the United States, in contrast to many European countries, for example, there appears to be a conflict between the 'wet' desires of many Americans and the 'dry' sentiments still left over from the Prohibition era. The result, it is argued, is a cultural ambivalence towards alcohol, and a complete lack of consistency in the rules and regulations governing its use (Room, 1976). To correct such a situation the integrationists argue for improved education about responsible drinking, and a co-ordinated effort to integrate drinking behaviour into the mainstream of cultural life, rather than leaving it at the fringes dangling like a bunch of forbidden fruit. It is also suggested that the best strategy for controlling the alcohol problem is not to reduce availability, but to distribute it more evenly, as part of a comprehensive effort to make responsible drinking the cultural norm within society.

Although the alcoholic beverage industry had not had things all its own way, by the middle of the 1970s it had not been seriously challenged, either by the providers of alcoholism services, or by the mainstream of social science research. By this time the drinking age had been lowered in most American states, and the *per capita* level of consumption had reached the highest level since before Prohibition (table 18.2).

Alcohol and Distribution: The Public Health Model

Beginning in the 1970s, a formidable challenge to the alcoholic beverage industry was launched, one that had an interdisciplinary base and was armed with cross-cultural evidence. Much of the early empirical work conducted on this issue was generated in Scandinavian countries (Kuusi, 1957), and the most widely circulated report was conducted by the Finnish Foundation for Alcohol Studies in 1975. This study concluded that 'changes in the overall consumption of alcoholic beverages have a bearing on the health of the people in any society. Alcohol control measures can be

TABLE 18.2.   Average alcoholic beverage consumption in the USA

	Spirits	Wine	Beer	Total
1930	0.9	—	—	0.9
1935	0.7	0.1	0.7	1.5
1940	0.6	0.2	0.8	1.6
1945	0.7	0.2	1.1	2.0
1950	0.7	0.2	1.1	2.0
1955	0.7	0.2	1.0	1.9
1960	0.8	0.2	1.0	2.0
1965	1.0	0.2	1.0	2.2
1970	1.1	0.3	1.2	2.5
1975	1.1	0.3	1.3	2.7
1980	1.1	0.3	1.4	2.8

Note: The figures indicate consumption of US gallons of absolute alcohol per capita aged 15 and over.

Source: Rorabaugh, 1979, p. 233; NIAAA, 1983, p. 2.

used to limit consumption: thus control of alcohol availability becomes a public health issue' (Bruun *et al.*, 1975, pp. 12–13).

This conclusion was based on what has become known as the *distribution of consumption (or public health) model* of alcohol use and abuse. It has been demonstrated that there is an empirical regularity between the mean level of consumption within a population and the proportion of heavy drinkers (Schmidt, 1977). Because heavy drinkers are more likely to develop alcohol-related problems, it follows that the proportion of problem drinkers can be predicted from the overall level of consumption. Empirical studies conducted in several countries had established that the distribution of consumption among the population is more or less lognormal, in other words positively skewed, with the majority being moderate drinkers, and a small proportion very heavy drinkers. Although there are still no generally accepted explanations for this phenomenon, it has been shown to hold in many different countries, regardless of the beverage preferences involved (Skog, 1980).

In *public health* terms this empirical regularity suggests that a solution to the growing problem of alcohol abuse would be somehow to reduce the mean level of alcohol consumption. This could be achieved by increasing the price of beverage alcohol, or by reducing its availability in any of a number of ways (Wittman, 1985; Smith and Hanham, 1982). For obvious reasons the model is not popular with the industry, or with the federal and state governments who generate a large share of their revenues from alcohol taxes and the sale of liquor licences. (Moore and Gerstein, 1981).

In spite of significant opposition from the industry and its supporters in the academic world, the public health approach and the drive to exert greater controls over the supply of alcohol have made some small but significant gains. Beginning in 1978, the National Institute of Alcohol Abuse and Alcoholism (NIAAA) rather tentatively embraced the traditional public health model of 'agent–host–environment' as it applies to the alcohol issue, and since then many individual state alcoholism agencies have followed suit (NYSDAAA, 1986). In 1982 the United States National Council on Alcoholism (NCA) announced a dramatic shift from its previous stance, and embraced a control perspective. In the announcement the following statement was made:

Today's environment is permeated by more than a billion dollars of advertising . . . which has promoted positive messages about alcohol use . . . in society as a whole. Drinking is associated with the 'good life', with health, with success, and with sexuality. In addition this has been matched by a general trend of relaxation on controls on availability and prices of alcoholic beverages which has, in turn, been followed by steady and frightening increases in alcohol-related problems . . . These problems are broadly based, and cannot be effectively approached except through broad, general measures of prevention policies . . . (Quoted in Room, 1984, p. 297).

Naturally the alcoholic beverage industry has registered its complaints about these developments, and has launched into a bitter conflict with the federal alcoholism agency (NIAAA), arguing that the government has been dragged into the alcohol control business by liberal academics and by research findings that are still equivocal (Room, 1984).

It is interesting to note that the public health approach can include an important role for geographers and planners in the development of alcohol policy. It is implicit in the distribution of consumption model, for example, that the level of consumption, and therefore the prevalence of alcohol-related problems, might prove to be susceptible to manipulations in the retail environment. In the last two decades we have learned a lot about the relationship between alcohol-related problems and the availability of alcoholic beverages, and there is some evidence that consumption patterns can be influenced by the location and density of outlets (Smith and Hanham, 1982; Room, 1984).

In the *urban areas* of the United States, localities (cities and counties) are uniquely placed to regulate the physical and temporal availability of alcohol. The presence of planning and zoning ordinances in approximately 6,000 municipalities and 3,000 counties offers a significant opportunity for localities to include whatever prevention-oriented language and procedures they consider to be appropriate. The research that has linked the prevalence of public health and social problems to the distribution of alcohol outlets solidly puts the regulation of outlets within the auspices of zoning law. Although planning and zoning ordinances are usually involved with innocuous land use controls, they become crucial when issues of the community's health and welfare are concerned. Patterns of permitted land uses that are written into the local zoning ordinances reflect the beliefs and social values of the residents, and are crucial in shaping the social and economic future of the community (Perin, 1977). It is reasonable to expect, therefore, that spatial variations in the retail availability of beverage alcohol will be an important issue for local planners and politicians.

It is evident that alcohol consumption is generally more widespread throughout the population in an urban area than elsewhere, and also more diversified (Room, 1983a). Cities report significantly fewer abstainers than small towns and rural areas, and generally have a higher per caput consumption rate (Cahalan and Room, 1974; Smith and Hanham, 1985). Alcohol consumption patterns in the city also involve drinking at a wide variety of times and places, particularly if there is an extensive tourist and entertainment business. All of these factors make it likely that the density of alcohol outlets will be considerably higher in cities than elsewhere. This is especially the case in certain parts of the city: for example in the urban core areas, where population has declined leaving, a high ratio of outlets per capita; and in areas that have been 'gentrifying', resulting in new outlets opening in bars and restaurants.

In California, Wittman (1985, 1986) has noted a number of other urban developments in which alcohol outlets have become considerably more prevalent in specific parts of the city, for example, in the commercial 'strip' areas, where many gas stations and convenience stores have recently received licences to sell alcohol; and in 'high risk' settings such as in the vicinity of sports stadiums. To monitor such developments it is essential for community groups and local planning and zoning officials to have access to the information they need to make sensible decisions. In a survey of 349 cities in California, Wittman and Hilton (1984) found that although cities are willing to use local ordinances to regulate the geography of alcohol outlets, they often lacked vital planning information about the outlets and the local problems associated with them.

In the legislative arena there is also evidence that the new control perspective has started to generate proposals for measures designed to prevent alcohol-related problems, in addition to the manipulation of the tax structure. In the keynote address at a national conference on alcohol control policy in 1986, Mosher (1986) listed some of the most common themes:

general adoption of the twenty-one drinking age law;

retail establishments held liable if they sell liquor to minors or people
   who are already intoxicated and who subsequently cause injuries to
   third parties;
all new and renewal applications for alcohol outlets should be subject to
   a mandatory 'environmental impact analysis', public hearings, and
   administrative approval;
gasoline stations and convenience stores should not be licensed for the
   sale of alcohol;
threshold limits should be established for the overall density of alcohol
   outlets in specific parts of the city (e.g. in the downtown area, and in
   the suburbs);
zoning moratorium on new licences in areas such as revitalized
   neighbourhood;
spacing requirements between outlets of similar type and between land
   uses that are incompatible (e.g. schools);
server training and server intervention programmes to produce responsible server behaviour.

In spite of the enthusiasm for the new public health perspective on
alcohol control, and the intense debate that has so far been generated,
little has yet actually been achieved. There are several possible reasons
for the apparent inactivity, not the least of which is the continual opposition of the alcoholic beverage industry to any significant attempts to
control availability. The industry argues that not only will they lose
money, but that the country as a whole will suffer economically, as it did
during Prohibition. Going beyond the confines of the industry, however, alcohol control policies are viewed by many people as an unnecessary intrusion by the state on to the rights of individual citizens. There is
also an occasionally voiced argument from the other side of the fence,
suggesting that alcohol controls would act as a regressive tax because the
heaviest drinkers are over-represented among the nation's poor and
unemployed. Another challenge to the public health approach comes
from the adherents of the medical view of alcoholism, who consider it
almost sacrilegious to challenge the supremacy of the *disease model* with
anything so ill-formed and unscientific as a *public health model* (Room,
1984).

The alcoholic beverage industry is not seriously threatened by the
public health approach to alcohol policy, and it would probably be in
its best interests to accomodate the new public health approach as it
earlier accommodated the other perspectives. This will require some
minor sacrifices, and perhaps the loss of some revenue, but it will
effectively leave the industry free to continue with its production and
distribution activities without significant interference.

Although there may be some opportunities for planners to be involved in the formulation and execution of alcohol policies, it is likely that these policies will hardly even scratch the surface of the industry's operations. Few legislators will be prepared to argue for any controls that seriously restrict the activities of the industry at the manufacturing, wholesale, or retail end of the trade. It would, therefore, be good public relations for the industry to comply with some of the public health recommendations, perhaps by beginning to exercise some degree of self-control in the area of advertising. Many of the industry's spokespersons are convinced that the public health measures will not work, and they have argued that the research evidence is equivocal, so they have little to lose by making some concessions.

It is important to point out that in the realm of public health it is not necessary to know all the answers, or even to know all the questions, before making some key interventions that might turn out to have positive health benefits. On the other hand, even some of the most ardent supporters of control policies have suggested that the only control measures that have had unequivocal impacts on the level of alcohol consumption have been changes in the level of taxation (Cook, 1981), and in the minimum drinking age (Moore and Gerstein, 1981). To date, isolated and small changes in other control measures have had mixed results. It is generally recognized that to be effective, control measures have to be part of a comprehensive set of preventive measures, including extensive education campaigns (Room, 1984).

In the absence of any really significant alterations in the overall pattern of alcohol availability, there may not be any noticeable impact on the structure of alcohol consumption in the near future. As a final alternative, therefore, it is important to look beyond where we have already come in practical terms, to where we might go in an idealized future, and to subject the issue of alcohol and problem drinking to the scrutiny of a political economy examination.

Alcohol and Production: The Political Economy of Alcoholism

Political economy approach to the alcohol issue is long overdue. In the first place there is a need to move beyond the limited and distorted views of medicine and the culture-bound studies conducted by many anthropologists and sociologists. In the second place it is clear that alcoholism is intimately connected with class and the distribution of power within society. A political economy approach has the potential for combining drinking studies from all classes and all cultures. Alcohol abuse has long been a problem in the cities of the developed world, but it has also become a problem in the Third World.

In approaching this topic it is useful to look in two directions. One way is to explore the manner in which alcoholic beverages are mass-produced and distributed, and how this fits into the inevitable drive within capitalism toward ever-greater accumulation and consumption. The second approach looks at the way drinking functions within a class-dominated society, and how the alienation and oppression inherent in industrial capitalism have contributed to the rising alcohol problem that we are witnessing today.

The production of alcohol is a multi-billion dollar industry that produces, for profit, a mind-altering drug. In that sense there is a clear link between the economic force driving the industry and the prevalence of alcohol-related problems within the population. In their search for profit, the corporations who make and sell alcohol must accept a major part of the responsibility for the way their product is used. The corporations themselves dispute this, choosing to argue that they are not responsible for the obvious fact that some people are addicted to alcohol, and others are likely to behave dangerously and unpredictably if they drink too much.

A historical perspective helps to spell this out more clearly. The spread of industrial capitalism created in the nineteenth-century city an entirely new set of pressures to drink (Smith, 1987; Johnson, 1978). It also enabled the alcohol producers to manufacture at a more rapid pace than ever before. The capitalist mode of production vastly expanded the array of goods that were reaching the market, but the unique feature of capitalism was that the working classes were required not only to produce the goods but also to consume them, thereby speeding up the circulation of capital. Commercial brewing was one of the earliest forms of manufacturing to be organized along the principles of capitalist production, both in the United States and in Britain, and the expanding supply of alcohol reaching the market was made easily available to the masses of thirsty workers. As Park (1983) has explained, alcohol producers went to great lengths to make sure drink was available to the workers, through tied houses or taverns under contract to one brewery.

During the colonial expansion and in more recent times alcohol has played a significant role in the relationships between developed and less developed countries. As Park (1983) has argued: 'Alcohol . . . caught up in the unending spiral of profit-making in the capitalist economy leads to high levels of consumption both within the producing countries and the world system of nations . . . this is what explains the world-wide rising tide of alcohol consumption observed during the last decades' (p. 60). This process has been particularly evident in the last decade, as alcohol producers in developed countries found their domestic markets were levelling off in the middle of the 1970s. When this happened they were forced to seek markets elsewhere around the globe, but particularly in the developing countries.

Through the sale of their products, the export of capital, and the sale of licences, it has been possible for the transnational corporations to increase the availability of alcohol in developing countries. This has resulted in some significant changes in consumption patterns, and increases in most of the usual indicators of problem drinking (Edwards, 1979). Of the 46 countries where beer output grew by more than half between 1975 and 1980, for example, 42 were developing countries; and by 1977, 36 developing countries depended on transnationals for more than one-fifth of their spirits consumption (Edwards, 1983). From 1960 to 1980 there had been a clear shift in the world pattern of alcohol production and consumption. The beer industry grew spectacularly—Latin American, Asian, and African output rose by over 400 per cent; and by 1980 the developing countries accounted for 18.3 per cent of the global output of alcoholic beverages.

Turning briefly to the consumer of alcoholic beverages, it is possible to make a connection between the alcohol problem and the social relations of production within capitalism. This allows a more comprehensive argument: namely that the capitalist mode of production provided the driving force for the continual expansion of production and an ever-wider distribution of alcohol, while at the same time the social relations of production under capitalism, and the character of the urban environment established to support capitalism, helped to develop appetites for strong drink and addictions to alcohol.

This point was made eloquently by Friedrich Engels (1980) in his classic work, *The Condition of the Working Class in England*, which was first published in 1845. In one expressive passage Engels captures some of the dynamics of problem drinking among the working-class poor:

The working man comes home from his work tired, exhausted, finds his home comfortless, damp, dirty, repulsive; he has urgent need of recreation, he must have something to make work worth his trouble, to make the prospect of the next day endurable. His unnerved, uncomfortable, hypochondriac state of mind and body arising from his unhealthy condition . . . is aggravated beyond endurance by the general conditions of his life, the uncertainty of his existence . . . and his inability to do anything towards gaining an assured position. His enfeebled frame, weakened by bad air and bad food, violently demands some external stimulus; his social need can be gratified only in the public house, he has absolutely no other place where he can meet his friends. How can he be expected to resist the temptation? It is morally and physically inevitable that, under such circumstances, a very large number of working men should fall into intemperance. (Engels, 1980, pp. 127–8)

Engels's description covers several facets of the role of drinking in the life of the poor, and much of what he wrote at that time is still applicable today. In the first place, alcohol provided much-needed recreation and an escape from the dirt, tedium, and danger of the factory. Getting drunk takes a person away from all this, to a narcotized sleep at least until the morning. At the same time drink keeps the working person satisfied with, or at least acquiescent to, his or her powerlessness. Communal drinking, usually in the working-class tavern, also provided one of the few places where working people could meet and exhibit the solidarity of their class; in fact some historians have suggested that heavy drinking often became a 'badge' for the working classes in the industrial city, to be worn angrily by an alienated and oppressed workforce (Johnson, 1978). Drinking also provided an excuse for certain behaviours that would not otherwise have been tolerated, such as fighting, abusing the family, and squandering all the food money on oneself. Engels was prepared to interpret these behaviours as natural coping responses to degraded conditions. In addition to all this, he pointed out that heavy drinking seriously damaged the health of many working people, exacerbating the effects of their squalid living and working conditions.

It would be foolhardy to try to impress upon representatives of the alcoholic beverage industry that they should take considerations such as these into their decision-making. In fact it can be argued that if a fully confrontational stance had been taken with the industry, it would not have been possible to make even the little headway that has so far been achieved. It appears, therefore, that pragmatism has dominated in the arena of alcohol policy. In a series of gradual and non-threatening steps a decidedly public-health-oriented philosophy has emerged as a dominant force in the debate. As this chapter has suggested, this philosophy is limited to the domain of alcohol distribution. The solutions generated by the debate will be equally limited, focusing on short-term, small-scale, technocratic efforts to tinker with the sales of alcoholic beverages. In spite of the obvious opportunity for geographers and planners to take part in the design of these solutions, they must be viewed as inherently simplistic, superficial, and ultimately subversive, in that they will tend to preclude a more in-depth search for some of the underlying causes of the alcohol problem.

Conclusion

This chapter has traced some of the developments in the debate over the alcohol policy in the United States during the last fifty years. In that time much has been achieved, and a concerted effort is now being made on a number of fronts to reduce the abuse of alcohol. After the highly politicized years leading up to Prohibition and its ultimate repeal, the alcohol issue was essentially depoliticized for about four decades (Gusfield, 1982). The 'disease' of alcoholism made the successful transition into the world of medicine, and this transition had a number of important advantages. It created a market for the development of therapeutic and research skills in the area of alcohol studies (Room, 1983*b*), and it helped to enhance the already dominant medical model of human behaviour. It also served to protect both the reputations and the incomes of the corporations who produce beverage alcohol, as well as those who promote it and make a living from its distribution. The extension of psychological and sociological models to explain alcohol abuse (Cahalan and Room, 1974), and the broadened definition of alcohol-related problems, did not change this basic situation. Alcohol abuse had been privatized: it was defined as a disease of the body, of the mind, of the family, or even the community—but its definition as an individual disease effectively neutralized it as a social problem, and normalized the socio-economic conditions that helped to produce it.

The alcohol issue has recently been repoliticized to some extent, but, as this chapter has suggested, the process has occurred mainly at the level of consensus politics. Legislative change have been called for, and in the current environment there is a chance that some of the legislation will be successful. This certainly represents an advance over the political dormancy of the last fifty years, but the alcoholic beverage industry has been able to ride the storm essentially unharmed. With the exception of some minor restrictions on its advertising practices, and its lukewarm public service announcements telling people to drink responsibly, the industry remains intact, in fact stronger than ever.

References

Aaron, P., and D. Musto (1981), 'Temperance and prohibition in America: a historical overview', in M. H. Moore and D. R. Gerstein (eds.), *Alcohol and Public Policy: Beyond the Shadow of Prohibition* (National Academy Press: Washington DC), 127–81.

Armor, D. J., M. J. Polich, and H. B. Stamboul (1976), *Alcoholism and Treatment* (Rand Corporation: Santa Monica).

Beauchamp, D. E. (1980), *Beyond Alcoholism: Alcohol and Public Health Policy* (Temple University Press: Philadelphia).

Bruun, K., G. Edwards, M. Lumio, K. Makela, L. Pan, R. E. Popham, R. Room, W. Schmidt, O. J. Skog, P. Sulkunen, and E. Osterberg (eds.), (1975), *Alcohol Control Policies in Public Health Perspective*, Publication 25, (Finnish Foundation for Alcohol Studies: Helsinki).

Cahalan, D., and R. Room (1974), *Problem Drinking Among American Men*, Monograph 7 (Rutgers Center of Alcohol Studies: New Brunswick, NJ).

Clark, N. H. (1976), *Deliver Us From Evil: An Interpretation of American Prohibition* (Norton: New York).

Cook, P. J. (1981), 'The effect of liquor taxes on drinking, cirrhosis, and auto accidents', in M. H. Moore and D. Gerstein (eds.), *Alcohol and Public Policy: Beyond the Shadow of Prohibition* (National Academy Press: Washington, DC) 255-85.

Edwards, G. (1979), 'Drinking problems: putting the Third World on the map', *Lancet* 25, Aug., 402-4.

—— (1983), Preface 6 'Alcoholic beverages: dimensions of corporate power', *Globe*, 4, Dec., 3-43.

Engels, F. (1980), *The Condition of the Working Class in England* (Progress Publishers: Moscow).

Gusfield, J. R. (1982), 'Deviance in the welfare state: the alcoholism profession and the entitlement of stigma', in M. Lewis (ed.) *Research in Social Problems and Public Policy* (J.A.I. Press: Greenwich, Conn.), 1-20.

Johnson, P. (1978), *A Shopkeeper's Millenium: Society and Revivals in Rochester, New York, 1815-1837* (Hill and Wang: New York).

Kuusi, P. (1957), *Alcohol Sales Experiments in Rural Finland*, trans. A Westphalen, publication 3 (Finnish Foundation for Alcohol Studies: Helsinki).

Moore, M. H., and D. R. Gerstein (eds.) (1981) *Alcohol and Public Policy: Beyond the Shadow of Probihition* (National Academy Press: Washington, DC).

Mosher, J. F. (1986), 'Bold new initiatives in alcohol policy', Keynote address at the Alcohol Policy IV Conference: 'Implications for prevention of alcohol problems', New York City, 11-13 Nov.

NIAAA (National Insitute on Alcohol Abuse and Alcoholism) (1978), *Third Special Report to the US Congress on Alcohol and Health* (US Dept. of Health, Education and Welfare: Rockville, Md).

—— (1983), *Fifth Special Report to the US Congress on Alcohol and Health* (NIAAA: Rockville, Md).

NYSDAAA (New York State Division of Alcoholism and Alcohol Abuse) (1986) *Focus on Prevention: 1986 Update to the Five Year Comprehensive Plan for Alcoholism Services in New York State* (NYSDAAA: Albany, NY).

Padavan, Frank (1986), 'Legislative priorities: a comprehensive strategy for the 1980s', paper presented at the Alcohol Policy IV Conference: 'Implications for prevention of alcohol problems', New York City, 11-13 Nov.

Park, P. (1983), 'Social class factors in alcoholism', in B. Kissin and H. Begleiter (eds.), *The Pathogenesis of Alcoholism: Psychological Factors* (Plenum: New York), 365-404.

Perin, C. (1977), *Everything In Its Place: Social Order and Land-use in America* (Princeton University Press: Princeton, NJ).

Room, R. (1976), 'Ambivalence as a sociological explanation: the case of cultural explanations of alcohol problems', *American Sociological Review*, 41: 1047-65.

—— (1983*a*), 'Region and urbanization as factors in drinking practices and problems', in B. Kissin and H. Begleiter (eds.), *The Pathogenesis of Alcoholism: Psychosocial Factors* (Plenum: New York), 555-604.

—— (1983*b*) 'Sociological aspects of the disease concept of alcoholism', *Research Advances in Alcohol and Drug Problems*, 7: 47–91.

—— (1984), 'Alcohol control and public health', *Annual Review of Public Health* 5: 293–317.

Rorabaugh, W. J. (1979), *The Alcoholic Republic: An American Tradition* (Oxford University Press: New York).

Schmidt, W. (1977), 'Cirrhosis and alcohol consumption: an epidemiological perspective', in G. Edwards and M. Grant (eds.), *Alcoholism: New Knowledge and New Responses* (Croom Helm: London), 15–47.

Skog, O. J. (1980), 'Social interaction and the distribution of alcohol consumption', *Journal of Drug Issues*, 10: 71–92.

Smith, C. J. and R. Q. Hanham (1982), *Alcohol Abuse: Geographical Perspectives* (Association of American Geographers: Washington, DC).

—— (1987), 'The social geography of prohibition', Department of Geography and Planning (State University of New York: Albany, NY), mimeo.

—— —— (1984), 'Regional changes and problem drinking in the United States, 1970–1978', *Regional Studies*, 19(2): 149–62.

—— —— (1985), 'What drives people to drink? Interpreting the effect of urban living on the use and abuse of alcohol', *Urban Ecology*, 9: 195–213.

Wilson, J. Q. (1975), *Thinking about Crime* (Basic Books: New York).

Wittman, F. D., (1985), 'Reducing environmental risk of alcohol problems' (Prevention Research Center: Berkeley), mimeo.

—— (1986), 'Issues in controlling alcohol availability', *Western City*, Nov., 9–13.

—— and M. E. Hilton (1984), 'Uses of planning and zoning ordinances to regulate alcohol outlets in California cities', paper presented at conference on 'Control issues in alcohol abuse prevention, II: impacting communities', Charleston, SC, 11–13 Oct.

PART III

Policy Response

19

Local Initiatives for Economic Regeneration

Andrew P. Church and John M. Hall

Few texts about British urban policy published in the 1970s included the phrase 'local economic initiatives' in their tables of contents or indexes. In less than a decade an extensive literature on the origins, nature, and impact of various initiatives had appeared (see for example, Morison, 1987; the recently established journal *Local Economy*; and reviews such as Vielba, 1986), and a number of agencies and organizations provide briefing documents on the latest changes in policies and instruments (e.g. the Centre for Local Economic Strategies in Manchester, producers of the monthly *Local Economic News*, and the Glasgow Planning Exchange's Local Economic Development Information Service). Our review of the literature will be selective rather than exhaustive, our focus firmly on Great Britain (and England more than Scotland or Wales), although there have been useful studies of West Germany and the OECD. We also concentrate on the major urban areas, and not the major regions (for which see Damesick and Wood, 1987), nor even the rural areas, although Mills and Young (1986) encountered numerous examples of economic initiatives in the shire counties, and the Ministry of Agriculture's package on rural development shows a philosophy similar to that followed in urban areas by the Department of the Environment (DoE) and Department of Employment (DE, (DoE/DE, 1987). (The latter department's involvement in promoting enterprise was to be transferred later to the Department of Trade and Industry.) In alighting on the key themes and debates in the topic we have four questions in mind, and we use the policy analysts' term 'intervention' rather than the politicians' 'initiative'. Why intervene? Who should intervene? How does intervention take place? What are the outcomes—indeed, is the effort justified, and are formal policy evaluations likely to overlook important intangibles such as local pride?

The Economic Context of Intervention: Urban Decline and Restructuring

Except in times of severe national recession or local industrial collapse, economic management has been regarded as a central government responsibility, focused principally on questions about exchange rates, inflation, money supply and borrowing, productivity, unemployment, and wage rates. While economic growth allowed broadly redistributive policies to bring central government support to, say, stagnating nationalized industries, and grants to the older industrial conurbations (through regional policy especially, both British, and latterly European Community supported) and to the more recently defined smaller areas of social hardship within selected cities (such as education and immigration priority areas), local authorities saw little need to be engaged in their own brand of economic management. But in times of national recession and local economic collapse, local authorities and local business consortia have understandably wished to prevent further job losses, arrest firms' financial losses, and hold back further declines in local rate income as premises are left derelict. And, more positively, they might seek not just to extinguish economic forest fires, but to create more attractive environmental, financial, and skill conditions locally with which to attract economic growth in future. Using a mixture of central and local government powers, measures have been adopted to stem job loss, diversify local economies (especially where manufacturing has been over-represented and producer services under-represented), and to attract incoming growth industries.

A desire to intervene, whether expressed by central or local government and private business consortia, is now commonplace, especially in the country's older urban and industrial areas. A widespread move of people and jobs from conurbation cores to fringes was documented with meticulous care by Hall *et al.* (1973). More recently, Begg *et al.* (1986) have shown that between 1951 and 1981 the inner areas of Britain's six largest conurbations lost 35 per cent of their population and 45 per cent of their jobs—mostly in manufacturing, hence an almost automatic use of the term 'industry' rather than 'industry and commerce' in the literature. In fact the manufacturing labour force contracted by about 2 million people between 1971 and 1981. The outer areas of these same cities also experienced losses: − 13 per cent for people; − 7 per cent for jobs during the same period. Even the seventeen next largest free-standing cities lost 15 per cent of their jobs in the thirty-year period. The causes of this urban-rural shift in the locus of job and population growth are well documented: changing residential preferences (and the financial wherewithal to express them), improvements in the accessibility of outer suburban and surrounding rural areas; the generally poor image of the inner city (Sunday supplement journalists' preoccupations with gentrifying yuppies notwithstanding), and of the now somewhat neglected grey or intermediate areas, such as central Lancashire and the Potteries, as described in the Hunt committee report (1969).

But Britain's job market is not, as the prime minister was so keen to emphasize in the early 1980s, part of a closed system. British firms, especially those in the manufacturing sector, were affected by the oil-price rises in the 1970s, global economic recession and foreign competition, mergers, and rationalizations. Was their plight also made worse by operating from an inner-city location? Analysts equivocate in the face of contradictory evidence about the physical constraints and cost penalities of inner urban locations. Certainly the Economy Group (1976) working on the Strategic Plan for the South East had no difficulty in finding an adverse 'London factor', whereby, when taken together, high rents and rates, site access problems and road congestion, high staff turnover, and a shortage of skilled labour severely disabled firms operating in the London compared with elsewhere. Begg *et al.* (1986) argue that the 'assorted cost disadvantages of city locations, planning restrictions and the policies of local authorities, and regional policy have all contributed to employment loss in city locations' (p. 14). Others, such as Robson (1987), while recognizing that land supply problems in cities may constrain existing firms and deter new investment, claim none the less that 'there is not, so far as I am aware, a convincing argument that (barring the problems arising from the cost, availability and dereliction of urban land) firms actually benefit from a non-urban location' (p. 14).

A different explanation for the geographically skewed pattern of the death of firms and relocations is provided by the restructuring thesis advanced by Massey and Meegan (1982) which derives from an analysis of international trends in the circuit of capital. In this view, inner urban job loss is the geographical outcome of macro level changes in the British and international economies. In the 1960s declining profits, combined with increased international competition, forced British industry to restructure organization, production methods, and labour requirements. To closures, mergers, and acquisitions were added capital intensification in production and the increasingly rapid switching of investment and productive capacity between countries by multi-national firms. Again uneven geographical outcomes were described; the process was especially detrimental for inner-city areas. So, rather than being seen as a result of physical constraints and changing costs, inner urban job loss was explained by companies' needs to maintain profit levels in an ever-changing and increasingly competitive international economic environment. And a further scythe-cut of restructuring has swept across the inner-city areas, the swing being driven by national government's restructuring of local government and public services such as education, health, housing, and transport, obeying Mrs. Thatcher's ideological commitment to reduced public expenditure and greater competitiveness in public quasi-monopolies. Even the naval dockyard towns in the otherwise favoured south of England have not been exempted (case studies are presented in Cooke, 1986).

Hence the view is now widespread among commentators and politicians that although local factors may contribute to economic decline in urban areas, such decline is not caused primarily by local forces. Given that the motive force seems to be national and international, an implication might be that local responses are likely to have but a small impact on redressing local employment declines. Nevertheless, numerous such responses have been formulated. But exactly what constitutes a *local* economic initiative? It is an action to stimulate or protect the economy within a defined local or sub regional area. In some cases the area will correspond to an entire administrative unit of local government, such as an English or Welsh county or district. In other cases it may be found that a locally implemented scheme is part of a nationally directed and evaluated policy programme, and is only local in the sense that implementation is organized in a particular locality. And to add to the diversity of forms, some national policies to protect a specific sector of industry or commerce, e.g. defence, may have an inadvertently disproportionate effect on the economic *success* of particular localities where the activity takes place (see Boddy *et al.*, 1986).

Why Intervene?

The desire to intervene is readily understood. Especially where the result is long-term unemployment and all-too-visible dereliction, job losses and ailing firms constitute a political embarrassment and domestic misfortune. 'Something must be done' is an entirely normal reaction. It is not just pay that is forfeited, but savings and pensions, and local purchasing power and rate income are reduced. Now if the market behaved perfectly, reduced demand in certain areas might lead to lower wages—people would buy themselves back into work—and rents and so firms' costs would fall. Labour might even migrate to areas of demand and workers retrain in the skills required. Given that one of the principal aims of post-war British land use planning was to reduce congestion and overcrowding, might not population decline and the thinning out of economic activity actually be *desirable* in certain circumstances? But, as is so often the case, individuals migrating from the inner cities have been younger, more vigorous and more skilled, leaving behind the less- and un-skilled and the poor generally in the deprived inner urban areas. When combined with the rigidities of the public housing market especially, job loss has allowed high levels of unemployment to develop and persist in the same inner-city areas, such that the British inner city problem is now viewed as a concentration of overlapping economic *and* social problems that are found throughout society (Hall, 1986; Pahl, 1986).

But there are arguments against focusing social programmes exclusively on the numerous *urban* poor. On equity grounds it can be argued that if a society chooses to tackle a problem that affects the lives of individuals (say, an unemployed person), then all of the individuals affected by the problem should be assisted, regardless of where they live. Further, why devise programmes to overcome locally exhibited misfortunes if the problem continues to grow at a national level? In such cases intervention may simply move the problem around the map. But, equally, broad equity considerations are raised by others as the justification for areally defined policies, including local economic interventions, especially if *concentrations* of people facing economic and social hardships can be shown to be more disadvantaged than those in similar circumstances who are not surrounded by like people. A related justification considers future costs, especially in areas of multiple deprivation in which riots might be precipitated and thereby result in significantly increased policy (and police) costs, and do possible harm to the regional or national economy. Also supporting area-based policies, but running counter to the equity argument, is the view that at a time when national resources are limited, the best value for money is obtained by targeting interventions on chosen localities with the severest problems. Only rarely, however, does the literature of economic regeneration begin with, or even include passing reference to, any theoretical justifications for action. Instead the 'something must be done' school predominates, often as a direct result of sharp increases in local unemployment rates.

Ward (1983) views politicians' recent penchants for local measures in a perspective from much earlier in the present century. An extra impetus was provided by local government reorganization (in Greater London in 1965, in England and Wales in 1974, and in Scotland in 1975) which established the upper-tier counties and metropolitan counties as strategic authorities with the resources to undertake large-scale local economic initiatives (Mawson and Miller, 1986). The recent significance of urban rioting, for long a fear of governments, should not be overlooked. Michael Heseltine himself—he was Environment Secretary when the Toxteth riots broke out in Liverpool in 1981—has written (1987, p. 164) that 'it is widely agreed that the jolt given by the urban riots of the 1980s provided the motive power' for his own particular style of interventions. These included businessmen's bus tours, private sector secondments, preferring Liverpool to Stoke-on-Trent for the country's first international garden festival on derelict inner-city land, and the broad approach followed by the Merseyside Development Corporation in seeking to change the image not just of the Liverpool waterfront and its former dock area, but of a whole conurbation now conceivably more commonly associated by non-Liverpudlians with economic death-watch-beetle than the Beatles. There was an interesting irony in Liverpool in 1984 at the time of the garden festival: how many of its five million visitors realized that they were inspecting a Conservative economic demonstration plot in what had become by then a militantly Labour-controlled city?

Who Should Intervene?

At present both national and local politicians want to be seen to be doing something for the economic plight of the inner city. Since the 1979 General Election, the three successive Conservative national governments have sought to use selected economic initiatives in chosen localities—such as in enterprise zones and in free ports—to foster broader national economic aims, such as encouraging small firms, limiting government controls (*Lifting the Burden* was the title of the related White Paper, Cmnd. 9571, of 1981), and fostering an entrepreneurial or enterprise culture. Centrally inspired and imposed local economic initiatives can be seen as a deliberate attempt to weaken local government. What is the true motive of the Conservatives' new fight for the inner city? Recovery in votes rather than the recovery of local employment? Not that local governments are without guile. From 1981 until their abolition in 1986 the six metropolitan counties and Greater London were all Labour-controlled, and all chose a particular form of economic interventions, sometimes labelled 'alternative economic strategies', which favoured job protection in the public sector, investment support and planning agreements, and policies to protect vulnerable employment groups, such as recent immigrants, women employed part-time, and the physically handicapped. By these means they also hoped that the electorate would understand Labour's economic ambitions if returned to power in Westminster. Since the seven counties were abolished in 1986, and especially since the third General Election victory in 1987, the Conservative government has gone on the offensive to capture the high ground of economic intervention.

It must be emphasized that the private sector also organizes help for business in particular localities (Owen, 1986, shows how). For example, Business in the Community's 1987 edition of the directory of enterprise agencies, trusts, and community action programmes lists some 280 local agencies—all 'business-led'—which, in addition to giving advice especially about small business creation and development, increasingly provide managed workshops and training courses. Nationally and locally, BiC seeks the active collaboration of major firms, local authorities, trade unions, and the voluntary sector. Enterprise agencies will often secure the secondment of experienced bank employees who are particularly able to assist small firms.

Even the nationalized industries, such as coal and steel, also engage in measures to promote new business ventures in areas where pits and ·steelworks have been closed. Such has been the function of British Steel Corporation (Industry) Ltd., founded in 1975, and British Coal Enterprise Ltd., founded at the height of the miners' strike in 1984.

Central–local relations

Such constructive partnerships at a local level are not always found between central and local government. In Britain there has long been open warfare, sometimes in skirmishes, sometimes in uprisings and rebellions, between the two administrative and political tiers. Textbooks on local government describe certain actions of local authorities being defined as *ultra vires* by parliament (in Latin, *beyond the powers* of such authorities to perform). Dawson (1985, p. 32) has characterized the main phases in parliament's rather grudging acceptance of local direction.

In the nineteenth century, urgent needs such as for clean water and sewage systems, and health and education services were viewed by parliament as suitable for private philanthropic funding or private enterprise, although local Acts would be framed for particular cases. During the early twentieth century, evolving powers were given in the main to *ad hoc* bodies, not to local authorities as such, but unevenness of provision by the private sector led parliament to pass permissive legislation. When responsibility was transferred to local authorities, the larger ones often performed well, and so compulsory national legislation was sometimes introduced to force other authorities to act, and to raise performance standards. Interestingly, Young (1986) considers that local authorities' economic development functions might currently be at this stage.

Most recently, since the upper tier counties were abolished in 1986 on the accusation of being 'wasteful and unnecessary', there has been a shift of concern from unevenness of *provision* to unevenness of *spending*, coupled with a concern to 'lift the burden' of supposedly stifling local controls and restrictions, and further attempts to reduce local authority spending as a proportion of the gross national product.

The debate about the extent of local government's powers, especially in relation to its accountability to the local rate-paying electorate through the ballot box, is of long standing. The view has long been advanced that by levying high rates local authorities may stifle local businesses, and should therefore have their powers curtailed sharply by central government. Contemporary evidence about the negative effect of rates is far from conclusive (Fothergill and Gudgin, 1982; Crawford *et al.*, 1985), although one can have some sympathy with the outbreak of the sentiment 'No taxation without representation' that followed the loss everywhere but in the City of London of the business rate-payers' vote in local government elections. In their proposals on the future of local government finance (Cmnd 9714, 1986) the government anticipated replacing the present rate demand which varies from one authority to another with a nationally uniform business rate, such that a local authority's income will be split in future between businesses, residents (through the community charge, or poll tax) and central government in the ratio 25 : 25 : 50. Such increasing centralization of control may fuel the view that central governments have come to view local government as an instrument for furthering central policy, in which case 'local administration' would be a more accurate term than 'local government'.

How Does Intervention Take Place?

So far we have described the broad context of intervention. We now move along the scale from broad ideology to policy, to programmes, and to specific projects. Ideological and policy shifts have become particularly marked in the 1980s, not least because of the rift between Conservative central government and Labour big city local governments. There are many examples of a clear breakdown in what for perhaps two decades had been a rather cosy consensus between political parties locally and nationally, in which many policy spheres (the nationalized industries most obviously exluded) showed little change as one party's hands succeded the other's on the levers of power. After Mrs Thatcher's first General Election success in 1979 the Conservative party gave a quite uncharacteristic ideological jerk to the levers. A similar but opposite jerk was given to the six metropolitan counties and the Greater London Council, all of which became Labour-controlled after 1981, mostly with a new breed of councillor in charge (who might also be a council employee and union representative in another authority).

TABLE 19.1. Conservative central government and Labour local government approaches to urban economic regeneration in England since 1979

Conservative central government approaches since 1979	'New Left' (Labour) local authority approaches, 1981–6
1. Focus on the *private sector* as the motor of economic development	See the *public sector* as the necessary stimulus for economic change
2. See public *land use planning* as a hindrance to economic regeneration, and aim to remove or reduce planning controls as a disincentive to investment	See *lack of socially responsible investment planning* as a major cause of economic decline, and aim to develop new forms of industrial and sectoral planning, supported by popular involvement
3. Give priority to the attraction of *new inward investment*	Give priority to the defence and development of *existing indigenous industries*
4. Focus on the *market* as the sphere for economic development	Focus on the sphere of *production* as the basis for economic regeneration
5. Want local government opened up by introducing market forces	Want local government opened up by giving greater attention to 'popular planning' (viewed in class struggle terms)

Source: Based on Benington, 1986.

The contrasting stances of Right in central government and Left in local government as regards urban economic policy are shown in table 19.1. On the Conservative side, new agencies and co-ordinating structures were created to emphasize private-sector financed, demand-led approaches to regeneration; Chandler and Lawless (1985) label this approach Neo-Liberalism. On the Labour side, in addition to property and marketing approaches, the New Left's quest for 'restructuring *for* labour, has given prominence to questions of workers' ownership and control in the workplace. Furthermore, particular Labour authorities— Liverpool and Sheffield come strongly to mind—have sought, despite rate capping and removal of grant, to maintain or expand their own local authority workforce in the face of rising local unemployment. In these cities earlier 'gas and water' socialism had been replaced by 'no cuts to jobs and services' socialism. In the middle politically, and not shown in table 19.1, are what Boddy in Boddy and Fudge (1984) has described as 'mainstream approaches' to economic and employment issues which seek public support to underpin the operation of private enterprise, usually through the economic development offices (described below). It is not unknown for a particular city to combine left, centre, and right approaches; for some authorities *any* aid that they can attract is welcome, whether from state bureaucracies or local business sponsors.

Local authority interventions

Broadly speaking, and neglecting local measures to combat economic hardships pursued in the 1920s and 1930s, it is only since the Local Government Act 1972, which brought a redistribution of powers and boundaries in 1974 in England and Wales, and the Local Government (Scotland) Act 1973, which did likewise in Scotland in 1975, that local authorities have become actively engaged in promoting economic growth and coping with the consequences of decline within their jurisdictions. Section 137 of the first Act and Section 83 of the second allow English and Welsh, and Scottish local authorities, respectively, to expend up to 2p for each pound of their rate income in the broad, otherwise undefined, interest of their area or its inhabitants. A survey for the Widdecombe committee by Ramsdale and Capon (1986) shows that almost exactly two-thirds of such discretionary spending is channelled into economic development initiatives. The Inner Urban Areas Act (1978) allows designated local authorities to direct specific financial aid to firms. A wide variety of national legislation, including education, employment and training, housing, and town and county planning Acts, allows local authorities to assist in training, housing key workers, and land assembly and servicing.

The most common form of local authority activity in the sphere of economic intervention has been the recent creation of economic development offices, the functions of which have been reported on in a recent survey by Mills and Young (1986). They distributed a questionnaire to all 456 local authorities (upper-tier counties and lower-tier districts) in England and Wales, and received usable replies from just over half of them. The picture of an economic development office that emerges is of a workload dominated by property-led functions, such as providing serviced sites, premises, factories, and workshops, together with associated local infrastructure support. Advice services are usually also offered, especially for small businesses, together with a variety of loans, grants, and rent concessions. Marketing is a third function, including advertising and publicity and displays at trade fairs, and in some cases specifically highlighting tourism, high-tech innovation and research, and development activities. Taking an example at random, Walsall Metropolitan District Council's Economic Development Unit lists six functions: to provide local economic information to policy-makers; to maintain a comprehensive list of sites and buildings on the market in both the public and private sectors; to encourage start-ups as well as indigenous firms to stay and grow in their current locality; to deliver programmes of grants or loans to companies for site or building improvements or job creating proposals; to ensure that training programmes are relevant to the needs of industry, and finally to encourage local self-help schemes for the unemployed.

Labour-controlled authorities show a propensity to create a specialist economic development unit within a department of the local authority; Conservative authorities show less affection for specialist units. Staff numbers engaged in economic development range in size between almost 300 in the former Greater London Council in 1984/85, to a mean in 1985/86 of about 27 in the six former metropolitan counties, 18 in the London boroughs, 11 in the metropolitan districts, 10 in the shire counties, and 2.5 in the shire county districts. The parent department is most commonly the planning department, followed by the chief executive's department—which often serves the key Policy and Resources Committee.

Turning to the professional officers, most economic development officers are male, with a local authority background, usually with a first degree in geography and a postgraduate planning qualification. Growing numbers are joining the Institute of Economic Development Officers, and they report wanting their own skills improved in such fields as investment appraisal, accounting and business finance, marketing, property development, and the generality of management. They are well informed about central government grants, liaise increasingly with the MSC, tourist boards and the Development Commission in rural areas, and in the assisted areas especially seeking funding from the European Community's Regional Development Fund and Social Fund. Deserving of investigation is the significance of any measurable correlation between levels of local economic distress and the magnitude of a local authority's response.

Of course other local authority departments are engaged in seeking to improve their areas's attractiveness for new inward investment, and to retain existing private and public sector enterprises. Although county planning departments are to lose their duty of preparing a structure plan, they have tried hitherto within the consultative framework of structure plans to co-ordinate public and private investment with a view to meeting economic as well as environmental and social objectives. Structure plans have proved of diminishing importance in an era of economic depression: what local authority willingly turns down almost *any* proposal for development that will bring jobs, whether new or transferred from elsewhere? Only a few green belt counties in south-east England will refuse new large-scale housing or retailing development. Further, many structure plans have been imperfect instruments for allocating locations and transport connections to the growing number of edge-of-town and out-of-town retail, commercial, and residential developments. And as we shall see, many local authorities have viewed the struggle to maintain their own employment levels and to promote equal opportunities in an attempt to offset what in the first half of the 1980s was a rapidly rising level of unemployment in most urban areas.

Central government policies for intervention

The list of current central government policies for intervention is extensive, as the following list shows, and is a composite mixture of programmes with varying degrees of central and local funding and control.

(a) = purpose; (b) = form of assistance; (c) = eligibility.

1. Urban development grant
   (a) To promote economic and physical regeneration of run-down urban areas by encouraging *private* investment which would not take place without grant.
   (b) Grant or loan; requires local authority's support (they contribute 25 per cent of grant).
   (c) Applications may be submitted by 57 designated districts in England.

2. Urban regeneration grant
   (a) Large-scale private sector redevelopment and refurbishment in areas affected by industrial change.
   (b) Outright grant, loan, or repayable grant for schemes not otherwise profitable.
   (c) Priority to schemes in areas of severe unemployment and derelict/disused property.

(£30m. was available for (1) and (2) in 1987/88. City grant replaces and simplifies (1) and (2) from May 1988).

3. Derelict land grant
   (a) To reclaim land so damaged by industrial or other uses that it cannot be used without being treated.
   (b) Grant payable as a percentage of the difference between the costs of reclamation and the increased value of the reclaimed land.
   (c) Grants paid at 80 percent in Assisted Areas and Derelict Land Clearance Areas; 50 per cent elsewhere.

(£81m. available 1987/8).

4. Urban programme
   (a) Focuses on economic, environmental, and social problems of inner cities, including enabling local authorities to assist private sector problems, ethnic minorities, and voluntary bodies.
   (b) Grants and loans for site preparation and improvements, rents, interest payments, workshops.
   (c) Inner Area Programmes may be submitted by 55 urban authorities in England.

5. Land registers
   (a) To bring under-and-un-used publicly owned land to the attention of private developers.
   (b) National and regional registers kept by DoE; local registers by local authorities.
   (c) Registers available for public inspection free of charge.

6. Urban development corporations
   (a) To regenerate its area by bringing land and buildings into effective use; encourage development of industry and commerce; ensure availability of housing and social facilities to encourage people to live and work in its area.
   (b) Acquiring, reclaiming, and servicing land for private sector development, and control of development within the urban development area.
   (c) Two UDC's initially (London Docklands, Merseyside), followed by Black Country (Cardiff *in Wales*), Teesside, Trafford Park, Tyne and Wear, four smaller corporations announced Dec. 1987: Bristol, Leeds, Manchester, Wolverhampton (their budgets will be taken out of categories (1)-(4) above. A new Lower Don Valley (Sheffield) UDC and extensions to Merseyside DC were announced March 1988.

7. Enterprise zones
   (a) To stimulate economic activity by lifting financial burdens and administrative controls.
   (b) Occupiers' rates paid to local authority by Treasury for ten years; tax liability offset against capital expenditure on industrial and commercial development in the zone; simplified planning control.
   (c) 17 in England; 25 in UK as a whole.

8. Co-ordination agencies
   (i) *City action teams (5 established in 1985; 2 added March 1988).* Joint ventures between DE, DoE and DTI (London CAT also includes DTp (with MSC/TI), and Home Office and is targeted principally on inner London boroughs of Hackney, Islington, and Lambeth). Priority themes:
       1. Enterprise: workshops, innovation, customer/supplier links;
       2. Mismatch between supply and demand in jobs and skills;

3. Leisure, tourism, and the environment, including possible employment effects.

(ii) *Task Forces (8 created in 1986, and a further 8 in 1987)*. DTI-led, with central and local government and private and voluntary sector involvement; aim to improve targeting of existing central programmes in four main areas:

1. Employment: more jobs for local people by removing impediments to recruitment of local residents, and encouraging creation of new firms and self-employment;
2. Enterprise: including financial and managerial assistance to firms.
3. Training: to improve employability of local people, including school-leavers; focusing on specific sectors and labour market gaps.
4. Environmental improvements; including service and leisure provision, crime reduction.

9. Related central departments' urban interests
   (i) *Department of Employment* and *Manpower Services Commission* (now renamed the Training Commission): youth and adult training.
   (ii) *Department of Education and Science*: curriculum development, City Technology Colleges, compacts, further and higher education and business links (with MSC).
   (iii) *Home Office*: ethnic minorities, policing, communications including cablevision; 'Safer cities' programme announced March 1988.

10. The enterprise initiative (Department of Trade and Industry) is not targeted on localities, but 'in all our work we will take account of the differing circumstances of the regions and of the Inner Cities to enable those who live there to help themselves' (Cm. 278, 1988, p. ii).
    (i) *Business review*: free consultant's advice (up to 2 days) for firms likely to be followed by specialized consultancy of 5–15 days' duration for which DTI pays 50 per cent of fee (2/3 in Assisted Areas and Urban Programme Areas); consultants' support is available as follows:
    (ii) *Design initiative*: managed for DTI by the Design Council.
    (iii) *Quality initiative*: managed for DTI by Production Engineering Research Association.
    (iv) *Manufacturing initiative*: for CAD/CAM, again managed by PERA.
    (v) *Business planning initiative*: help with formulation of a business plan.
    (vi) *Financial and information systems initiative*: for budget, control, and data services.

(DoE, 1987*c*; DTI, 1988*a*, 1988*b*; Cabinet Office, 1988)

In the case of Urban Development Grant, for example, private developers can propose schemes anywhere within the boundaries of 57 designated local authority districts (see figure 19.1), but applications require the district's support before the scheme can be considered by the

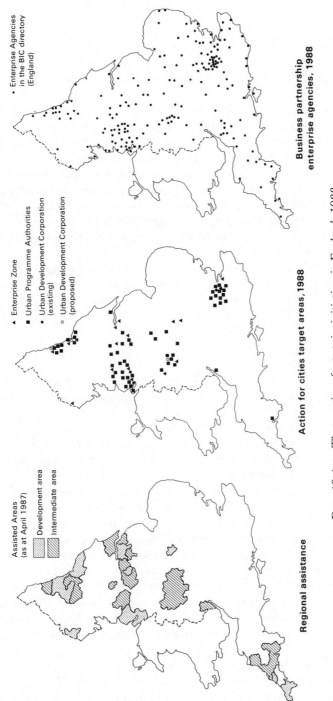

FIG. 19.1.   The targeting of enterprise initiatives in England, 1988

Department of the Environment. Alternatively, central government may delimit areas—that of the London Docklands Development Corporation is a particularly well-known example—where central policies will be implemented with, or in this case often without, local authority support.

Whereas local authorities can decide for themselves whether local economic conditions, currently or prospectively, justify the creation of a local economic development office or unit, central government has to make a selection of deserving areas which is broadly systematic and 'objective'. For this purpose census variables and other economic and social indicators can be used. But just as politicians and civil servants earlier responsible for regional policy had to respond to local authority delegations seeking inclusion (and, exceptionally, *not* wanting to be labelled as a problem area) in the national list of assisted areas, so authorities will lobby to be made eligible for the urban measures, and to be considered for, say, an enterprise zone or development corporation. Unless they are on the national list, many otherwise deserving authorities may not be eligible for the various social and regional funds allocated by the European Community.

Regeneration in action

Two case studies have been chosen to demonstrate the contrasting approaches of Conservative central government and Labour city government. For ease of comparison, both date from the early 1980s and both have operated within the same part of Greater London.

1. *The London Docklands Development Corporation (LDDC)*. Established in 1981 under the terms of the Local Government Planning and Land Act 1980, the London Docklands Development Corporation was a creation of central government designed to lever private sector investment into an area characterized by widespread dereliction following the closure of London's upstream docks, severe population loss, and employment decline in the port and other local industries. The model of private-sector-led regeneration—variously labelled 'demand-led planning', 'leverage planning' and more emotively 'a local monetarist experiment'—assumes that once the image of decay is overcome and infrastructure provided then private investment will be attracted, and that the wealth created will 'trickle down' into the local economy. By this means the area's pressing economic and social problems will be alleviated.

According to the Conservative central government, the scale of dereliction encountered in this downstream sector of the Thames close to the City of London (see figure 19.2) made the area a national priority

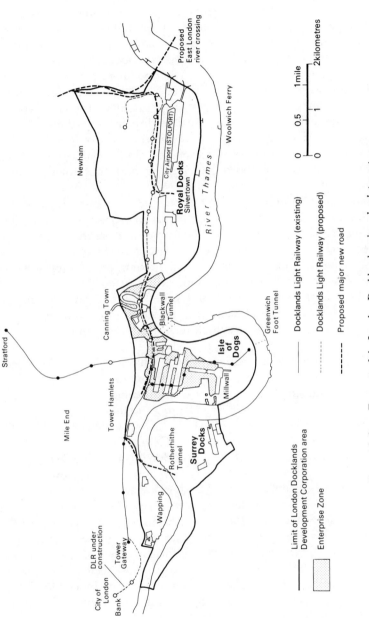

FIG. 19.2. *Features of the London Docklands urban development area*

requiring Treasury funding and a single-minded agency to attract growth firms capable of competing internationally. In this view also, the local (and GLC) Labour governments' recipe of muncipal socialism had failed signally to regenerate the ailing industrial and housing base. Among the armoury of LDDC powers, backed by Treasury funding of the order of £70m. a year, land acquisition is probably the most important. By 1986 the LDDC had acquired, and in many cases already serviced and released, some 560 of the 800 derelict hectares in the area. Because of the level of direct Treasury support, it was thought appropriate to make the corporation responsible directly to parliament, and thereby to remove planning control and various other functions (but not, for example, education, public housing, and social services) from the elected local London borough councils and the Inner London Education Authority.

A significant stimulus to economic regeneration was given by the designation of much of the Isle of Dogs as an enterprise zone for the ten years after 1982. Incentives in the zone are strongly property-orientated, including tax and rates concessions (see category 7 in the list above). During the first five years of its life, commercial interest in the zone was slow to grow, and development consisted largely of mixed low-rise high-tech units for rent and some bespoke owner-occupied buildings—whenever possible adhering to central government's menu of preferred sectors such as high-tech, telecommunications, and tourism.

The LDDC was also keen to encourage what it called 'catalyst projects' which would attract secondary growth or simply increase overall confidence. (That confidence has returned cannot be doubted: land values on the Isle of Dogs have risen from £100,000 to £7m. a hectare over a five-year period.) The London City Airport which opened in 1987 on the quayside of the abandoned King George V dock in the Royal Docks to offer direct flights for City of London business people especially to near mainland European capitals is such a catalyst development. Of even greater significance is the Canary Wharf office development scheme, agreed in 1987, which, the jolt of confidence from the stock market collapse of October 1987 notwithstanding, is expected by the mid- to late-1990s to have brought a million square metres of offices to a 30-hectare site in the Isle of Dogs enterprise zone. Canary Wharf is connected physically and symbolically to the post-'Big Bang' City of London (Hamilton, 1986, explains the significance of this) by the Docklands Light Railway (DLR). This single development site could employ some 40,000 people directly and maybe half as many again in related services. But will these jobs be new, or, as has happened with the recent moves of former Fleet Street and central London newspaper printing and publishing, merely transfers from within the labour market? In the period 1981–6 some 7,900 jobs came to the London Docklands, of which 5,600 were transfers from elsewhere, and over the same time 5,000 jobs were lost from the area's 1981 job total of 27,000.

Patently the scale of change is now set to increase dramatically, but will local residents benefit directly? Male unemployment in the area averaged about 30 per cent in the mid-1980s. Studies of the local labour market showed that although between 10 and 20 per cent of employees in new enterprise zone firms lived in the surrounding London borough of Tower Hamlets, this proportion was much lower than that of local residents employed in firms established in Docklands before the LDDC's designation in 1981. Considerable effort is now being devoted to training and specifically to collaboration between Olympia and York, the Canary Wharf developers, and Tower Hamlets, and prospectively between Rosehaugh Stanhope as a likely developer of a major new scheme in the Royal Docks and Newham borough there. Skillnet has been established as a brokerage to match local people to the training and skill updating courses that will make them more eligible for employment in the new Docklands. Further, part of Docklands and the surrounding borough of Tower Hamlets has been the locus for a novel British experiment called the London Compact, closely modelled on a scheme in Boston, Massachussetts, whereby a consortium of employers will guarantee to make job interviews available to local school-leavers who satisfy specified targets in scholastic motivation and achievement, and reliability of attendance.

Obviously it is premature to provide a definitive assessment of the impact of LDDC policies. For employment, evidence to date (Church and Ainley, 1987) shows that while a small proportion of local residents obtain jobs in firms new to Docklands, the incoming firms have had minimal impact on those most in need, such as young people in low-paid 'dead-end' and insecure jobs, and on the long-term unemployed. It can be speculated that a greater emphasis on training—especially if targeted on the most disadvantaged within the labour market—would have allowed more of the wealth created to have flowed, in the form of jobs, to local residents.

With respect to transport, clearly advantages have been brought for local residents and workers, primarily by the opening of the DLR. Such infrastructure and related environmental improvements may not directly affect employment prospects, but have certainly raised media interest in the area (e.g. in the airport) and its perceived accessibility to central and inner London by means of the DLR. With respect to housing, however, LDDC policies to encourage private housebuilding in an area almost totally dominated by council housing at the time of the 1981

Census have not alleviated housing hardship in the constituent east London boroughs. Despite preferential sales to council tenants and deliberately lowered house prices, only 4 per cent of the 809 surveyed households that had moved by 1985 into new private housing on land acquired by the LDDC in Newham had in fact moved from a Newham council property.

Clearly, market-led regeneration supported by a powerful, single-minded, and well funded agency of central government can result in rapid physical rebuilding; whether this process ameliorates the social and economic hardships faced by many existing residents of the area remains debatable.

2. *The Greater London Enterprise Board (GLEB)*. The opposition to the LDDC's market orientation and, as some local politicians and pressure groups opined, haughty unresponsiveness to local needs and established political structures led to an alternative economic initiative being established within the LDDC's boundary in 1983. The stimulus was the public planning inquiry into the London City Airport proposal (then called STOLport—short take-off and landing airport) at which local residents, supported by the GLC's People's Planning Centre, offered the *People's Plan for the Royal Docks*, in which there would be no airport, rather a job mix that recognized existing skills, public housebuilding, better social services, and environment improvements.

Coincidentally, the GLC had established—not without some internal administrative resistance (see Livingstone, 1987)—the Greater London Enterprise Board (GLEB) with the broad aim of developing projects that would aid the restructuring of production so as to benefit London residents directly. Enterprise boards presently number five in England (GLEB, Lancashire Enterprises, Merseyside EB, West Midlands EB and West Yorkshire EB—each has survived its founding, and now deceased, metropolitan county parent). They are economic development companies established by local authorities in response to the perceived failure of financial institutions to meet the need for long-term development capital of small and medium-sized firms (McKean and Coulson, 1987). GLEB's method was to target certain industrial sectors, manage a sizeable property portfolio, provide investment capital, develop technology networks for companies, and generally to pursue 'enterprise planning' in which social and equal opportunities goals were followed by assisted companies, most of whom were expected to explore methods of work and products for the social good.

One of the GLEB area teams was established in the Royal Docks. In the three years to 1986, before the GLC abolition caused a truncated budget and programme, the GLEB team tried to adhere to the People's Plan prescriptions, although was not able with the GLC to purchase the Royal Docks as the plan's authors had wanted. Financial support and advice was given to firms in the food and drink and the transport sectors, a training and co-operative business advice project for disabled people was inaugurated, and GLEB also produced economic analyses to influence the assessment of future projects. Obviously investment by GLEB in the Royals was negligible in comparison with the private sector schemes announced in 1987. GLEB staff would ask for their work to be judged by its value as a politically inspired pointer to local needs-based planning, in contrast to the volume of private capital investment measures by which the LDDC's success is judged.

What are the Outcomes?

Is this locally variable mixture of central government, local authority, and private initiatives worthwhile? As usual, it all depends: on how impacts are measured and related to often ill-defined objectives; on whether local initiatives can be disaggregated from wider policy interventions and even global economic conditions; on judging if doing nothing would have led to better or worse effects than doing something over a specified time scale during which circumstances might have changed markedly.

However, central government departments, who after all have to justify the financial returns on their spending programmes to the Treasury and parliament (through select committees and in answer to questioning MPs), have begun to commission and publish assessments. In the case of the Department of the Environment this includes evaluations of the employment effects of economic development projects funded under the urban programme (DoE, 1986), derelict land grant (DoE, 1987a), and enterprise zones (PA Cambridge Consultants for DoE, 1987; DoE 1987b). During the parliamentary session 1987–8 the Employment Committee has chosen to examine the employment effects of the first round of urban development corporations, the LDDC included; enterprise zones had earlier attracted the attention of the House of Commons Public Accounts Committee (1986).

All of this leads to the rather familiar conclusion that quoting figures of average national costs for, say, jobs saved or created, may mask locally highly significant effects, especially on intangibles like employees' and families' morale and even health, and on business confidence. Taking figures from various years and measured in different ways, the scale of job creation costs rises from £4,000 per job under the urban programme, £5,000 by enterprise boards, £10,600 under Local Jobs Plans (Campbell *et al.*, 1988), £11,000 in new industrial and commercial units, £19,000 in managed workshops, £35,000 in the assisted areas, and £68,000 per job in the enterprise zones (for regional policies see Moore *et al.*, 1986). At the lower end of the scale, creating a job equates broadly with the recurring annual cost to the Exchequer and to local authorities of supporting an unemployed person. Patently, in any such calculations the reporting and payback periods become critical, especially in enterprise zones where initial investment by central government on land purchase and infrastructure is high, and impacts such as increased land values may benefit subsequent owners but not necessarily appear in the Department of the Environment's formal accounts of government expenditure and private investment attracted.

Concluding Remarks

In this chapter we have seen how the retreat from full employment brought about by restructuring in international capital and the United Kingdom government's desire in the 1980s to shift many services from the public to the private sector, has hit particular localities harder than others, and the inner cities hardest of all. The response has been an entirely understandable desire by local authorities, central government, and private business groupings to stem further job losses, and to promote new enterprises both to offset decline and to establish a firm basis for future prosperity. Local authorities have used existing legislation, especially the powers to use the product of 2p in each £ of rate income, to develop various economic initiatives which are often promoted and co-ordinated by an economic development office or unit. A search for effective 'partnership' is widespread; a bond between central and local government permeated the inner-city White Paper of 1977 (Cmnd. 6845), and an even broader meaning to the word characterizes the approach of the Liverpool bishops Sheppard and Worlock (1988).

The efficacy of the various kinds of public intervention may pale against the scale of job losses: in the mid-1980s in Sheffield jobs were declining at 1,000 a month; the city's employment committee was creating or sustaining the same number over two years (Benington, 1986; Blunkett and Jackson, 1987). Nevertheless cities and counties consider the effort necessary and worthwhile. Sheffield in fact lobbied vigorously, and successfully, to attract the world student games for 1991, and will use the 'student olympics' to transform the image (and condition) of the Hyde Park flats near the city centre which currently boast the highest levels of youth unemployment in the country. So economic initiatives cannot be separated from the environmental and social.

In this necessarily brief review we have not paid any attention to

Scotland. Two recent books (Donnison and Middleton, 1987, and Morison, 1987) show respectively how in eastern Glasgow and more widely in Scotland effective co-ordination has been achieved among the various interests and tiers of government. We conclude by quoting a passage from Donnison (1988, p. 35) which points to the role of *leadership* in advancing local regeneration; we stress that there is a geography of enterprise which relates as much to the disposition of *people* with energy and enterprise as to the formal map of which districts are eligible for which grant.

Civic leadership itself . . . is a crucial element in urban renewal. Clydeside is making a better job of renewing itself than Merseyside, not because it has better laws and institutions, but because its politicians, officials and business people have been able to work more consistently and effectively together at central, regional and local levels of government, since they are all proud of the place. The first thing such people do is make their city cleaner, more beautiful, happier—a place where others who might have some choice about where they live might want to come.

References

Begg, I., B. Moore, and J. Rhodes (1986), 'Economic and social changes in urban Britain and the inner cities', in V. A. Hausner (ed.), *Critical issues in Urban Economic Development*, i (Clarendon Press: Oxford), 11–49.

Benington, J. (1986), 'Local economic strategies: paradigms for a planned economy?', *Local Economy*, 1: 7–24.

Blunkett, D., and K. Jackson (1987), *Democracy in Crisis: The Town Halls Respond* (Hogarth Press: London).

Boddy, M., and C. Fudge (eds.) (1984), *Local Socialism? Labour Councils and New Left Alternatives* (Macmillan: Basingstoke).

—— J. Lovering, and K. Bassett (1986), *Sunbelt City? A Study of Economic Change in Britain's M4 Growth Corridor* (Oxford University Press: Oxford).

Business in the Community (1987), *Enterprise agencies, trusts and community action programmes: 1987 directory* (BiC: London).

Cabinet Office (1988), *Action for Cities* (HMSO: London).

Campbell, M., M. Hardy, N. Healey, R. Stead, and J. Sutherland (1988), 'Economic sense: local jobs plan and the inner city', *Regional Studies*, 22: 55–60.

Chandler, J. A., and P. Lawless (1985), *Local Authorities and the Creation of Employment* (Gower: Aldershot).

Church, A., and P. Ainley (1987), 'Inner city decline and regeneration: young people and the labour market in London's Docklands', in P. Brown and D. N. Ashton (eds.), *Education, Unemployment and Labour Markets* (Falmer Press: Lewes), 71–92.

Cooke, P. (1986), *Global Restructuring: Local Response* (ESRC: London).

Crawford, P., S. Fothergill, and S. Monk (1985), *The Effect of Business Rates on the Location of Employment* (University of Cambridge, Department of Land Economy: Cambridge).

Damesick, P., and P. Wood (1987), *Regional Problems, Problem Regions, and Public Policy in the United Kingdom* (Oxford University Press: Oxford).

Dawson, D. A. (1985), 'Economic change and the changing role of local government', in M. Loughlin, M. D. Gelfand, and K. Young (eds.), *Half a Century of Municipal Decline, 1935–1985* (Allen and Unwin: London), 26–49.

DoE (Department of the Environment), Inner Cities Research Programme (1986), *Assessment of the Employment Effects of Economic Development Projects Funded under the Urban Programme* (HMSO: London).

—— (1987a), *Evaluation of Derelict Land Grant Schemes by Roger Tym & Partners in Association with Land Use Consultants* (HMSO: London).

—— (1987b), *Enterprise Zone Information 1985–1986* (HMSO: London).

—— (1987c), *Urban Regeneration: A Guide to Financial and other Assistance for Business* (Central Office of Information for HMSO: London).

DoE/DE (Department of the Environment and Department of Employment (1987), *Action for Cities* (HMSO: London).

DTI (Department of Trade and Industry) (1988a), *DTI—The Department for Enterprise*, Cm. 278 (HMSO: London).

—— (1988b), *The Enterprise Initiative* (Central Office of Information for HMSO: London).

Donnison, D. (1988), 'Competing cures', *Times Literary Supplement*, 8–14 Jan., p. 35.

—— and A. Middleton (eds.) (1987), *Regenerating the Inner City: Glasgow's Experience* (Routledge and Kegan Paul: London).

Duncan S. and M. Goodwin, (1985), 'The local state and local economic policy', *Policy and Politics*, 13(3): 227–53.

Economy Group, South East Joint Planning Team (1976), *Report of the Economy Group* (Department of the Environment: London).

Fothergill, S., and G. Gudgin (1982), *Unequal Growth, Urban and Regional Employment Change in the United Kingdom* (Heinemann: London).

Hall, P. (1986), 'From the unsocial city to the social city', *Planner*, 72(3): 17–25.

—— H. Gracey, R. Drewett, and R. Thomas (1973), *The Containment of Urban England* (2 vols., Allen & Unwin: London).

Hamilton, A. (1986), *The Financial Revolution: The 'Big Bang' Worldwide* (Viking: London).

Heseltine, M. (1987), *Where There's a Will* (Hutchinson: London).

House of Commons, Committee of Public Accounts (1986), *Enterprise Zones*, 34th Report of the Committee (HMSO: London).

Hunt, Sir Joseph (chairman) (1969), *The Intermediate Areas: Report of the Committee under the Chairmanship of Sir Joseph Hunt*, Cmnd. 3998, (HMSO: London).

Livingstone, K. (1987), *If Voting Changed Anything They'd Abolish it* (Collins: London).

McKean, B., and A. Coulson (1987), 'Enterprise boards and some issues raised by taking equity and loan stocks in major companies', *Regional Studies*, 21(4): 373–84.

Massey, D. and R. Meegan (1982), *The Anatomy of Job Loss* (Methuen: London).

Mawson, J., and D. Miller (1986), 'Interventionist approaches to local employment and economic development: the experience of Labour local authorities', in V. A. Hausner (ed.) *Critical Issues in Urban Economic Development*, i (Clarendon Press: Oxford), 145–99.

Mills, L., and K. Young (1986), 'Local authorities and economic development: a preliminary analysis', in V. A. Hausner (ed.) *Critical Issues in Urban and Economic Development*, i (Oxford University Press: Oxford) 89–144.

Moore, B., J. Rhodes and P. Tyler (1986), *The Effects of Government Regional Economic Policy* (HMSO for Department of Trade and Industry: London).

Morison, H. (1987), *The Regeneration of Local Economies* (Oxford University Press: Oxford).

Owen, T. (1986), *Mind Your Local Business* (Eurofi: Northill).

PA Cambridge Consultants (for Department of the Environment) (1987), *An Evaluation of the Enterprise Zone Experiment* (HMSO: London).

Pahl, R. (1986) 'Opinion: Hall's social city', *Planner*, 72 (4): 10.

Ramsdale, P., and S. Capon (1986), 'An analysis of local authority discretionary expenditure 1984–85', in Department of the Environment, Scottish Office, Welsh Office, *The Conduct of Local Authority Business, Research Volume IV: Aspects of Local Democracy*, Cmnd. 9801 (HMSO: London).

Robson, B. T. (1987), 'The enduring city: a perspective in decline', in B. T. Robson (ed.), *Managing the City: The Aims and Impacts of Urban Policy* (Croom Helm: Beckenham), 6–21.

Sheppard, D., and D. Worlock (1988), *Better Together: Christain Partnership in a Hurt City* (Hodder and Stoughton: London).

Smith C. J. (1987), 'Mental health and the fiscal crisis: the prospects of a socially conscious urban geography', *Urban Geography*, 8(1): 55–64.

Vielba, C. (1986), 'Government and industry: the local dimension', *Policy and Politics*, 14(4): 507–18.

Ward, S. V. (1983), 'Interwar Britain: a study of government spending, planning and uneven economic development', *Built Environment*, 7(2): 96–108.

Young, K. (1986), 'Economic development in Britain: a vacuum in central-local relations', *Government and Policy*, 4(4): 439–50.

20

Urban Policy? What Urban Policy? Urban Interventions in the 1980s

John Eyles

During the 1970s it was possible to identify a desire on the part of most governments in capitalist societies to intervene to alter the physical and economic structure of urban areas to engineer solutions to what were seen as pressing social problems. That desire is no longer as evident during the 1980s, although it is important to note that governments still focus much attention on the city. Some continue to formulate and even implement strategies for urban development and change. For example, the socialist government of France which held power in the early 1980s formulated ambitious interventionist and modernizing strategies for the Paris region, including the continuation of the new town programme, support for an urban industrial regeneration policy, and massive housing improvements, but it failed to implement any major projects and soon after its election in 1981 began to use the language of austerity (Dagnaud, 1983). Further, while the implementation of the Community Housing Improvement Programme in New Zealand has been eminently successful as a physical housing and environmental improvement scheme, budgetary restraints and partnership problems between central and local government have meant that its social aims of improving accessibility to good housing have not been met (Memon, 1986). In Japan, the problems of urban sprawl have meant the continuation of city containment policies. Through the establishment of national comprehensive development plans, national land use planning law, and specific acts to regulate urban growth, Japanese planners have tried to limit suburban expansion. The struggle has, however, been unequal. Restricted use of zoning regulations, the granting of exemptions for agricultural landowners and the fiscal constraints on planning in a market system have meant the attempts have not been very successful (Hebbert, 1986).

These examples show not only the continuing role of government but the contextualizing of its urban interventions. Indeed it is one of the main purposes of this chapter to examine the changing contexts of government actions because, it is asserted, this will provide an understanding of the ways in which urban problems are approached. With hindsight we may say that the 1970s were an optimistic period, in that public policies were seen as an efficacious way of tackling soluble problems. The dominant images of the 1980s are those of crisis, failure, and austerity. The chapter will, firstly and briefly, examine urban policy in the 1970s and go on to explore the forces that altered state and individual perceptions of what policy may achieve. Then it will exemplify the relationships between government activity and cities in the 1980s, and finally briefly address the issues that policy must tackle.

Urban Policy in the 1970s

The relationship between urban growth and uneven regional development has long been recognized, while the rapid urbanization of population has meant that urban problems in effect become national ones (James and Hoppe, 1969). But the realizations that urban containment and the new town programme had not greatly enhanced the material conditions of many city residents and that poverty, poor housing, and structural unemployment remained pressing concerns resulted in a reappraisal of regional policy and a desire to tackle the social as well as environmental problems of cities (Hall *et al.*, 1973; Hula, 1984; Lawless, 1986). While much of initial post-1945 urban policy had been physical in orientation, namely slum clearance and housing improvement, from the late 1960s onwards the social antecedents of government action came more to the fore. At this time, social malaise was still seen very much as an unintended consequence of affluence (Fuller and Stevenson, 1983), and welfare, including the need to intervene in deprived communities, was seen as necessary corrective to imbalances produced by economic growth. Welfare was very much the residual beneficiary of the growth state and focused on residual problems. Ways of improving the living conditions of urban areas relied greatly on the utilization of American ideas which emphasized community action and self-reliance, citizen participation, and organizational change (Eyles, 1979). These ideas, as well as American programmes like those connected with the War on Poverty or Model Cities, fired action in Britain, as did reports on urban housing problems, educational disadvantage, racial discrimination, and the difficulties of the organizational framework of social service provision.

The early 1970s, then, saw the culmination of the process of expanding state activity to tackle urban social problems. Historically, all government expenditures in the USA increased from $1.7b. in 1902 to more than $350b. in the early 1970s. Urban governments spent increasing proportions of their budgets on social expenditures such as education, public welfare, health, and safety, so that by 1976 these activities took 47 per cent of total urban spending (Blair and Nachmias, 1979). Similar rises can be documented for Britain, with social expenditure increasing from 4.2 per cent of GNP in 1910 to 28.8 per cent in 1975 (Gough, 1979). But despite these massive increases, as far as cities were concerned, the money was spread rather thinly. Thus, for example, the Model Cities programme (the rebuilding or restoring of slums and blighted areas to locally prepared plans by the concentrated and co-ordinated use of federal, local, and private resources) eventually covered some 150 cities. From this emerged the idea of general entitlement to funds found in the General Revenue Sharing Act (1972) and Community Development Block Grants (1974) (Eyles, 1987a), in which eligibility was determined by overcrowding, poverty, and blighted conditions. Most of the assisted cities and neighbourhoods were in the industrial north-east, and on a per caput basis two and a half times more aid went to the central cities than to the suburbs (Schwartz, 1981). Much aid, just as with the Model Cities programme, failed to target problem cities. Intervention became a programme of distribution rather than one of redistribution. Funds tended to be used to reduce local taxes rather than improve or expand services, and in any event the scale of funding meant that the resources allocated to any one city were insufficient to carry out the massive reforms required.

In Britain, the government response was even more parsimonious. The recognition of urban problems led to a desire to find the best strategy to tackle the issues through a series of low-cost experiments and inner area studies (because urban policy became increasingly to be seen as inner urban policy) and to the establishment of a funded urban programme. The background and detail of these approaches are well-documented (McKay and Cox, 1979; Edwards and Batley, 1978; Higgins *et al.*, 1983). Lawless and Brown (1986) see all government responses at this time (primarily 1967 to 1975) as experimentation. They identify three major types.

First, there were the resource-allocating projects of the Urban Programme. By as early as 1973 some 2,300 projects in 216 local authority areas had been funded to a value of £32m. In the main, the projects were small-scale, namely holiday schemes, day nurseries, playgroups and advice centres. Before its phasing out in 1986, the Urban Programme helped to improve access to services and facilities. Indeed it was predicated on the assumption that the key problem of deprived communities was one of access to resources which were often provided on a poorly co-ordinated basis. Better accessibility and co-ordination were required to discriminate positively in favour of those suffering from individual or social pathologies. Thus deprivation was seen as a residual, pathological phenomenon which changes in service provision would help to eradicate (see Wicks, 1977; Laurance and Hall, 1981).

The second type of experimentation concerns those charged with developing a more co-ordinated approach to the delivery of urban services. While all programmes attempted to emphasize this approach of involving all agencies, the comprehensive community programmes were entirely based on it. Their efforts were meant to identify a whole range of economic, social, and physical problems and co-ordinate effective policies. It was a management-oriented approach, and as the Home Secretary said 'it is not a question of providing extra money on top of the existing programmes. The real question is to find within existing programmes the right order of priority so that money is spent in urban areas of acute need rather then in other areas' (quoted in CDP, 1977, p. 15). While this statement demonstrates the general parsimony of urban policy, it also points to the essentially political nature of the programme's task. Only two—Gateshead and Bradford—were developed in any detail, but the whole programme was short-lived for political reasons. Better co-ordination, consultation, and management require a commitment to redistributive social change, and as Higgins *et al.* (1983) point out, that was lacking in both Labour and Conservative governments throughout the 1970s.

The third category of experimentation was in major investigative studies which changed the definition and explanation of urban deprivation. Particularly influential were the community development projects which saw the main cause of urban disadvantage as lack of income, or position in the economic and political system.

The problems of the 12 CDP areas are not reducible to problems of employment, housing, income and education. They are not isolated pockets suffering an unfortunate combination of circumstances. They are a central part of the dynamics of the urban system and as such represent those who have lost out in the competition for jobs, housing and educational opportunity . . . The problems in these areas are not going to be solved by marginal rearrangements to take account of their special minority needs. (CDP, 1974, p. 52)

Such research contextualized urban deprivation and saw it as part of the social order. These ideas were furthered by major research initiatives (DoE, 1974–6; Hall, 1981; *Regional Studies*, 1986) and had the impact of focusing attention both on the inner city and its problems and on the economic derivation of those problems. Thus the White Paper on the inner cities said that 'the decline in the economic fortunes of the inner areas often lies at the heart of the problem' (DoE, 1977, p. 2). But while structural decline was identified as a major cause of urban deprivation, that insight did not make policy formulation any easier. Area-based policies could still fail to target those in need. The recognition of the importance of context did not necessarily mean that policies of economic development, housing, land-use and transport would be co-ordinated. Indeed, the 1970s had witnessed the isolation of the issue of urban decline from mainstream political and professional discussion and practice (see McKay and Cox, 1979). And it remained possible that some urban policies would have unintended and potentially detrimental consequences on other areas or populations in the city. In the USA, for example, slum clearance can reduce a city's tax base, while welfare programmes may attract more poor to the urban area (see Blair and Nachmias, 1979). So, as the 1970s ended, in both the USA and the UK, there was recognition that urban problems must be seen in the context of their containing society and that government policy itself could only set the parameters for urban regeneration. Indeed, the context, with which policy itself was made, was changing.

The Context of Urban Interventions in the 1980s

As we have seen, up to the mid-1970s there was tremendous growth in state and urban expenditures, these in fact far outpacing expansion in the economy as a whole. Short (1982) points out for Britain, the details of policy implementation since the mid-1970s have been shaped by the recurring crisis in the British economy. The poor performance of the economy was reflected in low growth, high inflation, and increasing unemployment. The way out of this decline was seen to lie in the reduction of public expenditure which would reduce inflation, ease tax burdens, and free resources to increase the rate of economic growth, which would then provide the additional resources for any redistributive policies. Similarly in the USA, the rising trend of public expenditures was halted from the 1974–5 recession onwards. Rising inflation and unemployment, deteriorating trade balances, and slowing economy and productivity growth resulted in an 'urban fiscal crisis', represented by the gap between expenditure demands and available revenues. Glickman (1981) points to the importance of the changing international division of labour and capital shifts with their uneven spatial and urban impacts in this crisis, which was made more difficult in the USA by the division between federal, state, and local responsibilities (and tax-raising capacities) and the fragmentation of local government (Hill, 1984). Declining revenues have forced a reduction in traditional social programmes.

Importantly, then, the economic plight of cities was seen as a part of national economic malaise (Glickman, 1984; Pickvance, 1986), and all

social programmes would be dependent on national economic performance. Further, social problems, whether manifested in cities or not,
would be best solved by general improvements in economic well-being.
Thus the thrust of government policy became economic (and national)
rather than social (and urban). The first Reagan programme in the
USA—the program for economic recovery—focused on inflation, suggesting that prices could best be kept down by deflating the economy
through tight monetary policy, on the enactment of tax cuts to increase
growth and productivity, and on the reduction in government spending on
non-defence programmes (see Glickman, 1984). Such a programme is
remarkably similar to that outlined by the Conservative government in
Britain. Their strategic guidelines included the strengthening of incentives through tax cuts, greater freedon of choice through reducing the role
of the state, the reduction of public sector borrowing to allow the rest of the
economy to prosper, and firm monetary and fiscal discipline to control
inflation (see Eyles, 1987*b*).

It may be seen that the economic and political contexts of policy in the
1980s are conjoined. An important dimension was in fact the 'rolling back
of the state' to allow individual enterprise to flourish in the marketplace.
The idea of rolling back the state appeared to strike a chord with the electorates of both Britain and the USA. The expansion of government policies
and programmes appeared to mean not only increasing tax burdens but
also interference in individual lives. Further, the growth of government
did not seem able to solve or ameliorate adverse social and living conditions. Not only was government too big; it had also failed. In some ways, it
did not seem to know which way to turn. Thus, for example, Stewart (1987)
notes the confusion and hesitation over British urban policy from
mid-1970s onwards. This lack of success and of direction resulted in a
diminution in the state's confidence in its own ability to tackle problems.
Thus, President Carter in his State of the Union address in 1978 said: 'government cannot solve our problems. It can't set our goals. It cannot define
our vision. Government cannot eliminate poverty, or provide a bountiful
economy, or reduce inflation; or save our cities' (quoted in Tabb, 1984,
p. 257). This waning in the efficacy of correct policy choices and social
engineering solutions resulted in a disenchantment with government and
its programmes. The argument is well summarized by Mishra:

government growth, government failure and government overload thus form an
interweaving set of arguments in favour of a minimal state. Increasing state intervention in the ordering of economic and social affairs is neither necessary nor
beneficial. Government growth has been largely unprincipled, a product of
expedient and shortsighted action on the part of sectional interests . . . and has led
to government overload. Much is promised by politicians and a great deal
expected of governments: little is, and can be, delivered. (Mishra, 1984, p. 41)

The idea of the minimal state gained acceptance in many capitalist societies (see King, 1975; Sawer, 1983) and was provided with ideological support by the ideas and governments of the New Right. We have already seen how the state must be rolled back. The principal reason for this may be found in the primacy given to individual freedom, it being argued that the state (particularly in its welfare and social policies) reduces such liberty. The freedom of the individual is combined with a stress on the benefits of market principles, the importance of law, and the disadvantages of bureaucratic control of both economy and society. At root, then, the appeal is made to self-interest, traditional values, the family, and self-help and economic regeneration. These values and aims can be enhanced by deregulation, privatization, and the curbing of trade union power (see Blowers, 1987). The state's role is, therefore, to remove obstacles to private and individual endeavour. And it is interesting to note that not only did these ideas appeal to electorates but also that the juxtaposition of a minimalist state with economic crisis and the need for restraint seemed timely. The politics of austerity had come of age.

Urban Interventions in the 1980s

The politics of austerity added to the plight of particular cities and particular groups in those cities. In New York, wage concessions and increased city taxes and user fees illustrate the actions of urban fiscal retrenchment (Hill, 1984). But from the late 1970s and early 1980s onwards fiscal austerity became national policy in the USA. And more importantly, that austerity became anti-urban and asocial. We must, therefore, note in general public expenditure terms the disjuncture between rhetoric and reality. Thus in Britain, public expenditure in real terms increased by 8 per cent between 1979/80 and 1985/6 (Eyles, 1987*b*). Similar increases can be seen in Australia and the USA. In all cases, however, there has been a transfer of public expenditure between programmes, usually away from welfare, income maintenance, and housing and towards defence, law and order, and unemployment benefit. Further, there is a necessary continuity in policy implementations which even the most radical governments find difficult to break. In other words, in certain areas policy can only be transformed slowly and must build on what is already in place, especially in terms of legal and organizational frameworks. Thus, for example, the partnerships established by the White Paper on the inner cities, to review funding and co-ordinate urban strategies of local and central government agencies, and established by the Inner Urban Areas Act of 1978, were retained by the Conservative administrations of the 1980s, although the role of private and voluntary bodies became more important.

But, particularly in the USA, the urban realm and its problems became almost an afterthought. While this is not unusual, and indeed Goldsmith and Jacobs (1982) note that only the economic turmoil of the 1930s depression and the social unrest of the 1960s led to the institution of specific urban policies, the Reagan administration saw no need for an urban policy. Indeed, as Wolman (1986) notes, the Reagan urban policy largely ignored all previous arguments. In fact much of the Carter administration's urban initiatives had been at the level of rhetoric. A commitment to the cities was emphasized as were co-ordinated planning, fiscal relief, incentives for private investment, encouragement of neighbourhood and voluntary organizations, welfare services, and environmental programmes (Goldsmith and Jacobs, 1982). It was very much a people-oriented programme: the Livable Cities Program. But as Tabb (1984) has pointed out, in reality the policy emphasized loan guarantees to private business in depressed neighbourhoods. Federally subsidized loans meant that much of the risk was borne by the taxpayer. Further, the Urban Department Action Grants (UDAG) also emphasized the role of the private sector, with federal funds being used as leverage for private funds to help revitalize older urban areas. While some such partnerships were successful particularly with community participation as in South Bronx (Schwartz, 1981), other expenditures were used to develop luxury hotels and shopping malls, so that by the end of 1979, 15 per cent of UDAG had gone to neighbourhoods and over 50 per cent to commercial development (half of which funded hotel-related projects) (Tabb, 1984). Rose (1986), however, provides a more optimistic assessment of the job creation potential of UDAGs. With the Reagan urban policy, therefore, there may be practical continuity with the Carter years.

The Reagan administration has stated that 'a healthy economy is the most powerful tool for revitalizing our cities and improving their fiscal positions' (quoted in Wolman, 1986, p. 311). The principles of urban policy are that the workings of the market should not be impeded, that cities can best solve their own problems, that the states have ultimate responsibility for urban well-being, that federal expenditure may impede adjustments to change, and that it should not favour one region more than any other. This apparent evenhandedness means the reduction in measures to discriminate positively in favour of cities in general and the urban poor and old industrial cities in particular. Glickman (1984) calculates that urban outlays declined from a peak of 12.4 per cent of all federal outlays in 1978 to 7.8 per cent in 1984. Job creation, educational and mass transit assistance, and economic development programmes have also been reduced (Wolman, 1986). The solutions to urban problems are now seen to lie in private sector initiatives and investments, with public policy's role being to facilitate such expenditures. Thus, for example, the reduction in federal aid to cities and states has meant the contracting out or privatization of service delivery as well as increases in local taxes and fees. Denver, for example, has given part of its urban area to a joint private-public committee with power to regulate land use, pollution control, and construction design (Tabb, 1984). Further, the enterprise zone is now put forward as a way of utilizing the market to solve urban problems. Such zones require little in federal outlays, shift burdens to local areas, intensify competition between cities, and subsidize private investments. While the zones and their philosophy are more clearly articulated in Britain, the US experience points to some of the problems of relying on private investments to build infrastructure, create jobs, and provide services. Such investments are by definition profit-motivated, and it has been found that while such investments are not negligible, they are concentrated in downtown areas in office and retailing developments and in housing for the new service populations (financial, clerical, personal service workers). The real incomes, services, and housing conditions of the urban poor have worsened. In fact, metropolitan poverty has increased, as has its central city concentration. Explicit urban investments have thus created two central cities, or poverty amid prosperity, in New York, Boston, and Baltimore (Palmer and Sawhill, 1984; Ganz, 1985). And this does not take account of the urban effects of general social and economic policies, such as mortgage relief and tax policy, to which we shall briefly refer after a discussion of British urban interventions.

In Britain, a similar economic framework has been put in place during the 1980s, although there appears to be more continuity with past urban policy than in the USA. This may be because the political Left and Right share the empirically derived view (see Hall, 1981; Hausner and Robson, 1985) that urban (particularly inner city) problems are an extreme version of the woes of the British economy in general. But, as we have already noted, there has been a shift in emphasis in the nature of policy-making and in the policies themselves. While all divisions of policy type are perhaps more apparent than real, it is possible to examine the interventions of the 1980s as either direct or indirect ones, although all have a certain degree of remoteness when compared with direct public expenditures such as the Urban Programme. In the main, direct interventions are those specifically geared to confront urban issues, usually through institutional arrangements to improve co-ordination and management or through attempts to stimulate economic regeneration. Important in stimulating such regeneration in a minimal-state-market-oriented framework has been the enterprise zone. The decline in inner-city manufacturing employment has been well documented, it was argued that economic development and employment growth, the necessary spurs to social development and service provision, would be achieved by relaxing controls which hindered private enterprise. Indeed, Hall (1977) suggested a 'freeport' solution as an experiment because planning controls, health and safety, and welfare notions would have to be downplayed. While the Local Government, Planning and Land Act of 1980 gave legal status to the freeport idea as the enterprise zone, the exemptions were relatively modest (Taylor, 1981), relating primarily to tax and planning exemptions (Butler, 1981), In fact, Massey (1982) suggests that these exemptions make it likely that landowners and property developers inside the zones have most to gain from the policy. In any event, they favour the development of retail outlets, hotels, and, offices (Tyme and Partners, 1983, 1984) rather than manufacturing. The emphasis on small firms may make it difficult to generate sufficient jobs to replace those lost in redundancies. The number created has been small. Bromley and Morgan (1985) point out that less than 500 new jobs had been created in the Lower Swansea Valley Enterprise Zone up to December 1983. Many of the jobs created inside the EZ are relocations from outside the zone. In a study of Belfast EZ, O'Dowd and Rolston (1985) estimate that 55 per cent of new jobs could be seen in these terms, the vast majority being from within the Belfast urban area. It must be noted that even this success is dependent on other public investments such as site preparation. Relatively successful EZs—Belfast, Clydebank, Swansea, Corby—are thus dependent on regional aid or local government assistance. But such variation not only makes evaluation of policy difficult, but also leaves ample scope for 'success' to be emphasized as justifications of the policy and 'failures' to be explained in terms of local conditions inhibiting the flourishing of enterprise. And further to encourage enterprise and facilitate investment, simplified planning zones, which specify types of development which have advance planning permission, have been recently introduced (Trippier, 1987).

The other major direct intervention is in the form of institutional arrangements and rearrangements. The Conservative administrations have retained the partnership and programmes scheme. Initially introduced to co-ordinate urban strategies in seven partnership areas— London's Docklands, Lambeth, Islington, and Hackney, Birmingham, Liverpool, Manchester and Salford, and Newcastle and Gateshead— the scheme has been broadened to include other authorities. This perhaps recognizes the problems of identifying the urban areas with the worst problems (see Bentham, 1985) and the difficulties of effecting change without co-operation and co-ordination between agencies. Government still seems wedded, therefore, to a co-ordinated approach (perhaps because in theory it allows for efficient management and resource utilization), despite the abandonment of conherent strategies by the early partnerships and their failure to give priority to economic development (Nabarro, 1980). Co-ordination is also important to the programme authorities. In a case study of Nottingham, Aldridge and Brotherton (1987) show that, despite clumsy structures for liaison and the lack of central government commitment and funds, the local and health authorities want the programme to continue, as it provides resources and justification for innovative and redistributive schemes which would otherwise be politically and financially impossible to achieve.

Further, since 1981, new institutional arrangements has proliferated, mainly to increase both central government control and the involvement of the private sector in urban policy. The 1980 Local Government, Planning and Land Act established urban development corporations, which have wide powers to acquire, sell and develop land. The best developed UDC is the London Docklands Development Corporation which has taken control of some 5,000 acres of east London from the local authorities (see previous chapter). Its aim is to transform the social and economic base of area through encouraging private investments (LDDC, 1984), especially in financial, communication, and high technology industries. Despite its statements that it will consult local people and.ensure that there are affordable dwellings for them (LDDC, 1985, 1986), it has been accused of being remote and autocratic, and of gentrifying east London (GLC, 1984; JDAG, 1984; DCC, 1985). But Lawless and Brown (1986) put forward a counter-argument, suggesting that UDCs are an appropriate vehicle for urban regeneration, being able to operate quickly and with less bureaucracy than local authorities; to follow demand-led policies to attract the private sector; to encourage development in growth sectors; to propose socially balanced communities, and to advocate national rather than local solutions. Indeed, the government finds the UDC concept attractive and has established them in Merseyside, West Midlands, Cardiff, Trafford Park, and Tyne and Wear. It has also established (December 1987) four mini-urban-corporations in Leeds, Manchester, Bristol, and Wolverhampton, which will receive less public funds than the UDCs and will be more reliant on the private sector to revitalize what are essentially run-down or derelict industrial areas. These mini-corporations further diversify inner-city initiatives. As Stewart (1987) comments, the proliferation of these semi-autonomous and centrally accountable institutions dilutes local control and represents a major shift in the interest and power structure in inner-city policy. This, however, is not to say that all agency and local initiatives are centrally controlled and privately dominated. The Glasgow eastern area renewal scheme would not have been possible without Scottish Development Agency funding (Leclerc and Draffan, 1984; Eyles, 1987*a*), while Labour-controlled local authorities such as Birmingham and Sheffield have tried to establish their own employment generation and environment improvement initiatives (often with private sector involvement), but may fall foul of indirect interventions with respect to urban policy.

Indirect interventions are those resulting from broad-based policies directed at phenomena that are not specifically urban, for example local government, housing, industry, and public expenditure. With respect to the financing of local government, the government has stated that the economic regeneration of the country cannot be secured if the cost of local government is too great a burden for the private sector to carry (DoE, 1983). The limiting of rate levels by the Rates Act of 1984 (rate capping) has in practice been anti-urban, with the inner London boroughs and northern cities being particularly hard hit (see Lambert, 1986). Further, the real reduction in housing expenditure—down in real terms by more than two-thirds between 1979 and 1986—has again particularly affected run-down urban areas, while the 'right to buy' legislation of the Housing Act (1980) has removed not only better quality housing but also the more affluent tenant from the public housing system. As the housing capital programme is now virtually self-financing, it means few resources are available to improve this dimension of the urban infrastructure. The deregulation of many development controls has enhanced the significance of private interests in land-use planning (see Hooper, 1979; Blowers, 1987), while the centralization of decision-making has reduced the role of strategic planning. This reduction makes the tackling of urban problems more difficult, and the emphasis on local planning may mean that local authorities are less able to withstand the development demands of private, non-local interests for, say, industrial and residential developments. Other aspects of policy have had an indirect and often detrimental effect on urban areas. For example, mortgage tax subsidies and highway construction tend to favour suburban and small town communities rather than urban problem areas, which suffer disproportionately from reductions in welfare and social security programmes. Similar effects are found in the USA (Goldsmith and Jacobs, 1982; Wolman, 1986), where large defence expenditure also discriminates against older cities and poorer neighbourhoods (Vernez, 1980). It is, therefore, hard to disagree with Stewart (1987, p. 135): 'other policies, however (public expenditure, rate support grant, housing policy, social security rules, regional and industrial policy), have operated to contradict and wipe out the modest contributions of inner cities policy.'

Conclusions

This chapter has primarily reviewed those interventions, arising from economic crisis and changing political ideology, that are of the city or affect the city. These impacts have been illustrated mainly from the USA and Britain and in the context of the inner city. This is not to say that only policy responses or inner cities in these countries take these forms. Similar issues may be discerned in Australia (Fagan, 1986), Canada (Filion, 1987), Greece (Hastaoglou *et al.*, 1987), and West Germany (Zielinski, 1983). In many of these societies, it is questionable whether urban interventions and impacts are similar in form or function to the urban policies of the 1970s. A shift from *social* to *economic* 'policy' may be noted. This may mean that the principles underlying policy may have shifted too. If we adopt Townsend's (1979) classification of these principles—conditional welfare for the few, minimum rights for the many, and distributional justice for all, with the last-named being a redistributive ideal in so far as all past social policy is concerned—then there has been a shift from the entitlement programmes (including area policies) suggested by minimum rights, to conditional welfare in which inequality is seen as inevitable and the state's role is to provide a means-tested welfare safety net. A conditional welfare state is primarily concerned with facilitating private and market activity as well as the conditions to allow individual ability and opportunity to flourish, as evidenced through training and retraining schemes, city colleges, and task forces. This change from a minimum rights to a conditional welfare state may also be seen in shifts in emphasis in policy. Writing of the anti-poverty programmes, Berthoud and Brown (1981) suggest policy took three forms: institutional reorganization to achieve more equitable access to services; interventions in the market to, for example, ensure adequate housing or wage levels for the less affluent; and the redistribution of incomes and resources through the taxation and social security systems. These forms still exist. But institutional reorganization (e.g. programme authorities, UDCs, task forces) has as its main purposes increased central control and private sector involvement, while market 'interventions' (e.g. freeing of capital and exchange controls, EZs, development control deregulation) have been to facilitate greater entrepreneurial activity. The tax and social security systems have been utilized mainly to redistribute income and resources away from the poor and inner cities and peripheral public housing estates to the relatively affluent and the suburbs. The contexts of economic regeneration and political ideology have, therefore, altered the nature and purpose of intervention. The rhetoric of this intervention for facilitation is well expressed by the British inner cities minister: 'the aim of the government's policy . . . is to restore confidence, initiative, enterprise and choice. This is the only sure foundation for long term improvements in living conditions and prosperity' (Trippier, 1987, p. 235). Whether the reality will match this rhetoric is open to debate. There will inevitably be losers as well as gainers within such a regenerative strategy. And while it is unlikely to find redistributive area policies (even if it is accepted that these are efficacious in themselves) in societies with regressive tax and social security systems, the social problems of poverty, unemployment, poor housing, racial discrimination, youth disaffection, and so on which mainly manifest themselves in urban areas remain to be fully addressed by policy-makers. Until then, we seem to be entitled to conclude not only with the question 'what urban policy?' but also with 'why urban policy?'

References

Aldridge, M., and C. J. Brotherton (1987), 'Being a programme authority: is it worthwhile?', *Journal of Social Policy*, 16: 349–69.

Bentham, C. G. (1985), 'Which areas have the worst urban problems?', *Urban Studies*, 22: 119–31.

Berthoud, R., and J. C. Brown (1981), *Poverty and the Development of Anti-Poverty Policy in the United Kingdom* (Heinemann: London).

Blair, J. P. and D. Nachmias (1979), 'Urban policy in the lean society', in J. P. Blair and D. Nachmias (eds.), *Fiscal Retrenchment and Urban Policy* (Sage: Beverly Hills).

Blowers, A. (1987), 'Transition or transformation?—environmental policy under Thatcher', *Public Administration*, 65: 277–94.

Bromley, R. D. F., and R. H. Morgan (1985), 'The effects of enterprise zone policy', *Regional Studies*, 19: 403–13.

Butler, S. (1981), *Enterprise Zones* (Heinemann: London).

CDP (Community Development Project) (1974), 'Inter-project Report' (Information Unit: London).

—— (1977), 'Gilding the ghetto' (Inter-Project Team: London).

Dagnaud, M. (1983), 'A history of planning in the Paris region', *International Journal of Urban and Regional Research*, 7: 219–36.

DoE (Department of the Environment) (1974–6), *Inner Area Studies: Reports* (HMSO: London).

—— (1977), *Policy for the Inner Cities*, Cmnd. 6845 (HMSO: London).

—— (1983), *Rates*, Cmnd. 9008 (HMSO: London).

DCC (Docklands Consultative Committee) (1985) *Four year Review of the LDDC* (DCC: London).

Edwards, J., and R. Batley (1978), *The Politics of Positive Discrimination* (Heinemann: London).

Eyles, J. (1979), 'Area-based policies for the inner city', in D. T. Herbert and D. M. Smith (eds.), *Social Problems and the City* (Oxford University Press: Oxford).

—— (1987*a*), 'Poverty, deprivation and social planning', in M. Pacione (ed.) *Social Geography* (Croom Helm: London).

—— (1987*b*), *The Geography of the National Health* (Croom Helm: London).

Fagan, R. (1986), 'Sydney west', in D. Dragovich (ed.), *The Changing Face of Sydney* (Geographical Society of New South Wales: Sydney).

Filion, P. (1987), 'Concepts of the inner city and recent trends in Canada', *Canadian Geographer*, 31: 223–32.

Fuller, R., and D. Stevenson (1983), *Policies, Programmes and Disadvantage* (Heinemann: London).

Ganz, A. (1985) 'Where has the urban crisis gone?' *Urban Affairs Quarterly*, 20: 449–68.

GLC (Greater London Council) (1984), *London's Docklands* (GLC: London).

Glickman, N. J. (1981), 'Emerging urban policies in a slow-growth economy', *International Journal of Urban and Regional Research*, 5: 492–528.

—— (1984), 'The Reagan administration's urban policies', *Journal, American Planning Association*, 50: 470–8.

Goldsmith, W. W. and H. M. Jacobs (1982), 'The improbability of urban policy', *Journal, American Planning Association*, 49: 53–66.

Gough, I. (1979), *The Political Economy of the Welfare State* (Macmillan: London).

Hall, P. (1977), 'Greenfields and grey areas', *Proceedings of the Royal Town Planning Institute Annual Conference* (RTPI: London).

—— (ed.) (1981), *The Inner City in Context* (Heinemann: London).

—— H. Gracey, R. Drewett, and R. Thomas (1973), *The Containment of Urban England* (2 vols, Allen and Unwin: London).

Hastaoglou, V., C. Hadjimichalis, N. Kalogirou, and N. Papamichos (1987), 'Urbanization crisis and urban policy in Greece', *Antipode*, 19: 154–77.

Hausner, V. A., and B. T. Robson (1985), *Changing Cities* (ESRC: London).

Hebbert, M. (1986), 'Urban sprawl and urban planning in Japan', *Town Planning Review*, 57: 141–58.

Higgins, J., N. Deakin, J. Edwards, and M. Wicks (1983), *Government and Urban Poverty* (Basil Blackwell: Oxford).

Hill, R. C. (1984), 'Fiscal crisis, austerity politics and alternative urban policies', in W. K. Tabb and L. Sawers (eds.), *Marxism and the Metropolis* (Oxford University Press: New York).

Hooper, A. (1979), 'Land availability', *Journal of Planning and Environmental Law*, 18: 752–6.

Hula, R. C. (1984), 'Market strategies as policy tools', *Journal of Public Policy*, 4: 181–207.

James, D. C. and L. D. Hoppe (1969), *Urban Crisis in America* (National Press: Washington, DC).

JDAG (Joint Docklands Action Group) (1984), *Stifling the Island's Enterprise* (JDAG: London).

King, A. (1975), 'Overload', *Political Studies*, 23: 162–74.

Lambert, C. (1986) 'The changing context of local government finance in the 1980s', in M. Brenton and C. Ungerson (eds.), *The Yearbook of Social Policy in Britain 1985–6* (Routledge and Kegan Paul: London).

Laurance, S., and P. Hall (1981), 'British policy responses', in P. Hall (ed.), *The Inner City in Context* (Heinemann: London).

Lawless, P. (1986), 'Inner urban policy', in P. Lawless and C. Raban (eds.), *The Contemporary British City* (Harper and Row: London).

—— and F. Brown (1986), *Urban Growth and Change in Britain* (Harper and Row: London).

LDDC (London Docklands Development Corporation) (1984), *Corporate Strategy* (LDDC: London).

—— (1985), *Memorandum* (LDDC: London).

—— (1986), *Corporate Plan* (LDDC: London).

Leclerc, R., and D. D. Draffan (1984), 'The Glasgow eastern area renewal project', *Town Planning Review*, 55: 335–51.

McKay, D. H., and A. W. Cox (1979), *The Politics of Urban Change* (Croom Helm: London).

Massey, D. (1982), 'Enterprise zones: a political issue', *International Journal of Urban and Regional Research*, 6: 429–34.

Memon, P. A. (1986), 'Urban renewal policy in New Zealand', *Urban Law and Policy*, 8: 53–75.

Mishra, R. (1984), *The Welfare State in Crisis* (Wheatsheaf: Brighton).

Nabarro, R. (1980), 'Inner city partnerships', *Town Planning Review*, 51: 25–38.

O'Dowd, L., and B. Rolston (1985), 'Bringing Hong Kong to Belfast?', *International Journal of Urban and Regional Research*, 9: 218–32.

Palmer, J. L. and I. V. Sawhill (1984), *The Reagan Record* (Ballinger: Cambridge, Mass.).

Pickvance, C. G. (1986), 'The crisis of local government in Great Britain', in M. Gottdiener (ed.), *Cities in Stress* (Sage: Beverly Hills).

Regional Studies (1986), 'Theme issue: the changing urban and regional system in the United Kingdom', *Regional Studies*, 20(3).

Rose, E. A. (1986), 'Urban development grants', *Town Planning Review*, 57: 440–57.

Sawer, M. (1983), 'From the ethical state to the minimalist state', *Politics*, 18: 26–35.

Schwartz, G. G. (1981), 'Urban policy and the inner city in the US', in G. G. Schwartz (ed.), *Advanced Industrialisation and the Inner Cities* (D. C. Health: Lexington, Mass).

Short, J. R. (1982), 'Urban policy and British cities', *Journal, American Planning Association*, 48: 39–52.

Stewart, M. (1987), 'Ten years of inner cities policy', *Town Planning Review*, 58: 129–45.

Tabb, W. K. (1984), 'The failure of national urban policy', in W. K. Tabb and L. Sawers (eds.), *Marxism and the Metropolis* (Oxford University Press: New York).

Taylor, S. (1981), 'The politics of enterprise zones', *Public Administration*, 59: 421–39.

Townsend, P. (1979), *Poverty in the United Kingdom* (Penguin: Harmondsworth).

Trippier, D. (1987), 'Restoring confidence, initiative, choice', *Town and Country Planning*, 56: 235.

Tyme, R., and Partners (1983), *Monitoring Enterprise Zones* (Tyme: London).

—— (1984), *Monitoring Enterprise Zones* (Tyme: London).

Vernez, G. (1980), 'Overview of the spatial dimensions of the federal budget', in N. J. Glickman (ed.), *The Urban Impacts of Federal Policies* (Johns Hopkins University Press: Baltimore, Md).

Wicks, M. (1977), 'Social policy for the inner cities', in M. Brown and M. Baldwin (eds.), *The Yearbook of Social Policy in Britain in 1977* (Routledge and Kegan Paul: London).

Wolman, H. (1986), 'The Reagan urban policy and its impacts', *Urban Affairs Quarterly*, 21: 311–35.

Zielinski, H. (1983), 'Regional development and urban policy in the Federal Republic of Germany', *International Journal of Urban and Regional Research*, 7: 72–91.

Conclusion: From Social Problems and the City to the Social Problem of Injustice

David M. Smith

What we have come to refer to as social problems are place- and time-specific. Health or housing conditions that would elicit moral indignation and public interventions in Britain might be unremarkable in Sudan or Soweto, where attention would more reasonably be given to mass starvation and deprivation of the franchise. Similarly, perceptions of problems and the policy response can change over time, as the decade separating this book from its first edition shows. Indeed, writing at the end of the 1970s it would have been hard to predict the nature and extent of change that has taken place in Britain by the end of the 1980s, in terms of the way in which social problems are identified and understood—at least at the ideological level of government discourse and the policy prescriptions which follow. The fact that this has been, almost precisely, the decade of the rise of neo-conservatism associated with the election of Margaret Thatcher's government in 1979 is, of course, no coincidence. At the risk of giving undue emphasis to one ten-year period of change, which could be reversed or find a new trajectory in the 1990s, this conclusion will review briefly a number of ways in which the perspective on social problems revealed by our authors is different from that at the time of the original volume.

The first point, noted in the preface, is that the conditions selected for treatment have changed. This is not to say that in the latter part of the 1970s there was no problem of alcoholism, drug dependency, and civil disorder, that women were not in some special sense victims of inequality, or that the physical environment of our cities was non-problematic. It is that changing social experience along with its popular as well as academic articulation has heightened awareness of certain aspects of British (and American) urban life. There is also the fact that the appearance of what have been termed 'riots' on the streets of British cities, or more accurately their reappearance, is a phenomenon of the 1980s, just as is the sudden emergence of AIDS on the social agenda. Our list of contents makes no claim to being a comprehensive catagorization of contemporary social problems, but it does reflect a changing society.

Some of the changes in the societal context have been identified by Paul Knox. There has been a spectacular decline in manufacturing industry, with obvious implications for employment and the nature of work. Restructuring has led to de-skilling of some occupations, and with it the 'feminization' of jobs previously the province of men. The informal (black or underground) economy has provided alternatives to factory employment for some; for many, however, the outcome has been unemployment or daunting competition for low-skill, low-pay jobs in the growing service sector. Demographic change has increased the dependent (young or old) proportion of the population, and to the aged living alone has been added the single-(usually female) parent family among those recognized as especially vulnerable to poverty in its various manifestations. The conspicious affluence of those able to add to their array of consumer durables heightens the disadvantage of the homeless, lonely, alienated, or desperate. Income inequality increased in Britain in the 1980s.

Another dimension of change is in the geographical distribution of the poor or socially deprived. Knox refers to the dispersal of poverty within the city, associated with gentrification as well as with the urban renewal programmes which have displaced large numbers of the inner-city poor, especially in the United States. Even in Britain, residential redevelopment is rarely at original densities. Simplistic notions of an inner-city ghettoized underclass must yield to a recognition of a more complex pattern, including a concentration of social deprivation in outer-city local-authority housing estates. Some of these estates represented planned relocation from inner-city slums; some were tied more clearly to the changing needs of capital for large new plants on green-field sites and the associated dispersal of employment, and have themselves become redundant as a result of factory closures in a new round of economic structuring, as Roger Lee points out. There is also more awareness now of a rural deprivation, associated with difficulties of accessibility on the part of those dependent on declining public transport and with spatial concentration of services such as retailing, as well as with low wages in agriculture. Added to this are the problems of specialized one-industry towns based on iron and steel, coal, railway engineering, and the like, as vulnerable to rationalization of state-controlled activity as were the mill towns to private-sector changes a generation ago. Ian Gordon points out the compexity of the relationship between unemployment and local conditions, while Sarah Curtis shows something of the diversity and changing nature of inner-city populations and the consequent need for social services.

Changes in the understanding of social problem are evident in any review covering the 1980s. The editorial contribution to the first edition of this book reflected the competing (or complementary) academic understandings of the time, in which areal associations among phenomena, the spatial organization of human activity, and the structural focus of a political-economy perspective represented distinctive approaches in contemporary geographical inquiry. While human geography still has its competing 'isms', some largely unheard of ten years ago, the analysis of social problems in this edition is less self-consciously concerned with methodology or paradigm than in the earlier volume. There is now a broad if not universal acceptance of the structural origin of social problems, which are themselves seen as socially constructed. If there is some reticence in tracing back individual conditions to the ongoing dynamics of contemporary capitalism (even 'the reproductive imperative' or 'the law of value'), this reflects a more subtle understanding than was permitted by the somewhat deterministic versions of structuralism which predominated in the 1970s, allowing little room for human agency. It may also reflect a recognition that certain institutions and processes generating inequality or social deprivation under capitalism are more resistant to change than was thought, or hoped, in the 1970s. Changing understanding of social problems must also include some indications of a return to the thesis of individual responsibility and culture of poverty (or welfare dependency), as academics of the 'New Right' find comforting congruence between their analyses and Conservative government prescriptions which stress individual initiative and the benefits to be derived from an enterprise culture.

It is in the realm of government policy that the most obvious changes can be seen. John Eyles reminds us of the confidence of the 1970s in area-based policies directed towards what were regarded as residual, soluble problems of people somehow slipping through the safety-net of the welfare state. No sooner had the more fundamental structural origin of the problems been recognized than their underlying cause was seen, by government at least, to be national economic malaise rather than the endemic uneven development of a crisis-prone mode of production. The dominant theme of the 1980s thus became that of improving national economic performance so as better to fund social need. But to be more competitive the British economy has to use labour more efficiency, or so the prevailing understanding has it, which can require a reduction in the cost of production and reproduction of labour as well as further development of productive forces in the form of improved technology. The outcome has been shedding of labour and economizing on public service expenditure, as well as a strengthening predisposition towards technological solutions.

Michael Bradford identifies the changed agenda from the mid-1970s in the field of education as a shift from the objectives of equality of opportunity and' outcomes towards aspects of economic efficiency (including vocational relevance). This can be interpreted as a move from social equity to economic efficiency driven by consumer sovereignty. Economic priorities tend to suggest private sector and market-based solutions, and while this response may to some extent be an act of faith it can appeal to neo-classical economics for some semblance of academic legitimacy. Thus freedom of choice among services provided by competing producers is supposed to deliver to individuals and communities what they want (or need) at least cost, without the intermediary of state or local government bureaucracies which are too often self-serving. There is sufficient logic to this model to give it much intuitive appeal, especially when harnessed to an ideology emphasizing local control and value for tax or rate payers' hard-earned money. In spheres where market place evaluations cannot automatically differentiate among more or less satisfactory outcomes, then specific goal attainment can be monitored by performance indicators. The chapters by John Mohan on health care and Peter Kemp on housing, as well as Michael Bradford on education, provide illustrations of the range and similarity of market-based solutions across the public sector in Britain in the 1980s. The activities of local authorities in general are to be made more responsive to their populations by the so-called 'community charge' or 'poll tax' replacing rates, and giving every household or elector a vested interest in efficiency which will be more effective in holding down costs than the normal democratic process—or so it is argued by government ministers. Pressure to privatize certain local government services has been added to the emphasis on private sector initiatives in addressing the special problems of the inner cities.

An important element in the new political culture stressing self-reliance and individual responsibility is the rise of voluntary and informal responses to social problems. This is not (yet) an overt appeal to private charity and philanthropy, consistent with other aspects of what is sometimes held to be a desirable return to Victorian values. It is a call for people to take the initiative to help solve their own problems rather than relying on others or the state. This is connected with a re-emphasis on the role of the family, and also with local community action. Community care is a significant feature of contemporary political rhetoric, prompted initially by reaction to the dehumanizing aspects of medicalized and institutionalized strategies towards the elderly and mentally ill, for example, and subsequently found consistent with economization and the reduction of public expenditure. This policy change has generated a new set of problems, however. For those released 'into the community', local authority services are inadequate, already strained by the existing client groups. Community care may thus in practice mean no care at all, or family care which puts great pressure on the (usually) female carers, thus adding to other gender disadvantages in seeking employment or leisure.

While the emphasis in this book has been on the British experience, it should be noted that the ideological underpinnings of the Thatcher government's policy orientation bear a close resemblance to those articulated in the United States. Individual self-reliance, family solidarity, local or small-town community cohesion, and antogonism towards 'socialized' services and state control are central features of the culture and political rhetoric of the United States, only slightly exaggerated by Ronald Reagan. The import of specific policy initiatives from the United States has been rare, however, ministerial curiosity towards education and economic regeneration in American cities notwithstanding. American cities are significantly different, and so are important aspects of the institutional and cultural context of public policy. Reductions in social security payments, privatization, and other aspects of the erosion of the welfare state nevertheless bring Britain closer to the United States in actual practice.

Changes in policy have been associated with changes in polity. Most notable has been the change in central–local government relations. Ten years ago the 'local state' tended to be viewed as largely a local arm of a central state, acting in the interests of capitalist class hegemony; there was little room for local autonomy, or for conflict. As Keith Hoggart points out, this interpretation was not sufficiently sensitive to geographically and historically different practices. The 1980s have seen central (Conservative) and local (Labour-controlled) government in often bitter conflict, culminating in the abolition of the Greater London Council and similar bodies responsible for Britain's other major metropolitan areas. Local perceptions of needs, priorities, and necessary expenditure became increasingly discordant with those of central government, and especially with its squeeze on public spending (as Bennett shows). Control of significant sources of local government revenue as well as a substantial parliamentary majority enabled central government to impose severe constraints on local freedom of action, with reductions in the scope of local service provision (e.g. in education) further weakening the 'local state'. Far from being an instrument of central control, local government is increasingly an irrelevance.

Thus the British social formation is different in important respects from that of ten years ago. The societal context of social problems has changed, and so has the public response. This is part of a broader process of change, driven by the national repercussions of a turbulent international economy and guided by a government unusually inclined to place ideological commitment before pragmatism. What would have been unthinkable in the 1970s is now not only thought but executed, from privatization of former public authorities running telephone services, gas supplies, and so on, to the possibility of opting out of state services on a hitherto unimaginable scale. A largely compliant press far to the right of that of a decade ago helps to articulate the new libertarianism, with such imaginative inversions as 'Power to the People' in a newspaper headline announcing the privatization of electricity supply. Even the BBC has been cowed into submissive avoidance of stands that could be construed as political partiality. The balance of contemporary discourse and of common-sense understanding has shifted towards what, in the 1970s, would have been judged the extreme Right. What was then soft socialism is now 'hard Left'. The socialist commitment to equality has almost vanished as a potent political force, and with it a degree of concern for the poor.

That the 'popular authoritarianism' of the late 1980s has a coherence is explained by Susan Smith. The emphasis of government policy has been on the so-called 'first sphere' of state intervention: shaping the legal infrastructure, maintaining a strong defence, and upholding moral values (in public rhetoric if not necessarily in private conduct). Redistribution in response to social need clearly has second place. The social problems which have elicted most government attention have themselves been significant, even symbolic. The stress on law and order, drug abuse and, most recently, AIDS, represent a politicization of practices which raise issues of morality and of what is 'normal' conduct, thus reinforcing a popular consciousness of a normal society as law-abiding, drug-free and heterosexual, at least for those lacking the resources or privilege necessary to keep their 'deviance' discreet.

This kind of society is not without its contradictions, as these last observations suggest. Perhaps the greatest is between the ideology of individual liberty and the practice of central control. Thus, for example, greater parental choice in education is to be provided, up to schools opting out of local education authorities; yet there is to be a centrally determined core curriculum. Free inquiry in the universities is increasingly constrained by budget cuts and government preference for industrially relevant activity which, arguably, needs the free inquiry of basic research to sustain it. Local community control is applauded and to some extent facilitated, but not for the Metropolitan Police. Public expenditure must be cost-effective and monitored by performance assessment (even for academics, if not yet for painters and musicians), yet, as Susan Smith reminds us, there is little demonstrable effect on crime rates from further investment in the police force, which is nevertheless a privileged beneficiary from public expenditure. Such contradictions are crucial features of the societal context of social problems.

That social problems are socially constructed is no more evident anywhere than in terms of crime. Great attention continues to be given to property crime and crime 'on the streets' such as mugging. Yet we see barely the tip of the iceberg of corporate crime, and much financial business appears to hover around the fringe of illegality. The definition of certain crimes makes it hard for some people in some places to avoid committing them, as part of a daily life which includes resisting what may be regarded as wrongful arrest and contending for space in ritualized conflict with the police; this may be the case in some black neighbourhoods, as Michael Keith explains. Keith refers to the essential rationality and normality of black resistance and other manifestations of 'crime'. Geoffrey Pearson echoes this in his comments on the normality of drug use and its acceptance in some places and cultures at some times. It was acceptable for Sherlock Holmes in Victorian England, and possibly for pop stars, media persons and even rich undergraduates if done discreetly in Britain today, but for working-class youth in Brixton or Kirkby it is another matter. Whether some acts are high spirits or hooliganism depends on who performs them, and where. One of the most significant and, to some, ominous changes in policing in Britain in the 1980s was its politicization, notably in response to the miners' strike, along with a militarization which contrast uneasily with the image of the Dixon of Dock Green 'bobby'. The miners' strike clearly expressed what Keith identifies as the two contradictory police roles, those of law-enforcer and representatives of a particular social order. It was a particular strategy of law enforcement as well as changes in the law which made criminals out of some of those whose strike was seen as a challenge to the political strategy of reducing trade union power. Picketing, for example, had been transformed from a solution to a social problem.

What of the future? As was suggested earlier, there is a danger in preoccupation with a relatively short period of time. A new oil crisis, mega-power miscalculation, or domestic mishandling of a crucial issue could produce dramatic change before this second edition runs out of print. Nevertheless, the general trajectory of continuing change over the next few years in Britain, and possibly elsewhere in the advanced capitalist world, seems fairly clear. A few predictions will thus be made to round off this conclusion. If proved wrong by the passage of time, so would a similar exercise have been ten years ago.

As government perception and understanding of social problems changes, along with possible range of response, we are entering a period of innovation in policy. As Tony Warnes says of policies towards the aged, earlier strategies are being abandoned for 'chaotic, pragmatic and hesitant experiments to find effective mixtures of individual, market, and state support services'. So it is in health care, as what is popularly perceived as a crisis in NHS funding is generating a bewildering variety of possible alternatives. And the Education Reform Bill embodies approaches to secondary and higher education that might more properly be described as revolutionary, so profound are some of the implications. While there may be a degree of hesitation in some fields, the government and its ministers seem more to exude confidence, not only in the rectitude of the measures proposed but also in the kind of society they seek to create. They also appear confident in a particular model of individual conduct and social development, implicit for the most part, which guides the implementation of policy.

The emphasis on freedom and choice and (constrained) local control, exercised within some kind of market with competing service producers, could enhance efficiency and improve quality by eliminating expensive and/or poor services. However, this depends on a degree of consumer knowledge, rationality, and mobility which stretches credibility. Choice among shirts and competing clothes shops may not be fully informed, but a mistake is trivial and quite easily rationalized. An individual choosing a school or surgeon is unlikely to be well-informed, and mistakes can be irreversible if not fatal. The well-known shortcomings of the free market model based on consumer sovereignty are all the greater as services replace goods. Furthermore, markets respond most to people with most money (or power or influence) who thereby become further advantaged, unless the state steps in. This, together with a growing distinction between private provision for those who can afford it (e.g. in education and health services) and an inevitably more limited or inferior public service for the rest, promises increased inequality among individuals, groups, and locality-based communities. Trends towards greater socio-economic polarization or cleavage are already evident in British cities, as Brian Robson points out. Racial as well as socio-economic exclusivity may be encouraged, for example in housing, where few blacks live on local authority estates where the 'right to buy' has been popular, and in schools 'opting out' which could lead to selective entry on racial as well as financial grounds. As Michael Bradford says of education, the integration of the 1960s is likely to be replaced by greater segmentation, segregation, and separation.

Thus, for those with the resources, there will be superior services, as well as the ever-increasing array of goods the consumption of which is encouraged by a culture of individual material self-interest. For others, however, there will remain the dole queue, dirty street, damp bedroom, and bad chest, along with inferior education and health services, and lower levels of social security than today. In theory an economy revived by the new enterprise culture will generate the wealth required to maintain or increase public expenditure on social services. In practice those who have benefited from privatization may prefer things as they are, and in any event there will be a further round of innovation in electronic entertainment, home computing, or automobile technology to take up the slack of disposable income; capital accumulation depends on material fulfilment never being quite fully filled. Of course, the poll-tax-paying masses may march on the town hall, figuratively speaking, to demand new or more efficient services. But this depends on a rationality on their part consistent with that of those who devise policies based on such assumptions, a rationality not necessarily shared by those for whom some people's deviance is the norm. To avoid registration and hence payment of the poll tax may be the rational response, like the avoidance of income tax by otherwise law-abiding people. As to the strategy for change, it may take threats to social order on the part of the deprived—threats to social reproduction—to shift the balance back significantly towards well-funded public services.

Threats to social order were a marked feature of the 1980s in Britain, just as they were in the United States in the 1960s. To prevent or control such unrest has been high on the political agenda, from challenges to trade union power to policing strategy in black neighbourhoods. It is customary to condemn violent disorder; its consequences can be discomforting, not least to some of the participants. But it is part of the process of change, part of the struggle whereby those who are socially deprived, discriminated against, or otherwise see themselves as hard-done-by seek to improve their conditions. Societies may seem at times to be little more than their institutions, but, as Roger Lee reminds us, they are made by people:

Societies cannot be assumed away but they can be changed. We have to start from the here and now rather than from some idealized alternative, and we must recognize the power and social distinction of the historical geography that has brought us to the here and now. The clock cannot be turned back: a return to an idealized past is neither possible nor desirable. The desire to return to the Victorian city, for example, is at best a grotesquely ill-informed anachronism.

Thus what is sometimes referred to as Thatcher's Britain, like Reagan's America, will be part of the future, people compliantly or contendedly moulding to it, or struggling to change it. If change rather than consolidation is the outcome, then the motivation may come not only from the experience and reaction of the poor in an increasingly unequal and divided society, but also from a renewed sense of fairness and justice. At the end of the 1980s in Britain there are increasing calls for moral standards, including exhortations on the part of the government for the church to take the lead. What conservative politicians have in mind appears to be a combination of a return to the Protestant ethic in the form of hard work by the masses and reasonably honest hustling in business and finance, along with more prudence in sexual conduct (preferably hetero). What might possibly be released is moral unease if not outrage at the degeneration of contemporary life into rampant materialism, devil-take-the-hindmost and let-the-weak-go-to-the-wall, and at its outcome, an increasingly unequal society.

Social justice has almost become unfashionable as a sphere of discourse in the 1980s, compared with the 1970s and 1960s. Yet is it no less pertinent today to ask what justifies the evident disparities in level of living between people whose shared humanity is arguably more important than what may largely be the good fortune of the right family, education, or job in the right place? After all, as Michael Keith reminds us, civil disorder is rooted in an unjust society: there is *a social problem of injustice* no more clearly expressed anywhere than in the city.

INDEX

access crisis in housing 166
access to facilities 215–16
acid rain 82, 95
agency co-ordination 177, 345–67 *passim*
AIDS 319, 387, 392
air pollution 81–98
alcoholism 323–39
alcohol abuse 10, 323–39
alcohol control policy 323–39
alternative economic strategies 350
attitudes to council housing 170
Audit Commission 21, 112–16, 168

black population 9, 43, 247–67
  and demography 247, 249
  and disadvantage 251
  and discrimination 251, 257, 267
  and migration 248–9
  and spatial concentration 251–2, 256–7
built environment 214–15, 274

capital accumulation 65–7
careerism 142–3, 148–53
central government policies 356–60, 365
  city action teams 357
  derelict land grants 356
  land register 357
  urban development grants 356, 358, 365
  urban regeneration grants 356
central–local government relations 21, 55–7,
    101, 104, 115, 351–2, 374, 391
'chasing the dragon' 315
child care 213, 221, 227–8
children in care 189, 221
choice in education 142–3, 154–6
circuit of capital 65–71, 73
City Technology College 149, 151–2, 155–6
class conflict 65
cocaine 309–11
Commission for Racial Equality 265
commodification 142–3, 153–4, 156
community control 142–3, 155–6, 377
community programmes 373
community welfare 176–94, 373
consumption model 332
contraction in education 142–5, 156
corporate capitalism 66, 147–8
cost-cutting in education 142–3, 145–8
counter-urbanization 1, 250
creative accounting 116, 118

crime 9, 35, 271–85, 323–5
  and the elderly 279
  and ethnic groups 280–2
  and surveys 273
  and women 279

decentralization 25, 26, 66, 68, 74, 107, 156,
    190, 192
de-institutionalization 42, 207
demand-led planning 360
demographic change 42, 198, 247–9, 250
disadvantage 32–45, 251
disease model 328–30, 334
District Health Authorities 127–31, 135, 137
domestic violence 214, 216, 221, 227–8, 324
domestic work 213, 219–20, 227
drug abuse 10, 307–20, 323
drug dependency units 313
dual state hypothesis 53, 54

economic base 100, 102
economic development offices 354
economic regeneration 345–67
economic restructuring 110, 248–50, 346–65
    passim
education 6, 43, 110–11, 142–56, 372
elderly 8, 40, 43, 198–210, 280–2
  and crime 279
  as economic burden 198, 201
  and poverty 203–5
  and social problems 201–3
  as women 216, 219, 279
élitist theory 51–3
Employee Assistance Programme 326
enterprise culture 350
enterprise zones 120, 326, 357, 365–6, 378–9
equality of opportunity 142, 146, 154
  for women 227
ethnic minorities 184–6, 188, 247–67, 205,
    216, 220, 237–8, 265–6
  and crime 276, 280–2
  and housing 260–3
  and policies 247, 264–7
  and unemployment 260, 262
  as women 216, 220–1, 279

family 218–20
fear of crime 278–81
finance 5, 6, 100–25, 156, 352
fiscal climate 109

fiscal crises 67, 103, 122, 374
fiscal migration 103
flexible accumulation 68
flexible workforce 224–5
floods 86, 92
Fordism 60, 62, 64
fossil fuels 91

gentrification 1, 43
ghetto 22, 32, 33, 312
global urban system 68
grant programmes 107, 119
Greater London Enterprise Board 364–5

health care 6, 126–8, 176, 182–3, 213, 216,
    372
  and alcohol 323
  and elderly 208–9
hegemony 71, 73
heroin 307–22
  and British social policy 312–15, 318–20
  and crime 312, 318
  and deprivation 315–18, 320
homelessness 111, 166–7, 221
home ownership 164–5, 167, 169, 171
home workers 219, 225
Hospital Plan (1962) 127
housing 7, 36, 43, 65, 110, 154–73, 216, 220–2,
    371
  and elderly 205–8
  and ethnic groups 260–3
  and women 216
housing estates 36, 232–3, 237, 276, 280, 315
housing tenure 235, 243
humanism 3, 4

immigration 247–8, 264
income support 202
individualism 235, 376
induced migration 235
information-rich environments 29
inner city 1, 2, 4, 32, 36–8, 120, 122, 128, 146,
    149–50, 153, 188–9, 191, 209, 241, 276–7,
    280, 283, 347–9, 366, 373, 382, 388
institutional problems 176

job creation schemes 365
job loss 249–50
joint planning 191

karst 84
Kondratiev waves 66

law enforcement 271–2, 278, 285
leisure and tourism 27, 29, 354–5
lesbians 216
local economic initiatives 11, 345–67

local government 60, 64, 115
  and ethnic groups 265–6
  and reorganization 349
local labour markets 151–3
local state 53, 70, 279–80, 284, 391
London Docklands Development 66, 360–4,
    379–80

managerialism 51–2, 56, 148
Marxist theory 49–53
mass housing 154, 168
mass production 68
mass urbanization 65
Maternity Services Liaison Scheme 188
minimal state 376, 378–9
morphine 310
mud-slides 83

narco-terrorism 319
neighbourhood change 281
New Left 115–17, 122, 353
New Right 271, 389
new towns 24

opium 309–10, 319

patriarchy 214, 227
pluralism 51–3, 147–8
police accountability 272, 283–4
policing 281–5, 293–302
policy communities 56–7
policy culture 121
political economy of alcoholism 335–8
political power 48
poll tax 24, 107, 119–20, 352, 390
pollution 93
Poplarism 60
positivism 3
post-industrial thesis 17, 62, 70
post-modernism 68, 73
power relations 294–9
prevention policies:
  alcohol 327
  crime 278
primary health care 129, 131–4, 208–10
private health care 134–6, 208–9
privatization 42, 168–9, 171–2, 192
  and alcohol 328–30
producer services 68, 70–1
Prohibition 323, 325, 327–8, 330–9
property tax 101
public health model 330–5, 338
public health movement 131, 161, 190, 324
public services 213, 220, 222, 225–6

quality-adjusted life year 137

racism 295–306 *passim*
rate-capping 116
rate support grant 21, 108, 146
'red-lining' 153
regional audits 25
Regional Health Authorities 127, 130, 135
Resource Allocation Working Party 127–8, 130–1, 137
resource base 102
resources for the city 100–25, 186–7
retirement towns 200

sale of council houses 168–9, 171
school closures 146–7, 149, 156
service sector 222, 224, 226
sewers 84, 94–5
shrink-swell 84
single parent families 218, 219, 221
single women 216, 221
smog 85, 95
social dependency 109–11
social disadvantage 178–82
social indicators 4, 33–40
social justice 149
social relations 71–4, 337
social reproduction 63–75, 294
social services provision 185, 207
social targeting 26
standardized mortality ratios 127–8, 130, 181
State 48, 161
    autonomy 50
    intervention 65, 160–2, 272
stigmatization 244
structuralism 3, 50, 235
subsidence 93
surplus value 61

TVEI 149–51
task forces 120, 358
Thatcherism 55–6, 387, 395
theories of state 49–53
transport 213, 216, 228

unemployment 110–11, 232–45, 363
    and crime 275

and ethnic minorities 260, 262
    and heroin 315–18, 320
urban age structures 199–200
urban blacks:
    and housing 260–3
    and policy 264–6
    and unemployment 260–2
Urban Development Action fronts 356–60, 365, 377
Urban Development Corporations 21–2, 121, 357, 380
urban disorder 10, 289–306
urban heat island 85
urban impact assessment 25
urban management 111–14
urban policies 11, 120, 356–67, 370–83
urban programme 4, 19, 22, 120, 190, 265, 357, 372, 378
urban redundancy 61, 69–70
urban riots 289–306
    in UK 290–306, 349
    in US 289–91
urban thunderstorms 85
urban underclass 17, 22, 32–3, 110, 120

victimization 32–45, 275–8
voluntary sector 192–3

welfare 7, 110, 176–94, 372, 382
women 214–28
    and committees 223
    and employment 213, 217–19, 222–7, 238, 243
    and inequality 216–27
    and safety 215, 227–8
    and subordination 213–14
    and units 228
    and work 217–19
World Health Organization 131, 138

youth unemployment 243, 366
yuppification 186

zoning 332–4